A Logical Journey

Representation and Mind
Hilary Putnam and Ned Block, editors

A Logical Journey

From Gödel to Philosophy

Hao Wang

The MIT Press
Cambridge, Massachusetts
London, England

This book was set in Palatino by Asco Trade Typesetting Ltd., Hong Kong.
Printed and bound in the United States of America.

Library of Congress Cataloging-in-Publication Data

Wang, Hao, 1921–
  A logical journey: from Gödel to philosophy / Hao Wang.
    p.   cm. – (Representation and mind)
  Includes bibliographical references and index.
  ISBN 978-0-262-23189-3 (hc : alk. paper)
        978-0-262-52916-7 (pb : alk. paper)

  1. Gödel, Kurt. 2. Logicians—United States—Biography. 3. Logicians—Austria—Biography. I. Title. II. Series.
QA29.G58W357   1996   96-32568
193—dc20   CIP

Contents

Ren tong ci xin, xin tong ci li. *There are sages from the East; there are sages from the West: all of them have the same kind of mind-heart; all their minds have the same kind of intuition.*
Lu Jiuyuang, 1139–1193

It is only after profounder acquaintance with the other sciences that logic ceases to be for subjective spirit a merely abstract universal and reveals itself as the universal which embraces within itself the wealth of the particular.
Hegel, *Greater Logic*

Preface

In this book I propose to discuss Kurt Gödel's philosophical views within the context of my own conception of the mansion of philosophy and its many rooms. Beginning with the actual discussions between Gödel and me, I have broadened the meaning of *conversations* to include the interplay between my continual reflections and the available relevant material by and about Gödel. In this way, I hope to attain a coherent understanding of his life and thought within the framework of my own evolving perspective, reconstituting and completing the actual discussions between us so as to bring out their implications. It is therefore obvious that this project has become an integral part of my own ongoing pursuit of a comprehensive view of things.

This book is a continuation of my *Reflections on Kurt Gödel*, which I completed in June of 1986 and published in 1987. Among other things, it attempts to present a more transparent survey of Gödel's life and work than is given in the earlier book. My original purpose was to bring out in a generally understandable form my fragmentary and chaotic records of our wide-ranging conversations. This turned out to be a much more formidable task than I had anticipated. As the effort continued and as time went on, I felt increasingly that I was trying to reconstitute an immense puzzle from the distorted images of a few scattered pieces. To borrow some light, I consulted Gödel's own writings; but unfortunately much of the unpublished notes he made remain concealed behind his Gabelsberger shorthand. To understand his comments on Leibniz, Kant, Hegel, Husserl, and Einstein, I have also tried to study some of their relevant work.

Earlier, in my *From Mathematics to Philosophy*, I had made use of discussions I had with Gödel between 1967 and 1972; I completed that work in June of 1972 and published it in January of 1974. In particular, I included there, without comments, about ten pages of Gödel's own summary of what he wanted to see published. The present book contains elaborations of these pages too.

All along I have thought of my study of Gödel's ideas as a way to arrive at and communicate what I take to be the most reasonable of his views on the issues he studied, rather than an attempt to depict faithfully the body of his philosophical thought. His total thought, inevitably, like that of every great thinker, is difficult to bring into focus, if taken as a whole, and contains parts of varying degrees of clarity. In the process of trying to resolve various ambiguities in my notes, I have selected, interpreted, and extrapolated from some of his observations along paths that are congenial to me. Moreover, I have tried to find an inclusive framework within which the salient features of alternative philosophies—such as his and Wittgenstein's—can be seen as complementary rather than as contradictory to each other. By doing these things, I have been led beyond the scope of the planned book and find it hard to locate a suitable boundary between what should be included and what should be excluded here. This has added an obstacle to the completion of the project.

Worse still for this limited goal, I began to realize more and more my own ignorance and prejudices, both generally and in regard to the literature relevant to the specific issues considered; but these deficiencies can be corrected only gradually. At the same time, I began to sense that there are ways of looking at philosophy superior to what I had been accustomed to. This feeling of facing new vistas is exhilarating, but it also accentuates the familiar tension between a desire to conclude a piece of work and a natural urge to enter the promised land of better views. For all these reasons, I had to decide more or less arbitrarily where and when this book was to stop.

Since I am trying to preserve in this book a fairly complete record of what Gödel said in our discussions, it would be awkward to include also my own extended reflections on the central topics of Platonism in mathematics, the nature of logic, and the contrast of minds with computers. I am, therefore, planning to put that material in a separate book, to be entitled *The Formal and the Intuitive: From Computation to Wisdom*.

Another complication is my belief that many of the topics considered here are intrinsically of more than isolated interest. But to communicate this belief successfully requires a gift for presenting the material in such a way that the common reader will not be put off by preconceived ideas about what he or she can understand. Even though I have spent much energy in organizing the material to motivate the more specialized considerations so that the reader can see them as a natural refinement of our shared concerns, I am not sure how far I have succeeded.

In 1946 Gödel's mother Marianne heard that Gödel and Einstein were close friends. She began to ask about Einstein in her letters and wanted to know more about him. In December of 1950 Gödel recommended to her Philipp Frank's biography *Einstein: His Life and Times* (1947, the original German manuscript was published only in 1950); Marianne obtained the German version of this book and found it difficult. In January of 1951 Gödel wrote to her: "Is the book about Einstein really so hard to understand? I think that prejudice against and fear of every 'abstraction' may also be involved here, and if you would attempt to read it like a novel (without wanting to understand right away everything at the first reading), perhaps it would not seem so incomprehensible to you."

I have myself found this advice helpful in studying trustworthy works. It must be a fairly common experience to realize that what we thought was difficult turns out to be quite understandable with a bit of effort. The seemingly difficult parts of this book are, I hope, of this kind. In any event, the understanding of one part of it does not depend upon familiarity with preceding parts, or even, in most instances, with the chapter that contains it.

The writing of this book has continually occupied me for nearly a decade; in the process I have written much preliminary and related material, parts of which have been published elsewhere while other parts remain unfinished. I have derived benefits from various sources in one way or another.

I am grateful to Marie Grossi for her skill and patience through these years in executing the interminable work of turning the numerous fragments into accurate typescripts, with sympathetic understanding and constructive suggestions.

To the Institute for Advanced Study I am grateful for permission to use material from Gödel's literary estate. To the Wiener Stadt- und Landesbibliothek I am grateful for permission to quote from Gödel's letters to his mother.

In connection with different parts of the book, I have profited in various ways from comments by Paul Bernays, Leigh Cauman, Juliet Floyd, Zhao-wu He, Hong-kuei Kang, Ray Monk, Sidney Morgenbesser, Charles Parsons, G. H. von Wright, Qing-he Wang, Sian-jun Wang, Yi-Ming Wang, and Rei-yuan Wu.

On several specific topics I have had the good fortune of obtaining the help of experts: from Howard Stein, on the concept of time in physics and in philosophy; from Richard Tieszen on the views of Edmund Husserl; from Wayne C. Myrvold on the algorithmic character of physical laws; from Palle Yourgrau, on the ideas of Gottlob Frege, and from Sher-min Hsei, on the work of John Rawls. Discussions with Hanne Tierney and Palle Yourgrau on many aspects of the book have been extensive and especially helpful.

For the past two years or so, Anthony Everett has helped me by making an index and an outline of the reconstructed notes of my discussions with Gödel. His acute comments on a draft of the book have enabled me to eliminate various repetitions and other errors. Moreover, he has consented to make an index for the book.

HW

Hao Wang died on May 13, 1995, after this book was submitted for publication but before it was ready to go to press. The final checking that he would ordinarily have done was done instead by his friends Palle Yourgrau of Brandeis University and Leigh Cauman of the *Journal of Philosophy* (retired), at the request and with the approval of Hao's widow, Hanne Tierney. We apologize to Hao and to you, his readers, for any deficiencies in our effort to render the manuscript as clear and faithful to Hao's intentions as possible.

We should also mention one specific problem: Professor Wang realized that the book is repetitious, and he spoke to Prof. Yourgrau about this on a number of occasions. Some of the repetition is inevitable, because of the structure of the book, but some he would have eliminated if he had lived longer or if his health in his last years had allowed him to do more work. This is a defect that we in his absence are not in a position to address— a very small defect, we feel, in what seems to us a beautiful and extraordinarily useful book.

PY and LSC

Introduction

Philosophers should have the audacity to generalize things without any inhibition: go on along the direction on the lower level, and generalize along different directions in a uniquely determined manner.
Gödel, 13 September 1972

Hegel seems to me to be always wanting to say that things which look different are really the same. Whereas my interest is in showing that things which look the same are really different.
Wittgenstein, Autumn 1948

In order to see Gödel's work as a contribution to philosophy as we know it today, it is helpful to relate both his philosophical assertions and his philosophically significant work in logic to familiar philosophical concerns. In particular, his most famous result on the mechanical inexhaustibility of mathematics is relevant to the current debate over the mind's superiority to computers. By his own account, Gödel's Platonism was important to his work in logic. In addition, he speculated on several traditional topics which have, by a sort of unspoken consensus, been largely abandoned in contemporary philosophy: topics such as the likelihood of an afterlife, the existence of God, and the project of an exact metaphysics—preferably in the form of a monadology.

Consequently, in order to discuss Gödel's views in such a way as to benefit one's own study of philosophy, it seems necessary to review briefly the conceptual and the historical motivations behind both contemporary philosophy and Gödel's somewhat different philosophical interests. Particularly relevant in this connection are the relations of philosophy to logic and to science, which may be seen as two subproblems of the general issue of the nature of philosophy and its place in human life. The transition from logic to philosophy in Gödel's own work is a convenient place to begin.

0.1 The Logician and His Theorem

It is generally accepted that Kurt (Friedrich) Gödel (1906–1978) was the greatest logician of the twentieth century. In February 1951, when Gödel was sick in a hospital, Robert Oppenheimer told the attending physician that "Your patient is the greatest logician since Aristotle." At the memorial meeting on 3 March 1978, André Weil observed that it would be banal to affirm that in 2,500 years Gödel was the only person who could speak without exaggeration of "Aristotle and me." In the seventies John Wheeler said that "if you called him the greatest logician since Aristotle you'd be downgrading him" (quoted in Bernstein 1991:141). Gödel himself felt his greatest kinship with Leibniz. In any case, no one denies that his position among logicians is comparable to Einstein's among physicists.

Einstein himself, who had a really warm and very close relationship with Gödel from 1942 until his death in 1955, considered Gödel's work as important to mathematics as his own work was to physics: "Now that I've met Gödel, I know that the same thing does exist in mathematics" (quoted in Wang 1987a, hereafter *RG*:31–32).

Gödel's work has revolutionized modern logic, greatly raising its level of significance both mathematically and philosophically. Moreover, in his hands mathematics and philosophy are exceptionally meaningful, beautiful, and free from rancor. The deep respect he enjoys among diverse groups of thoughtful people is rare in the modern world. In a world where people compete constantly with one another, he raised himself above competition. For all contemporary branches of logic, his work serves as a foundation and a life force. In philosophy, by contrast, much of his writing remains unpublished, and opinions of it are tentative and divided.

On 17 June 1952 Harvard University awarded Gödel an honorary doctorate as "the discoverer of the most significant mathematical truth of this century." In a letter to his mother (22 July) Gödel describes this citation (which was written by Willard Van Orman Quine) as "unquestionably the most beautiful." "But this matter," he continues, "has nothing to do with Einstein, whose discoveries are not mathematical but physical." He points out that the citation should not be taken to say that he is the greatest mathematician of the century, but, rather, that the phrase *most significant* means "of the greatest *general* interest outside of mathematics."

The truth so honored was discovered by Gödel in 1930 at the age of 24. It is his best known work, usually referred to simply as *Gödel's theorem*, even though he discovered a number of other fundamental theorems as well. The theorem can be stated in any one of the following alternative forms:

GT Mathematics is inexhaustible.

GT1 Any consistent formal theory of mathematics must contain undecidable propositions.

GT2 No theorem-proving computer (or program) can prove all and only the true propositions of mathematics.

GT3 No formal system of mathematics can be both consistent and complete.

GT4 Mathematics is mechanically (or algorithmically) inexhaustible (or incompletable).

These propositions remain true when we replace "mathematics" by "arithmetic" (i.e., number theory or the theory of natural numbers, the simplest and the most fundamental part of pure mathematics). In brief, Gödel's theorem reveals the algorithmic inexhaustibility (or incompletability) of mathematics (and even of arithmetic). This fact of algorithmic inexhaustibility shows, according to Gödel, that either the human mind surpasses all computers or that mathematics is not created by the human mind, or both. It is therefore clear that the theorem is relevant to both the philosophy of mind and the philosophy of mathematics.

In terms of philosophical discourse, the theorem helps to clarify the dialectic of logic and intuition, of formalism and content, of the mechanical and the mental, of language and thought, of truth and provability, and of the real and the knowable.

Gödel's theorem has been celebrated in poetry ("Homage à Gödel" by Hans Magnus Enzenberger) and in music (the second violin concerto of Hans Werner Henze). It has been quoted in the Broadway play *Breaking the Code* (1988), about the life of Turing, and in the related biography, *Alan Turing: The Enigma* (Andrew Hodges, 1983). Turing's theory of computers built on and strengthened Gödel's theorem.

The original 1931 article in which Gödel proved the theorem is available in several English translations; this article and Gödel's lectures on it (at Princeton in 1934) were published both in *The Undecidable* (a 1965 collection of the basic papers closely related to the theorem, edited by Martin Davis) and in the first volume of Gödel's *Collected Works* (*CW*1 1986). Expositions of the proof of Gödel's theorem have proliferated in articles and books aimed at smaller and larger groups. Of those aimed at the common reader, the most notable are Ernest Nagel and J. R. Newman, *Gödel's Proof* (1958); Douglas Hofstadter, *Gödel, Escher, Bach: An Eternal Golden Braid* (1979); Rudy Rucker, *Infinity and the Mind* (1984); and Roger Penrose, *The Emperor's New Mind* (1990).

Gödel in person narrowly missed the widespread fame his theorem acquired through Hofstadter's best-selling book, which appeared the year after Gödel's death. This colorful work links the theorem with the music of J. S. Bach (1685–1750) and the drawings of M. C. Escher (1902–1972) all seen as diverse manifestations of self-reference, or "strange loops." Hofstadter sees strange loops or "tangled hierarchies" as "the crux of consciousness" and proposes a "metaphorical fugue on minds and machines." The constructions in Gödel's proof buttress the project of artificial intelligence (AI) by offering "the notion that a high-level view of a system may contain certain explanatory power which simply is absent on the low levels" (Hofstadter 1979:707). In a somewhat similar spirit, Judson Webb (1980) argues in *Mechanism, Mentalism and Metamathematics* that Gödel's theorem supplies evidence for (rather than against) the faith of many AI researchers.

Another extreme view, represented by Roger Penrose, is that "from consideration of Gödel's theorem ... we can see that the role of consciousness is non-algorithmic when forming *mathematical* judgments, where calculation and rigorous proof constitute such an important factor" (Penrose 1990:416). Gödel himself, like a majority of those who have thought about the question, looked for additional insights which, in combination with his theorem, would lead to a conclusive proof of our natural belief that the human mind does indeed surpass all computers, preferably just by demonstrating the mind's superior capacity to decide specifically mathematical questions.

Gödel's theorem occupies a central position in the development of recursion theory, proof theory, and computer science. Furthermore, it has been taken up enthusiastically by philosophers, linguists, and psychologists. People have asked whether an analogous theorem can be proved for physics. (Compare *RG*:156.) In response to a proposal to generalize his theorem to human affairs, Gödel once proposed what he considered a reasonable formulation (in the draft of a letter—I forget to whom—dated 15 March 1961):

0.1.1 A completely unfree society (i.e., one proceeding in everything by strict rules of "conformity") will, in its behavior, be either inconsistent or incomplete, i.e., unable to solve certain problems, perhaps of vital importance. Both of course, may jeopardize its survival in a difficult situation. A similar remark would also apply to individual human beings.

The theorem is fast becoming one of those seminal contributions to twentieth-century thought which everyone has heard about and acknowledges to be important, although appreciations of its significance differ in depth and in interpretation. In this respect, it is like Freudian psychology, Einstein's theory of relativity, Bohr's principle of complementarity and Heisenberg's uncertainty principle, Keynesian economics, and the double-helix model of DNA.

Gödel's other major contributions to logic, although important in logic and philosophically significant, have not acquired comparable public attention. His philosophical work remains largely unpublished, except for a few articles and fragments. Only his sketch of his philosophy of mathematics is fairly familiar. During my conversations with him, however, I realized that this sketch is highly inadequate and misleading, like one tip of an iceberg. Even the part of the iceberg that has been exposed to me reveals a much grander structure than is suggested by the familiar picture.

There is much more in Gödel's philosophy of mathematics than is commonly believed. For instance, contrary to the general impression, Gödel affirms the fallibility of our mathematical intuition and investigates the different degrees of clarity and certainty that exist within mathematics. Also, he recognizes the epistemic priority of natural numbers over arbitrary sets and of objectivity over objects.

And there is more in his philosophy than his philosophy of mathematics. Unlike most philosophers today, he has definite views on many difficult issues which appear to be so far beyond what we know that we are hard put to form strong convictions one way or the other. What is more, his views are usually contrary to the spirit of the time. This speculative boldness is undoubtedly linked to his belief that "there are many relationships which today's science and received wisdom haven't any inkling of" (letter to his mother [hereafter LM] dated 12.9.61, reproduced in Chapter 3).

In 1975, in response to a request from a popular magazine to report on some of my discussions with Gödel, I wrote a paper putting together some of his observations on the relations between mind, matter, mathematics, and computing machines. In commenting on a draft of this paper, Gödel asked me to add the following paragraph:

0.1.2 Gödel told me that he had certain deep convictions regarding mind and matter which he believed are contrary to the commonly accepted views today. The reasons for his convictions are of a very general philosophical nature and the arguments he possessed are not convincing to people with different convictions. Hence, he had chosen to state only those parts or consequences of his convictions which are definite even without reference to his general philosophy (Wang 1978).

The distinction between his deep convictions and his reasons for holding them indicates that Gödel possessed no persuasive formulation of his general philosophy. Judging from our limited knowledge of his literary estate, it appears that he did not work out and put into writing much of his general philosophy. My impression is that he did not develop his general philosophy nearly as thoroughly as he did some parts of his philosophy of mathematics. It is even possible that the informal and loosely structured conversations he had with me—and which I am using freely in this book—will turn out to be the fullest extant expression of the diverse components of his inadequately articulated general philosophy. If this conjecture is correct, there will be a great deal of room for alternative interpretations of his philosophical views.

Although I give an extended account of Gödel's mental development, in Chapter 2, it may be useful here to provide a brief sketch of some of the high points.

Stimulated by an introductory textbook in calculus, Gödel became interested in mathematics in 1921. In the summer of that year he read a biography of Goethe which led him, indirectly, to an interest in Newton's ideas and physics in general. He began to read the work of Kant in 1922. He entered the University of Vienna to study physics in 1924; but his interest in precision led him away from physics into mathematics in 1926 and, in 1928, to mathematical logic. Two revealing pieces of information about this period, as gleaned from his letters, are his early adherence to Platonism and his image of himself as someone going against the contemporary intellectual climate:

0.1.3 I have been a conceptual and mathematical realist since about 1925 (letter of 19.8.75, Quoted in *RG*:20).

0.1.4 I *don't* consider my work a "facet of the intellectual atmosphere of early twentieth century," but rather the opposite (ibid.).

From 1929 to 1933 Gödel did fundamental work on predicate logic and the foundations of arithmetic and began to think about set theory. From roughly 1933 to the beginning of 1943, he was mainly occupied with set theory and made fundamental contributions to it. This shift of his attention related to a conscious decision to concentrate only on basic problems. For instance, in early 1937 he told my college teacher, Wang Sian-jun, that

0.1.5 The nature of number theory is basically clear now as a result of my own and related work. The present task is to understand set theory (*Jetzt, Mengenlehre*).

Between 1927 and 1939, the mathematician Karl Menger had frequent contacts with Gödel. In 1981 he described Gödel's conduct during scientific discussions:

0.1.6 Gödel was generous with opinions and advice in mathematical and logic questions. He consistently perceived problematic points quickly and thoroughly, and made replies with greatest precision in a minimum of words, often opening up novel aspects for the inquirer. He expressed all this as if it were completely a matter of course, but often with a certain shyness, the charm of which awoke warm and personal feelings for him in many a listener. (Compare Menger 1994: 201.)

Gödel studied the work of Leibniz from 1943 to 1946. According to Menger, "Gödel had already begun to concentrate on Leibniz" around 1932 (1994:210). He published his Russell paper in 1944 and the first version of his Cantor paper in 1947. Between 1946 and 1950 he devoted himself mainly to what he called a "digression"—the study of the problem of time, with special reference to Kant's philosophy and Einstein's theory of relativity—producing two mathematical and two philosophical papers as a result.

In 1951 he wrote and delivered his Gibbs lecture, which was primarily an attempt to argue for Platonism in mathematics. In 1958 he published the Bernays paper, which interprets intuitionistic number theory by a slight and natural extension of Hilbert's finitary mathematics. From 1953 to the beginning of 1959 he spent a great deal of his effort on the Carnap paper, in which he tries to prove that mathematics is not syntax of language and argues in favor of some form of Platonism. In the end he decided not to publish this paper. He wrote to P. A. Schilpp, the editor, on 3 February 1959:

0.1.7   I have completed several different versions, but none of them satisfies me. It is easy to allege very weighty and striking arguments in favor of my views, but a complete elucidation of the situation turned out to be more difficult than I had anticipated. The subject matter is closely related to, and in part identical with, one of the basic problems of philosophy, namely the question of the objective reality of concepts and their relations. In view of widely held prejudices, it may do more harm than good to publish half-done work.

In 1959 Gödel began to study the work of Edmund Husserl. In 1964 he published a revised and expanded version of his Cantor paper; and from 1966 to 1969 he expanded the Bernays paper by adding three new notes. In December 1967 and March 1968 he wrote two letters to me explaining the importance of his Platonism for his work in logic. (I later published the letters, with his consent, in *From Mathematics to Philosophy* (Wang 1974a, hereafter *MP*:8—11). After explaining the relation of Platonism to his work on predicate logic, he continued:

0.1.8   I may add that my objectivistic conception of mathematics and metamathematics in general, and of transfinite reasoning in particular, was fundamental also to my other work in logic.

During 1971 and 1972 Gödel and I had extensive philosophical discussions, and he commented on a book manuscript of mine. As a result, he decided to formulate and make public some aspects of his own philosophical outlook through that book; these concise statements of his were duly published in *MP*:9—13, 84—86, 189—190, 324—326). We resumed our discussions in October of 1975 and continued them until June 1976. I am trying to make a full report of these conversations in the present book.

0.2 Gödel's Philosophy: Program and Execution

Gödel's program in philosophy is to find an exact theory of metaphysics, presumably in the form of a monadology. He felt, however, that he himself was far from reaching that goal. He did not even know, he said, what the right primitive concepts are. What he had done was to deal carefully with certain more manageable subproblems and to communicate his general attitude and some methodological recommendations. I discuss these items at greater length in Chapter 9. My purpose here is to explain the motivation behind the philosophical discussions reported there by viewing them, quite apart from their direct contact with current philosophy, as parts of Gödel's grand project.

Gödel characterized his philosophical outlook in this way:

0.2.1 My theory is a monadology with a central monad [namely, God]. It is like the monadology by Leibniz in its general structure.

0.2.2 My theory is rationalistic, idealistic, optimistic, and theological.

To carry out his program, Gödel had to take into account Kant's criticisms of Leibniz. He saw Husserl's method as promising a way to meet Kant's objections. This is why, as reported in Chapter 5, he criticized positivism and defended Husserl.

The idealistic component of Gödel's theory is, I believe, to be construed as affirming the primacy of mind and its powers. It is in this sense that he rejected materialism. This is implicit in the very conception of monadology, for the monads are seen as spiritual beings and they constitute the fundamental substances. Given the prevalence of the view that there is no mind separate from matter, Gödel had to try to disprove that view. Since the range of what matter can do is not as transparent as the range of the capabilities of computers, he assumed that the brain functions basically like a computer. He then tried to prove the superiority of mind over computers by arguing, in the first place, that minds can do more mathematics than computers can. This topic is central to the observations considered in Chapter 6, on "Minds and Machines."

In other words, in order to argue for his idealism, Gödel tried to bring the dialectic of the formal and the intuitive to a level at which a precise resolution is more likely to be attained. This is not unlike his work on the foundations of mathematics, where his precise results in logic constituted a plausible and precise refutation of a positivistically oriented formalism. Along a less decisive line, his solutions of Einstein's field equations were motivated by—and used by Gödel to support—his belief that our intuitive concept of time is not objective.

The rationalistic component of Gödel's theory argues in support of both Platonism and the superior power of the mind, because rationalism—at least as Gödel understood it—puts universals at the center and views them as stable and knowable by us. Immediately relevant to his grand project would be the independent existence and knowability of the sharp primitive concepts of metaphysics or monadology—so that we can find the governing axioms and see them as true.

But we do not even know what these primitive concepts are. In any case, from our experience in the history of philosophy, we are inclined to believe that the familiar candidates for the primitive concepts of metaphysics are not sufficiently sharp and knowable for us to see—with stable intersubjective agreement—that their axioms are true. Typically, instead of facing this problem directly, Gödel concentrated on a related more definite subproblem: that of Platonism (or objectivism) in mathematics, which is the subject matter of Chapter 7. He then seemed to apply implicitly his principle of uninhibited generalization (and analogy) to infer that, if we think hard enough and see things in the right way, metaphysical concepts become as sharp and can be seen as clearly as the concepts of mathematics.

The optimistic and the theological components of his theory are intended to provide us with more ammunition. The principle of uninhibited generalization is a major application of optimism. Other specific applications of these two components are well illustrated by Gödel's arguments for an afterlife and for the existence of God. These bold speculations are reported and discussed in Chapter 3. It seems clear that he himself realized, however, that these two components could not convince those who did not already believe the proposed conclusions. Indeed, they could have only a heuristic value in philosophy: one who believes in them could arrive at certain conclusions by applying them and subsequently look for or find more universally convincing arguments to support the conclusions.

Chapter 8 is devoted to set theory and logic as concept theory. In this connection, Gödel discussed extensively a conception of logic which seems to me to be a natural refinement of Frege's inconsistent conception of logic as concept theory. In both cases, logic includes set theory as a part. The difference is that Gödel rejected Frege's assumption that the range of every concept is a set. As a result, even though set theory enriches logic greatly, concept theory is not parallel to it and has yet to be developed. We are at present far from knowing what the main axioms of concept theory are. Apart from the intrinsic significance of set theory, Gödel was interested in capturing the essence of mathematics, as an additional support for Platonism in mathematics and as a substantive part of logic in his sense, which is an elementary part of monadology:

0.2.3 Logic deals with more general concepts; monadology, which contains general laws of biology, is more specific.

In the foregoing section I have tried to see the views of Gödel considered in this book as parts of his grand project. Most of us today do not, I am sure, see any plausible way of approaching the grand goal of his project in its full splendor: that is, as an exact theory that does for metaphysics what Newton did for physics. Nonetheless, it is possible to envisage fruitful work in the direction of this grand goal which would, say, capture in a satisfactory way the skeleton of a monadology.

For instance, if we enrich the theory of the world in Wittgenstein's *Tractatus* by distinguishing between concepts and objects (the monads and all sets of objects), taking perception and appetition as the primitive faculties of the monads, and using as axioms some of the Leibnizian principles and some of the rudimentary laws governing the operation of perception and appetition, we may hope to arrive at a reasonable theory which agrees with our crude intuitions and to see, in particular, that the true propositions of logic in Gödel's sense are all true in every possible world according to such a theory. If we think about the relevant ideas discussed later in Chapter 9, it seems to me possible to interpret Gödel's project in this apparently weakened sense.

In terms of the present state of philosophy and my own concerns in the study of philosophy, I believe it possible to distinguish two parts in what I know of Gödel's philosophical views and to evaluate these two parts separately. On the one hand, the speculations on God and an afterlife and the inclusion of a central monad in monadology are beyond my informed concerns; I am not able to see the reasonableness of the optimistic and the theological parts of his philosophy well enough to derive any benefit from them. On the other hand, Gödel's methodological observations and his comments on familiar philosophers are highly suggestive and helpful in broadening one's outlook; his extended discussions of logic and set theory, minds and machines, and Platonism in mathematics are stimulating contributions to the continuing dialogue in the European philosophical tradition.

Indeed, it may even be said that in the second (methodological) part of his philosophy Gödel was addressing the basic problems of this tradition, which puts the philosophy of knowledge at the center and directs its attention primarily to the universal and the theoretical. It has to do with the dialectic of the universal and the particular (arguably *the* central problem of Greek philosophy) and that of the subject and the object (arguably *the* central problem of modern philosophy from Descartes to Kant and onwards). For instance, Plato's theory of Ideas is an attempt to solve the problem of universals, and is commonly taken to be the backbone of Plato's philosophy. Yet it is only one philosopher's philosophy of knowledge, not a definition of the general task.

In a discussion of Plato's Academy, Harold F. Cherniss formulated the task of philosophy as follows (1962:83):

0.2.4   Moreover, there are two things in which Plato is more interested than in the theory of ideas itself, for that theory is, after all, only his way of satisfying these two requirements: first, there is such a thing as mind which can apprehend reality, and second, this reality which is the object [subject matter] of knowledge has absolute and unqualified existence.

These two requirements can be met in different ways. In fact, we all believe that they are as a matter of fact satisfied, as we know from experience. Yet when we try to reflect on them, we find it difficult to determine just what reality is, or what we mean by *reality*, as well as the sense and the extent to which our mind can apprehend it.

Much of traditional philosophy may be seen as attempts to capture our notion of this unqualified, absolute reality and to characterize the mind's capacity to apprehend it. We have a good deal of experience of the mind's apprehension of reality, its successes and its failures. We are convinced that the physical world is real, and life as we know it, including the surprising success of science and technology, shows us that in some sense the mind can apprehend it.

Yet, even for our most rudimentary knowledge, our minds have to use concepts, such as *red, chair,* and so on, which are not *in* the physical world in the same sense as that in which particular red chairs are. We are faced with the task of determining the status of concepts. It is therefore not surprising that for fifty years Gödel adhered to and continually tried to find convincing reasons to support some form of Platonism.

Following the suggestion of Cherniss (0.2.4), we may say that the main problems of the philosophy of knowledge are (1) the range and the nature of objective reality, and (2) the range and the nature of the mind's capacity to know objective reality.

Most people agree that the physical world is part of objective reality. One basic problem of philosophy is what is known as (1*a*) the problem of universals, which asks, in the first place, whether and in what sense concepts, or universals, and their relations are objectively real. (Another part of that problem is the relation between universals and particulars.) Another basic question is (1*b*) the problem of time, which asks whether time and change are objectively real.

We know from experience that the mind does know a lot about the physical world, as is evident both from our everyday knowledge and from physics as we now have it, and about the mathematical world, to the extent that we have reliable and rich mathematics. Most people agree that sense experience plays an important part in our knowledge; but it is by no means clear that sense experience alone can account for our conceptual knowledge, which plays an important part in physics and, even more strikingly, in mathematics.

A natural problem is (2*a*) the range and the nature of the mind's capacity to have conceptual knowledge—in particular, to know mathematics and be able to apply it. Because we feel we now know the physical world well and because we tend to think of our brains as part of it, we are interested in (2*b*) the relation between minds and brains and, in particular, the comparison between their capacities. Moreover, since computers operate in a more transparent manner than either brains or minds, another familiar question is (2*c*) whether brains or minds function like computers and whether or not they can do more than computers can.

The five vaguely formulated problems I have listed are notoriously elusive and controversial. In discussing them we typically talk at cross purposes, and so are rarely able to discover where, behind the vehement antagonisms, true disagreements lie. Two interrelated strategies for reducing the frustrations in this situation are, first, to work out fully all the ramifications of a position so as to reveal more definite spots of its peculiarity; and, second, to divide up the issue into less complex parts and plan to begin with the parts that admit of more precise treatment. It seems to me that much of Gödel's work can be viewed as a pursuit of philosophy by using the second strategy.

Gödel's philosophical observations and his major mathematical discoveries can mostly be seen as directed to the five major problems just listed, usually to restricted or derived parts of them. He restricts 1*a*, the problem of universals, largely to mathematical concepts and their relations, striving to establish and fix the content of his conclusion that they are objectively real. Indeed, in his philosophical writings and in his conversations he has said more on this topic than on any other. With regard to 1*b* (to be discussed in Chapter 9), he believes with Kant (and Parmenides and the "modern idealists") that time and change are merely subjective (not objectively real). In particular, he uses his solutions of Einstein's field equations—a precise mathematical result—as support for this belief.

On 2*a*, the mind's capacity for conceptual knowledge, Gödel again concentrates primarily on mathematical and logical concepts. He urges that our intuition goes beyond Kantian (or, according to him, concrete) intuition and that, indeed, we can also *perceive* concepts. Kant's *Anschauung* is restricted to space-time (or sensory) intuition; it accounts more or less for Hilbert's finitary mathematics, which carries us beyond the finite to a simple form of the potential infinite. Hilbert himself had expected to use his finitary mathematics to safeguard more advanced mathematics by proving it to be consistent, but Gödel's theorem frustrated this expectation. As I elaborate in Chapter 7, Gödel implicitly suggests and contributes to an approach alternative to Hilbert's original program, which aims to reveal how we can extend Hilbert's finitary mathematics step by step by adding plausible new abstract concepts, so as to obtain more and more advanced mathematics.

Gödel is also much interested in problems 2b and 2c, that is, in studying the relations between minds, brains, and computers, and, especially, in comparing their capacities. He believes that "the brain functions basically like a digital computer." With this assumption, he offers a "scientifically provable" conjecture that the mind can perform more operations than the brain (thus construed as a computer). In addition, he suggests several directions along which we may hope to prove that the mind can do more mathematics than any computer can. Specifically, he seeks additional plausible premises that can be combined, separately or together, with his theorem that mathematics is mechanically inexhaustible, to yield the desired conclusion that minds are superior to computers in mathematics.

Concepts are of central importance for the mind's capacity to apprehend reality. There is endless debate on the question of whether, when we come up with a new concept, we are discovering, creating, or inventing that concept—the answer being dependent on one's position regarding problem 1a, the problem of universals. However, regardless of one's position on this issue, the ability of the human mind to learn or come up with new concepts is a remarkable and hard-to-capture attribute. This constant development, Gödel and many of us feel, is quite beyond the capacity of computers. Yet it is hard to see how one could prove convincingly that this is so. To me, the phenomenon of the mind's learning or coming up with new concepts is the central mystery that philosophy tries but fails to deal with clearly and adequately. I am inclined to think that a lot of philosophical controversies are a consequence of this fact. Problem 1a is but one of them.

Gödel applies his principle of uninhibited generalization not only to draw such strong conclusions as reason's power to answer its own questions, but also to extend the range of certain concepts by analogy. As a result, some of his terminology may be misleading and may even conceal some difficulties.

For example, he asserts, in analogy to our perception of physical objects, our ability to *perceive* concepts too. It is necessary to remind ourselves, however, that by this he means primarily our capacity to understand and see that certain assertions about the concepts are true. He also regards perceiving concepts or intuiting essences as a kind of *observation*. His conception of the axiomatic method, which he regards as nothing but clear thinking, seems to be broader than the usual conception and to require some conjectural interpretation, which I attempt to provide later in this chapter.

Contrary to the familiar conception of *concept* as something originally conceived by the mind, Gödel construes concepts as real entities—specifically "as the properties and relations of things existing independently of our definitions and constructions" (Gödel 1994:128). There is a problem of distinguishing such concepts from notions introduced by us for the purpose of orientation and understanding: clearly we do use such notions, regardless of whether we also recognize real concepts in Gödel's sense. He himself mentions a species of such notions in the just-quoted context. I discuss this issue further in the Epilogue.

Gödel distinguishes *creation*, in the sense of making something out of nothing, from *construction* or *invention*, in the sense of making something out of something else. His strict adherence to this distinction has the consequence of giving creation for him a narrower range than we are accustomed to. In particular, he sees concepts and other things constructed by us as discoveries rather than creations. As a result, for instance, he disagrees with Brouwer, saying that we construct—rather than create—the natural numbers from our original intuition of two-oneness. In Chapter 7 I consider some of the ramifications of this insistence on his favorite sense of creation.

In the present work, I usually construe *intuition* and *idealization* in their broad and comparatively stable senses, which, I believe, agree with Gödel's primary conception. I also think of all primitive concepts as obtained or discovered (in his sense) by idealization. I regard the realm of intuition as consisting, in the first place, of what Rawls calls our "considered judgments in reflective equilibrium" (a concept I discuss in the Epilogue).

0.3 Relation of Philosophy to Mathematics and Logic

The surprising centrality of logic and mathematics within European philosophy is a familiar phenomenon, undoubtedly because these subjects are exceptionally precise and, at the same time, concerned with what is maximally universal. It is generally agreed that mathematics played an important part in Plato's philosophy and that Aristotle was the founder of logic. The works of Descartes and Leibniz also are important in both philosophy and mathematics, and Spinoza presented his *Ethics* in the order of geometrical demonstrations. Even though Kant relegates formal logic to a peripheral place, his transcendental logic is central in his philosophy. Hegel's science of logic is his metaphysics, or first philosophy.

When we come to the twentieth century, the phenomenon of the influence of mathematics and logic on philosophy is especially striking. Frege (1848–1925), Husserl (1859–1938), Russell (1872–1970), and Wittgenstein (1889–1951) all began with a strong interest in the foundations of mathematics. We are all familiar with the importance of their work and their influence in recent and contemporary philosophy. Moreover, Dedekind (1831–1916), Cantor (1845–1918), Poincaré (1854–1912), Hilbert (1862–1943), Brouwer (1881–1965), and Turing (1912–1954), though known primarily as mathematicians, have exercised considerable influence in the philosophy of mathematics. Peirce (1839–1914), Whitehead (1861–1947), C. I. Lewis (1883–1964), Bernays (1888–1977), Carnap (1891–1970), Ramsey (1902–1930), Gödel (1906–1978), and Quine (1908–) all worked on both logic and philosophy; their work exhibits several different ways of relating logic to philosophy.

The characteristic feature of effective thinking is an appropriate blending of the formal and the intuitive. Mathematics and logic are important because they provide us with a model and a frame of reference for the interplay between the formal and the intuitive. In everyday life and in scientific thinking we implicitly or explicitly use logic and mathematics. In philosophy we are concerned, in addition, with their nature and their relationship to each other and to philosophy.

Philosophy sees in mathematics a model of clear thinking, with sharp concepts and indubitable conclusions as well as a universe of discourse in which order prevails and the power of pure reason is most impressive. Plato and Gödel both used our experience with mathematics as their primary evidence for the independent existence of sharp concepts. Spinoza, as noted, formulated and presented his system of philosophy as an axiomatic theory in the manner of geometry. Frege's attempt to attain a precise foundation for mathematics led to a general framework for the philosophical study of our concepts of meaning and truth in all scientific discourse. In contrasting alternative philosophies as different worldviews, Gödel perceived mathematics as the ultimate stronghold of his own favorite type of philosophy, which chooses to view the world as an orderly and purposeful whole.

The influence of philosophy on mathematics is less conspicuous and pervasive. Cantor did try to borrow support from theology for his set theory, and Russell turned to mathematics as a source of security and consolation after he failed to find a rational ground for religious faith. G. H. Hardy and some other mathematicians seem to find the philosophy of Platonism helpful in a general way for their mathematical work. Gödel was exceptional in asserting that—and explaining specifically how—his adoption of Platonism in his philosophy of mathematics was fundamental to his mathematical work in logic.

The relation of philosophy to logic is more direct and intimate than its relation to mathematics. Logic is taught as a branch of philosophy, and in some philosophies logic in one form or another occupies a central place. As we know, however, there are different conceptions not only of the nature of logic but also of its range. We all implicitly apply logic in our thinking, but not many people study logic consciously as a subject in itself.

Logic as an activity—the art of thinking—serves to adjudicate the interplay or dialectic, as one thinks, between belief and action, which involves and is often replaced, in our thinking process, by the dialectic of the subject and the object, the known and the unknown, the subjective and the objective, form and content, the universal and the particular, the formal and the intuitive. This adjudicative function of logic is present in all sorts of thinking. As an art or a method, logic is neutral relative to the subject matter of our thought.

The vague but suggestive word *dialectic* is commonly used to describe the interactions of contradictory or opposite forces that lead to a higher and more unified stage in some processes. Traditionally, dialectic is closely associated with logic. Indeed, throughout the Middle Ages the word *dialectica* designated what we now call *logic*. For Hegel, logic is the science of the dialectical process—the continual unification of opposites in the complex relation of parts to a whole—which is pervasive both in human thought and in world history.

The familiar characterization of the subject matter of logic begins by agreeing that logical truths consist of all and only those propositions which are *valid* in the sense of being true no matter what the concepts and objects are in the actual world. The concepts of logic—the logical constants—are then the concepts that appear essentially or irreplaceably in these valid propositions. Examples are: everything is identical with itself; every proposition implies itself; either a proposition or its negation is true but not both; something is true of everything if it is true of all things. These are valid propositions because they are true, whatever the concepts and the objects are. And the concepts of identity, implication, negation, universalization (all), and so on, which occur essentially in these propositions, are logical constants.

Moreover, all propositions are built up from simple propositions of predication—that is, propositions that apply certain concepts to certain things—by using these familiar logical constants. In order to deal effectively with propositions in a uniform way, logicians from Aristotle to Frege have contrived increasingly adequate structures and notations to codify the intuitive process of building up propositions. Indeed, what is generally accepted today as the system of *predicate logic* (or elementary or first-order logic) is, in its general form, the system articulated by Frege in 1879. Practically nobody denies that predicate logic is definitely a part of logic.

A familiar controversy is over the issue of whether predicate logic is the whole of logic. It is possible to reformulate predicate logic in such a way that it can be seen as concerned only with the rules of inference that govern its logical constants—namely, identity, the propositional connectives, and the quantifiers. For instance, we can design a complete system of predicate logic by using self-identity of things and self-implication of propositions as the only axioms, leaving the substance of the system to natural deductive rules—such as the rule that authorizes inference from two given (asserted) propositions to their conjunction—which capture the intuitive meaning of these logical constants. With such a reformulation of predicate logic, those who wish to restrict logic to predicate logic can support their thesis by appealing to the familiar conception of logic as the science of valid rules of inference.

To determine the range of objects, we may begin with the familiar physical objects. When we think about concepts, we are led to a natural extension of the realm of objects: with respect to most familiar concepts, we have in each case a corresponding *set* which is the *extension* of the concept, in the sense of a collection of all the things to which the concept is applicable. It is, however, natural, as emphasized by Frege, to think of an extension as an object. In this way, we are led to the view that sets of objects are objects too.

Since logic is concerned with the *necessary*—in the sense that the logically true propositions are true in all possible empirical worlds—it has nothing to say about the contingent fact that this or that empirical object or concept exists in the actual world. Hence, it would appear, logic has little material to begin with.

However, even without recognizing any empirical thing, we realize that there must be some empty concept which applies to nothing and, therewith, the *empty set* which is the extension of every empty concept. Therefore, there is at least some object—namely the empty set—in every possible world. But given any objects, we can form their sets and the sets of their sets, and so on. In this way, we obtain the familiar hierarchy of *pure* sets which are the subject matter of set theory. And we may say, therefore, that set theory is also a part of logic.

It is also possible to envisage an analogous theory of pure concepts and argue, on the same grounds, that it is a part of logic too. However, as we know, there are certain concepts whose ranges of applicability are not sets: for instance, the concept of concept or the concept of set. Consequently, pure concept theory is not entirely a duplicate of pure set theory. In fact, even though we have by now a satisfactory and rather well-developed set theory, we are far from possessing today a comparably mature concept theory. In this sense, much fundamental work remains to be done even in setting up the basic framework of logic—if it is construed as including pure concept theory as an essential part. As I said before, this conception of logic agrees, I believe, with Frege's intention and Gödel's declaration.

The relation between philosophy and logic in this sense is comparable to the relation between science and mathematics. Just as mathematics studies the universal and abstract aspect which belongs to the intersection of the concerns of all sciences, the subject matter of logic may be seen as the intersection or the limit of all our philosophical concerns as we go from the more substantive to the more abstract. We may also see logic as a form of ontology which constitutes a fundamental part of metaphysics.

A less abstract approach to the relation between logic and philosophy is to adopt the view that philosophy as worldview aims at capturing and formulating the universal and comprehensive frame of our inner resources by means of which we receive, digest, and interpret all our thoughts about the world and about ourselves. From this perspective, logic makes up a major part of philosophy and may even be identified with what might be called *pure philosophy*. In my opinion, Hegel's conception of logic and Wittgenstein's conception as developed in his *On Certainty* tend toward this interpretation of logic and its relation to philosophy (compare Wang 1994: section 1).

Each of us learns to believe a number of things and gradually forms a picture of the world as a system of beliefs. We learn to act according to these beliefs, among which some tend to stand fast, like the riverbed, and some are more or less liable to shift, like the moving waters. Logic is concerned with the beliefs that stand fast in all systems of belief. The belief in certain empirical propositions belongs to our frame of reference too, even though they are not part of logic. Mathematics is a part of logic. Although the same proposition may be treated both as a rule for testing and, at other times, as something that must be tested by experience, logic is not an empirical science.

Given this vague characterization of logic based on a paraphrase and an interpretation of Wittgenstein's text, there remain different possibilities for explicating this ambiguous conception. For instance, Hegel and Wittgenstein, although both of them can be said to be applying this conception, offer different answers—undoubtedly conditioned to a large extent by their different attitudes toward sameness and difference, as well as their different ideas of what is taken to be known. In any case, it is clear that logic according to this conception forms an important part of philosophy. If we add the requirement of precision to this conception of logic, we could, I think, also view the Frege-Gödel conception as an explication of it.

One way to link this conception of logic—as the common part of different systems of beliefs—to our familiar shared concerns is to compare it to John Rawls's effort to replace comprehensive political theory with a political conception of justice intended to represent the *overlapping consensus* in a modern democratic society (Rawls 1993:xvii). If we consider the intersection or the universally overlapping consensus of conflicting philosophical worldviews, we seem to have a comparatively tangible way of gradually determining the vague domain of the a priori, in the sense of those concepts and beliefs which we could, potentially, all obtain and accept independently of our specific individual experiences. In other words, without restricting ourselves to one type of society, we may try to look for the concepts and the beliefs about them which all the different worldviews share. If we identify the range of logic with that of the a priori, or perhaps the maximally universal part of it, we have in logic a common basis on which we may hope to adjudicate between conflicting comprehensive philosophies.

Mathematical logic as it is commonly understood today consists roughly of recursion or computation theory, proof theory and constructive mathematics, model theory, and set theory. It is a branch of mathematics and of science. If we restrict logic to mathematical logic in this sense, then the relation between philosophy and logic is a special case of the general relation between philosophy and science. On the whole, the development of mathematical logic, especially at its early stages, has been much influenced by philosophical concerns: ... conversely, it has had a great deal of impact on the substance of the philosophy of mathematics and, therefore, also on several basic parts of general philosophy.

There are different attitudes toward the relation between philosophy and science. For instance, Einstein said: "The reciprocal relationship of epistemology and science is of noteworthy kind. They are dependent upon each other. Epistemology without contact with science becomes an empty scheme. Science without epistemology is—insofar as it is thinkable at all—primitive and muddled" (1949:683–84). Yet most practicing physicists today pay little attention to epistemology. Similarly, unlike Gödel, most practicing mathematical logicians today have at most a peripheral interest in philosophy. These differences in attitude undoubtedly relate to the current stage of a particular science and the specific problems investigated by a given scientist.

Analogously, different philosophers may value or deplore a positive relation between philosophy and science, depending on their own conceptions of the two subjects and the parts of philosophy they consider important. Gödel sees the interaction between science and philosophy as fruitful for both. Wittgenstein, on the other hand, finds science harmful because it strengthens "our craving for generality," which is responsible for bad philosophy (1975:18). He sees true philosophy as insulated from mathematics (1953:124)—despite his occasional declaration that philosophy may help get science on the right track of attending to our real need (1974:381 and 1980:62).

We do, as a matter of fact, draw philosophical consequences from scientific results—whether fruitfully or confusedly. As we all know, there have been conflicts between science and religion, and our whole picture of the world has been changed by the development of science. Professional philosophy has been affected by such major scientific advances as Newtonian physics, Darwinian biology, relativity theory, quantum physics, and molecular genetics. Among others, Gödel himself has repeatedly considered the philosophical implications of his own incompleteness theorem.

In the opposite direction, the influence of philosophy on science, we know that many scientific ideas had their beginnings in philosophy. It is likely that the theological view of God as promulgating the laws of nature had a positive effect on the persistent quest for order in nature by physicists like Newton. In this century, both Einstein and Gödel have alluded to the beneficial effect philosophy had on their scientific work.

A striking example of the interaction of philosophy and science is the set of fruitful mathematical problems proposed in Hilbert's program, which had been distilled with imagination and skill from philosophical debates on the foundations of mathematics. In cases like this, the solution to scientific problems can serve to clarify the original philosophical problem as well. Gödel saw one function of philosophy as the suggestion of seminal ideas—atomic theory, for example, was suggested by Democritus—and another as the reduction of philosophical to scientific problems, which was the intention of his own proposal (considered in Chapter 6) to clarify the philosophical issue of mind and matter by looking for a scientific proof of mind's superiority to matter. Moreover, Gödel's belief in the feasibility of finding an exact metaphysics seems to have been based on a bold—though unconvincing—extrapolation from his reflections on our experience with mathematics and physics.

0.4 From Gödel to Logic as Metaphilosophy

This book has two purposes: first, to present Gödel's life and work as completely and coherently as I can, and, second, to use his outlook as an illustration of how one might try to arrive at a comprehensive philosophy—or some substantive part of one—with recognition of our limited knowledge and with awareness that numerous reasonable alternative positions exist.

The parts of Gödel's outlook are of different degrees of clarity and certainty; they are linked together by certain more or less uninhibited generalizations of different degrees of persuasiveness. The mathematical part of his work is definitive. His conception of logic as concept theory defines a fairly precise and attractive task, although we do not know at present how productive it would be to concentrate on developing such a system.

Gödel's Platonism in mathematics is instructive and admits of a spectrum of weaker and stronger interpretations, from the easily acceptable to the powerfully ideal. For most of us his implicit analogy of metaphysics to mathematics is hard to accept; at the same time, it suggests possibilities which are consonant with his intent, but less substantive and more feasible.

Undoubtedly different people will accept different parts of Gödel's outlook, and derive different lessons from it. Most philosophers will, I believe, agree more or less with my division and evaluation of the different degrees of conclusiveness and persuasiveness of the several parts of his work. Some people may wish to clarify and develop further those of his ideas which they find attractive and plausible. Others may choose to disregard most of his philosophical ideas as unreasonable, contrasting his bad philosophy with his good work in logic.

One aim of this book is to report and interpret Gödel's views in a unified manner, providing its readers with an opportunity to reflect on their own positive or negative reactions to the different parts of Gödel's philosophy on the basis of additional data. Another aim is to use the material to clarify and formulate my own philosophical beliefs in order to address my own principal philosophical concerns.

Although I grew up in China, I have concentrated during my professional life mainly on Western philosophy, specializing in both general philosophy and mathematical logic. This background undoubtedly has much to do with my preoccupation with the prevalence of disagreement in philosophy: instead of concentrating on different parts of the same subject (as do most specialists in mathematical logic), philosophers arrive at conflicting conclusions while trying to answer the same question.

As a result, one of my primary concerns in studying philosophy has been to consolidate and apply the range of beliefs on which reasonable people agree, rather than to engage in detailed debates or present bold views that stimulate and provoke responses. Logic, at least by intention, stays within the domain of the overlapping consensus of philosophers, and so it is desirable to apply logic to adjudicate between alternative views. If we can see that certain conflicting answers to the same question are in fact answers to different questions, we can begin to decompose our disagreements through specialization and division of labor.

I find in the work of John Rawls an illuminating example of the use of shared beliefs. Rawls recognizes the existence of deep conflicts among reasonable comprehensive philosophies but sees no prospect of resolution. How, he asks, is a just and free society possible under such conditions? His answer is to formulate a political theory of justice which, he believes—falls within the range of an overlapping consensus.

Rawls sees his own political theory, like Kant's moral theory, as a form of *constructivism* and contrasts it with *rational intuitionism*, which is a form of Platonism. As we know, the conflict between constructivism and Platonism, which I consider in Chapter 7, is widely debated in the philosophy of mathematics. In order to clarify the perspective, which, I believe, I share with Rawls, it may be helpful to compare the two contrasts. There are, indeed, several instructive ramifications in this comparison, which I discuss in the Epilogue.

As they are commonly interpreted, constructivism and Platonism in mathematics contradict each other in a number of ways. Roughly speaking, the crucial step in a decomposition of this conflict is to reduce it to a familiar difference in attitudes: different combinations of attitudes depend on one's choice of whether to require or permit a higher or lower degree of clarity and certainty, or weaker or stronger idealizations. This choice, in turn, depends on other factors, such as the relation of the chosen position to the development and application of mathematics, one's knowledge and judgment of the naturalness of the major idealizations, and so on. Moreover, as I shall elaborate, each form of constructivism in mathematics already admits (or at least is compatible with) some form of Platonism; and within each meaningful form of constructivism or Platonism there is room for specialized investigations. Thus we arrive at a comprehensive perspective which replaces a major part of the conflicts of views about the same subject matter with choices to specialize in fairly well-defined mathematical domains of one degree of certainty and clarity or another.

This rough sketch of a dialectical approach to the philosophy of mathematics illustrates my proposal of a way to realize the familiar ideal of finding an appropriate way to see alternative philosophies as complementary parts of a cooperative project. The idea is to find and apply a shared criterion of rationality, so that we can assign different probabilities—relative to what we know now—to different parts of each philosophy and make explicit the distinct aims of each philosophy. In this way, one can choose and develop a philosophy according to one's aims and learn to tolerate philosophies with other reasonable aims. To arrive at a most plausible position for a shared aim, one can try to select and organize different beliefs directed toward that aim, according to their separate and conjoined probabilities.

It is usual to see the purpose of logic as the formation and application of a criterion of rationality that is acceptable to all reasonable people and serves to adjudicate between alternative views. When logic is seen in its role as the adjudicator between alternative philosophies, it becomes a kind of *metaphilosophy* which provides a methodology for finding and organizing, with due reflection, our considered judgments at all levels of generality.

Given, however, our gross ignorance of the truth or falsity of many assertions in philosophy, there are, of course, many disagreements over the probabilities to be assigned to them. In order to improve one's capacity to judge, it is necessary to reflect on the interconnection of the parts of some attractive system of beliefs and check them against one's own considered convictions on all the relevant levels of generality and certainty. This cautious approach tends to lead to an initial restriction to areas that promise continued stable agreement and to assertions of vague or qualified generalities which are reasonable but hardly striking.

In this sense, logic as metaphilosophy is a retrospective and preparatory approach to philosophy which tries to see alternative philosophies as complementary and to compare a philosophy (or some part of it) continually with our intuitions or judgments in reflective equilibrium. In the background are our large practical concerns, which give direction and ultimate motivation to our philosophical speculations.

Truth and *objective reality* are idealizations which derive meaning and are acceptable to us by way of our anticipation of intersubjective agreement, either universally or within a significant type of society, ideally if not actually. Philosophy is impoverished by an inappropriate resistance to abstraction and idealization, which, however, have to be restrained by attention to the requirement of foreseeable potential agreement. For instance, the conflict between constructivism and Platonism can be decomposed by breaking the relevant contested beliefs into parts that have fairly direct contact with our intuitions or considered judgments; we can thus localize the disagreement and choose among different forms of constructivism and Platonism within each domain, whether mathematics or moral theory or political theory.

I discuss these ideas more fully in the Epilogue. Even so, I am under no illusion that I am doing more than groping for an illustration of a program which I find attractive.

The first two chapters of this book are devoted to the life and mental development of Gödel. The third chapter illustrates the quest for final solutions and grand unifications of knowledge and action by discussing Gödel's written speculations on God and an afterlife. Chapter 4 supplies the background and a chronological summary of my conversations with Gödel in the 1970s, together with a report of his isolated general and technical observations.

Chapter 5 considers Gödel's comments on philosophies and philosophers, including his schema for classifying alternative worldviews, his support of Husserl's phenomenology, his criticism of positivism and empiricism, and his digressions on Kant and Wittgenstein. Chapter 6 concerns his attempt to demonstrate the superiority of minds over brains and computers, with special emphasis on the contrast between minds and computers.

The three chapters from 7 to 9 are intimately connected through Gödel's governing ideal of philosophy as an exact theory. He seems to see mathematics and Newtonian physics as models for philosophy and metaphysics. The strategy appears to be this: reflections on the nature of mathematics and logic support Platonism in mathematics; reasoning by analogy, he conjectures that Platonism in metaphysics is true as well; so it is possible to develop metaphysics as an exact theory.

His argument for Platonism in mathematics is the subject matter of Chapter 7. Chapter 8 is devoted to set theory and to logic as concept theory, which Gödel viewed as a sort of bridge between mathematics and metaphysics. In Chapter 9 I present an organized report and interpretation of our conversations, supplemented with my own comments and relevant material drawn from Gödel's writings. I try to combine Gödel's fragmentary metaphysical speculations and brief statements on his conception of philosophy. These programmatic observations provide a framework within which to place the more substantive assertions in Chapters 5 to 8, making it possible to discern the motivating force behind them. These substantive views are, of course, also of interest to those who do not share his optimistic belief in the feasibility and fruitfulness of his ambitious program for metaphysics.

Finally, in the last chapter, the Epilogue, I sketch my own approach to philosophy, in contrast to what I take to be Gödel's outlook.

Chapter 1
Gödel's Life

To develop the skill of correct thinking is in the first place to learn what you have to disregard. In order to go on, you have to know what to leave out: this is the essence of effective thinking.
Gödel, 15 March 1972

Roughly speaking, Gödel spent the first half of his life in Central Europe and the second half in America. He was born at Brünn in Moravia in 1906 and lived there until the autumn of 1924, when he left for the University of Vienna. Subsequently he lived and worked primarily in Vienna, paying three extended visits to America between 1933 and 1939. He left Austria in January 1940 and from March 1940 until his death in January 1978 made his home in Princeton, New Jersey. There he was a distinguished member of the Institute for Advanced Study. The time between 1929 and January 1940 was the most eventful and dramatic period of his life and work.

He was a student from 1912 to 1929 and engaged in academic research from 1929 to 1976. His most famous work, all in mathematical logic, was done in Vienna between 1929 and 1938. Yet, by his own account, his primary interest was philosophy, and he spent more effort in doing philosophy as he understood it than on anything else. From 1943 on, he said, he was chiefly occupied with philosophy. A central feature of his life and work, accordingly, was his choice to concentrate on what he considered to be fundamental, disregarding other issues.

At about the age of four, Gödel acquired the nickname *der Herr Warum* (Mr. Why) because he persistently asked the reasons for everything. He came from a quite wealthy family and grew up in a villa with a beautiful garden. He did exceptionally well and was much praised in school and, especially, in college. By the time he was twenty-five years old he had already done spectacular work, and he received wide recognition very soon afterward.

When he was about eight years old Gödel had a severe bout of rheumatic fever. Thereafter he was somewhat hypochondriacal; and his constant preoccupation with his health was accentuated by his excessive distrust of doctors. In 1976 he said that his generally poor health had, at certain periods, prevented him from doing serious work. He was about five feet six inches tall, usually underweight, and, in his later years, exceptionally sensitive to cold and prone to eating problems.

Gödel is remembered as a cheerful but timid child who became acutely troubled whenever his mother left the house. Throughout his life he avoided controversy and confined his personal contacts to a small circle of people. He liked women and even as a school boy developed romantic interests. Around 1928 he met his future wife, Adele, and from then on, despite the disapproval of his family, they remained together.

In Gödel's lifetime little was generally known of his personal life, although in 1976 he gave me an account of his intellectual development. After his death, his papers, his letters to his mother, and the reports of others—such as his brother Rudolf, Karl Menger, and Georg Kreisel—revealed more details about his life. In *Reflections on Kurt Gödel* (Wang 1987a, hereafter referred to as *RG*) I reported on the available facts about him, bringing together, in loosely organized manner, material from these sources.

In the rest of this Chapter I present a more coherent sketch of Gödel's life, digesting and structuring a selection from the data now accessible. These data include, apart from the material used in *RG*, a history of the family by his brother Rudolph Gödel (1987) and interviews with other people who knew him, conducted in May of 1986 by Eckehart Köhler, Werner Schimanovich, and Peter Weibel; I also make extensive use of Gödel's letters to his mother. I consider the details of his mental development separately in Chapter 2, even though I realize that, in a case like his, life and work are intimately intertwined.

Work and personal relationships are the two central concerns for most people. For Gödel, health occupied a comparable place as a third conspicuously determinative factor. From his birth in 1906 until 1928 he enjoyed a happy and harmonious period of preparation. During the most turbulent stretch of his life, from 1929 to the beginning of 1940, he did outstanding work and achieved great fame; he also experienced several mental crises, suffered deep personal conflicts, and reluctantly made the disruptive transition from Central Europe to America. From March 1940 until his death in January 1978 he lived an externally uneventful life in Princeton, except that during his last few years his health problems and those of his wife became his dominant concern.

1.1 A Sketch

Kurt (Friedrich) Gödel was born on 28 April 1906 at Brünn (in Moravia), which was known then as the Manchester of the Austro-Hungarian

Empire. The city was renamed Brno when it became a part of Czechoslovakia after the First World War. His German-speaking family cultivated its German national heritage. According to Kreisel (1980:152), Gödel wrote an essay at the age of fourteen extolling the superiority of the austere lives of Teutonic warriors over the decadent habits of civilized Romans. Whatever such youthful opinions may have meant for Gödel at the time, he was, as an adult, known to be peace-loving and cosmopolitan in his general outlook.

Gödel's paternal grandfather was born in 1848 and died before the turn of the century, apparently by suicide. His father, Rudolf, who was born in Brünn on 28 February 1874, did not grow up with his parents but lived with his Aunt Anna, a sister of his father. He did poorly in grammar school and was sent to a weaver's school at about the age of twelve. He completed his study with distinction and immediately obtained a position at the then famous textile factory of Friedrich Redlich. He worked in this firm till his premature death in 1929, rising first to manager and later to part-owner.

Gödel's mother, Marianne Handschuh (1897–1966), grew up in a large and happy family at a time when Europe was at peace. She had a broad literary education and for some time attended a French school in Brünn. A lively and cheerful young woman with many friends, she loved music, theater, poetry, sports, and reading. Her family occupied an apartment in the same house as the Gödels.

Marianne and Rudolf Gödel were married on 22 April 1901 and moved to their own apartment soon thereafter. Their first son, also christened Rudolf (and called Rudi in the family) was born in February 1902. Marianne was brought up as a Lutheran, and her husband was only formally Old Catholic. Their sons received no religious training. Gödel's brother remained indifferent to religion. Gödel himself, however, had a lifelong dislike of the Catholic Church and developed quite early theological interests. In 1975 he gave his religion as "Baptized Lutheran" (but not a member of any religious congregation). He wrote, "My belief is *theistic*, not pantheistic, following Leibniz rather than Spinoza." In 1978 Adele said that Gödel read the Bible in bed on Sundays although he did not go to church.

According to Gödel's brother, the union of their parents, though not a "marriage of love," was satisfactory. Marianne was undoubtedly impressed by the energetic efficiency of her husband and appreciated the material comfort he provided for the family. And he, who was duller and more solemn, enjoyed her cheerful friendliness. Both sons were in closer personal contact with their mother than with their father. Marianne always regretted, however, that neither of her children shared her interest in music.

Later in life Marianne recalled many details from Gödel's childhood which, in her opinion, presaged his later development into a world-famous intellect. Gödel's maternal grandmother, who often played with him before her death in 1911, had prophesied a great future for him.

In 1913 when Gödel was seven and his brother eleven, the family moved into a new villa with a fine garden. The boys had lots of fun with their two dogs, a Doberman and a small ratter. They played mostly with each other and had few friends; they played with building blocks, train sets, a sandbox, eight hundred tin soldiers, and board games.

From September 1912 to July 1916 Gödel attended the *Evangelische Volkschule*, a Lutheran school in Brünn. He then began his eight years in the *Staatsrealgymnasium mit deutscher Unterrichssprache*, a grammar school using the German language. He received private tutorials in English and did not take the elective course in Czech. He chose instead to study (from 1919 to 1921) Gabelsberger shorthand, of which he later made extensive use. (This is the reason why so much of his unpublished writing remains inaccessible today.)

Throughout his twelve school years Gödel received top marks in every class except for gymnastics and, once, mathematics. He was most outstanding, at first, in languages, then in history, and then in mathematics. To the astonishment of his teachers and classmates, he had already mastered the university material in mathematics when he was about seventeen. He was less attached to the family and less interested in their garden than his brother was.

Gödel entered the University of Vienna in autumn 1924 to study theoretical physics. His interest in precision led him from physics to mathematics in 1926 and to mathematical logic in 1928. He concluded his student days in the summer of 1929 by writing his important doctoral dissertation which proved the completeness of predicate logic. As students he and his brother lived together, each occupying his own room. Both prepared themselves for careers in Austria, rather than Czechoslovakia.

Gödel's student days were largely trouble-free and enjoyable. Gifted, diligent, well prepared in all relevant subjects, and the son of a well-to-do family, he possessed all the preconditions to benefit from the excellent intellectual nourishment the University of Vienna offered at the time. He was liked, and his talent was generally appreciated. He undoubtedly learned and digested a great deal in these years, principally in mathematics, physics, and philosophy. According to the recollection of Olga Taussky, a fellow student, "He was well trained in all branches of mathematics and you could talk to him about other things too—his clear mind made this a rare pleasure" (quoted in *RG*:76).

He was comfortable with his brother, and Brno was not far away, enabling them to enjoy family vacations and visits to and from their parents.

Even though they did not spend much time together because of their different schedules, the brothers got along with each other well enough.

On 23 February 1929 Gödel's father died unexpectedly. His mother moved to Vienna in November 1929 to live with her sons in a large apartment. For a number of years, the three of them often went to the theater together and had long discussions about what they had seen. In November of 1937 Gödel's mother moved back to Brno, and Gödel and his brother each acquired his own domicile in Vienna. Gödel married Adele Porkert in September 1938. His brother never married and lived with their mother in Vienna from 1944 until her death in 1966.

After Gödel's death, his brother revealed that:

1.1.1 The family was unhappy with his choice. Of course, she was not a match for him intellectually, but this would lie in the nature of things. She came from a very simple background. Her parents also lived in Langegasse. Her father was a photographer. (R. Gödel 1987.)

As I said before, the period from 1929 to the beginning of 1940 was the most turbulent in Gödel's life. He did his most famous work and received wide recognition. He traveled to the United States four times, and the last time he came to stay. He suffered several mental crises. He lived with Adele but had to contrive elaborate arrangements to deal with the disapproval of his family.

From the spring of 1929 to the autumn of 1930 Gödel made truly fundamental contributions to logic and was quickly recognized all over the world. He became a Privatdozent in March 1933. He received something like a standing invitation from the Princeton Institute for Advanced Study, and visited there from October 1933 to May 1934, from October to November 1935, and from October 1938 to January 1939. He also taught at the University of Notre Dame from January to May 1939.

Even after World War II began in September 1939, he apparently still wanted to remain in Vienna. In November 1939 he and Adele bought an apartment there and spent a good deal of money improving it. After the Anschluss, however, he had difficulty regaining even his modest position as Dozent under the new Nazi requirements. And, to his surprise, he was found fit for military service. He even considered obtaining a position in industrial research in the autumn of 1939. At the last minute he appealed to Oswald Veblen in Princeton and had to go through the unpleasant process of getting visas and permits to enable him and Adele to leave Vienna for America on 18 January 1940.

According to Gödel's brother Rudolf, their father had left each of them some money, and Gödel spent his share with Adele over the next seven or eight years. Rudolf believed that when they were still living with their mother, Gödel had secretly rented his own apartment and had probably used it with Adele. From November 1937 until November 1939, after their mother returned to Brno, Gödel lived—undoubtedly with Adele—at Himmelstrasse 43 in Grinzing, the famous Viennese wine district.

For many years Gödel kept his association with Adele almost entirely separate from his family and professional life. Their official marriage took place on 20 September 1938 at a registry office with only few people—including Adele's parents and Gödel's mother and brother—present. Apparently Gödel had never introduced Adele to his family before this occasion. Two weeks after the wedding, Gödel again left for America, alone, and stayed away almost nine months.

The months before his arrival in Princeton with Adele in March 1940 were hectic and disturbing for Gödel. Without a position in Austria and threatened with military service, he nevertheless bought an apartment and moved into it. Then, after the grueling process of obtaining visas and exit permits in the midst of the hurried exodus of Austrian Jews and intellectuals, he and Adele faced the long journey through Siberia and Japan to get to Princeton.

The strain of these experiences on a personality liable to periodic bouts of depression could have been—but apparently was not—excessive. According to his brother, around the end of 1931, not long after the publication of his most famous work, Gödel suffered from what "one would now call an endogenous depression—at that time neither the term nor the diagnosis was in existence yet." (R. Gödel 1987:00). This was Gödel's first serious nervous crisis and included suicidal tendencies. On this occasion he was sent to the Purkersdorf Sanatorium and, at another time, to Rekawinkel.

Gödel had a similar disturbance after his return from his first trip to America in June 1934. In the autumn of 1935 he cut short the visit, pleading depression and overwork. When he reached Paris he talked to his brother by telephone for about an hour. Rudolf then went to Paris and brought him back to Vienna by train. Gödel had another breakdown after the assassination of his teacher and friend Moritz Schlick on 22 June 1936. Decades later Adele told several people that Gödel was once sent to a sanatorium against his will and that she had rescued him by catching him as he jumped out of a window. This event presumably occurred in 1936. Gödel's papers contain a 1936 receipt for Dr. and Frau Gödel from a hotel at Aflanz for a two-week stay, which may have been made in the aftermath of the rescue.

In September 1931 Rudolf Carnap reported in his diary that Gödel had read Lenin and Trotsky, was in favor of socialism and a planned society, and was interested in the mechanism of such social influences as those of finance capital on politics. In 1939, on the other hand, Karl Menger complained of Gödel's indifference to politics when he was at Notre Dame.

Around 1935 Gödel was often seen reading at the department library, deeply sunk in thought and studying the same page over and over again. When he lectured at the university, he always faced the blackboard, and the audience dwindled rapidly as the course continued. A plaque in his honor now hangs in the room where he taught.

During the eventful years from 1929 to early 1940, Gödel produced the major part of the work he published in his lifetime, from the most famous papers to brief notes and reviews. He also did all the extended teaching in his life (three courses in Vienna, two in Notre Dame, and two famous series of lectures in Princeton), gave over a dozen single lectures at colloquia and professional meetings, and made his seven intercontinental trips.

In March 1940 a tranquil new chapter of his life began. In Princeton Gödel was appointed to the Institute for Advanced Study annually from 1940 to 1946. He became a permanent member in 1946 at the age of forty and a professor in 1953 at the age of forty-seven. At first he and Adele lived in rented apartments. In April 1948 they became citizens of the United States, and in August 1949 they bought the house on Linden Lane where they spent the rest of their lives. Adele took seven extended trips to Europe between 1947 and 1966, but Gödel confined his travels to summer vacations at places close to Princeton. He retired from the institute in 1976 at the age of seventy.

Even though Gödel wrote a good deal during his decades at Princeton, he published little in those years—mostly in response to requests. Of the seven articles published in this period, three were written to honor Bertrand Russell (1944), Albert Einstein (1949), and Paul Bernays (1958); two for invited lectures, to the Princeton University Bicentennial Celebration (1946, first published 1965) and the International Congress of Mathematicians (1950); and one in response to an invitation to write an expository article on Cantor's continuum problem (1947). The only unsolicited paper was the one giving his new solutions to Einstein's field equations, which was published in the *Reviews of Modern Physics* in 1949. In the 1960s he made brief additions to five of his earlier works, meticulously prepared for new editions.

Between 1940 and 1951 Gödel gave a number of lectures, but none, as far as I know, after 1951. In 1940 he delivered four lectures on constructible sets at Princeton in April and one on his consistency proof of Cantor's continuum hypothesis at Brown University on 15 November. In 1941 he gave some lectures on intuitionism in Princeton and one at Yale University on 15 April, entitled "In What Sense Is Intuitionistic Logic Constructive?" There were also the two (later published) lectures of 1946 and 1950 mentioned in the preceding paragraph. Finally, he lectured in Princeton on rotating universes in May of 1949 and gave his Gibbs lecture—"Some Basic Theorems on the Foundations of Mathematics and Their Philosophical Implications"—to the American Mathematical Society in Providence in December of 1951.

By his own account, Gödel worked principally on logic during his first three years in Princeton and then turned his attention to philosophy. From 1943 to about 1958, as I report at length in Chapter 2, Gödel concentrated on philosophy as it relates to mathematics and, to a lesser extent, to physics. From 1959 on he turned his attention to general philosophy, to tidying up certain loose ends in his earlier work, and to an unsuccessful attempt to solve Cantor's continuum problem.

From autumn 1944 on Gödel tried periodically to get in touch with his mother and his brother in Vienna. In a letter dated 7 September 1945, he wrote that he had received their letters of July and August. More than two hundred of his letters to his mother Marianne, from then until her death on 23 July 1966, have been preserved; these letters are a valuable source of information about his daily life and his views on various matters over this extended period.

On the whole, the letters deal with the ordinary concerns of a middle-class couple without children. In the early years, there is a good deal about packages and money orders sent to their families in Vienna. Every year there were exchanges of gifts, and messages were sent for Christmas, Mother's Day, Gödel's birthday, and Marianne's birthday. There were reports and comments on health and diet, on summer vacations, on friends and relatives, on Marianne's travels, on their apartments and their house, on maids and gardeners, on pets (dogs and parrots), on films and operas, on books, on radio and television, and so on.

In addition, the letters record a number of important events in Gödel's life and work between 1946 to 1966. They include his study of Einstein's relativity theory and its relation to Kant's philosophy (from 1947 to 1950) and his two lectures and three published papers on this work. They also mention his Gibbs lecture in 1951 and the invitation, in May 1953, to write a paper on the philosophy of Rudolf Carnap. Over the next few years he mentions this work in his letters several times, but he did not publish the paper in his lifetime. In 1956 he was invited to write a paper to honor Paul Bernays; he published it in 1958.

In a letter in April of 1976, Gödel speaks of the growth of his own reputation since the 1930s: an enormous development over the first ten or fifteen years, but afterwards kept up only in part. He also mentions a number of events that exemplified the recognition of his work: the invited lectures of 1950 and 1951, the honorary degrees from Yale in 1951 and from Harvard in 1952, the Einstein Prize and the promotion to professor in 1953, and an article on his work in *Scientific American* in June 1956.

On 14.12.58, in reply to his mother's concern about his health, he wrote: "Yet I was only really sick twice in the nineteen years since I have been here. That means then once in ten years. But that is really not much." The two instances he refers to, apparently, were a bleeding ulcer in February 1951 and a psychic disturbance in 1954, which was accompanied by the feeling that he was about to die. The letters also indicate that he was not well during the early part of 1961.

For almost ten years, Gödel periodically planned visits to his mother in Vienna but each time changed his mind. Finally in 1957 he invited his mother to visit him instead. His mother and his brother visited Princeton in the spring of 1958, the spring of 1960, the autumn of 1962, and the spring of 1964. In 1966 his mother wanted to come for his sixtieth birthday but was too ill to make the trip.

In the letters to his mother and, occasionally and briefly, to his brother, Gödel writes a good deal about Adele, about Einstein, about politics, and about his own health and daily life. Every now and then he makes some general observations on his life and outlook, which seem better dealt with in a separate section later in this chapter. He said little about these matters in his conversations with me, except to offer some remarks about his health, which I also include in the section on this subject.

Gödel's marriage and his relationship with Einstein are especially well documented and interesting aspects of the human relations in his life. We know considerably less about his relations with other people. According to Rudolf, neither of the brothers had any close friends at home. In his Vienna days, Gödel was friendly with some of his contemporaries, including Marcel Natkin, Herbert Feigl, John von Neumann, Alfred Tarski, G. Nöbeling, and Abraham Wald. Among his teachers, he seems to have interacted fairly extensively with Hans Hahn, Moritz Schlick, Rudolf Carnap, and Karl Menger. His other teachers included Hans Thirring, Heinrich Gomperz, and Philipp Furtwängler. At Princeton he is known to have been friendly with Oskar Morgenstern, Hermann Broch and Eric Kahler, and to have had some measure of contact with Oswald Veblen, John von Neumann, Emil Artin, Alonzo Church, Paul Oppenheim, Paul Erdos, Marston Morse, Deane Montgomery, and Hassler Whitney. He found all the directors of the Institute well disposed toward him. He was, at various times, comfortable with a number of logicians who saw him as their master, among them William Boone, Paul J. Cohen, Stephen Kleene, Georg Kreisel, Abraham Robinson, Dana Scott, Clifford Spector, Gaisi Takeuti, Stanley Tennenbaum, and me. He corresponded with Paul Bernays over many years and invited him to the Institute several times.

I know of no source of information about Gödel's life after July 1966 comparable in detail to his letters to his mother for the earlier period. We know that he resumed work on Cantor's continuum problem more than two decades after his original study (1943) and spent time expanding his 1958 paper on an interpretation of intuitionistic logic. In 1967 and 1968 he wrote me two careful letters to explain the relation between his philosophical views and his mathematical work in logic.

In early 1970 Gödel was suffering from poor health and thought he was about to die. After his recovery he had extensive discussions with me between the autumn of 1971 and the spring of 1976.

In 1974 Gödel was hospitalized for a urinary tract problem but declined to have an operation, and from then on he had to wear a catheter. For the last few years of his life his health problems and those of Adele became his central concern, especially after the spring of 1976.

Gödel arranged to have me visit the Institute for 1975 and 1976, but he mostly stayed at home and talked with me by telephone. We had many extended conversations between October of 1975 and March of 1976. After he was briefly hospitalized around the end of March theoretical discussions virtually ceased. In June of 1976, however, he spoke to me at some length about his intellectual development.

Near the end of May 1977, urged by William Boone, I tried to persuade Gödel to go to the Graduate Hospital at the University of Pennsylvania, where some excellent doctors were prepared to deal with his health problems as a special patient. He asked for and took down all the relevant information, but, in the end, would not give his permission to be taken there.

In July of 1977 Adele had an operation and subsequently stayed away from home for about five months. I myself was out of the country from mid-September to mid-November of that year. When I returned, I found Gödel very depressed and full of self-doubt. Once he complained that there was no one to help him at home. I asked Hassler Whitney, who had taken it upon himself to look after Gödel's needs, about this; Whitney told me he had sent several nurses to the house, but Gödel had refused to let them in.

On 17 December 1977 I visited Gödel and brought, at his request, a roasted chicken and some biscuits. He asked me to break up the chicken into pieces, but did not eat any while I was there. On this occasion, he said to me: "I have lost the power to make positive decisions. I can only make negative decisions." A few days later Adele returned home, and on 29 December Whitney arranged to have Gödel taken to the Princeton Hospital. He died there on Saturday 14 January 1978. According to the death certificate, he died of "malnutrition and inanition, caused by personality disturbance." A small private funeral service was held on 19 January and a memorial meeting took place at the Institute on 3 March.

1.2 Health and Daily Life

In a letter of 29 April 1985, Gödel's brother wrote to me:

1.2.1   My brother was a cheerful child. He had, it is true, a light anxiety neurosis at about the age of five, which later completely disappeared.

1.2.2   At about the age of eight my brother had a severe joint-rheumatism with high fever and thereafter was somewhat hypochondriacal and fancied himself to have a heart problem, a claim that was, however, never established medically.

In his later years, Gödel's preoccupation with his health was well known. It is likely that this preoccupation began quite early, perhaps not long after his rheumatic fever. It appears, however, that he enjoyed good health on the whole for the first twenty-five years of his life. As far as I know, no one, including himself and his brother, has mentioned any other illness during this period, and we have no direct information about the state of his health before 1931. We do know, however, that he performed extraordinarily well in school, in college, and in his early research without any apparent interruptions for health or for other reasons. Indeed his powers of concentrated and sustained work were clearly evident from these early achievements. According to Kreisel, these powers "continued into the sixties when his wife still spoke of him, affectionately, as a *strammer Bursche* [vigorous youth]" (Kreisel 1980: 153).

There are several stories of Gödel's early romantic interests. When his mother was visiting Lugano in 1957, he wrote her (9.8.57), "I still remember the Zillertal and also that I experienced my first love there. I believe her name was Marie." There is no indication of when this took place, and it probably came to nothing. While he was still in school, his brother recalled, he fell in love and conversed easily with the daughter of some family friends who visited frequently. The young woman was more than ten years older than he was, and his family objected strongly, and successfully.

Rudolf once told me that, in his student days in Vienna while the brothers were living together, they often ate at a nearby restaurant on the Schlesingerplatz because Gödel was interested in a waitress there. It was a family business: the father was the cashier, the mother cooked, and their attractive young daughter waited on the customers.

At about this time, according to Olga Taussky-Todd, a fellow student at the university, Gödel was seen with a good-looking young girl who "wore a beautiful, quite unusual summer dress." This girl "complained about Kurt being so spoiled, having to sleep long in the morning and similar items. Apparently she was interested in him, and wanted him to give up his *prima donna* habits" (Taussky, "Remembrances of Kurt

Gödel", in P. Weingartner and L. Schmetterer, eds., *Gödel Remembered*, 1987, Bibliopolis, Napoli; hereafter Taussky 1987; see p. 32).

During university vacations, Gödel often accompanied his family to resort areas. Even though he apparently never drove later in life, in those days he sometimes drove the family car, a Chrysler, and was, according to his brother, a fast driver.

I have mentioned earlier the turbulent decade of Gödel's life between 1929 (when he was twenty-four) and 1939 (when he was thirty-four). During these years he made most of his famous discoveries, began his lifelong intimacy with Adele, did all his intercontinental travels, and, according to Adele and his brother, was mentally ill several times. In his conversations with me, however, he said nothing about his various mental crises, although he did mention a severe tooth problem in 1934 and a period of poor health in 1936. From 1940 to 1943, he told me, his health was good, and it was exceptionally poor in 1961 and in 1970.

His letters to his mother after he moved to Princeton and was able to reestablish contact with her near the end of the war, provide more information about his health and his daily life. My quotations from these letters are prefixed by their dates.

6.4.46 I am glad that you have in Vienna at least good plays for a diversion. We never go to the theater here but often to the cinema, which is a good substitute for it, since there are really many good pieces. What is also incomparably better here is the music on the radio (i.e., light music, I cannot judge the others).

Probably in 1942, Oswald Veblen or Paul Oppenheim introduced Gödel to Einstein, and they became close friends for the dozen years or so before Einstein's death in April of 1955. Almost every day they walked together to and from the Institute. At this time Einstein and Gödel each had a large office on the ground floor of Fuld Hall. According to Deane Montgomery, whose office was (from 1948) next to Einstein's, Gödel ordinarily stopped at Einstein's house about ten or eleven in the morning, and they walked together to Fuld Hall. They worked until one or two in the afternoon, and then walked home together. They usually approached Fuld Hall from the side near Olden Lane and used the side entrance. Gödel's mother must have heard about her son's friendship with Einstein and asked him about it. In his letter of 27.7.46, Gödel mentioned Einstein for the first time; from then on, Einstein was a frequent topic of their correspondence.

19.9.46 Mostly I am so deeply absorbed in my work, that I find it hard to concentrate so much on something else, as is necessary for writing a letter.

19.1.47 We always spend Sundays in very much the same way. We get up toward noon and after eating I do the weekly account and read the newspaper.

Generally I only subscribe to the newspaper (the *New York Times*) for Sunday and find this alone still too much. [Gödel usually wrote his letters to his mother on Sundays too, mostly in the evening.]

19.1.47   I have also enough exercise, since I walk daily to and from the Institute, that is easily half an hour each way. Moreover, in the afternoon I often go to the university or the town center, which takes again at least half an hour to get there and come back.

On 2 May 1947 Adele sailed for Europe and stayed away for about seven months.

12.5.47   Naturally I am now very lonely, especially the Sundays are even more lonesome than the other days. But I have anyhow always so much to do with my work, not much time is left for me to brood over it. Making the bed is a healthy gymnastic exercise and anyhow I have otherwise nothing to do.

One day in December of 1947 Oskar Morgenstern drove Gödel and Einstein to Trenton for Gödel's citizenship examination. Einstein called it "the next to last examination," evidently having in mind death as the last one. On 2 April 1948 Gödel and Adele took their citizenship oath together.

17.2.48   Although my hair is already turning grey and greyer, my youthful elasticity has not diminished at all. When I fall, I spring back on my feet again like a rubber ball. That is probably a remnant of my gymnastic suppleness.

In 1949 the Gödels bought their house on Linden Lane. They moved in at the beginning of September and lived there for the rest of their lives.

In February of 1951, Gödel was hospitalized for delayed treatment of a bleeding duodenal ulcer requiring massive blood transfusions. The undue delay was apparently caused by his distrust of doctors. In February 1978, shortly after Gödel's death, his brother wrote that "My brother had a very individual and fixed opinion about everything. Unfortunately he believed all his life that he was always right not only in mathematics but also in medicine, so he was a very difficult patient for his doctors" (1987:26).

Dr. Joseph M. Rampona was for many years Gödel's physician in Princeton, probably from 1935 to 1969. In an interview in May 1986 (see Schimanovich et al. 1995?), he said that Gödel had refused to go to the hospital to be treated for the ulcer and that they had to ask Einstein to persuade him. The relationship between Gödel and Einstein was, according to Rampona, "very very close. I felt that Einstein in his presence was like a blanket for him. He felt confident then. He could really speak to the world at that moment. Einstein was for him a kind of protection." The very morning when Dr. Rampona put Gödel in the hospital, J. Robert Oppenheimer, director of the institute, telephoned him and said, "Believe it or not, doctor, but there is the greatest logician since the days of Aristotle!"

In autumn 1935, while he was still living in Vienna, Gödel cut short a visit to Princeton because of depression and overwork. Before leaving he apparently went to see Rampona about his depression and continued to consult him when he moved permanently to Princeton. Dr. Rampona recounted that he saw Gödel about once a week until, probably, not long before February 1970. "Someone told him to take digitalis," Rampona recalled. "He had no reason for taking it, no shortness of breath, no swelling of the ankles. So I refused to give it. And I kept on refusing and refusing. Finally he went to another doctor! That was the first time he went to another doctor."

His friends knew that in his later years Gödel ate very little as a rule. As early as a letter of 19 January 1947, he argued that it is better to eat less than to eat more. Later the traumatic experience of the bleeding ulcer led him to adopt a stringent diet, one apparently designed largely by himself. His brother believes that not eating enough was the central problem of his health, at least after around 1950. Dr. Rampona, commenting generally on Gödel's health seems to concur:

1.2.3 He had no diseases, he was just a weakly built man. I do not think he ever took exercises in his life and he never built himself up as a young man. He grew up, probably with good health, and grew to the age he did.

1.2.4 When you do not eat anything and your nutrition is bad, things in your mind do not work the way they do when you are normal. He was never really sick, just did not eat. He lived on the tissues of his own body. [That was also one reason why] he had the feeling that someone was going to poison him. He was very fearful of strangers giving him something to eat.

I have found no exact information about the date of Gödel's 1951 hospital stay. His letter of 8 January 1951 gives no indication of the forthcoming crisis, and his next letter, dated 17 March, says he is sufficiently recovered to write. Two telegrams to his brother on 5 March and 23 March say that he was all right. —Judging by these indications, it is plausible to conclude that the hospitalization took place in February.

31.10.52 My acquaintances tell me that I had not looked so well for a long time already.

1.6.54 I still always do gymnastic exercises regularly in the morning, i.e., I began to do it again a few years ago and it does me much good.

In the autumn of 1954, however, according to his letters of 4 October and 10 December, Gödel was again in poor health. (There were also two telegrams to his brother on 1 December and 10 December.) In the letter of 14 December quoted below, he recalls being sick only twice in the last nineteen years; undoubtedly the bleeding ulcer was the first time and this occasion in 1954 was the second.

10.12.54   A major part of my trouble was undoubtedly psychically conditioned. For some time [*zeitlang*] I was in a very remarkable psychic state. I had the irrepressible feeling that I have only still a short time to live, and that the familiar things around me, the house, the books, etc., are nothing to me. This paralyzed me in such a way that I could rouse myself to attend to none of my ordinary tasks [*Tätigkeiten*]. This has now also abated, but naturally I have been somewhat reduced in my powers through the whole thing. My whole state is similar to the tooth business in 1934. The causes may even be similar. [In each case he suffered from a minor infection.]

5.1.55   I am also not at all so lonesome as you think. I often visit Einstein and also get visits from Morgenstern and others. I now live [by] myself more than necessary in the past.

5.1.55   I have in any case no time for a hobby, but it is also not necessary at all: since I have various interests outside of my vocation, e.g., in politics, also often view plays and variety programs on television, so that I have sufficient diversion from mathematics and philosophy.

14.3.55   My health is now again quite normal; I have also reached again my former weight. Only my sleep is not quite so good as before. I often wake up early about six and cannot sleep again. This then naturally has the effect that one is less fresh all day long and works more slowly.

Einstein died on 18 April 1955, not long after his seventy-sixth birthday. Gödel was surprised and shaken.

25.4.55   The death of Einstein was of course a great shock to me, since I had not expected it at all. Exactly in the last weeks Einstein gave the impression of being completely robust. When he walked with me for half an hour to the Institute while conversing at the same time, he showed no signs of fatigue, as had been the case on many earlier occasions. Certainly I have purely personally lost very much through his death, especially since in his last days he became even nicer to me than he had already been earlier all along, and I had the feeling that he wished to be more outgoing than before. He had admittedly kept pretty much to himself with respect to personal questions. Naturally my state of health turned worse again during last week, especially in regard to sleep and appetite. But I took a strong sleeping remedy a couple of times and am now somewhat under control again.

21.6.55   That people never mention me in connection with Einstein is very satisfactory to me (and would certainly be to him, too, since he was of the opinion that even a famous man is entitled to a private life). After his death I have already been invited twice to say something about him, but naturally I declined. My health now is good. I have definitely regained my strength during the last two months.

18.12.55   There was yesterday a symphony concert here in remembrance of Einstein. It was the first time I let Bach, Haydn, etc. encircle me for two hours long. Nonetheless, the pianist on the occasion was really fabulous.

In March 1956 Adele returned from a trip to Vienna with her eighty-eight-year-old mother, who lived with them until her death about three years later.

30.9.56   Tomorrow the semester begins again with its faculty meetings, etc. The very thought already makes me nervous. I often think of the nice days with nostalgia, when I had not yet the honor to be professor at the Institute. For that, however, the pay is now higher!

23.3.57   [Marcel] Natkin (from the Schlick Circle) [See Chapter 2] is now in America and I have recently met with him and [Herbert] Feigl in New York. The Schlick Evenings are now thirty years ago, but both of them have really changed very little. I do not know whether this is also the case with me.

27.8.57   I constantly hope that my life comes for once in a calmer track, which would also include, that my oversensitivity to food and cold stops, and that unexpected things do not keep on intruding.

12.12.57   It is indeed true that there are mental recreations in Princeton. But they are mostly classical music and witty comedies, neither of which I like.

10.5.58   Where are the times when we discussed in the Marienbad woods Chamberlain's book on Goethe and his relation to the natural sciences?

14.12.58   Yet I was only really sick twice in the nineteen years since I have been here. That means then once in ten years. But that is really not much.

30.7.59   Recently I have once again very deeply involved myself in work, for which Adele's being away has given the occasion.

11.11.60   My life-style has changed, to the extent that I lie for a couple of hours in the garden.

During the long gap between Gödel's letters of 16 December 1960 and 18 March 1961, he had an extended stretch of ill health.

18.3.61   I always go to sleep very early now, for that I get up rather early and go to the Institute about one hour earlier than before. I am actually much more satisfied with this life-style than my previous one. That my health is now really much better, you surely see sufficiently from Adele's letter.

25.6.61   You could give me a great joy, if you could send me in autumn a price-catalogue (or at least a prospectus) of Mühlhauser or Niennes or their successors. It would interest me very much to know what progress the toy industry has made in the last forty-five years. Are there not also already small atom bombs for children? [This request and the one in his letter of 12 September 1961 were replies to his mother's inquiry about what he wanted for Christmas gifts.]

Adele left for Italy in July and stayed away for more than two months. During her absence Gödel wrote several long letters to his mother which included extended considerations about the afterlife. These passages will be reproduced in Chapter 3.

23.7.61 I live here rather lonesomely and have occupied myself with reading and work all day long—but just in this way I do feel fine. As far as my "normal" eating is concerned, I of course still never eat so much as before this whole business.

12.9.61 You could give me most joy with good books in philosophy, also with classical works. E.g. I would be very glad to have the "Critique of Judgment" by Kant or also the "Critique of Pure Reason" at home, in order to read in them whenever I have the time.

18.12.61 The right Christmas mood one has only in childhood, of which I have once again been vividly reminded by the pretty toy catalogue. [The catalogue was undoubtedly sent in response to Gödel's request in June, quoted above.]

12.6.65 Adele does not play the piano very often, but still many times she does play old Viennese melodies.

13.5.66 We do not socialize with anybody here.

As far as I know, Gödel's health was moderately good from 1962 to 1969. In the beginning of 1970 he was again unwell and thought he was going to die soon. In February 1970 he consulted Dr. W. J. Tate of the Princeton Medical Group, probably after Dr. Rampona had refused to prescribe digitalis. Later that month he called and, after some delays on his part, eventually met with Dr. Harvey Rothberg. The disturbance seems to have been more mental than physical.

In 1974 Gödel was hospitalized for a urinary-tract problem related to the state of his prostate. Dr. James Varney and Dr. Charles Place, two urologists, advised him to have an operation. In addition, Marston Morse recommended to him Dr. John Lattimore, a urologist at the Presbyterian Hospital in New York. Apparently after consulting Lattimore, Gödel decided not to have the operation. Instead, he wore a catheter in his last years.

As mentioned before, by the spring of 1976 his own health problems and Adele's had become Gödel's chief preoccupation. His condition deteriorated rapidly between July and December 1977, after Adele had a major operation and had to be attended to elsewhere while he lived alone at home.

In the 1950s Gödel once wrote that in recent years his weight never exceeded fifty-four kilograms. In 1970 he weighed eighty-six pounds. At his death in 1978 he weighed only sixty-eight pounds. These figures appear to support Dr. Rampona's theory that he had for many years lived off the tissues of his own body.

During our conversations Gödel said little to me about his own or Adele's health problems. In 1976, however, he mentioned these problems several times. In April, after he returned from a brief stay in the hospital, he told me he had a cold and spoke of a thirty-year-long kidney infection, of being sensitive to cold, of a prostate blockage, and of using increased dosages of antibiotics. He admitted having sent out the wrong manuscript on the continuum problem at the beginning of 1970—the result, he said, of taking certain pills that had damaged his mathematical and philosophical abilities.

18.4.76 I had written the paper when I was under the illusion that my ability had returned. Can't expect wrong sayings from one of the greatest logicians. The pills had also affected my practical ability in how to behave, and I did things which were not so beautiful.

10.5.76 I had not been well last night.

11.5.76 Psychiatrists are prone to make mistakes in their computations and overlook certain consequences. Antibiotics are bad for the heart. [E. E.] Kummer was bad in large calculations.

1.6.76 My health problems include my not having enough red blood cells and my indigestion—feeling like a rock.

3.6.76 I have arthritis caused by my cold and received some antibiotic treatment in the hospital.

6.6.76 Mrs. Gödel had a light stroke last autumn. She sleeps in the daytime. Her head is heavy and she can't sit up. She is seventy-six years old and worries about many things. A nervous weakness affects her legs. She was once delirious in Vienna. We employ a nurse. A second stroke may have occurred.

6.6.76 I do not accept the doctors' words. They have special difficulties with me. There is a psychological component in this.

22.6.76 My wife is in the hospital for tests. I cook once every few days.

31.3.77 I need and use a catheter for urinating because of a prostate problem.

17.12.77 I have lost the power for positive decisions. I can only make negative decisions now.

1.3 Some of His General Observations

As I mentioned in the first section of this chapter, Gödel's letters to his mother and brother sometimes included general observations embodying aspects of his outlook. They are mostly brief, written in widely accessible language, and can be understood independently of their original contexts. I have included a number of them, without comment, in the following pages.

17.2.48   I would not say that one cannot polemicize against Nietzsche. But it should of course also be a writer [*Dichter*] or a person of the same type to do that.

18.10.49   Marriage is of course also a time-consuming institution.

28.10.49   That one is not pleased in every respect with the vocation is, I believe, unavoidable, even if one has chosen it purely out of one's love for the subject.

27.2.50   What you say about sadness is right: if there were a completely hopeless sadness, there would be nothing beautiful in it. But I believe there can rationally be no such thing. Since we understand neither why this world exists, nor why it is constituted exactly as it is, nor why we are in it, nor why we were born into exactly these and no other external relations: why then should we presume to know exactly this to be all [*gerade das eine ganz bestimmt zu wissen*], that there is no other world and that we shall never be in yet another one?

3.4.50   One cannot really say that complete ignorance is sufficient ground for hopelessness. If e.g. someone will land on an island completely unknown to him, it is just as likely that it is inhabited by harmless people as that it is by cannibals, and his ignorance gives no reason for hopelessness, but rather for hope. Your aversion against occult phenomena is of course well justified to the extent that we are here facing a hard-to-disentangle mixture of deception, credulousness and stupidity, with genuine phenomena. But the result (and the meaning) of the deception is, in my opinion, not to fake genuine phenomena but to conceal them.

In December 1950 Gödel recommended to his mother Philipp Frank's biography *Einstein: His Life and Times* (1947, the original German manuscript was published only in 1950). Apparently Marianne obtained the German version and found it difficult. In reply, Gödel wrote:

8.1.51   Is the book about Einstein really so hard to understand? I think that prejudice against and fear of every "abstraction" may also be involved here, and if you would attempt to read it like a novel (without wanting to understand right away everything at the first reading), perhaps it would not seem so incomprehensible to you.

12.4.52   But the days are much too short, each day should have at least forty-eight hours.

25.3.53   The problem of money is not the only consideration and also never the most important.

10.5.53   And is there anyone you know who lives in a paradise and has no conflicts on anything?

26.7.53   With the aphorisms you have hit upon my fancy. I love everything brief and find that in general the longer a work is the less there is in it.

21.9.53   It is interesting that in the course of half a year *both* the main opponents of Eisenhower (Stalin foreign political, Taft domestic political) have died.

Moreover, the president [sic] of the Supreme Court (a creation of Truman's) has now also died. Something so peculiar, I believe, has never happened before. The probability for this is one in two thousand.

28.9.55 If you wish to send me the Einstein biography, please, if possible, send the original text. Or is it neither German nor English? In that case the English version would be preferable, because, as I have already often remarked, translations into English are mostly much better than translations into German.

24.2.56 Ordinarily the reason of unhappy marriages is: jealousy (justified or unjustified), or neglect of the wife by the husband, or political or religious disagreements.

7.11.56 As you know, I am indeed also thoroughly antinationalistic, but one cannot, I believe, decide hastily against the possibility that people like Bismarck have the honorable intention to do something good.

23.3.57 About the relation of art and kitsch we have, I believe, already discussed many times before. It is similar to that between light and heavy music. One could, however, hardly assert that all good music must be tragic?

7.6.58 I believe that half of the wealth of America rests on the diligence of the Americans and another half depends on the ordered political relations (in contrast to the constant wars in Europe).

28.5.61 Recently I have read a novel by Gogol and was altogether surprised how good it is. Previously I had once begun to read Dostoevski but found that his art consists principally in producing depression in his readers—but one can of course gladly avoid that. In any case I do not believe that the best in world-literature is the German literature.

12.11.61 It is always enjoyable to see that there are still people who value a certain measure of idealism.

17.3.62 It is surely rather extraordinary for anybody to entitle an autobiography "The Fairy Tale of My Life," since life is indeed mostly not so pretty. It may of course be that Slezak simply leaves out all the nonpretty, since it is not enjoyable to write about them.

14.5.62 The Slezak biography is, as I see it, chiefly meant humorously. But I doubt that anybody has experienced only the humorous.

17.3.62 You are completely right that mankind does not become better through the moon flight. This has to do with the old struggle between the "natural" and the "human" ["*Geistes*"] sciences. If the progress in history, legal and political science [*Rechts-und Staatswissenschaft*], philosophy, psychology, literature, art, etc. were as great as that in physics, there would not be the danger of an atomic war. But instead of that one sees in many of the human sciences significant regress[ion]. This problem is very actual especially here, inasmuch as, according to American tradition, the human sciences were favored in the middle schools, a fact which certainly played a considerable part in the ascent of America over Europe. Unfortunately the European influence, with the Russian concurrence (see Sputnik), turns this relation around, as America on the whole, not to its advantage, becomes more and more like Europe.

4.7.62 Recently I have discovered a modern writer [Dichter] "Franz Kafka," hitherto unknown to me. He writes rather crazily, but has a really vivid way of portraying things. For instance, his description of a dream had the effect on me, that I had two lively dreams the next night which I still remember exactly—something that never happened to me otherwise.

24.3.63 Of all that we experience, there eventually of course remains only a memory, but just in this way all lasting things retain some of their actuality.

20.10.63 I have yet to read the article in "Entschluss" about my work. It was in any case to be expected that sooner or later use of my proof would be made for religion, since it is indeed justified in a certain sense.

16.7.64 An "editor" of our letters would certainly be surprised at the repetitions.

21.4.65 Only fables present the world as it should be and as [if] it had a meaning, whilst in the tragedy the hero is slaughtered and in the comedy the laughable (hence also something bad) is stressed.

3.6.65 I at least have always found that one rests best at home.

Over the years Gödel's views about America changed with the political situation. But he undoubtedly found that his position at the Institute for Advanced Study suited him, and he always expressed the view that the institute treated him well. In the spring of 1953, shortly after he was told of his promotion to a professorship, he wrote:

25.3.53 The Institute pays its members without requiring any performance in return, with the whole purpose that in this way they can pursue their scientific interests undisturbed. I shall as professor also have no obligation to teach. Moreover, the pays here are even higher than those of the universities.

Gödel had no wish to return to Europe and expressed a strong aversion for Austrian academic institutions:

28.4.46 I feel very well in this country and would also not return to Vienna if some offer were made to me. Leaving aside all personal connections, I find this country and the people here ten times more congenial than our own.

Later he refused honorary membership in the Academy of Sciences in Vienna, as well as the Austrian national medal for arts and sciences.

In 1948 he explained his reluctance to visit Europe this way:

9.6.48 I am so happy to have escaped from the beautiful Europe, that I would on no account like to expose myself to the danger, for whatever reason, of my not being able to return [to Princeton]. I believe that this danger really exists under the present conditions.

Three years later he wrote:

12.11.51   Except for the fact that you live in Vienna, I am not at all eager to go to Europe, and especially to Austria.

To his mother's observation that evil forces were at work in Europe, he responded:

31.10.52   This is of course true here too, the difference is only that they are in Europe enduring at the helm, here only temporarily and partly.

1.4 Marriage

Adele Porkert was born 4 November 1899 and died 4 February 1981. She was six-and a-half years older than Gödel and came from a family much poorer and less cultured than his. She had little formal education or intellectual aspiration and was slightly disfigured by a facial birthmark. Her first, brief marriage to a photographer named Nimbursky was apparently unhappy. According to Gödel's description in 1953,

14.4.53   Adele is by nature certainly harmless and good-natured, but evidently has a nervous streak that was aggravated by her experience, especially the strict upbringing at home and her first marriage.

When Gödel first met her in 1928, Adele was living with her parents near the apartment shared by Gödel and his brother. At the time, Adele was working at Der Nachtfalter, a nightspot located at Petersplatz 1 where Gödel often went to visit her after they became acquainted. Later, in America, Adele still recalled those ventures into Viennese nightlife vividly and with delight.

Gödel's parents objected strongly to this relationship. After his father's death in February of 1929, his mother's objections seem to have been the main reason why Gödel kept his relationship with Adele separate from his family life and did not marry her until 1938. Undoubtedly the need to separate these two close relationships imposed a great mental burden on Gödel during these years and may well have contributed to the crises he suffered in 1931, 1934, and 1936.

Gödel's mother moved from Brno to Vienna in November of 1929 and lived with her sons in a large apartment until November of 1937. Gödel and Adele were married on 20.9.39. (When I wrote up what Gödel had told me about his intellectual development in 1976, I added, from standard references, the date of his marriage. He asked me to delete the sentence, on the ground that his wife had nothing to do with his work.)

Later in life Adele expressed regret that they had had no children. They began their settled married life after they moved to Princeton in March 1940, and at first Gödel was appointed to the institute annually. Only in the beginning of 1946 was he offered a permanent position. It seems likely that Gödel did not want children, at least not before getting a secure position. By 1946, however, Adele was already forty-six, rather old to bear a first child. For Adele life in Princeton was not nearly as satisfactory as it was for Gödel himself, even though he undoubtedly shared her sense of loss at having moved away from the familiar places of their youth. There are several references to her state of mind in his letters:

16.4.46 Unfortunately Adele does not share my enthusiasm for this country at all.

16.3.47 Adele does not like the apartment but would like to live in a fairly new house. She does not like living in a small town. But the main reason for being dissatisfied is to be separated from her folks. And she has great difficulty in relating herself to the people here.

11.9.49 [The first problem was resolved after they moved into their own house at 129 Linden Lane.] Adele is very happy and works from morning till night in the house.

In May 1986 Alice (Lily) von Kahler, who also came from Vienna and was for many years a close friend of the Gödels in Princeton, spoke about Adele's life there and her marriage with Gödel (quoted in Schimanovich et al. 1995):

1.4.1   For her the matter [of adapting to life in Princeton] was not so simple [as for me], because she could not even manage with English so well, having come from another social circle. Even though she was very intelligent, there was perhaps some difficulty in her being accepted here.

1.4.2   She was not a beauty, but she was an extraordinarily intelligent person and had an extremely important role [in his life], because she was actually what one calls the life-line. She connected him to the earth. Without her, he could not exist at all.

1.4.3   A complicated marriage, but neither could exist without the other. And the idea that she should die before him was unthinkable for him. It is fortunate that he died before her. He was absolutely despondent when she was sick. He said, "Please come to visit my wife."

1.4.4   She once told me, "I have to hold him like a baby."

Georg Kreisel, who often visited the Gödels from the mid-1950s to the late-1960s, made similar observations about Adele and the marriage (Kreisel 1980:151, 154–155):

1.4.5   Gödel himself was equally reticent about his personal history, but his wife talked more freely about it, usually in his presence.

1.4.6   It was a revelation to see him relax in her company. She had little formal education, but a real flair for the *mot juste*, which her somewhat critical mother-in-law eventually noticed too, and a knack for amusing and apparently quite spontaneous twists on a familiar ploy: to invent—at least, at the time—far-fetched grounds for jealousy. On one occasion she painted the I.A.S., which she usually called *Altersversorgungsheim* (home for old-age pensioners), as teeming with pretty girl students who queued up at the office doors of the permanent professors. Gödel was very much at ease with her style. She would make fun of his reading material, for example, on ghosts or demons.

Gödel's mother was critical of Adele, and so naturally Adele was uncomfortable in her presence. This conflict created many difficulties for Gödel, as his letters to his mother show quite clearly. Friends noticed the problem too. As Dorothy Morgenstern observed, "I am not sure that Mrs. Gödel really approved of her daughter-in-law, so I always have the feeling that, when she came, they were both sort of suffering."

Given Adele's discomfort in Princeton, it is not surprising that she wanted to travel and visit her own family. Because Gödel was not willing to travel, especially to Europe, Adele made a number of extended trips by herself, leaving Gödel alone in Princeton. This was a major source of resentment for Gödel's mother, both because of the expense and because she believed Adele was not taking proper care of her husband. Gödel had to make many explanations in defense of Adele, and on several occasions he noted that he worked exceptionally hard when Adele was away.

In 1947 Adele went back to Vienna to spend about seven months with her family. After more than seven years, this was her first opportunity to go—because of the war and its aftermath. For the next few years she stayed in America, vacationing with Gödel at the seashore near Princeton in the summers, enjoying their house, and avoiding the expense of a trip to Europe. In March of 1953, after Gödel received the Einstein Prize (two thousand dollars) and was promoted to professor, Adele took her second trip to Europe when she learned her sister was dangerously ill.

Judging from Gödel's letters, his mother was very angry about this trip, and for the next few years she and Adele were estranged from each other. In his letter of 25 March 1953, Gödel defended Adele's trip and her "sudden" arrival in Vienna by air. He had sent his brother Rudi a telegram in advance, but, for some reason, their mother had not seen it. The fare for a tourist-class flight was not much more expensive than travel by boat.

25.3.53   There is certainly no ground to say that Adele keeps me isolated. As you well know, I like best to be alone and to see nobody except a couple of intimate friends.

25.3.53   In any case one cannot say at all that she prevents me from coming; on the contrary, she steadily urges me to travel.

25.3.53   For you to come here in Adele's absence is of course hardly possible now—just when you are afflicted with her.

In the next letter Gödel again pleaded for Adele, this time in connection with money matters.

14.4.53   There is also no ground for you to be bitter over my writing that I spend for myself only what is necessary, since the "necessary" includes yearly summer vacations and arbitrarily many taxis. In other words, I do not spare anything for myself and can spend no more on myself even if I had the most frugal wife in the world. As you know, I have no need to travel, and to buy books would have little sense, since I can get all that interests me more simply and more quickly through libraries. When you write that, you now see, you have "always judged Adele right" and that Adele plays comedy and theater, it is definitely false.

14.4.53   It is a difficult matter here to restrict a wife in her spending, since it is the *general* custom that man and wife have a joint account and the wife can use the account as she will.

In February of 1956 Adele went to Vienna for the third time and visited Gödel's mother. On 24 February 1956 Gödel wrote, "I am very happy to hear that Adele visited you and everything has again become all right." That March, Adele brought with her to Princeton her own mother, who lived in their house and died about three years later.

For about eight years Gödel made plans to go to Europe to see his mother (in Vienna or Leipzig or Hanover), but each time he changed his mind. Finally, on 11 November 1957 he wrote inviting her to Princeton. She and his brother came in May of 1958, and she repeated the visit in 1960, 1962, and 1964. In 1966 his mother wanted very much to be with him on his sixtieth birthday in April but was too weak to travel. She died in July.

Adele did not travel while her mother was living with them. After her mother's death in March of 1959, Adele took a summer vacation in the White Mountains of New Hampshire, then went to Vienna from October to December. Gödel's mother again objected to the European trip and Gödel wrote in reply:

6.12.59   There is really nothing special at all about Adele's travel, when one reflects that many of my colleagues travel there almost every year and bring their wives with them. It is true that in these cases they usually reduce the travel costs through lectures over there. But just because I do not do this, I will nonetheless not let Adele suffer for it, especially this year when she needs after all a diversion after the death of her mother.

Adele again went to Vienna in the autumn of 1960 and again Gödel feared a clash between his mother and Adele.

18.11.60   That my last letter was written in an irritated tone is unquestionably a false impression, because I was not at all testy. As I wrote it, I was only afraid that another disharmony between you and Adele might arise—a situation which would of course have very unfavorable consequences for our life here.

In 1961 Adele was in Italy from July to September. Gödel wrote to his mother on 23 July to express the hope that she was not upset by this. On 12 September he said: "You wrote that everyone condemns her going away for so long. But since I have nothing against it and am well taken care of, I do not know what there is to object to." The next year, on 27 August 1962, Gödel wrote that "This year Adele is, for the first time in a long while, spending the whole summer here, and has gladly spent the money thus saved in beautifying our home."

In earlier passages I extensively documented Gödel's health situation and his preoccupation with it. Given Adele's importance to him, it is easy to understand why he was also very much concerned with Adele's health. Indications of his concern began to appear in the mid-1960s; on the whole Adele's health seems to have been good up to that time.

On her first trip to Italy in the summer of 1961, she enjoyed a stay in Ischia that, according to a letter Gödel wrote to his mother in 1965, enabled her to cure her maladies:

3.6.65   Adele is now in the middle of preparing for her trip. She will in June travel again to Ischia for cure, because her rheumatism and other maladies, which were completely cured in Ischia, have returned.

3.6.65   [To his brother.] Adele went to see Dr. Rampona and he said to me that Ischia is unquestionably the right place for her pains in the limbs.

In his letter of 19 August 1965 Gödel said he had recently been very much worried over Adele's state of health. On the one hand, she felt wonderful after taking the baths. On the other hand, the baths were bad for her high blood pressure and she had to get injections:

1.4.7   That there is something wrong with her health, one can also see from the fact that she has lost all her zest for adventure and would have liked best to come home already at the beginning of August, but had obeyed the doctor to continue the cure. I have now booked for her a direct flight from Naples to New York on the 24th, and hope that the travel will do her no harm.

In his letter of 23 September 1965 he apologized that, for the first time in twenty years, he had completely forgotten his mother's birthday (on 31 August): "This probably has to do with my (unnecessary) worry on account of Adele in August."

My impression is that Adele's health really became a matter for serious concern only in the 1970s. As I mentioned earlier, Gödel told me about various problems in 1976, and, subsequently, about the major operation she underwent in July of 1977. She also had two strokes before then, probably some time after 1974 or 1975. It was clear to me by the spring of 1976 that Gödel's chief concern in life was with his own health and Adele's.

I met Adele only a few times. In June 1952 when she and Gödel came to Cambridge to receive the honorary degree from Harvard, I met them at the dinner and the reception at the home of W. V. Quine. On this occasion Adele had prepared some special food for Gödel, and she urged him to move to Harvard because people there were so nice to them. I also visited them at the guest house next door to the Faculty Club, bringing for Adele the newspapers reporting on the honorary-degree ceremony, as she had requested.

In September 1956 Georg Kreisel took me to their house for afternoon tea. Adele was present but did not say much. I remember that we discussed Turing's suicide and that Gödel asked whether Turing was married. On being told that he was not, he said, "Perhaps he wanted to get married but could not." This observation indicated to me the importance Gödel attributed to marriage for a man's, and perhaps also for a woman's, life and death.

Two days after Gödel's death on 14 January 1978 I went to see Adele, having learned the news from Hassler Whitney that morning. On this occasion Adele told me that Gödel, although he did not go to church, was religious and read the Bible in bed every Sunday morning. She also gave me permission to come on 19 January to the private funeral service, where, of course, I saw her again.

1.5 Politics and His Personal Situation

Gödel was a cautious man in practical matters. As far I know, he never took any political stand in public. It is generally assumed that he had little interest in politics. As I mentioned before, Karl Menger complained that Gödel appeared indifferent to politics even in 1939, when the situation in Europe so much affected his own life. On the other hand, apart from his reported interest in socialism in 1931, the only indications of political opinions are in the letters he wrote between 1946 and about 1963. Perhaps this was the only period in his life when he took a strong interest in politics, as the following selection from his letters suggests.

Gödel admired Roosevelt and Eisenhower, disliked Truman, detested Joseph McCarthy, and liked Henry Wallace and Adlai Stevenson. On 31 October 1951, toward the end of Eisenhower's first presidential campaign, he wrote "I have occupied myself so much with politics in the last two months that I had time for nothing else." (Einstein found his preference for Eisenhower over Stevenson very strange.) On 5 January 1955, in reply to a question from his brother about his "hobby," he wrote "I could at most name politics as my hobby; it is in any case not so completely unpleasant in this country as in Europe." By 7 August 1963 his interest in politics had gradually reached a low point: "I have more or less lost contact with politics, nowadays I very rarely look at the newspaper."

After the victory of the Republican Party in the mid-term congressional elections in 1946, Gödel wrote to his mother:

22.11.46 You have probably already read about the "landslide" result of the election here fourteen days ago. So the Republicans (i.e., the reactionaries) are now again in power (for the first time since 1933). The development has indeed already gone in this direction since Roosevelt's death [on 12 April 1945] and I have the feeling that this, incredible as it may sound, has also already shown itself in everyday life in various ways. E.g., the films have decidedly become worse in the course of the last year. Princeton University is now, throughout many months, celebrating the two hundredth year jubilee of its founding. Remarkably this is linked to a great secret-mongering: I.e., the scientific lectures and discussions are in part only open to invited guests, and even when something is public, one speaks, as much as possible, only about banalities, or a lecturer is selected who speaks so unclearly that nobody understands him. It is downright laughable. Science has now (chiefly because of the atom bomb) on the whole the tendency of turning itself into secret-science here.

Gödel often expressed his admiration for Roosevelt and for Roosevelt's America:

5.1.47 When you say it is good that the Americans have the power in hand, I would unconditionally subscribe to it only for the Rooseveltian America. That Roosevelt could no longer exert influence on the conclusion of the peace treaties and the establishment of the new League of Nations [sic] is certainly one of the most deplorable facts of our century.

29.9.50 True, I have already often critized America: but only just in the last few years; formerly I was still thoroughly enchanted.

According to a book on Einstein in America, "Einstein was so disgusted with Truman's reckless handling of foreign policy that he vigorously supported the quixotic, third-party candidacy of Henry Wallace in 1948." Gödel apparently shared Einstein's views on Truman and Wallace.

9.6.48 The political horizon here also appears to be brightening up somewhat. You have perhaps heard about the great success that Henry Wallace, a close colleague of Roosevelt's, had on his campaign tour. This seems to prove yet at least that the country is not as reactionary as the present regime. It remains, however, very questionable whether he can receive enough votes to become the president.

26.2.49 What do you think of the beautiful expression, which President Truman inflicts on his political opponents in his public speeches? In any case he said, according to the local habit, only the initial letters S.O.B. (son of a bitch).

With regard to the Korean War, Gödel wrote on 1 November 1950: "But at any rate it is clear that America, under the magic word 'Democracy,' carries on a war for a completely unpopular regime and does things in the name of 'policing' for the UN, with which the UN itself is not in agreement."

Several of his letters contain comments in favor of Eisenhower:

10.3.52 It would be nice if Eisenhower would get elected in autumn.

6.1.54 You question my opinion about the political development. But I find that good things have happened under Eisenhower. 1. The cease-fire in Korea, which has, in my opinion, saved us from a third World War. 2. The reduction of the military budget by about three billion dollars. 3. the cessation of the inflation, which has lasted six years. I believe, however, that is just the beginning, since a new president certainly cannot get into a new course in one day.

16.1.56 It is a gross exaggeration to say that today the political climate in America is symbolized by [Joseph] McCarthy (who is undoubtedly the American Hitler). The influence of McCarthy has sunken almost to zero since Eisenhower became president. [In his letter of 5 May 1954 Gödel credited the Eisenhower regime with "the unmasking of McCarthy."]

16.12.60 I believe that people generally underestimate what Eisenhower has done in the last eight years for mankind. When he leaves, much will turn to the worse, especially also with regard to the peace of the world.

Although Gödel preferred Eisenhower over Stevenson for the presidency, he also thought well of Stevenson:

26.7.65 Stevenson is dead. He was one of the few sympathetic politicians. He is difficult to replace: the U.S. foreign policy will probably become even more unreasonable through his death.

Gödel's opinion of Kennedy changed between 1961 and 1963:

30.4.61 With regard to the new president, one sees quite clearly already where his politics is leading: war in Vietnam, war in Cuba, the belligerent Nazis or fascists (in the form of "anticommunist" organizations) beginning to bloom, more rearmament, less press freedom, no negotiations with Khrushchev, etc.

28.5.61 In other aspects Kennedy now looks more congenial than before the election and I believe that Adele is right that he often has an insidious expression in the eyes.

24.3.63 In the realm of politics it appeared for a long time that an atomic war could break out any day. But fortunately Khrushchev and Kennedy are both rational in this regard.

20.10.63 With regard to the politics and the gold reserve in America, I had little time in recent months to devote myself to such matters. But in general the international situation has certainly improved substantially and Kennedy has proven himself to be a better president than was to be expected originally and by the Cuban adventure.

Gödel was unambiguously against the American involvement in the war in Vietnam:

21.10.65 Have you heard about the belligerent demonstrations against the war in Vietnam? They are right. It took Eisenhower to end the war in Korea. But scarcely had he returned, exactly the same thing began in Vietnam.

20.1.66 The peace offensive in Vietnam is very welcome, but Johnson has waited so long in this matter, till people here have already nearly thrown rotten eggs at him (if not also literally).

1.6 Companion of Einstein

From about 1942 to April of 1955 Einstein and Gödel frequently walked together while conversing. They were a familiar sight in the neighborhood of the Institute for Advanced Study. Although others have occasionally noted their close friendship, few details are known, for it was primarily a private matter, and there is scarcely any record of their discussions, which were almost certainly undertaken entirely for their own enjoyment. According to Ernst G. Straus, who was with them a good deal in the 1940s,

1.6.1 The one man who was, during the last years, certainly by far Einstein's best friend, and in some ways strangely resembled him most, was Kurt Gödel, the great logician. They were very different in almost every personal way—Einstein gregarious, happy, full of laughter and common sense, and Gödel extremely solemn, very serious, quite solitary, and distrustful of common sense as a means of arriving at the truth. But they shared a fundamental quality: both went directly and wholeheartedly to the questions at the very center of things (in Holton and Elkena 1982:422).

They were both great philosopher-scientists—a very rare breed indeed, which appears to have become extinct as a result of intense specialization, acute competition, obsession with quick effects, distrust of reason, prevalence of distractions, and condemnation of ideals. The values that governed these philosopher-scientists are to a large extent now considered out of date, or at least no longer practicable in their plenitude. Admiration for them takes the form of nostalgia for a bygone era, or they are regarded as fortunate but strange and mysterious characters. Their lives and work also suggest questions for somewhat idle speculation: What would they be doing if they were young today? What types of cultural, social, and historical conditions (including the state of the discipline) are likely to produce their sort of minds and achievements like theirs?

There is a natural curiosity about the life and work of people like them. Much has been said about Einstein, and there are signs indicating that a good deal will be said about Gödel as well. Their exceptional devotion to what might be called "eternal truth" serves to give a magnified view of the value of our theoretical instinct and intellect. Reflections on their primary value may also provide an antidote to all the busy work now going on; they may supply a breath of fresh air, and even point to the availability of more spacious regions in which one could choose to live and work.

Both Einstein and Gödel grew up and did their best work in Central Europe, using German as their first language. In the "miraculous" year of 1905, when he was about 26, Einstein published articles on Special Relativity, on the light-quantum, and on Brownian motion. Gödel had done his work on the completeness of predicate logic and on the inexhaustibility of mathematics before reaching the same age. Einstein went on to develop General Relativity, and Gödel moved to set theory, where he introduced an orderly subuniverse of sets (the "constructible" sets), which yielded the consistency of the continuum hypothesis and which has been to date the single most fruitful step in bringing order into the chaos of arbitrary sets. (His work on Einstein's equations followed, as a digression and a byproduct of his study of the philosophical problem of time and change. He once told me that it was *not* stimulated by his close association with Einstein.) During the last few decades of their lives, both of them concentrated on what are commonly thought to be unfashionable pursuits: Einstein on the unified theory and Gödel on "old-fashioned" philosophy.

The combination of fundamental scientific work, serious concern with philosophy, and independence of spirit reaches in these two men a height that is rarely found and is probably unique in this century. The supreme level of their intellectual work reminds one of the seventeenth century, sometimes called the "century of genius," when important work was given to the world by such geniuses as Kepler, Harvey, Galileo, Descartes, Pascal, Huygens, Newton, Locke, Spinoza, and Leibniz.

One indulgence leads to another. If we pair Einstein with Gödel, why not extend the familiar association of Einstein with Newton by analogy? The riddle is, then, to look for an x such that Einstein is to Gödel as Newton is to x. The obvious candidates are Descartes and Leibniz. Gödel's own hero is Leibniz, another great logician. Moreover, Gödel considers Leibniz's monadology close to his own philosophy. At the same time, the clean and conclusive character of Gödel's mathematical innovations may be more similar to Descartes's invention of analytic geometry, and his sympathy with Husserl appears to be closer to Descartes's predominant concern with method, with a new way of thinking and the beginning of a new type of philosophy. Another likely candidate is Pascal, who, like Gödel, often went against the spirit of his time.

During his lifetime Gödel was much less well known to the general public than his friend. In a 1953 letter to his mother, undoubtedly in response to a question from her, Gödel comments on the burden of fame:

9.12.53 I have so far not found my "fame" burdensome in any way. That begins only when one becomes so famous that one is known to every child in the street, as is the case of Einstein. In that case, crackpots turn up now and then, who desire to expound their nutty ideas, or who want to complain about the situation of the world. But as you see, the danger is also not so great; after all, Einstein has already managed to reach the venerable age of 74 years.

Gödel's fame has spread more widely since his death in 1978. The growing attention to him and his work is undoubtedly related to the increasingly widespread application of computers. For example, one symposium held as a memorial to him announced its theme as "Digital Intelligence: From Philosophy to Technology." Indeed, it may be that the connection between Gödel's work and computers is closer than that between Einstein's work and the atom bomb, about which Gödel says in a 1950 letter to his mother:

11.5.50 That just Einstein's discoveries in the first place made the atom bomb possible, is an erroneous comprehension. Of course he also indirectly contributed to it, but the essence of his work lies in an entirely other direction.

I believe Gödel would say the same thing about the connection between his own work and computers. The "entirely other direction" is fundamental theory, which constituted the (central) purpose of life for both Gödel and Einstein. This common dedication, their great success with it (in distinct but mutually appreciated ways), and their drive to penetrate deeper into the secrets of nature—the combination of these factors undoubtedly provided the solid foundation for their friendship and their frequent interactions. Each of them found in the other his intellectual equal who, moreover, shared the same cultural tradition. By happy coincidence, they happened to have been, since about 1933, thrown together in the same "club," the Institute for Advanced Study.

Gödel was generally reluctant to initiate human contacts and was comfortable with only a small number of individuals, especially during his Princeton years. There were undoubtedly a number of other people who would have enjoyed social interaction with him; but few had the confidence or the opportunity. In the case of Einstein, of course, there was no problem of confidence, and there was plenty of opportunity. Moreover, both of them had thought exceptionally deeply and articulately about science and philosophy on the basis of a wealth of shared knowledge. There is every indication that both of them greatly enjoyed each other's company and conversation. Indeed, their relationship must have been one of the most precious experiences of its kind.

Oskar Morgenstern, who knew Gödel well and was also acquainted with Einstein (probably through Gödel), wrote to the Austrian government toward the end of 1965 to recommend honoring Gödel on his sixtieth birthday:

1.6.2   Einstein has often told me that in the late years of his life he has continually sought Gödel's company, in order to have discussions with him. Once he said to me that his own work no longer meant much, that he came to the Institute merely 'to have the privilege to walk home with Gödel.' [The "late years" probably began in 1951, when Einstein stopped working on the unified theory.]

The letters to his mother make it clear that Gödel valued Einstein's company just as highly as Einstein valued his. What was involved is, I think, a fascinating example of human values which may perhaps be helpful in testing ethical theories in particular, such theories as, John Stuart Mill's "principle of preference," which proposes to guide the ranking of pleasures. More than a quest for definite results or even an airing of personal troubles, their talks may appropriately be considered to have served a "purposeless purpose" based on a "disinterested interest." From a common and ordinary perspective, they might be thought to have engaged in a "useless" activity. Yet their genuine enjoyment strikingly reveals a type of value many of us can only dimly see or have experienced only in a limited degree. Could we, perhaps, call this underlying value that of *pure and free inquiry*—which is usually a solitary affair—*as an end in itself*? Surely, the devotion of Gödel and Einstein to this value had much to do with their extraordinary level of intellectual achievement.

After Einstein's death, Gödel responded to an inquiry from Carl Seelig by saying that he and Einstein had talked particularly about philosophy, physics, politics, and, often, about Einstein's unified field theory (although, or perhaps because, Einstein knew that Gödel was very skeptically opposed to it). What is presupposed in Gödel's statement is, I am sure, a large area of agreement in their tastes and in the value and importance they placed on particular questions and ideas. They shared also a good deal of knowledge (including judgments on what is known and what is not), as well as a great talent for expressing their thoughts clearly. In the rest of this chapter I contrast their outlooks by looking at some of their agreements and disagreements.

Both Einstein and Gödel were concerned primarily, and almost exclusively in their later years, with what is fundamental. For example, Einstein (Schilpp 1949:15; Woolf 1980:485) often explained his choice of physics over mathematics partly in terms of his feeling that mathematics was split up into too many specialties, while in physics he could see what the important problems were. He said to Straus, however, that "Now that I've met Gödel, I know that the same thing does exist in mathematics." In other words, Einstein was interested in problems fundamental to the whole of mathematics or the whole of physics, but could initially discern them only in the case of physics. Gödel once told me, almost apologetically (probably to explain why he had so little of what he considered success in his later decades), that he too was always after what is fundamental.

Neither Einstein nor Gödel (contrary to prevailing opinion in the physics community of their time) considered quantum theory to be part of the ultimate furniture of physics. Einstein seems to have been looking for a complete theory within which quantum theory would be seen as a derivative ensemble description. In physics, according to Gödel, the present "two-level" theory (with its "quantization" of a "classical system," and its divergent series) was admittedly very unsatisfactory (Wang 1974:13).

In the letters to his mother, Gödel often explains Einstein's attitude with sympathy. In 1950 he commented on an article calling Einstein's theory "the key to the universe," and declared that such sensational reports were "very much against Einstein's own will." He added, "The present position of his work does not (in my opinion) justify such reports at all, even if results obtained in the future on the basis of his ideas might perhaps conceivably justify them. But so far everything is unfinished and uncertain." This opinion, I think, agreed, essentially, with Einstein's own.

These and other examples of agreement between Einstein and Gödel reveal a shared perspective which was contrary to common practice and the "spirit of the time" and which constituted a solid foundation for their mutual appreciation. Against this background, their disagreements and differences were secondary. Indeed, in other aspects as well, the opposition of their views can usually be seen as branchings out from a common attitude.

Both of them valued philosophy, but they disagreed on its nature and function. They were both peace-loving and cosmopolitan in outlook, but, unlike Einstein, Gödel took no public political positions. They were both sympathetic to the ideal of socialism, but Gödel's skepticism toward prevalent proposals on how to attain it contrasts with the less restrained view expressed in Einstein's 1949 essay "Why Socialism?" (reprinted in 1954). There is a sense in which both men could be seen as religious, but Einstein spoke of accepting Spinoza's pantheism, while Gödel called himself a theist, following Leibniz. (In 1951 Gödel said of Einstein, "He is undoubtedly in some sense religious, but certainly not in the sense of the church.")

They both read Kant in school and developed a strong taste for philosophy when young. Einstein turned against it because of its vagueness and arbitrariness; Gödel went on to devote a great deal of energy to its pursuit, aiming at "philosophy as a rigorous science." According to Einstein, "Epistemology without contact with science becomes an empty scheme. Science without epistemology is—insofar as it is thinkable at all—primitive and muddled" (Schilpp 1949:684). Gödel, by contrast, shows less interest in epistemology and believes that the correct way to do philosophy is to know oneself. For Gödel, science only *uses* concepts, whereas philosophy analyzes our primitive concepts on the basis of our everyday experience.

In the 1950s Einstein, like most intellectuals, preferred Stevenson to Eisenhower, but Gödel strongly favored Eisenhower. (On the other hand, Gödel shared his colleagues' great admiration for Franklin D. Roosevelt.) Einstein's love of classical music is well known; music seems to have been of little interest to Gödel. On the other hand, Gödel's reported liking for modern abstract art was presumably not shared by Einstein. Einstein married twice, had two sons and two stepdaughters, and was a widower for almost two decades. Gödel married only once and relatively late, had no children, and was survived by his wife.

In Gödel's letters to his mother he frequently mentions seeing Einstein almost daily and comments on Einstein's health, usually in optimistic terms. He also explained Einstein's public activities and made observations on books and articles about Einstein.

In 1949 there was mutual gift-giving on the occasions of Einstein's seventieth birthday and the Gödels' housewarming. In the summer of 1947, Gödel reported to his mother that Einstein was taking a rest cure: "So I am now quite lonesome and speak scarcely with anybody in private." In January of 1955, he wrote: "I am also not at all so lonely as you think. I often visit Einstein and get also visits from Morgenstern and others."

A week after Einstein's death on 18 April 1955, Gödel wrote that the death of Einstein had been a great shock to him, for he had not expected it at all, and that, naturally, his state of health had worsened again during the last week, especially in regard to sleep and appetite. Two months later, however, he said, "My health now is good. I have definitely regained my strength during the last two months."

In terms of the contrast between participating in history and understanding the world, both Einstein and Gödel were primarily engaged in the task of understanding. In the process, they contributed decisively to their own special subjects. But, unlike Gödel, Einstein participated in history in other ways and was much more of a public figure. Gödel kept a greater distance from the spirit of the time, speculating and offering novel ideas on a number of perennial issues that interest some specialists but are, shunned by most of them. For example: Is mind more than a machine? How exhaustive and conclusive is our knowledge in mathematics? How real are time and change? Can Darwinism provide an adequate account of the origins of life and mind? Is there a separate physical organ for handling abstract impressions? How precise can physics become? Is there a next world?—Einstein, I believe, paid much less attention to such questions.

While Einstein concentrated on physics throughout his life, Gödel at first shifted his interest from theoretical physics to mathematics and, later, to logic; then, after his great success in logic, he involved himself deeply in several philosophical projects. It is true that Einstein too left his last work, the unified field theory, unfinished. Yet Gödel was more liable to embark on new voyages, apparently pursuing several important lines of work without bringing them to completion. One might say that Gödel did not plan his life as well as Einstein did, and that Einstein had a sounder sense of what was feasible. But then none of us is equipped to foretell with any assurance what fruits our unfinished work will bear in future. Moreover, as Gödel says, even though the present is not a good time for philosophy, this situation may change. We have a tendency to expect the dominant trend to continue in the same direction, but history is full of swings of the pendulum. There is no solid evidence that would preclude the appearance of many other powerfully effective intellects of the type represented by Einstein and Gödel—perhaps even in the not-too-distant future.

Chapter 2
Gödel's Mental Development

The world and everything in it has meaning and sense, and in particular a good and unambiguous meaning.
Gödel, 6. October 1961

At an early age Gödel's quest for security and certainty led him to a preoccupation with meaning and precision. A summer's reading at the age of fifteen seems to have led him to a decision to concentrate, as a starting point, on theoretical physics, which promised to provide precise answers to his why-questions on a global scale. From eighteen to twenty-two, his interest in precision led him from physics to mathematics and, then, to (mathematical) logic.

With his exceptional talent and thoroughness of preparation, Gödel quickly gained command of contemporary logic. He went on to do revolutionary work in logic from 1929 to 1943—before he reached the age of thirty-seven. During this period he also studied a good deal of philosophy. When, in 1943, he decided to abandon active work in logic, he turned his principal attention to philosophy.

From 1943 to 1958 Gödel approached philosophy by way of its relation to logic and mathematics—with a digression, from 1947 to 1950, to study the problem of time and change, linking Einstein's relativity theory to the work of Kant. By 1959 he had concluded that this approach revealed its own inadequacy and that philosophy required a method different from that of science.

In 1959 Gödel began to study the work of Husserl and subsequently suggested, with some hesitation, that phenomenology might be the right method for philosophy. Even though there are traces of Husserl's influence in some of Gödel's very limited number of available writings after 1959, it is not clear that his work actually derived much benefit from his study of Husserl. In 1972, he stated that had not found what he was looking for in his pursuit of philosophy.

2.1 His Life in Its Relation to His Work

A familiar ideal, both for each person and for society at large, is the enjoyment of one's work. For most of us, however, work is a necessary component of our lives, governed mainly by the demands of society. If work could become generally enjoyable—a need rather than a necessary evil—not only would everyone have a better life but we would also have a better society. As it is, as Karl Marx pointed out, working people are commonly "alienated" from their work and so they "live only when they are *not* working." For a majority of people, work is no more than the unavoidable means of making a living, a precondition for realizing a life of one kind or another.

In the case of those, like Gödel, who have done outstanding work, the rest of us are primarily interested in the end product of that work. At the same time, we may also be curious about the process of the work and its place in the life of the person. On the whole, this relationship tends to be more revealing in the case of artists, writers, and philosophers than it is in that of scientists. Gödel divided his attention between science and philosophy. His scientific work borders on philosophy and is avowedly linked intimately to his philosophical views. I have come to believe that it is rewarding to speculate on the relation of Gödel's work to his life as an instructive example for studying the interconnections between various philosophies and different ways of life and different types of work.

A fundamental determinant of human behavior is our desire for security and order. Since complete security is rare, it is natural for us to try to see the world as fundamentally orderly. Alternative worldviews propose alternative ways of reconciling the apparent disorder we find with our desire for order; they either cultivate an ability to live with uncertainty or contrive some way to perceive order beneath the phenomenon of contingency. Gödel is of special interest from this perspective because he strove especially hard and with great power to find and articulate a consistent and comprehensive view of an orderly and rational world. His life and work were conspicuously governed by his dominant wish to see order and attain security.

One task of philosophy is to reconcile the phenomenon of time and change with our desire for *Sicherheit* (security and certainty). We cannot deny that we experience change, and that change brings about new situations which may threaten our sense of security unless we can anticipate and prepare for them. (Incidentally, as a way of giving us a certain general sense of security, Gödel proposed a doctrine [considered in Chapter 9] according to which time and change are not objectively real.) Our desire for security leads in this way to a craving for generality, for laws that tell us what changes to expect. Typically this quest takes the form of a why-question, which asks for the cause or the reason *A* that produces or accounts for a given situation *B*. The situation *B*, whether encountered or imagined, may be either desirable or else something we wish to avoid or need to prepare for. In either case, we feel more secure if we can find, among the complex factors surrounding *B*, some *A* that is the why of *B*.

The quest for reasons has a tendency to expand beyond the practically relevant and to become an end in itself, either from curiosity or from habit. Indeed, we are inclined to formulate, both as an empirical generalization and as a heuristic principle, a sweeping universal proposition to the effect that everything has a reason. This may be viewed as a form of what Leibniz calls the "principle of sufficient reason." And Gödel seems to believe strongly in this principle, even though it is, most of us would think, neither provable nor refutable. Like Leibniz, Gödel takes this principle to be a given fundamental truth. More explicitly, he attributes to Leibniz (in a letter to his mother reproduced in the next chapter) the idea, which he shares, that everything in the world has a meaning; this idea, he says, "is, by the way, exactly analogous to the principle that everything has a cause, which is the basis of the whole of science" (Gödel 1945–1966, hereafter *LM*).

When Gödel was about four, he was nicknamed Mr. Why by family and friends because he always wanted to get to the bottom of things with his intensive questioning. This early disposition may be viewed as the beginning of his persistent quest for reasons, carried out even then in a more careful manner than that of most children. Conditions were, as I have mentioned in Chapter 1, favorable for him to continue this pursuit.

In China, some trees are famous for their shape, age, size, location, or historical association, and so on—either locally or more widely. If we consider the growth from a seed to a large tree that lends shade to passersby and provides a home to other living beings, we are inclined to think in terms of the continuing interaction of heredity (as initially contained in the seed) and environment (such as the soil and the climate) through the different stages of the life of the tree. In his *Erewhon* (or "nowhere," 1872) Samuel Butler envisages machines that metabolize, reproduce, evolve, maintain themselves, and seem to have an aim in life. Like people, these trees and machines adapt themselves to the environment. They are all, to use a currently popular term, "complex adaptive systems"—a comprehensive category that is challenging but difficult to study systematically. For instance, the phenomenon of (our felt) freedom is an essential ingredient of human beings, which may or may not be construable as part of the connotation of the concept of an adaptive system.

If we compare Gödel to a famous tree (or perhaps the big tree between him and Einstein in the photograph of 1950) (Wang 1987a:142, hereafter *RG*), we find in him a seed with potentially strong intellectual power (unmistakably revealed quite early) planted in healthy soil (a wealthy and enlightened family) and growing up under proper care (a normal good education) in a congenial climate (with stable intellectual standards, appreciative teachers, and increasingly well-defined tasks for him to accomplish).

Gödel's ability was, as I mentioned before, demonstrated quite early. His maternal grandmother, who often played with him as a child, prophesied a great future for him. In later years his mother told many stories about him as a child, which in her view suggested even then that he would become a world-famous intellect. These anecdotes suggest strongly that Gödel as a child had already acquired confidence in his own capabilities, a state of mind usually necessary for great work later on. Moreover, this confidence was abundantly confirmed in school and at university, where he was widely recognized as an exceptionally able student. He was known to possess great capacities for methodical concentration, accuracy, and thoroughness, for separating the essential from the inessential, and for getting quickly to the heart of the matter.

At the same time, there were early signs that Gödel's mental and physical health was not robust. At about five, he often exhibited states of anxiety when his mother left the house; he suffered at about this time from a light anxiety neurosis. From about the age of ten he enjoyed playing chess but became very upset when he lost, which happened rarely.

These incidents indicate that Gödel was more easily upset than most people when his expectations were frustrated. Clearly, being upset is a state one would like to avoid, and so we learn to distinguish important (including long-range) expectations from unimportant ones, to adapt our expectations to our ability, to regulate circumstances to reduce uncertainty, and to cultivate our capacity to anticipate and tolerate disappointment. A conspicuous feature of Gödel's life is the choice he made to concentrate on reducing uncertainties. His entire life and work make clear that he was greatly concerned with *Sicherheit*. Undoubtedly he also had great expectations for himself; he seemed to be disappointed in himself in his last years.

Gödel must have worked hard to find ways to assure himself of *Sicherheit* and, at the same time, do good work. His later behavior gives some indication of his solution to this problem. He tended to enter every situation—be it human contact, publication, or competition—thoroughly prepared. He generally avoided controversy, knowing it would upset him. He tried to make his work definitive and acceptable to all sides. In particular, he procrastinated over his decisions to see people, to publish his work, to respond to questions or requests, and so on. On the whole, he adhered to the principle of "fewer, but better." (Wittgenstein's attitude toward publishing his work was quite similar to Gödel's.)

With regard to his work, Gödel often chose to do (and especially to publish what was more definitive rather than things that were less conclusive, even when the latter seemed more important to him. This appears to account for his preference for seeking philosophically relevant (and therefore important for him) scientific (and therefore precise and definitive) results. The success he achieved by following this strategy in logic is conspicuous, but his solutions of Einstein's field equations are also illustrative. Moreover, he spent much time and effort (especially between 1960 and 1970) in consolidating and extending his old work. Since, however, definitive and precise work itself is hardly possible in philosophy, it is not surprising that he felt he had not found what he looked for in philosophy.

The sort of anxiety he had displayed when he was losing at chess may explain in part why Gödel published so little in philosophy. It may also explain his later success in cultivating other ways of dealing with competition. By opening up new directions and thinking through their implications, he generally entered into competitive situations only when he was sure of success. When there was any danger of being involved in a controversy over priority, he refrained from contention; for example, he did not stress the fact that he was first to prove that truth in a language is not definable in that language. He also tried to minimize in public the extent to which he had pursued the independence problems in set theory in his unpublished work.

In 1972 I asserted that Gödel was "above competition." He smilingly expressed skepticism over the phrase but did not deny the assertion. He was, I think, aware of his concern over competition but managed to deal with it magnanimously. In 1976 he checked my report "Some Facts about Kurt Gödel" (RG:41–46) and then told me I could publish it after his death. I believe he would, likewise, have no objection to my publishing his other sayings after his death, since he is no longer in any danger of being upset by criticisms to which he has no conclusive replies.

We do not know enough about Gödel's childhood to understand why his sense of security was so vulnerable. One familiar approach in such cases is to look at the person's sibling relations. In Gödel's case the only sibling was his brother Rudolf, who was a capable and pleasant boy four years older than he. Rudolf was apparently closer to their parents than he was. Kurt may have felt insecure because he thought, rightly or wrongly, that Rudolf was the more favored child. (In this regard too, Wittgenstein was similar to Gödel; he was a youngest child with a brother, Paul, also four years older.) However that may be, it seems better simply to accept as a given that Gödel was, from childhood on, exceptionally preoccupied with *Sicherheit*.

Closely related to this concern is the matter of Gödel's physical health. At about eight or nine, he had a severe case of rheumatic fever. He was somewhat hypochondriacal thereafter and fancied that he had a heart problem. He may have developed his exceptional distrust of physicians at this early period. Since medicine is far from a rigorous science, his demand for precision and certainty may well have contributed to this distrust. In any case, his refusal to follow the advice of physicians had serious adverse effects on his later health. In particular, in early 1951, as mentioned in Chapter 1, he delayed treatment of a bleeding duodenal ulcer and, apparently, designed a strange diet for himself, which he continued to follow, to the detriment of his general health.

Judging from the available data, however, it appears that Gödel was in generally good health during the 1920s and 1940s. In the 1930s he suffered several periods of mental disturbance: at the end of 1931, in mid-1934, in late 1935, and in 1936. Between the spring of 1929 and the summer of 1938 he was doing most of his important work in logic, and the intense concentration may have weakened his resistance. He also took two long trips during this period, unaccompanied by his future wife Adele. In later years he occasionally mentioned his loneliness during his visits to America in 1933 and 1934 and, briefly, in 1935.

According to Gödel himself, his health was, as mentioned before, exceptionally poor in 1936, 1961, and 1970. From the spring of 1976 until his death in January of 1978, his health problems and those of his wife Adele were his principal concerns. According to his physician, he had become depressive and was at times troubled by feelings of inferiority. His death certificate says that he died of "malnutrition and inanition" caused by "personality disturbance."

Most of the time Gödel was able to protect his delicate health and sensitivity by judiciously restricting the range of his activities, commitments, and human contacts. In his later years, however, he was not able to protect himself similarly from disappointment. His early success in logic seems to have led to expectations of similarly definitive work in philosophy; these expectations were not realized, and so his self-confidence and his feelings of security were damaged. It is possible that he would have done more effective philosophical work if he had required less precision and less definite conclusions in philosophy than in science. It is also possible that he would have developed his philosophy further if Europe had been at peace and he had continued his work there. But of course these are mere speculations, especially since our knowledge of his unpublished work and of the probable long-range effect of his philosophical ideas remains limited.

Gödel's exceptionally strong desire for security and certainty caused him to be generally cautious and somewhat legalistic. He was reluctant to publicize those aspects of his views which he thought were unpopular. In practical matters he was willing to accept established authority but insisted on doing and requiring what he saw as legally correct. As a result, some of his behavior appeared unreasonable. For instance, in the spring of 1939 when Gödel was in America, he insisted on returning to Austria, against the advice of friends. Menger thought his major reason for going was to defend his rights: "He had complained earlier about the withdrawal of his Dozent position at the University of Vienna by the Nazi regime, and he spoke with great precision about his violated rights" (Menger 1994).

Menger also recalled in 1981 that Gödel, while living on the campus of the University of Notre Dame in the spring of 1939, sometimes made an issue of very minor matters:

2.1.1 He had quarrels with the prefect of his building for all sorts of trivial reasons (because of keys, etc.). I always had to settle them, which was not easy, because the prefect was an old priest, very set in his ways, and with Gödel maintaining his rights. Later Veblen told me that [in Princeton] Gödel had similar but more serious household difficulties (in particular because of a supposedly dangerous refrigerator), which Veblen only alleviated with great difficulty (Menger 1994).

Morgenstern told Menger a story about Gödel's legalistic bent from his last years, when he was admitted to a hospital but insisted that he had no right to one of the benefits proffered: "And in his judicial precision Gödel unshakably maintained his ground, even though the hospital routine was disturbed, inconvenience arose on all sides, and, of course, what was the most grievous, he himself was deprived of urgently needed medical help" (Menger 1994).

2.2 Conscious Preparation (1920–1929)

Curious children are likely to ask "Why?" when surprised by something unusual, such as an exceptionally long nose. Then, at some stage we begin to ask for reasons for ordinary things as well, which, by definition, fall into groups, and we are on our way to asking more and more *universal* questions. Moreover, we often have the urge to ask "Why?" again in response to the answer to a previous question. When this urge arises from genuine curiosity, we may come to ask more and more *fundamental* questions.

In this way, the quest for reasons is transformed into an ideal: we search for what is more universal or more fundamental, and then for what is most universal or most fundamental. There are, of course, alternative approaches to this formidable task; one may choose philosophy or poetry or religion or history, and, within each approach, any of a variety of ways of selecting and arranging the preparatory steps.

From the beginning, Gödel's pursuit of reasons was tempered by and combined with his quest for security and certainty, with precision as a criterion. Given this central concern, it is not surprising that he chose a course that begins with what is certain and precise. It is then also natural that he decided to approach the ideal of seeing all reasons through philosophy, specifically philosophy by way of physics and mathematics.

At the *Gymnasium* (secondary school) in Brunn which he attended from 1916 to 1924, Gödel was an outstanding student, excelling, at first, in languages, then in history, and finally in mathematics. In 1920 (at the age of fourteen) he began to take a strong interest in mathematics (on reading an introduction to the calculus), and at sixteen or seventeen he had already mastered the university material in mathematics. This achievement must be seen as the result of an interaction between Gödel's native talent and his quest for certainty, precision, the universal, and the fundamental. Even then, he was undoubtedly aware that the study of mathematics is good preparation for a wide range of intellectual pursuits.

In 1985 I came upon a passage in a 1946 letter Gödel wrote to his mother, which appeared to offer a clue to Gödel's choice of vocation.

26.8.46 The book " Goethe" by Chamberlain, mentioned in your letter, brought to my mind many memories from my youth. I read it (strangely exactly twenty-five years [ago] now) in Marienbad and see today still the remarkable lilac-colored flowers before me, which then pervaded everything. It is incredible how something can be so vivid. I believe I have written you already in 1941 from the Mountain Ash Inn, that I found there again the same flowers and how peculiarly this touched me. This Goethe book also became the beginning of my occupation with Goethe's *Farbenlehre* and his *Streit mit Newton*, and thereby also indirectly contributed to my choice of vocation. This is the way remarkable threads spin through one's life, which one discovers only when one gets older.

At the time I found the letter I was at a loss for a clue to what it meant. Later I had an opportunity to ask his brother what had happened in the summer of 1921 in connection with the biography of Goethe. Rudolf told me that the two boys had had extended discussions of Goethe's views about the natural sciences and that afterwards Gödel had concluded that he favored Newton over Goethe. This experience undoubtedly touched off his interest in theoretical physics, and so, when he entered the University of Vienna in 1924 he at first specialized in physics.

Meanwhile, in 1922, Gödel's first reading of (some of) the work of Kant was, as he told me in 1975, important for the development of his intellectual interests. In January of 1925, shortly after beginning his university studies, he requested from the library Kant's *Metaphysical Foundations of*

Natural Science, which studies the philosophical (partly a priori) foundations of Newtonian physics. This fact suggests to me that Gödel's interest was less in physics itself than in its philosophical foundations and significance.

Judging from his later development, it seems likely that Gödel was dissatisfied with Kant's subjective viewpoint and with the lack of precision in his work. Gödel apparently saw even physics as insufficiently precise, as can be seen from his observation that his interest in precision had led him from physics to mathematics. Moreover, in 1975 he said that he had been a sort of Platonist (a "conceptual realist" or a "conceptual and mathematical realist") since about 1925; this Platonist stance is clearly an objectivist position, in contrast to Kant's subjective point of view.

From 1925 to 1926, while still specializing in physics, Gödel also studied the history of European philosophy with Heinrich Gomperz, the philosophy of mathematics with Moritz Schlick, and number theory with P. Furtwängler. We see, then, that he was becoming more involved with philosophy, mathematics (in particular number theory), and the philosophy of mathematics. This impression is confirmed by the fact that in 1926 he transferred from physics to mathematics and, coincidentally, became a member of the Schlick Circle (commonly known as the Vienna Circle).

For a short period Gödel was much interested in number theory, which is exceptionally "clean" (pure) and, in a general way, philosophically significant in that it offers a strong supporting example for Platonism in mathematics. Yet specific results in this area are of no philosophical significance. Moreover, definite advances in number theory depend more heavily on technical skills than on conceptual clarification, and by his own account Gödel was better at the latter. At any rate, the pull toward logic soon became very strong, both for its apparent overall philosophical importance and for its promise of precise conceptual results of philosophical significance.

From 1926 to 1928 Gödel attended the meetings of the Schlick Circle regularly, and the group aroused his interest in the foundations of mathematics. Undoubtedly this was the period when, in Gödel's own words, his interest in precision led him from mathematics to logic. This was a time when mathematical logic was widely believed (certainly by the Circle) to be (1) the key to understanding the foundations of mathematics; (2) the main tool for philosophical analysis; and (3) the skeleton and crucial instrument for erecting and fortifying a new (logical) empiricism (or positivism). Underlying (3) was the idea that the main drawback of empiricism had been its failure to give a satisfactory account of mathematics; mathematical logic promised to remedy that defect by showing that mathematical truths are "analytic" or "tautologous" or "without content," like such sentences as "there are three feet in a yard"—to use Russell's example.

Gödel himself rejected this idea even then. Indeed, he saw the work in logic he was soon to undertake as a refutation of point (3) and its underlying idea. At the same time, he found points (1) and (2) congenial. Hence, he had a negative reason (to refute empiricism) as well as positive reasons for studying mathematical logic, even if his basic goal was restricted to the pursuit of philosophy. An additional impetus was provided when he became familiar with Hilbert's program, which proposed to settle crucial philosophical issues by solving precise mathematical problems.

Gödel agreed to have his name included in the list of members of the Schlick (or Vienna) Circle in its manifesto of 1929. Nonetheless, he was eager, over the years, to dissociate himself from the main tenets of the Circle, as he did, for instance, in letters he wrote to his mother in 1946 and to Burke D. Grandjean in 1975:

15.8.46 The article on Schlick arrived and has interested me very much. You need not wonder that I am not considered in it. I was indeed not a specially active member of the Schlick Circle and in many respects even in direct opposition to its principal views (*Anschauungen*).

19.8.75 (draft) It is true that my interest in the foundations of mathematics was aroused by the "Vienna Circle," but the philosophical consequences of my results, as well as the heuristic principles leading to them, are anything but positivistic or empiricistic.

Apparently Gödel started to concentrate on mathematical logic by the autumn of 1928, when he also began to attend Rudolf Carnap's lectures on "the philosophical foundations of arithmetic." In 1929 he began his research for the dissertation and soon proved the completeness of predicate logic. With the completion of this work, he left the stage of preparation and entered the stage of his most productive work in logic.

The thoroughness of Gödel's preparations and the acuteness of his youthful mind were observed and reported by Olga Taussky and Karl Menger, among others. According to Taussky, Gödel "was well trained in all branches of mathematics and you could talk to him about any problem and receive an excellent response." Menger described how "he always grasped problematic points quickly and his replies often opened new perspectives for the enquirer" (Menger 1994:205).

2.3 The First of the Three Stages of His Work

Gödel's preparations up to 1928 included a thorough mastery of a great deal of mathematics, a good knowledge of theoretical physics, and development of a philosophical viewpoint of objectivism which went well with his work in theoretical science. From 1929 to 1942 he revolutionized logic by doing philosophically important mathematics. Until 1939 he was spectacularly successful, and he was satisfied with his work. But by the beginning of 1943 he was frustrated by his unsuccessful attempt to further clarify Cantor's continuum problem and turned his main efforts to philosophy.

From 1943 to 1958 Gödel was engaged in seeking ways to repeat, in suitably selected parts of philosophy, his success in logic. From 1943 to 1946 he studied the work of Leibniz and, at the same time, took stock of his own work in logic from a philosophical perspective. From 1947 to 1950 he enjoyed a digression into the problem of time, linking philosophy to physics. In 1958, or shortly before, he was able to write and publish a paper on the problem of evidence in the context of his own interpretation of intuitionistic arithmetic—a technical result he had obtained in 1941. Yet his principal concern from 1951 to 1958 seems to have been the attempt to apply and extend his work in logic so as to draw definite philosophical conclusions in favor of his own objectivistic or Platonistic position. He was not satisfied with his efforts and found it difficult to attain "a complete elucidation" of his philosophical beliefs concerning conceptual realism.

By about 1959 he began to look for a new way of doing philosophy and, by his own account, initiated his study of Husserl in 1959. Still he was unable to settle on, develop, and apply a new method far enough to satisfy himself. In 1972 he told me he had not developed his philosophical views far enough to give a systematic account of them but could only apply them in making comments on what other philosophers had to say.

The three stages in Gödel's work may be seen as a special case of the effort to approach the philosophical ideal of understanding the meaning of the world and everything in it, by doing the best work within one's power as a contribution toward the ideal. The influence of the Vienna school put the nature of mathematics at the center of philosophy and suggested that mathematical logic was the best path for advancing understanding of the nature of mathematics. It was, therefore, natural for Gödel to *contract* or narrow his philosophical ideal and to begin his quest by doing work in logic. Later he continued this pursuit by *expanding* his work to larger issues, first without altering his method, and, finally, by searching for a *new method* of dealing directly with general philosophy.

During his association with the Vienna Circle from 1926 to 1928 Gödel had frequent discussions with some younger members of the group and attended the seminars. As noted earlier, this association aroused his interest in the foundations of mathematics, and in 1928 he began to concentrate his attention on mathematical logic. In the autumn of 1928 his library requests are mostly for works in logic; and he was attending Carnap's course on the foundations of arithmetic.

When Gödel began to do research in 1929, he was well equipped with powerful mathematical tools, a fruitful guiding philosophical viewpoint, a clear understanding of the fundamental issues in the foundations of mathematics, and a command of nearly all the important results in mathematical logic—which were not much at all at that time. In March 1928 he attended two stimulating lectures by L. E. J. Brouwer, given in Vienna. Carnap's course had undoubtedly introduced him to the relevant work of Frege Gottlob, David Hilbert, and Brouwer. In short, by 1929 Gödel had a clear picture of what was known and what remained to be discovered at the time, within the whole field of mathematical logic and in the foundations of mathematics.

Early in 1929, he obtained and studied the newly published *Grundzüge der theoretische Logik* (1928) by Hilbert and W. Ackermann, in which the completeness of predicate logic was formulated and presented as an open problem. Gödel soon settled this problem by proving the completeness, and wrote up the result as his doctoral dissertation, which he submitted on 15.10.29. The dissertation, which has been published in the first volume of his *Collected Works* (1986, hereafter *CW*1) reveals not only his thorough familiarity with much of the literature but also his clear understanding of the relevant philosophical issues, such as the distinction between provability as such and provability by certain *precisely stated formal means* and his observation that there is no need to restrict the means of proof in this case.

All Gödel's famous definite results in mathematical logic were obtained during the period from 1929 to 1942. These include (1) his proof of the completeness of predicate logic (1929); (2) his method of constructing, for any formal system of mathematics, a number-theoretical question undecidable in the system (1920); (3) his proof that the consistency of any of the formal systems for classical mathematics cannot be proved in the same system (1930); (4) his translation of classical arithmetic into intuitionistic arithmetic (1932); (5) his introduction of a definition of general recursive functions (1934); (6) his sketch of a proof that the length of a proof in a stronger logic can be much shorter than any proof of the same theorem in a weaker logic (lecture of 19.6.35); (7) his introduction of constructible sets and his immediate application of them to prove the consistency of the axiom of choice (1935); (8) his further application of constructible sets to prove the consistency of the (generalized) continuum hypothesis (1938); (9) his interpretation of intuitionistic arithmetic in terms of a slight extension of finitary arithmetic (1941); and (10) his preliminary proof of the independence of the axiom of choice (1942).

Gödel obtained many of these results with the help of his objectivistic philosophical viewpoint—a fact that, in turn, supports his viewpoint by demonstrating its fruitfulness. In 1967 he wrote to me to explain the importance of this viewpoint for discovering his proof of the completeness of predicate logic (1 above); he then added: "My objectivistic conception of mathematics and metamathematics in general, and of transfinite reasoning in particular, was fundamental also to my other work in logic." He went on to elaborate this assertion by considering the crucial importance of the viewpoint to his discovery of (2), (3), (7), and (8) above.

The completeness theorem (1) may be seen as the successful conclusion of our quest for a satisfactory formulation of what Gödel calls "the logic for the finite mind." This theorem also supplements the incompleteness theorems (2) and (3) so as to demonstrate both the powers and the limitations of mechanization and concrete intuition. The implications of (2), (7), and (9) provide us with instructive examples of our capacity to find new axioms and new concepts. In particular, the proof of (2) gives us a general way of seeing new axioms, by exhibiting, for each substantive consistent formal system, certain new axioms not provable within it. The connections established by (9) and (4) are significant as a kind of ladder to raise us from the potential infinite (based more directly on our concrete intuition) to the actual infinite. Observation (6) offers an early example in the study of the complexity of proofs and computations—an area of lively investigation for the last few decades.

When Gödel began his research in 1929, there were at least three challenging areas concerned with the relation between logic and the foundations of mathematics. In the first place, formal systems for several parts of mathematics had become available, and Hilbert had proposed, and argued forcefully for the importance of, the problems of consistency, completeness, and decidability of these systems. In (1), (2), and (3) Gödel settled the questions of completeness and (finitary proofs of) consistency for all these systems. His proposal (5) offered one way of settling the questions of decidability, which were shortly afterwards answered negatively by Alonzo Church and, in a more convincing manner, by Alan Turing.

In the second place, there was the problem of evidence in mathematics, which received sharper formulations from Hilbert's finitary viewpoint and Brouwer's intuitionism. The connections discovered by Gödel in (9) and (4) made an important contribution to this problem by revealing explicitly what is involved essentially in expanding finitary arithmetic to intuitionistic arithmetic and then to classical arithmetic.

The third challenging area was set theory. In 1976 Gödel said he first came across Hilbert's outline of a proposed "proof" of Cantor's continuum hypothesis in 1930 and began to think about the continuum problem. He read the proof sheets of Hans Hahn's book on real functions in 1932 and learned the subject. Around this time he attended Hahn's seminar on set theory, as well.

The continuum problem is, in Gödel's words, "a question from the 'multiplication table' of cardinal numbers." The fact that it was so intractable indicated to Gödel the need to clarify the very concept of set. That Gödel saw the need for such clarification is also clear from Menger's 1981 recollection that "in 1933 he already repeatedly stressed that *the right [die richtigen] axioms of set theory had not yet been found* " (Menger 1994:210).

Early in 1937 my teacher Wang Sian-jun traveled to Vienna, intending to study with Gödel. When he visited Gödel, Gödel told him that the situation with arithmetic was essentially clear as a result of his own work and its further development by others; the next major area to clarify, he said, was set theory—*jetzt, Mengenlehre*. Gödel undoubtedly saw the continuum problem not only as intrinsically important but also as a catalytic focus and a convincing testing ground for his reflections on the concept of set. In a letter to Menger in 1937, he wrote;

15.12.37   I have continued my work on the continuum problem last summer and I finally succeeded in proving the consistency of the continuum hypothesis (even the generalized form) with respect to general set theory. But for the time being please do not tell anyone of this. So far, I have communicated this, besides to yourself, only to von Neumann, for whom I sketched the proof during his latest stay in Vienna. Right now I am trying to prove also the independence of the continuum hypothesis, but do not yet know whether I shall succeed with it.

Set theory was clearly one of Gödel's main interests, and the continuum problem occupied him for many years. It seems likely that from 1935 (or perhaps even 1932) to 1942, it was the principal concern of his work. By his own account, the frustrations caused by his failure to apply his method to prove the independence of the continuum hypothesis played a major part in his decision, in early 1943, to abandon research in logic. More than two decades later, after the independence of the continuum hypothesis was proved by Paul J. Cohen in 1963, Gödel attempted to go beyond compatibility results and settle the continuum problem completely by introducing plausible new axioms. He continued work on this (unsuccessful) project for several years, probably up to 1973 or 1974.

From 1930 to 1940 Gödel published a large number of papers and short notes, which are now generally available in his *Collected Works*. He also attended several courses and seminars. In 1976 he said he had continued his study of logic and mathematics, including the foundations of geometry and the beautiful subject of functions of complex variables, between 1930 and 1933. Menger recalled: that he also continued his study of philosophy:

2.3.1   In addition, Gödel studied much philosophy in those years, among other topics post-Kantian German idealist metaphysics. One day he came to me with a book by Hegel (unfortunately I forget which one) and showed me a passage which appeared to completely anticipate general relativity theory. ... But Gödel already then began to concentrate on Leibniz, for whom he entertained a boundless admiration. (Menger 1994:209–210)

In the autumn of 1927 Gödel attended Menger's course on dimension theory. Menger recalled him as a "slim, unusually quiet man. I do not recall having spoken with him then. Later I saw him again in the Schlick Circle; however, I never heard him take the floor or participate in a discussion in the Circle." After one session in which Schlick, Hahn, Otto Neurath, and Friedrich Waismann had talked about language, Gödel said, "The more I think about language, the more it amazes me that people ever understand each other at all." In contrast, to his reticence in the Circle he was very active in Menger's mathematical colloquium, which he began to attend on 24.10.29 at Menger's invitation:

2.3.2   From then on he was a regular participant who did not miss a single meeting so long as he was in Vienna and in good health. In these gatherings he appeared from the beginning to feel quite well and spoke even outside of them with participants, particularly G. Nöbling and a few foreign visitors, and later on frequently with A. Wald. He took part enthusiastically in diverse discussions. His expression (oral as well as written) was always of the greatest precision and at the same time of exceeding brevity. In nonmathematical conversations he was very withdrawn. (Ibid.:201)

There are indications that Gödel was also interested in economics. (I mentioned earlier Carnap's 1931 report that Gödel was interested in the influence of finance capital on politics.) While Gödel was in Princeton from 1933 to 1934, George Wald obtained results on certain equations about economic production and reported on them in Menger's colloquium. After his return to Vienna in the summer of 1934, Menger reports, he wanted to know them: "Gödel was very interested in these investigations and asked Wald to bring him up to date, since the first session of the year 1934/35 was to begin with another report by Wald on these equations" (Ibid.:212).

At the session of 6 November 1934, Gödel suggested a generalization of Wald's studies to systems with the price of the factors included: "Actually, for each individual entrepreneur the demand also depends on the prices of the factors of production. One can formulate an appropriate system of equations and investigate whether it is solvable." In his introductory note to this remark, John Dawson reports (CW1:392) that Gödel also discussed the foundations of economics with Oskar Morgenstern in those days and that Morgenstern, shortly before his death, named Gödel as one of the colleagues who had most influenced his work.

2.4 The Two Later Stages

From 1943 to 1958, Gödel was chiefly concerned with developing a philosophy of mathematics, both as a prolegomenon to metaphysics and as a
relatively precise part of general philosophy. In particular, he drew consequences from his mathematical results of the previous period. In the
process of trying to find a self-contained definitive account of the nature
of mathematics, he concluded that (a) the task requires an understanding
of knowledge in general, and (b) philosophy requires a method different
from that of science.

Gödel also studied Leibniz intensively from 1943 to 1946 and made,
in his own words, "a digression " (probably from 1947 to 1950) on the
problem of time. He found a group of novel solutions of Einstein's field
equations and used them to support the Kantian thesis that time and
change are purely subjective, or in some sense "illusions." He published
three articles on Kant and Einstein in connection with this digression.
Among the unpublished material there are also several versions of a long
philosophical essay entitled "Some Observations about the Relationship
between Theory of Relativity and Kantian Philosophy."

Gödel's main concern from 1943 to 1958 was the nature of mathematics and its relation to definite results, on the one hand, and philosophical issues, on the other. Over this period he wrote five articles on this
subject, of which three were published: the Russell paper (1944), Cantor
paper (1947), and Bernays paper (1958). These essays on the whole adhere closely to the goal of demonstrating a direct interplay between
his philosophical perspective and definite mathematical results and problems. They may be said to be applications, rather than direct expositions,
of his philosophical perspective, which is either shown in them implicitly
or suggested only briefly and tentatively. In contrast, the two essays
he did not publish were devoted to proving his philosophical position
of Platonism or conceptual-realism. These are his lively Gibbs lecture
(written and delivered in 1951) and the six laborious versions of his
Carnap paper which he prepared between 1953 and about 1958. In reply
to my question about his "philosophical leanings," Gödel wrote in 1975:
"I was [have been] a conceptual and mathematical realist since about 1925.
I never held the view that mathematics is syntax of language. Rather this
view, understood in any reasonable sense, can be *disproved* by my results."

The Gibbs lecture, which was a preliminary attempt to prove Platonism
in mathematics, concluded with an explicit formulation of that position
and an expression of faith:

2.4.1 I am under the impression that after sufficient clarification of the conclusion
in question it will be possible to conduct these discussions with mathematical
rigor and the result will be that (under certain assumptions which can hardly be
denied—in particular the assumption that there exists at all something like mathe-

matical knowledge) the Platonistic view is the only one tenable. Thereby I mean the view that mathematics describes a non-sensual reality, which exists independently both of the acts and the dispositions of the human mind and is only perceived, and probably perceived very incompletely, by the human mind. (*CW*3:323)

An illuminating aspect of the Gibbs lecture is the systematic approach to a proof of Platonism (in mathematics) envisaged by Gödel in 1951. He saw the task as that of disproving each of three theories alternative to Platonism and showing that they exhaust all the possibilities. These three alternative views are what he called: (1) the creation view, (2) psychologism, and (3) Aristotelian realism. What he called "nominalism " he saw as an extreme form of (1). The major part of the Gibbs lecture was devoted to a disproof of this special case of one of the three alternatives to Platonism: "The most I could assert would be to have disproved the nominalistic view, which considers mathematics to consist solely in syntactical conventions and their consequences" (*CW*3:322).

As far as I know, Gödel never made any serious effort to revise the Gibbs lecture for publication or to pursue the systematic program of refuting all three alternatives to Platonism. He did not include the Gibbs lecture in his list of major unpublished articles, even though he told me once or twice in the 1970s that "it proved Platonism." Instead, in his next project, one of the most extended in his work, he concentrated on refuting more thoroughly the extreme position of "nominalism", that is, the syntactical conception of mathematics.

On 15 May 1953 P. A. Schilpp invited Gödel to contribute a paper, to be entitled "Carnap and the Ontology of Mathematics" to a projected volume in which various philosophers would discuss Carnap's work (with Carnap himself). The manuscripts were to be due on 2 April 1954. Gödel replied on 2 July 1953, agreeing to write a short paper on "Some Observations on the Nominalistic View of the Nature of Mathematics." For the next five years or so Gödel spent a great deal of time and energy on this paper, writing six different versions of it under the revised title "Is mathematics syntax of language?" Finally, on 2 February 1959, he wrote to Schilpp to say that he was not going to submit his paper after all.

The Carnap paper is of special interest for the insights it gives into both Gödel's work and his life. It was undoubtedly his most sustained effort to defend Platonism in writing, and it illustrates his tendency to concentrate on a special case and then generalize without inhibition. I have often been struck by Gödel's readiness to infer Platonism in general from Platonism in mathematics, apparently seeing no need for offering additional reasons; this he does in the Carnap paper. Notably in the fifth and sixth versions, he refutes the syntactical view of mathematics by arguing that (1) mathematical intuition cannot be replaced by conventions about the use of symbols and their applications; (2) mathematical propositions are not devoid of content; and (3) the validity of mathematics is not compatible with strict empiricism. Thus, by refuting an extreme position opposed to Platonism in mathematics he was at the same time showing the plausibility of his own position.

The various manuscripts of the Carnap paper also illustrate the thoroughness of Gödel's working habits, his preference for brevity, and his appreciation of the value of serious views alternative to his own. The earlier versions include many references and footnotes, whereas the last two versions are much shorter and include no footnotes. By appreciating the value of an alternative view, we can better understand its appeal and, at the same time, see that it serves a useful purpose even though it is not true. The final two sections of the second version of the Carnap paper are good examples of Gödel's attention to this point.

48. I do not want to conclude this paper without mentioning the paradoxical fact that, although any kind of nominalism or conventionalism in mathematics turns out to be fundamentally wrong, nevertheless the syntactical conception perhaps has contributed more to the clarification of this situation than any other of the philosophical views proposed: on the one hand by the negative results to which the attempts to carry it through lead, on the other hand by the emphasis it puts on a difference of fundamental importance, namely the difference between conceptual and empirical truth, upon which it reflects a bright light by identifying it with the difference between empirical and conventional truth.
49. I believe that the true meaning of the opposition between things and concepts or between factual and conceptual truth is not yet completely understood in contemporary philosophy, but so much at least is clear: that in both cases one is faced with "solid facts," which are entirely outside the reach of our arbitrary decisions.

In my opinion the negative results Gödel had in mind include his own results on the mechanical inexhaustibility of mathematics and on the impossibility of proving consistency by finitary means, which show also the inadequacy of the conventionalist view of mathematics, since the consistency of the conventions goes beyond the conventions themselves. In this sense the Hilbert program, by leading to these negative results, may be viewed as a contribution, indeed a major one, of the syntactical conception to the clarification of the situation. From this perspective, it is surprising that Carnap continued to adhere to the syntactical conception even after Gödel's negative results had been obtained and were known to him.

Hilbert's contribution, on the other hand, lies not in his suggestion of the syntactical conception but in his formulation of precise problems as a way to test it, even though he himself expected it to be confirmed rather than refuted. The syntactical conception is a typical example of what is commonly called *reductionism*. Other examples include the physical and the computational conceptions of mental phenomena. These reductionist views are similarly useful—at least potentially—in helping us to clarify the situation with respect to our thought processes, that is, to understand what alternative views of mind are available to us at present and what the issues are that divide them. It seems to me, however, that no one has so far succeeded in formulating fruitful problems to test these alternative conceptions of the mind—problems that are as precise and as close to resolution as Hilbert's problems were when he proposed them.

When Gödel worked on the Carnap paper in the 1950s, the inadequacy of the syntactical conception had been recognized not only by him but also by others, among them Ludwig Wittgenstein and Paul Bernays. It is therefore somewhat surprising that he chose to spend so much effort trying to refute it. One reason seems to have had to do with his personal history, specifically his youthful association with the Vienna Circle and, in particular, with his teachers Hahn, Schlick, and Carnap, who were all proponents of the syntactical conception in one form or another. Even after the publication of Gödel's decisive results in 1931, the conception remained popular and influential among philosophers for many years. He must have been much struck and bothered by the strange phenomenon of philosophers who put logic and mathematics at the center of their philosophy, uphold an erroneous conception of mathematics based on an inadequate understanding of the nature of the subject, and yet continue to exert a great deal of influence. And it was surely natural for him to wish to settle once and for all a fundamental disagreement with his teachers which had lasted over three decades.

Another reason was probably Gödel's initial belief that, by conclusively refuting the syntactical conception, an extreme opposite of his own Platonism in mathematics, he would be strengthening his own position, and the whole situation would be clarified. By 1959 he seems to have concluded that this expectation had not been and would not be fulfilled. In 1971 he told me he regretted getting involved in the project and had finally decided not to publish the paper, because, even though he had proved that mathematics is *not* syntax of language, he had not made clear what mathematics *is*.

The sustained struggle with the project of his Carnap paper seems to have lad Gödel to the conclusion that philosophy was harder and more different from science than he had expected and that his approach to philosophy until then had not been on the right track. His February 1959 letter to Schilpp explaining that he had decided not to submit his paper, gave three reasons: (1) he was still not satisfied with the result; (2) his manuscript was quite critical of Carnap's position; and (3) since it was too late for Carnap to reply, he felt it would be unfair to publish it. Schilpp tried to persuade him to change his mind but had no success. Among other things, Gödel said in this letter:

2.2.59 It is easy to allege very weighty and striking arguments in favor of my views, but a complete elucidation of the situation turned out to be more difficult than I had anticipated, doubtless in consequence of the fact that the subject matter is closely related to, and in part identical with, one of the basic problems of philosophy, namely the question of the objective reality of concepts and their relations.

In 1972 Gödel told me he had begun to study Husserl's work in 1959. It seems likely that he saw in it the promise of "a complete elucidation of the situation" that would settle "the question of the objective reality of concepts and their relations." That question is the question of Platonism, or conceptual realism: How do we determine the sense in which concepts and their relations are objectively real and find convincing reasons for believing that the proposition so interpreted is true?

Over the last period of his active life, from 1959 to 1976, Gödel seems to have devoted his efforts partly to tidying up his previous work and partly to sketching his broader philosophical views. In the first effort, he expanded and commented on several of his previously published article. He also tried, unsuccessfully, to find reasonable new axioms to settle the continuum hypothesis. In the second effort, he seems to have attempted, again unsuccessfully, to articulate his own philosophical views into a "theory." Yet, because of the inaccessibility of much of his later work, our knowledge of his thoughts and writings over this period is limited to the few pieces noted in the following paragraphs.

There is a bundle of undated loose sheets, possibly from around 1960, which includes a statement of a "philosophical viewpoint" and which consists of fourteen strong theses. (I reproduce this list and discuss it in Chapter 9.) Around 1962 he wrote a brief essay on the classification, the past, and the future of philosophy, with special emphasis on its relation to mathematics. This essay gives some indication of what he hoped to see developed from something like Husserl's approach. It is contained in an envelope from the American Philosophical Society, to which he was elected in 1961. Probably the essay (which I discuss in Chapter 5) was the draft of a lecture intended for the society.

In 1963, Gödel completed "a supplement to the second edition" (1947) of his Cantor paper, which was published in 1946, together with a revised version of the original paper. This supplement offers a more extended and categorical exposition of his Platonism than is found in his previously published writings, and contains brief but decisive observations on mathematical intuition, creation, and his agreements and disagreements with Kant.—These few pages have been much discussed in the literature and are considered in some detail in Chapter 7. A historical question is their relation to Gödel's study of Husserl, even though they make no explicit reference to Husserl. It has been reported, however, that in the 1960s Gödel recommended to several logicians Husserl's treatment of "categorial intuition" in the last part of his *Logical Investigations*. In our discussions in the 1970s he suggested to me that *Ideas* and *Cartesian Meditations* are the best of Husserl's books.

In 1967 and 1968 Gödel wrote two letters to me explaining the relation between his objectivistic viewpoint and his major mathematical results in logic. Around this time he also added a number of philosophical notes to the Bernays paper of 1958. In both cases he was expounding his philosophical viewpoint primarily in the context of definite results and problems of a scientific character.

From October of 1971 to December of 1972 and from October of 1975 to March of 1976, Gödel freely expressed many of his philosophical ideas during extended discussions with me. Early in 1972 he decided to edit and expand my notes on what he considered to be the important parts of what he had told me. By June of 1972 he was satisfied with a condensed formulation of this material in several fragments, and he authorized their inclusion for publication in my book *From Mathematics to Philosophy* (1974a, hereafter *MP*), which appeared in January of 1974.

From 1975 to 1976 Gödel and I also experimented with the idea of writing up for publication some of his discussions with me, but nothing much came of the idea at the time, except for one or two observations in my article "Large Sets" (completed in 1975 and published in 1977) and in the biographical article "Some Facts about Kurt Gödel" (1981b).

The records of Gödel's extensive conversations with me include informal formulations of many facets of his philosophical position, which are, unfortunately, hard to reproduce or paraphrase or organize or evaluate. The purpose of much of this book is, as I said in the Introduction, to report and evaluate what he said to me within an appropriate organizational framework.

2.5 Some Facts about Gödel in His Own Words

Before his retirement in the autumn of 1976, Gödel arranged for me to visit the Institute for Advanced Study, and from July of 1975 to August of 1976 I was given a house on Einstein Drive. During my stay he almost never went to his office, and we met there only once, by previous agreement, on 9 December 1975. We had, however, frequent and extended conversations by telephone. Between October of 1975 and March of 1976, we discussed mostly theoretical matters. Around the end of March he was briefly hospitalized, and thereafter he avoided topics that required concentration.

On 28 May 1976 he mentioned a small conference held at Königsberg in the autumn of 1929. This gave me the idea of asking him about his intellectual development, and I prepared a list of questions for him on 1 June. He agreed to answer them and suggested I could write up his responses and keep a record for publication after his death. The result was the aforementioned "Some Facts about Kurt Gödel"—a title he suggested. He read and approved the text, which was first published in the *Journal of Symbolic Logic* (1981b); it is reproduced in my *Reflections on Kurt Gödel* (1987a), hereafter *RG*:41–46.

Recently it occurred to me that a presentation of the basis of the published text—that is, of what he told me in more or less his own words—may be of interest as an informative complement that retains much of the subtle personal flavor of his own account. For this reason, I reproduce in the rest of this section, as far as feasible, his own account of his mental development, rearranged according to the chronology of the events, together with some of my own explanatory comments and references (enclosed in square brackets).

I graduated from high school in 1924, studied physics from 1924 to 1926, and mathematics from 1926 to 1929. I attended philosophical lectures by Heinrich Gomperz whose father [Theodore] was famous in Greek philosophy. I became a member of the Schlick Kreis in 1926, through Hans Hahn. My dissertation was finished and approved in autumn 1929, and I received my doctor's degree in 1930.

When I entered the field of logic, there were 50 percent philosophy and 50 percent mathematics. There are now 99 percent mathematics and only 1 percent philosophy; even the 1 percent is bad philosophy. I doubt whether there is really any clear philosophy in the models for modal logic.

Shortly after I had read Hilbert-Ackermann, I found the proof [of the completeness of predicate logic]. At that time I was not familiar with Skolem's 1922 paper [the paper reprinted in Skolem 1970:137–152; the relevant part is remark 3, pp. 139–142]. I did not know König's lemma either—by the same man who had the result on the power of the continuum. [For some details relevant to these observations, compare *RG*:270–271.]

In summer 1930 I began to study the consistency problem of classical analysis. It is mysterious why Hilbert wanted to prove directly the consistency of analysis by finitary methods. I saw two distinguishable problems: to prove the consistency of number theory by finitary number theory and to prove the consistency of analysis by number theory. By dividing the difficulties, each part can be overcome more easily. Since the domain of finitary number theory was not well defined, I began by tackling the second half: to prove the consistency of analysis relative to full number theory. It is easier to prove the *relative* consistency of analysis. Then one only has to prove by finitary methods the consistency of number theory. But for the former one has to assume number theory to be true (not just the consistency of a formal system for it).

I represented real numbers by predicates in number theory [which express properties of natural numbers] and found that I had to use the concept of truth [for number theory] to verify the axioms of analysis. By an enumeration of symbols, sentences, and proofs of the given system, I quickly discovered that the concept of arithmetic truth cannot be defined in arithmetic. If it were possible to define truth in the system itself, we would have something like the liar paradox, showing the system to be inconsistent. [Compare Gödel's letter of 12.10.31 to Ernst Zermelo, in which the easy proof of this is given, in *RG*:90–91.] This aspect of the situation is explicitly discussed in my Princeton lectures of 1934, where the liar paradox is mentioned as a heuristic principle, after the proof of the incompleteness results has been given. The liar paradox itself refers to an empirical situation which is not formalizable in mathematics. In my original paper [published in 1931] there is [in addition] an allusion to Richard's paradox, which is purely linguistic and refers to no empirical fact.

Note that this argument [about truth not being definable in the system itself] can be formalized to show the existence of undecidable propositions without giving any individual instances. [If there were no undecidable propositions, all (and only) true propositions would be provable in the system. But then we would have a contradiction.] In contrast to truth, provability in a given formal system is an explicit combinatorial property of certain sentences of the system, which is formally specifiable by suitable elementary means. In summer 1930 I reached the conclusion that in any reasonable formal system in which provability in it can be expressed as a property of certain sentences, there must be propositions which are undecidable in it. [This preliminary result was, according to Carnap's diary, announced to Carnap, Feigl, and Waismann at Cafe Reichsrat on 26.8.30. For a more formal explication of the last three paragraphs compare Wang 1981b:21–23.]

It was the anti-Platonic prejudice which prevented people from getting my results. This fact is a clear proof that the prejudice is a mistake.

I took part in a little conference at Königsberg in autumn 1930. Carnap and [John] von Neumann were there. The meeting had no "discussion." I just made a remark and mentioned my [incompleteness] result. [The meeting was the second *Tagung für Erkenntnislehre der exakten Wissenschaften*, at which Gödel presented his proof of the completeness of predicate logic, obtained in 1929, on 6 September, and mentioned incidentally his new result during the discussion session the next day.]

At that time, I had only an incompleteness theorem for combinatorial questions (not for number theory), in the form as described later in the introduction of my [famous] paper. [See *CW*1:147, 149, where the main idea of the proof is sketched in terms of integers (for the primitive signs), sequences of integers (for sentences), and sequences of *these* (for proofs).] I did not yet have the surprising result giving undecidable propositions about polynomials [by using the Chinese remainder theorem].

I had just an undecidable combinatorial proposition. I only represented primitive symbols by integers and proofs by sequences of sequences of integers. The undecidable proposition can be given in fragments of type theory (and of course in stronger systems), though not directly in number theory.

I had a private talk with von Neumann, who called it a most interesting result and was enthusiastic. To von Neumann's question whether the proposition could be expressed in number theory I replied: of course they can be mapped into integers but there would be new relations [different from the familiar ones in number theory]. He believed that it could be transformed into a proposition about integers. This suggested a simplification, but he contributed nothing to the proof because the idea that it can be transformed into integers is trivial. I should, however, have mentioned the suggestion; otherwise too much credit would have gone into it. If today, I would have mentioned it. The result that the proposition can be transformed into one about polynomials was very unexpected and done entirely by myself. This is related to my early interest in number theory, stimulated by Furtwängler's lectures.

On the matter of an undecidable number-theoretic problem, von Neumann didn't expect to be quoted. It was to get information rather than to stimulate discussion: von Neumann meant so but I didn't expect so. He expected that I had thought out everything very thoroughly. [Stanislaw] Ulam reported that von Neumann was upset that he didn't get the result. It is surprising that Hilbert didn't get it, maybe because he looked for absolute consistency.

Ulam wrote a book [*Adventures of a Mathematician* , 1976] and I was mentioned in it at several places. Ulam says that perhaps I was never sure whether I had merely detected another paradox like Burali-Forti's. This is absolutely false. Ulam doesn't understand my result, which is proved by using only finitary arithmetic. As a matter of fact it is much more. [I take this sentence to mean that the proof is not only precise but perfectly clear.] How can Wittgenstein consider it [Gödel's result] as a paradox if he had understood it?

Shortly after the Königsberg meeting, I discovered the improved undecidable proposition and the second theorem [about consistency proofs]. Then I received a letter from von Neumann nothing independently the indemonstrability of consistency as a consequence of my first theorem. Hilbert and von Neumann had previously conjectured the decidability of number theory. To write down the results took a long time. [This undoubtedly refers to his famous paper. The "long time" certainly included the period between 7 September (when the initial result was announced) and 17 November 1930 (when the paper was received for publication). It is also possible that he had spent a long time writing an early version before the September meeting.]

The proof of the (first) incompleteness theorem in my original paper is awkward because I wanted to make it completely formalized. The basic idea is given more clearly in my Princeton lectures [of 1934].

I wrote Herbrand two letters, the second of which he did not receive. He had a good brief presentation of my theorems.

I visited Göttingen in 1932 and talked about my work. [C.] Siegal and [Emmy] Noether talked with me afterwards. I saw [Gerhard] Gentzen only once. I had a public discussion with Zermelo in 1931 [at the mathematical meeting on 15 September at Bad Elster]. I had more contact with Church and Kleene than with Rosser in Princeton.

In 1930–33 I had no position in the University of Vienna. I continued my studies of *Principia Mathematica* and of pure mathematics, including the foundations of geometry and functions of complex variables (a beautiful theory). Hahn wrote his book [on real functions]; I read the proof sheets and got acquainted with the field [probably in 1932]. It is an interesting book. I was active in Menger's colloquium and Hahn's seminar on set theory. I also took part in the Vienna Academy.

Also, I was thinking about the continuum problem. I heard about Hilbert's paper ["On the Infinite," 1925] about 1930. One should not build up the hierarchy in the constructive way; it is not necessary to do so for a proof of [relative] consistency. The ramified hierarchy came to my mind. One doesn't have to construct ordinals. Here again the anti-Platonistic view was hampering mathematics. Hilbert didn't believe that the continuum hypothesis (CH) could be decided in [the familiar system] ZF; for example, he added definitions. In addition, Hilbert gave [claimed to give] a consistency proof of set theory.

When I came back to Vienna from America in 1934, I became ill with an infection of my bad teeth. I continued my work on set theory from summer 1934 to 1935. (Hahn died in 1934). At first I did not have CH, only the axiom of choice. It must have been in 1935. I was sick in 1936 (very weak). In 1937 I studied consequences of CH. I found the consistency proof of CH in summer 1938. [Sometimes the date has been given as summer 1937; possibly Gödel was not satisfied with his earlier proof.] In 1940–43 I was in the U.S. and my health was relatively good. I worked mostly in logic. I didn't accomplish what I was after. I was disturbed by reviews in Vienna. [I have no idea what this sentence might be referring to.]

I was ill in 1936 and had other things to do in 1937. I obtained the consistency proof of the CH in spring 1938 and extended it to the generalized GCH shortly afterwards. I came to America in the autumn and gave lectures [on my results].

The conjecture, rather than the proof, of the consistency of CH [by using the constructible sets] was the main contribution. Nobody else would have come upon such a proof [such an approach].

The observations in the preceding four paragraphs were made by Gödel on several different occasions. They suggest that he had probably already begun to think about CH around 1931 or 1932, and that his consistency proof may be seen as a modification of Hibert's approach along three directions: (1) not to prove CH outright but to prove only its consistency, (2) to use "first-order definable" properties rather than just recursive functions, and, most remarkably, (3) to assume all ordinal numbers as given rather than try to construct them from the bottom. The idea of (3) depends strongly on Gödel's Platonistic conception of mathematics. I give a more formal explication of these ideas in Wang 1981b:128–132.

My original proof of the consistency of CH is the simplest, but I have never published it. It uses a submodel of the constructible sets, countable in the lowest case. This construction is absolute. I switched to the alternative in my 1939 paper [reprinted in CW2:28–32] to assure absoluteness more directly. The involved presentation in my 1940 monograph was to assure metamathematical explicitness. [Reprinted in CW2:33–101, this was Gödel's longest single published work.]

The observations so far principally concern Gödel's work from 1929 to 1939: the completeness of predicate logic, the incompleteness theorems, and the constructible sets with their applications. In April 1977, he stressed that

I have discussed extensively the conceptual framework of my major contributions in logic in the letters and personal communications published in your book [MP:7–13]. My work is technically not hard. One can see why my proofs work.

I was at the Institute [for Advanced Study] in [the academic year] 1933 to 1934, for [part of] the first term of 1935, and appointed annually from 1938 to 1946. I became a permanent member in 1946.

In 1940 or so I obtained a metamathematical consistency proof of the axiom of choice. It is more general than the proof using constructible sets. It uses finite approximations. Only the initial segment is known. Ask whether, say, 2 will occur: yes or no. Every proposition is transformed into weaker propositions. I should think it would go through in systems with strong axioms of infinity which give nonconstructible sets. Certain large cardinal axioms would be weaker in the absence of the axiom of choice. [Gödel mentioned this proof on several occasions. I urged him to write it up. He probably looked up his notes as a result of my suggestion, because in May 1977 he told me:] My unpublished new proof of the consistency of the axiom of choice is not clear and the notes are confused.

I obtained my interpretation of intuitionistic arithmetic and lectured on it at Princeton and Yale in 1942 or so [should be 1941]. [Emil] Artin was present at the Yale lecture. Nobody was interested. The consistency proof of [classical] arithmetic through this interpretation is more evident than Gentzen's. [The interpretation was eventually published in the Bernays (or *Dialectica*) paper in 1958. The Yale lecture on 15.4.41, was entitled "In what sense is the intuitionistic logic constructive?" Gödel also gave a course of lectures on intuitionism, including this interpretation, at Princeton in the spring of 1941.]

In the late forties a report had already begun to circulate among logicians that Gödel had a proof of the independence of the axiom of choice in finite type theory. After Paul J. Cohen had used his method of "forcing," in 1963, to prove the independence of the axiom of choice and CH from the axioms of ZF Gödel convinced himself that his own method could also be applied to get these independence results. He made a number of observations on this matter in his conversations with me. According to his notebooks, he obtained the crucial step in his proof in the summer of 1942, when he was vacationing at Blue Hill House in Hancock County, Maine. For the next half year or so he worked intensively on trying to use his method to prove the independence of CH as well, but had no success. He seems to have dropped the project in the early part of 1943.

In 1942 I already had the independence of the axiom of choice. Some passage in Brouwer's work, I don't remember which, was the initial stimulus. Independent sets of integers are used. Many irregular things are introduced. There is no choice set as required by the axiom, because things are irregular. Details of the proof are very different from those in the proof that uses forcing. They have more similarity with Boolean models than intensional models in which the same set might be represented by different properties. [I am not sure that I have correctly reconstructed this sentence from my confusing notes.] I worked only with finite type theory. The independence of the axiom of constructibility is easier to prove. If it were provable in ZFC, it would also be provable in ZF.

Exactly the same method, which wouldn't be mathematically so elegant, can give the independence of CH. It is surprising that if CH is independent of ZF, then it is easy to prove its independence from ZFC. For the special method of proof, a negative formulation works: there exists no sequence of aleph-two increasing functions. It should be easier to prove the stronger [positive] formulation [of CH], but it is not so.

In substance my own independence proofs use Boolean models. It is a surprising fact that the axiom of choice holds in the Boolean models. One would have expected the opposite. We don't take care of the axiom of choice: it is magic that it works for Boolean models. The topology is just the simplest that one has. My proofs use topological logic. The problem was to find the right topology. I have to design it specially. [This paragraph appears to be concerned with a proof of the independence of CH by using Gödel's own methods.]

My proof is easy to see. It shows the way one arrives at it. This is like my results on undecidable propositions and on the consistency of CH. One sees the idea behind it.

Cohen's models are related to intuitionistic logic and double negation.

I tried to use my method to prove the independence of CH [in 1942 to 1943] but could not do it. The method looked promising. I always had no elegant formulation at the beginning. At the time I developed a distaste for the whole thing: I could do everything in twenty different ways, and it wasn't visible which was better. Moreover, I was then more interested in philosophy, more interested in the relation of Kant's philosophy to relativity theory and in the universal characteristic of Leibniz.

I am sorry now. If I had persisted, the independence of CH would have been proved by 1950 and that would have speeded up the development of set theory by many years.

There should be a new model theory that deals with intensionality. The shape of the intensional would correspond to the structure of the extensional.

The preceding observations largely concern Gödel's work in logic from 1940 until the beginning of 1943, when, as mentioned earlier, he turned his attention to philosophical matters, including a careful study of the work of Leibniz (which he pursued from 1943 to 1946).

I have never obtained anything definite on the basis of reading Leibniz. Some theological and philosophical results have just been suggested [by his work]. One example is my ontological proof [of the existence of God]. Dana Scott has [a copy of] the proof. It uses the division between positive and negative proerties [proposed by Leibniz]. But I have inserted changes in these quotations. My mathematical results (such as the "square axioms" [proposed by me for deciding CH]) have nothing to do with my study of Leibniz.

Paul Erdos said that, though both of them studied Leibniz a good deal, he had always argued with Gödel and told him: "You became a mathematician so that people should study you, not that you should study Leibniz." He didn't say how Gödel responded. Gödel did tell me that his general philosophical theory is a Leibnizian monadology with the central monad (namely God), although he also stressed, Leibniz had not worked out the theory.

I went home with Einstein almost every day and talked about philosophy, politics, and the conditions of America. Einstein was democratically inclined. His religion is much more abstract, like that of Spinoza and Indian philosophy. Mine is more similar to church religion. Spinoza's God is less than a person. Mine is more than a person, because God can't be less than a person. He can play the role of a person.

There may exist spirits which have no body but can communicate with us and influence the world. They stay in the background and are not known [to us]. It was different in antiquity and in the Middle Ages when there were miracles. We do not understand the phenomena of *déjà vu* and thought transference. The nuclear processes, unlike the chemical ones, are irrelevant to the brain.

My work on rotating universes was not stimulated by my close association with Einstein. It came from my interest in Kant's views. In what was said about Kant and relativity theory, one only saw the difference, nobody saw the agreement of the two. What is more important is the nature of time. In relativity there is no passage of time, it is coordinated with space. There is no such analogy in ordinary thinking. Kant said that the ordinary notion was wrong and that real time is something quite different. This is verified [by relativity theory], but in a way contrary to Kant's intentions. [By what is verified Gödel meant, I believe, the view that time is only subjective.] One half is different. The other half, being not knowable, is not falsified. [I think that by the "different half" Gödel means the issue of whether space is Euclidean and that by the "other half" he means the status of space and time in the world of things in themselves, which was unknowable for Kant.]

This work [about rotating universes] was done in the late forties [probably from 1946 or 1947 to 1950]. It was only a digression. I then spent one year on the Gibbs lecture [1951].

The Carnap paper caused me tremendous trouble. I wrote many versions in the fifties [probably from 1953 to 1957 or 1958].

In later years I merely followed up with work in logic. In 1959 I started to read Husserl. My health is [generally] poor: ulcer all the time and sometimes very sick. My heart has been sick since I was eight or nine years old when I had rheumatic fever. As my duty at the Institute, I read papers of the applicants. I am much more talented in doing work of my own [than evaluating the work of the applicants].

I am always out for important results. It is better [more enjoyable?] to think than to write for publication. I have neglected to publish things. I should publish my paper on Kant and Einstein, my Gibbs lecture, and my Carnap paper. Of mathematical results I should publish my "general method of proving the consistency of the axiom of choice" and several things on recursive functions. [This observation was made in June 1976; in May 1977, as I mentioned before, he said his notes for the "general method" were not clear.] The footnote in Heijenoort toward the end of the paper could be made into a very elegant paper. [The reference is, I believe, to the note dated 18.20.66 in van Heijenoort 1967:616–617, reprinted as footnote 1 in *CW*1:235.]

In June of 1976 Gödel talked about the expanded English version of his Bernays paper of 1958, which has now been published in *CW*2:271–280, 305–306. Apparently he worked on this expanded version from 1967 to 1969. It seems to have been a response to an invitation by Bernays to contribute a paper to a symposium on the foundations of mathematics to be published in the journal *Dialectica*.

My interpretation of intuitionistic number theory gives a proof of its consistency. There is an objection to the proof that, as a consistency proof of intuitionistic number theory, it is circular, on the ground that, in order to define primitive recursive functionals, intuitionistic logic is used to some extent. I found a way to avoid this objection. A very much narrower concept of proof is sufficient to carry out the proof. It is complicated to show this completely. I only give the idea and have not given all the relevant details—also it is too condensed. It spends a lot of time discussing foundations. The negative interpretation stays in lower types: this is stimulating. There is something good in the idea of finitism. [There is much in this paragraph which I don't understand. For other comments on the expanded version, compare *RG*:288–291.]

The expanded English version was meant for "the second Bernays volume" in *Dialectica*. It was already in proof sheets. I had expected to make some changes and additions, but was prevented [from doing so] by my illness in 1970. I now think that no major revision is necessary.

As I now recall, at some stage Gödel asked me to write a letter to Bernays to ask him to simply correct the proof sheets and publish it. And then he wanted to make some minor changes and told me that he had two sets of the proof sheets. I asked him to let me have one set with the changes so that I could pass it along to Bernays. He never did send me the set and, as a result, I didn't write to Bernays about the matter.

Apparently Gödel was stimulated by Cohen's independence proof of CH in 1963 to resume his search for new axioms to decide CH. There is a report on some of his attempts in this direction between January of 1964 and 1970 (or a little later) in *CW*2:173–175, compiled by Gregory H. Moore. In 1972 Oskar Morgenstern told me that Gödel was writing a major paper on the continuum problem. I asked Gödel about this in 1976. In April and June 1976 he made the following two overlapping observations:

The continuum hypothesis may be true, or at least the power of the continuum may be no greater than aleph-two, but the generalized continuum hypothesis is definitely wrong.

I have written up [some material on] the continuum hypothesis and some other propositions. Originally I thought [I had proved] that the power of the continuum is no greater than aleph-two, but there is a lacuna [in the proof]. I still believe the proposition to be true; even the continuum hypothesis may be true.

[I wrote a draft of "Some Facts about Kurt Gödel" around 20 June 1976. On 29 June he commented,] "I doubt whether anybody would be interested in these details."

[In April 1976 Gödel spoke about his own reputation:] An enormous development over ten or fifteen years—afterwards it has only kept up in part. I feel that my reputation has declined: the doctors do not treat me as so special any more.

[On 22.11.77 he called me to say] I did not do enough for the Institute—considering the salary.

2.6 His Own Summaries

During his lifetime, Gödel published altogether fewer than 300 pages, mostly between 1930 and 1950; about half are taken up by his incompleteness results and the work related to constructible sets. Given the importance and wide range of his work, the total of his published work is surprisingly small. The reason for this disproportion is partly that he wrote so concisely and partly that a great deal of his work remained unpublished. The first two volumes of his *Collected Works* reprint nearly all his previously published work; two additional volumes, devoted to a selection of his unpublished writings, are under preparation. The present volume, which includes some of his oral communications, may be viewed as a supplement to these volumes.

Around 1968 Gödel prepared a bibliography of his own published work for the proceedings of a conference which had celebrated his sixtieth birthday in 1966. The bibliography was published in the resulting *Foundations of Mathematics* (Buloff, Holyoke, and Hahn 1969:xi–xii). An accompanying sheet found in his papers gives an overview and brief evaluation of the items in this bibliography. I reproduce both the bibliography and his notations on its items below, with a view to capturing, to some extent, Gödel's attitude toward his own published work at that period.

In addition, in 1984 John Dawson discovered among Gödel's papers and sent to me a sheet headed "My Notes, 1940–70." This sheet, written by Gödel in 1970 or 1971, summarizes his unpublished writings and provides us with some indication of his own evaluation of his later work. It seems desirable to try to explain this list as well. The fact that it begins in 1940 is not surprising, since he published what he took to be his important work before that year.

Bibliography of Gödel Prepared by Himself around 1968

1. Die Vollständigkeit der Axiome des logischen Funktionenkalküls. *Monatshefte für Mathematik und Physik* 37 (1930):34–360. See item 28.

2. Einige metamathematische Resultate über Entscheidungsdefinitheit und Widerspruchsfreiheit. *Anzeiger der Akademie der Wissenschaften in Wien* 67 (1930):214–215. See item 28.

3. Diskussion zur Grundlegung der Mathematik. *Erdenntnis* 2 (1931/32):147–151.

4. Über formal unentscheidbare Sätze der Principia Mathematica und verwandter Systeme I. *Monatshefte für Mathematik und Physik* 38 (1931):173–198. Italian translation in Introduzione ai problemi dell'assiomatica, by Evandro Agazzi, Milano 1961. See also items 27, 28.

5. Zum intuitionistischen Aussagenkalkül. *Anzeiger der Akademie der Wissenschaften in Wien* 69 (1932):65–66.

6. Ein Spezialfall des Entscheidungsproblems der theoretischen Logik. In *Ergebnisse eines mathematischen Kolloquiums* ed. by Karl Menger, vol, 2 (1929/30):27–28.

7. Über Vollständigkeit und Widerspruchsfreiheit. In *ibid.*, vol. 3 (1930/31):12–13. See item 28.

8. Eine Eigenschaft der Realisierungen des Aussagenkalküls. In ibid.:20–21.

9. Eine Interpretation des intuitionistischen Aussagenkalküls. In *ibid.* 4 (1931/32):39–40.

10. Über Unabhängigkeits-beweise im Aussagenkalkül. In *ibid.*:9–10.

11. Zur intuitionistischen Arithmetik und Zahlentheorie. In *ibid.*:34–38. See item 27.

12. Bemerkung über projektive Abbildungen. In *ibid.* 5 (1932/33):1.

13. Über die Länge von beweisen. In *ibid.*, vol. 7 (1934/35):23–24. See item 27.

14. Zum Entscheidungsproblem des logischen Funktionenkalküls. *Monatshefte für Mathematik und Physik* 40 (1933):433–443.

15. On Undecidable Propositions of Formal Mathematical Systems (Mimeographed notes of lectures given in 1934).

16. The Consistency of the Axiom of Choice and of the Generalized Continuum-Hypothesis. *Proc. Nat. Acad. Sci. USA* 24 (1938): 556–557.

17. The Consistency of the Continuum Hypothesis. In *Annals of Mathematics Studies*, vol. 3, Princeton University Press, 1940; 2nd printing, revised and with some notes added, 1951; 7th printing, with some notes added, 1966.

19. Russell's Mathematical Logic. In *The Philosophy of Bertrand Russell*, ed. by P. A. Schilpp, pp. 123–153. Evanston and Chicago, 1944. See item 26.

20. What Is Cantor's Continuum Problem? *Amer. Math. Monthly* 54 (1947):515–525. See item 26.

21. An Example of a New Type of Cosmological Solution of Einstein's Field Equations of Gravitation. *Rev. Modern Physics* 21 (1949):447–450.

22. A Remark about the Relationship between Relativity Theory and Idealistic Philosophy. In *Albert Einstein, Philosopher-Scientist*, ed. by P. A. Schilpp, pp. 555–562. Evanston, Ill., 1949. German translation, with some additions to the footnotes in *Albert Einstein als Philosoph und Naturforscher*, pp. 406–412. Kohlhammer, 1955.

23. Rotating Universes in General Relativity Theory. In *Proceedings of the International Congress of Mathematicians in Cambridge, Mass., 1950*, vol. 1, pp. 174–181.

24. Über eine bisher noch nicht benützte Erweiterung des finiten Standpunktes. *Dialectica* 12 (1958):280–287. Revised English edition to appear in *Dialectica*.

25. Remarks before the Princeton Bicentennial Conference on Problems of Mathematics. In *The Undecidable*, ed. by Martin Davis, pp. 84–86. New York, 1965.

26. A reprint of item 19 and a revised and enlarged edition of item 20 were published in *Philosophy of Mathematics*, ed. by P. Benacerraf and H. Putnam, pp. 211–232, 258–273. Englewood Cliffs, N. J.: Prentice-Hall, 1964.

27. English translations of items 4, 11, 13 and a revised and enlarged edition of item 15 were published in *The Undecidable*, ed. by Martin Davis, pp. 4–38, 75–81, 82–83, 39–75. New York, 1965.

28. English translations of items 1, 2, 4, 7, with some notes by the author, were published in *From Frege to Gödel*, ed. by Jean van Heijenoort, pp. 583–591, 595–596, 596–616, 616–617. Cambridge, Mass., Harvard University Press, 1967.

This completes my reproduction of the bibliography prepared by Gödel around 1968. There are some peculiar features in Gödel's ordering of this bibliography. He evidently violated normal chronological order in order to list all his significant contributions to Karl Menger's colloquium in one block (items from 6 through 13). The placement of item 25 (the Princeton Lecture of 1946) is determined by the date of its first publication; it would, I think, be more accurate to put it between items 19 and 20.

I discovered a marked copy of this bibliography which adds dates to a number of the items in the list, linking it to the sheet mentioned earlier which summarizes and evaluates the items in the bibliography. Adding these dates and other markings (in square brackets), I reproduce the sheet below:

Jahresz. [year]		Meine Publikat.	[my publications]
30	W Compl.	[1]	
30		[6]	W-*wichtig* [important]
31	W Undecid.	[4]	
31		[7]	17 papers
32		[5]	
32		[9]	
32		[11]	
33		[14]	
34		[15]	
35		[13]	
5 >			
40	W Cont.	[18]	
4 >			
44		[19]	
46		[25]	
47		[20]	
49		[21]	
49	W Rotating	[22]	
50		[23]	
8 >			
58	W Dialectica	[24]	
4 >			
64	Putnam	[26]	
65	Davis	[27]	
67	Heijenoort	[28]	
69	Dialectica 12		

Reedited: Putnam 2, Russell, *Cont*; Davis, *Vorl.*, int., leng., Bicen., Und.; Heijenoort, comp1., Menger Note, Ac. note, undec., *Hilbert.*

A lot of information is packed into this sheet. Disentangling its different components is an amusing puzzle. In the first place, seven of the 28 items in the original list—2, 3, 8, 10, 12, 16 and 17—are left out. The motive for this deletion is undoubtedly that in Gödel's mind the seven papers are either unimportant (8 and 12) or do not add much to related items that are included (4 for 2 and 3, 5 for 10, and 18 for 16 and 17). Moreover, the double line between 58 and 64 indicates that the items below it are not new publications but rather revisions and expansions of previous papers. In this way, we arrive at a count of eighteen—rather than his count of seventeen—papers. One way to eliminate the discrepancy might be to treat [4] and [7] as one paper.

The paragraph under "Reedited" is more or less self-explanatory. *Putnam* refers to item 26, which includes versions of the Russell paper (19) and the Cantor paper (20). *Davis* refers to item 27, which includes versions of the 1934 lectures (15) as well as items 11, 13, 25, and 4. *Heijenoort* refers to 28, which includes versions of 1, 7, 2, 4, and a quotation from Gödel's letter of 8.7.65 (p. 369), commenting on the relation between Hilbert's and his own work on the continuum hypothesis.

The last entry, [19]69 Dialectica 12, indicates that at the time of writing the list Gödel expected the expanded English version of his 1958 paper (published in German in volume 12 of *Dialectica*) to appear in 1969 (in volume 23). Since the paper did not appear in 1969, and since he included information on his publications up to and including 1967 (namely, item 28), the two documents must have been prepared around 1968.

The mark W (for *wichtig*) of course indicates the published work Gödel took to be his most important. Five categories, esch represented by one (or two) publications, are marked with this letter: (1) the completeness of predicate logic [1]; (2) undecidable propositions (on incompletability) [4]; (3) the continuum hypothesis [18]; (4) rotating universes [21, its mathematical aspect, and 22, its philosophical aspect], and (5) interpretation of intuitionistic arithmetic [24, together with its expanded English version].

The eighteen publications selected by Gödel can also be grouped as follows: (a) predicate logic, [1], [6], and [14]; (b) undecidable propositions, [4], [7], [15], and [13]; (c) intuitionism, [5], [9], [11], and [24]; (d) set theory (with the continuum problem as its focal point), [18] (possibly with [20]); (e) rotating universes, [21], [22], and [23]; (f) philosophy of logic and mathematics, [19], [25], and [20] (with its expanded revision, as indicated under [26]).

The relation of the items under (f) to the items under (a), (b), and (d) may be seen as an analogue of the relation between the two parts of [24] or that between [22] and the two mathematical papers under (e) or that between [20] and [18]. In each case, there is an interplay between philosophy and mathematics. We may also say that (a) is concerned with predicate logic, (b) with arithmetic, (c) with intuitionism and concrete intuition, and (d) with set theory. The isolated group (e) is concerned with time and physics.

The numbers (marked with the symbol >) between some of the years evidently point to the lapse of years between publications; they indicate four stretches of more than two years between 1930 and 1969. They are, however, somewhat misleading. The number 5 between 1935 and 1940 gives only a rough idea of the comparatively long period of preparation for the work in set theory. The number 4 between 1940 and 1944 is associated with Gödel's transition from logic to other matters. The number 8 between 1950 and 1958 covers, implicitly, his extended efforts on his Gibbs lecture and, especially, on his Carnap paper, which he decided not to publish. The number 4 between 1958 and 1964 coincides with another period of transition but shows on the surface an arithmetical error. One interpretation is that already in 1962 he had essentially completed some of his revisions and additions, even though they were not published until 1964 or a little later.

After 1967 Gödel published nothing under his own name. Yet from a letter he wrote in 1975 and his related reply to a request for "a particularly apt statement" of his philosophical point of view (RG:20 and answer to question 9, p. 18), it is clear that he considered his statements quoted in Wang 1974 as his own publication: "See what I say in Hao Wang's recent book 'From Mathematics to Philosophy' in the passages cited in the Preface." In fact, in our conversations he made it clear that he valued highly the ideas he had expressed in these statements and that he was rather disappointed by the indifference with which they were received. One purpose of the present work is to consider these statements extensively in the hope of calling people's attention to them.

Gödel's Statement in "My Notes, 1940–70"
As I mentioned at the beginning of this section, I propose to provide an explication of Gödel's statment, in his "My Notes, 1940–70," in which he summarizes and evaluates his own unpublished work.

In order to discuss this statement, it is necessary to say something about the current state of Gödel's unpublished papers. His will bequeathed his entire estate to his wife Adele, who then presented all his papers and books, with minor exceptions, to the Institute for Advanced Study. Later, her will gave the Institute literary rights as well. Between June 1982 and July 1984, John W. Dawson, with the assistance of his wife, Cheryl Dawson, classified and arranged the papers and issued a typescript catalogue of the collection, "The Papers of Kurt Gödel: An Inventory." The papers have since been donated to the Firestone Library of Princeton University, where they have been available to scholars since 1.4.85. The Institute retains publication rights.

The collection consists of about nine thousand items, initially occupying 15 Paige boxes and one oversize container—altogether about 14.5 cubic feet. They are divided into twelve categories. The following four categories are relevant to our considerations:

Series 03 Topical notebooks. Boxes 5, 6, and 7. About 150 items; 125 folders (and one oversize folder). Mostly in Gabelsberger shorthand.

Series 04 Drafts and offprints (of lectures and articles). Boxes 7, 8 and 9. About 500 items; 154 folders (and 15 oversize folders).

Series 05 Reading notes and excerpts; bibliographic notes and memorands. Boxes 9, 10, 11. About 250 numbered groups; 78 folders (and one oversize). Largely in Gabelsberger shorthand.

Series 06 Other loose manuscript notes. Boxes 11 and 12. About 800 items; 52 folders (and 7 oversize folders).

Most of the items were found in envelopes labeled by Gödel himself. On the whole, his original order has been retained or restored. Folders are numbered sequentially within each series, the first two digits serving as series designation. Each document is also given its own number.

The statement labeled "My notes 1940–70" is in folder 04/108. It consists of six entries numbered 1 to 6, written mostly in English, with footnotes and parenthetical remarks in a mixture of shorthand, English, and abbreviations. A line drawn between entries 3 and 4 evidently indicates that entries 1 to 3 pertain to philosophy, whereas entries 4 to 6 are more scientific in nature. A pair of large square brackets surrounds entry 5, probably because it deals with results in mathematical logic which bear a complex relation to recent developments and may, therefore, involve questions of priority that Gödel was generally eager to avoid.

Let me try to reproduce, the summary as best I can, using the headings *S1* to *S6* (*S* for summary) in place of the original 1 to 6 for convenience in future reference.

S1 About 1,000 stenographic pages (6 × 8 inches) of clearly written philosophical notes [a footnote here: also philological, psychological] (= philosophical *assertions*).

S2 Two philos. [philosophical] papers almost ready for print. [A complicated footnote is attached to the end of this line. The footnote begins with "On Kant and Syntax of Lang." (The words *on* and *and* in shorthand), so that it is clear which two papers Gödel had in mind. What is complicated is what he seems to have added as afterthoughts: first, there is an insertion referring to his ontological proof; next, in parentheses, is a mixture of items that seems to begin with five minor mathematical pieces and to continue with two parallel additions, one of them evidently referring to (his notes on?) his new consistency proof of the axiom of choice, while the other appears to refer to the collection of his "Notes."]

S3 Several thousands of pages of philosophical excerpts and literature.

S4 The clearly written proofs of my cosmological results.

S5 About 600 clearly written pages of set-theoretical and logical results, questions, and conjectures (to some extent *outstripped* by recent developments.) [*Hefte* is written between the second and third lines of this entry, evidently referring to his *Arbeitshefte*, which are contained in folders 03/ 12 to 03/28.]
S6 Many notes on intuit. [intuitionism] & other found. [foundational] questions, auch Literat. [also literature.] [In parentheses after the word *questions* is an insertion largely in shorthand which appears to say: "the whole Ev. on Main qu. and another (pertaining to the Dial. work and another work)." Presumably Ev. stands for Evidenz or Evidence. Here, as with the footnote to S2, it is not easy to determine exactly what Gödel is referring to. Among other things, he certainly has in mind all the material related to his 1958 Bernays (*Dialectica*) paper and its expanded English version (together with the three added notes.) Maybe this is all the parenthetical insertion is saying. It is reasonable to say that the main or central question of foundations is, both generally and according to Gödel's view, the problem of evidence. His interest in intuitionism is undoubtedly a result of the importance he attaches to this problem. And he certainly viewed his work on the Bernays paper as a definite contribution to the problem of evidence in mathematics.]

Much of the material mentioned in this statement is written in Gabelsberger shorthand, and awaits transcription. Gödel once told me that his writings in shorthand were intended merely for his own use—undoubtedly because they were not in a sufficiently finished state to communicate effectively to others what he had in mind. Even though the statement gives an indication of what he took to be of value among his unpublished writings, it is hard to identify exactly which pieces he had in mind. Moreover, we have no reliable estimate of how reasonable his evaluation is.

The ordering of items in Gödel's statement suggests that he valued most the one thousand pages of philosophical assertions (*S1*). There are fifteen philosophical notebooks labeled "Max" (in 03/63 to 03/72) and two theological notebooks (in 03/107 and 03/108). The bulk of the philosophical notebooks contains material written in the period from 24.8.37 to June 1945 or December 1946. Folder 06/43 includes philosophical material from 1961 or later, and folder 06/42 contains philosophical remarks written between early 1965 and about 20.8.67. Folder 06/31 contains Gödel's notes on Husserl's *Cartesian Meditationen, Krisis* (and its English translation), and *Logische Untersuchungen*. Notes on general observations found in 06/115 include these longhand markings: (1) Aufsatz im "Entschluss" Sept. to Dec. 1963; (2) Axiom Wahrheitsbegr. u. intens. funktionen [the concept of truth and intensional functions]; (3) Bem. Phil.

Math. (Allg.) [Remarks on the philosophy of mathematics (general). This bundle has recently been transcribed by Cheryl Dawson]; something on P. J. FitzPatrick's "To Gödel via Babel," *Mind* 75 (1966):332–350.

The "two philosophical papers almost ready for print" (S2) are easy to identify. The first, S2.1, "Some Observations about the Relationship between [the] Theory of Relativity and Kantian Philosophy," was probably written in the late forties. There are various versions (marked A, B, C, but with variants). Folder 04/132, marked "Einstein & Kant (längere Form)," contains manuscripts A and B. Typescript version A consists of 28 pages (including 43 footnotes), while B is a revision of A, with 52 footnotes. Folder 04/133 contains a handwritten manuscript C, which consists of 30 pages of text and 19 pages of footnotes (about 66 of them). A typed version of C with only 14 pages of text (with references to handwritten footnotes) is contained in 04/134.

Gödel worked on the second paper (S2.2), "Is Mathematics Syntax of Language?," from 1953 to 1957 or 1958. It exists in six different drafts, of which the last two versions are the shortest and quite similar to each other.

The ontological proof mentioned in the statement seems to exist only in a preliminary form. S2.3, an ontological proof of the existence of God in Folder 06/41 is identified as "ontologischer Beweis." An accompanying date (10.2.70) apparently refers to the time when Gödel first allowed it to circulate. It also is marked "ca. 1941," presumably the date of its initial conception.

Surprisingly, another manuscript, which Gödel had mentioned to me several times in the seventies was not included under S2. It is S2.4, the text for the Gibbs Lecture, "Some Basic Theorems on the Foundations of Mathematics and Their Philosophical Implications." This text, handwritten in English, was composed in 1951 and delivered in December of that year. He apparently left it unaltered. Its content overlaps with S2.2. Folder 04/92 contains a draft in shorthand; 04/93 contains a 40-page text; the manuscript in 04/94 adds 18 pages of 52 insertions; and, finally, the version in 04/95 has 25 pages of footnotes.

The other items in the footnote to S2 are more difficult to identify. As I have mentioned before, in 1977 Gödel found that his notes for his new consistency proof of the axiom of choice were confusing and unclear. Although the idea was probably conceived in 1940, I could find only a few notes on pp. 8–11 of volume 15 of his *Arbeitsheft* in folder 03/27. The "five minor mathematical pieces " were presumably written before 1943. There are several possible candidates: (1) "Simplified Proof, a Theorem of Steinitz" (in German) in folder 04/124, (2) "Theorem on Continuous Real Functions" in 04/128; (3) "Decision Procedure for Positive Propositional

Calculus" (in German) in 06/09; (4) "Lecture on Polynomials and Undecidable Propositions" (undelivered) in 04/124.5.

The several thousands of pages of philosophical reading notes and excerpts from literature under S3 are probably mostly to be found among the papers in Series 05, although some are included in Series 06, folders 06/06, 06/11, and 06/15, and a large part of the folders from 06/24 to 06/44. Gödel retained many of his library request slips. These are stored in folders 05/54 to 05/63, giving us some indication of the books and articles he studied or intended to study. Folders 05/07 and 05/08 appear to contain the "programs" of what he planned to read from, roughly, 1959 to 1975.

Among the seventy-eight folders in series 05, I noticed the following items: Leibniz, 05/24 to 05/38; Husserl, 05/22; Hegel and Schelling, 05/18; phenomenology and existentialism, 05/41; C. Wronski, 05/53; theology, 05/47 to 05/50; philosophy, 05/05, 05/09, 05/42, 05/43, 05/44, 05/60, and 05/62; contemporary authors (including S. K. Langer and N. Chomsky), 05/44; history, 05/19 to 05/21; women, 05/51, 05/52; psychology, neurophysiology, psychiatry, 05/06. Folder 05/39 includes notes on Brouwer's doctoral dissertation (1907, in Dutch), on Hilbert's paper, "On the Infinite" (1925), and on Hilbert's 1928 Bologna address, which pulled together the open problems of the foundations of mathematics at that time.

In S4 Gödel speaks of the "clearly written proofs" of his cosmological proofs, suggesting that they are for the results in his 1950 address on "rotating universes," which had been published in 1952 with less than complete proof. The relevant folders probably include 06/13, 06/14, and 06/45 to 06/50.

Entries S5 and S6 in Gödel's statement are concerned with logic and the foundations of mathematics. The "about 600 clearly written pages of set-theoretical and logical results, questions, and conjectures" of S5 are of a mathematical character. It seems likely that the chief sources for these 600 pages are the three sets of notebooks labeled by Gödel: (1) *Arbeitshefte* (sixteen volumes plus one index volume, totaling more than a thousand pages, found in 03/12 to 03/28); (2) "Logic and Foundations" (six volumes with pages numbered consecutively from 1 to 440, plus one index volume, in 03/44 to 03/50); and (3) "Results on Foundations" (four volumes with pages numbered consecutively from 1 to 368, plus one index volume, in 03/82 to 03/86). Probably (1) is the more important, since the latter two sets appear to include a good many reading notes (rather than notes on his own research). (I conjecture that the major portion of these three sets of notebooks was written between 1940 and 1943, when, by his own account, his health was relatively good and he worked primarily on logic.)

The "Many Notes on Intuitionism and Other Foundational Questions" of S6 are more philosophical in character than the material classified under S5. A typical example is the material related to his Bernays paper. What Gödel included in his conception of "foundational questions" is a little ambiguous. It is not, for instance, clear whether some the material in the three sets of notebooks might fall under S6 too, and if so, how much. In any case, I do not know enough about the unpublished papers to speculate about what Gödel meant to include under S6.

Chapter 3
Religion and Philosophy as Guides to Action

The philosophers have only interpreted *the world, in various ways; the point, however, is to* change *it.*
Marx, *Theses on Feverbach,* 1845

Philosophy as an attempt to find the key to life and the universe has been suffering increasingly from the difficult choice between plausible irrelevance and exciting but unconvincing speculation. The quest for universality gets frustrated by our growing realization of the intimate connections between contingency and relevance and of the strong dependence of truth on both the context of the observed and the position of the observer. Individual situations vary from person to person, and the cumulative human experience changes from one year to the next. As a result, one's conception of what constitutes an appropriate combination of relevance and plausibility is neither invariant across subjects nor stable over time.

For most people, academic philosophy today is largely irrelevant to their deep concerns. Those individuals who ask for more than what business, science, technology, and ordinary politics have to offer look elsewhere for satisfaction: to the traditional religions or to popular psychology, combined, perhaps, with Zen, Taoism, or body mysticism, or with such grand philosophies and ideologies as Marxism, liberalism, conservatism, or neo-Confucianism.

Philosophy today faces sharper demands than do other disciplines, sharper also than the demands faced by philosophy itself at other times: to illuminate its own nature and place, and to answer not only questions *in* philosophy but also questions *about* it. For those of us who are interested in philosophy as a vocation, it is natural and helpful, both in order to satisfy ourselves and to justify our choice to others, to ask a string of questions: Why philosophy? What is the place of philosophy in life? What is the motivating force in the pursuit of philosophy? What are the original aims and problems of philosophy? How and why have they been transformed into seemingly pointless and fruitless questions? Would the work of bringing to light the process of this transformation revitalize philosophy and restore our faith in the possibility of finding appropriate philosophical combinations of relevance and plausibility?

A number of familiar traditional philosophical ideals are easy to appreciate, for they are obviously important if attainable. Can we, for instance, prove the existence of God and an afterlife? Can we offer a plan for bringing about an ideal society? Can we learn how to live a satisfactory life? Clearly, believing that such ideals are attainable through philosophy would provide strong motivation for studying philosophy. Yet very few contemporary philosophers hold this belief. Gödel is an exception. He not only offers, in private, arguments in favor of belief in the existence of God and an afterlife; he also suggests that philosophical investigations hold promise of yielding definitive reasons for such beliefs, clearer and more convincing than his own tentative unpublished arguments.

Because Gödel's thoughts are both akin to familiar traditional ideas and, at the same time, contemporary in character, they are well suited for my purpose of beginning the discussion of philosophy with familiar and obviously important issues. On the one hand, we can see at once how Gödel's philosophy is directed to our central common concerns; and, as we shall see, some of Gödel's, uninhibited generalizations, centered on his rationalistic optimism, may be viewed as an outer limit to the inclination of philosophers to speculate boldly about the plenitude of the universe. On the other hand, Gödel connects these audacious views with his more finished and articulate work, which is very much a part of what is actively investigated in contemporary professional philosophy. His thoughts thus provide us with a living example of how to link up current and traditional concerns in philosophy.

A natural starting point in looking for the motivation to study philosophy and determine its nature and its place in our lives is the universal concern with bridging the gap between our wishes and their consummation. We are constantly aware of this separation between our desires and their fulfillment, between what we wish for and what we find, between what is and what ought to be. Often, however, we do not know either what is or what ought to be. We work only with our beliefs, testing them when we can, directly or indirectly, rigidly or flexibly. There is, accordingly, much room for modifying our beliefs and desires, so as to give us hope that, by behaving in an appropriate manner, we may be able to maximize the satisfaction of our desires.

Wishes produce forces that drive us toward their consummation. A belief in new possibilities broadens the range of wishes and the possible ways of satisfying them. Values serve to modify and rearrange existing wishes. We have a natural inclination to look for a highest value—*the* good or the one thing to will—that could serve as a guide in selecting from among our different wishes and as a step toward unifying them.

Furthermore, the universal experience of passing through childhood yields a tendency to appeal to someone who possesses power, with one's mother and father as the prototypes. As we grow up, we transfer our appeal to more remote authorities—the tribal chief, the prince, the emperor, God, or history. There is, however, a dilemma: on the one hand, familiarity breeds contempt; on the other hand, ignorance leaves us in the dark as to the commands of the authority.

It is reasonable to conclude that the gap between our wishes and their consummation can be reduced either by increasing one's power or by decreasing one's wishes. Buddhism and Taoism put a high value on the ideal of decreasing wishes, especially when our wishes depend for their consummation on factors beyond our own control. On the other hand, a wider range of wishes has the advantage of providing more possible selections and combinations, a richer reservoir of choices from which to work out a satisfactory life.

Belief in an afterlife offers the promise of an opportunity to complete tasks left unfinished in this life. If this belief is combined with faith in the existence of a suitable God, the afterlife can also be seen as a stage at which another gap will be bridged—the gap between fact and our wish for just rewards and punishments.—There are, as we all know, many different conceptions of God. A desirable conception must endow God with a selection of desired properties in such a way that, given what we believe we know, it is not only possible but also probable that these properties coexist. The various attempts to *prove* the existence of God all aim at establishing this possibility, and also at resolving the issue of communication between God and human beings.

For those who do not believe we can possibly settle in a reasonably convincing manner the question whether a consequential God exists, there remains the challenge of finding a web of beliefs to serve as a framework for organizing our desires, beliefs, and activities. This challenge of finding an articulate worldview seems to me the natural central concern that most people associate with philosophy as a vocation.

Given the ambiguity of this ambition, its formidable range, and its remoteness from what we really know, this challenge is hard to meet. In the history of mankind, exceptional people have occasionally come up with influential value systems which summarize human experience in more or less novel and convincing ways. One set of such philosophers might include Confucius, Plato, Aristotle, Kant, and Marx. Philosophy today, however, seems to have lost touch with such unifying systems. Philosophy has taken many shapes; it has been split into many specialized parts, and we detect no clear pattern in an accumulation of its fruits. Nonetheless, it seems to me desirable to link the major parts of contemporary philosophy to the central challenge, both directly and with the help of traditional concerns.

In his *Poetics* (1451) Aristotle says that "poetry is something more philosophic and of graver import than history, since its statements are of the nature rather of universals." I see in this observation the broad suggestion that it is most effective to deal with a general situation by way of appropriate examples. Focusing on examples often provides us with a better way of clarifying and communicating our thoughts than directly confronting the complex subject matter itself. In particular, it seems to me, certain philosophical issues can be treated effectively by concentrating on the views of a few suitably selected representative philosophers. That is why I have tried to combine my own study of philosophy with a study of the views of Gödel and a few others.

The rest of this chapter is devoted to some illustrative discussions of Gödel's formulations of his thoughts on the existence of God and an afterlife, together with some thoughts of my own derived from my tentative groping for a grand philosophy. Some of Gödel's related observations on his monadology, rationalistic optimism, and his general philosophical viewpoint will be considered in Chapter 9.

3.1 Gödel on an Afterlife

Between July and October of 1961 Gödel wrote four long letters to his mother in which he offered, among other things, a discussion of the possibility of an afterlife. This discussion is of interest because it links a familiar and fundamental human concern with more or less abstract philosophical deliberations. Just as the relation of his philosophy to Gödel's mathematical results provides us with a firm reference point for certain indefinite philosophical issues, so—from a different direction—this connection with a shared and lively wish helps us to give concrete meaning to the relevant abstract speculations.

Because some atheists believe in an afterlife (Schopenhauer is an example mentioned in Gödel's letters), Gödel feels free to consider that issue apart from the problem of the existence of God and of God's intervention in bringing about just rewards or punishments.

At one stage in his argument, Gödel cites his awareness that we are grossly ignorant in many ways: "Of course this supposes that there are many relationships which today's science and received wisdom haven't any inkling of. But I am convinced of this [the afterlife], independently of any theology." I see in this passage an important recognition that plays a significant part in Gödel's thinking. However, though I agree with him that we should always remember the fact of our ignorance, I am often not convinced of the consequences he seems to draw from it.

3.1.1 A Summary of Gödel's Argument

Science shows that order pervades the world. This order provides some degree of evidence for the belief that the world has meaning. Granted that the world has meaning, there must be an afterlife. This follows because, given that human beings in this world realize only a very small part of their potentialities, these potentialities would be a meaningless waste if there were no afterlife.

Moreover, science supports the belief that this world of ours had a beginning and will have an end, thereby opening up the possibility of there being another world. On the other hand, we can, through learning, attain better lives, and we learn principally through making mistakes. This is how we are. As we grow older, we get better at learning; yet before we can realize a significant portion of our possibilities, death comes. There-fore, since there ought not be such meaningless waste, we must envision the greater part of learning as occurring in the next world.

Gödel rejects the idea, put forth by his mother, that the intellect is not the appropriate faculty for studying this issue. (By the way, this idea of his mother's was widely shared and was endorsed, for instance, by Witt-genstein.) Gödel compares the status of his own view with that of atomic theory at the time of Democritus, when it was introduced "on purely philosophical grounds." Gödel suggests that his belief in an afterlife may prevail in the future, just as the atomic theory prevails today. He admits that we are a long way from justifying this view scientifically, but he believes it is "possible today to perceive, by pure reasoning," that it "is entirely consistent with all known facts."

To perceive this consistency, Gödel says, was what Leibniz attempted to do 250 years ago, and what he also is trying to do in his letters. The underlying worldview is that the world and everything in it has meaning, or reasons; this view is analogous to the "principle that everything has a cause, which is at the basis of the whole of science."

3.1.2 The Text of the Letters

In each of the four letters, Gödel presented the discussion in one con-tinuous paragraph. I have broken them up into smaller segments. The English translation is by Yi-Ming Wang.

23.7.61   In your last letter you asked the weighty question, whether I believe that we shall meet again in an afterlife [ob ich in ein Wiedersehen glaube]. About this, I can only say the following: If the world [Welt] is rationally constructed and has meaning, then there must be such a thing [as an afterlife]. For what sense would there be in creating a being (man), which has such a wide realm of possibilities for its own development and for relationships to others, and then not allowing it to realize even a thousandth of those [possibilities]? That would be almost like someone laying, with the greatest effort and expense, the foundations for a house, and then letting it all go to seed again.

But does one have reason to suppose that the world *is* rationally constructed? I believe so. For it is by no means chaotic or random, but, as science shows, everything is pervaded by the greatest regularity and order. Order, however, is a form of rationality [*Vernünftigkeit*].

How would one envision a second [another] life? About that there are naturally only guesses. However, it is interesting that it is precisely modern science that provides support for such a thing. For it shows that this world of ours, with all the stars and planets in it, had a beginning and most probably will also have an end (that is, it will literally come to "nothing"). But why, then, should there exist only this one world—for just as we one day found ourselves in this world, without knowing why and wherefrom, so can the same thing be repeated in the same way in another world too.

In any case, science confirms the apocalypse [*Weltuntergang*] prophesied in the last book of the Bible and allows for what then follows: "And God created a new Heaven and a new Earth." One may of course ask: Why this doubling [*Verdopplung*], if the world is rationally constructed? But to this question too there are very good answers. So now I've given you a philosophical lecture and hope you've found it comprehensible.

14.8.61 When you write that you worship the Creation [*die Schöpfung*], you probably mean that the world is everywhere beautiful where human beings are not present, etc. But it is precisely this which could contain the solution of the riddle why there are two worlds. Animals and plants, in contrast to human beings, have only a limited capacity to learn, while lifeless things have none at all. Man alone can, through learning, attain a better existence—that is, give more meaning [*Sinn*] to his life. But one, and often the only, method of learning consists in first making mistakes. And indeed, that actually happens in this world in sufficient measure.

Now one may of course ask: Why didn't God create man so that he would do everything correctly from the very start? But the only reason that this question appears justified to us could very well be the incredible state of ignorance about ourselves in which we still find ourselves today. Indeed, not only do we not know where we're from and why we're here, we don't even know *what* we are (that is, in essence [*im Wesen*] and as seen from the inside).

But were we once able to look deeply enough into ourselves using scientific methods of self-observation in order to answer this question, it would probably turn out that each of us is a something with very specific properties. That is, each person could then say of himself: Among all possible beings [*Wesen*], "I" am precisely this combination of properties whose nature is such and such. But if it is part and parcel of these properties that we do not do everything correctly from the start, but in many cases only first based on experience, it then follows that, had God created in our place beings who did not need to learn, these beings would just not be *we*. It is natural to assume that such (or quite similar) beings, also in some way, exist or will exist. That is, we would then not exist at all. According to the usual view, the answer to the question "What am I?" would then be, that I am a something which of itself has no properties at all, rather like a clothes hanger on which one may hang any garments one wishes. One could naturally say a lot more about all these things.

I believe there is a lot more sense in religion—though not in the churches—than one usually thinks, but from earliest youth we (that is, the middle layer of mankind, to which we belong, or at least most people in this layer) are brought up *prejudiced against* it [religion]—from school, from poor religious instruction, from books and experiences.

12.9.61   That you had trouble understanding the "theological" part of my last letter is indeed quite natural and has nothing to do with your age. Indeed, I expressed myself very briefly and touched on many rather deep philosophical questions. At first sight, this whole set of views [*Anschauung*] that I expounded to you indeed seems highly implausible. But I believe that if one reflects on it more carefully, it will show itself to be entirely plausible and reasonable.

Above all, one must envision the greater part of "learning" as first occurring only in the next world, namely in the following way: that we shall recall our experiences in this world and only then really understand them; so that our present experiences are, so to speak, only the raw material for [this real] learning. For what could a cancer patient (for example) learn from his pain *here*? On the other hand, it is entirely conceivable that it will become clear to him in the next world what failings on his part (not as regards his bodily care, but perhaps in some completely different respect) caused this illness, and that he will thereby learn to understand not only this relationship [*Zusammenhang*] with his illness, but other similar relationships at the same time.

Of course, this supposes that there are many relationships which today's science and received wisdom [*Schulweisheit*] haven't any inkling of. But I am convinced of this, independently of any theology. In fact, even the atheist Schopenhauer wrote an article about the "apparent purpose in the fate of the individual."

If one objects that it would be impossible to recall in another world the experiences in this one, this [objection] would be quite unjustified, for we could in fact be born in the other world with these memories latent within us. Besides, one must, of course, assume that our understanding [*Verstand*] will be considerably better there than here, so that we will grasp everything of importance with the same absolute certainty as $2 \times 2 = 4$, where a mistake is objectively excluded. (Otherwise, for example, we wouldn't have any idea if we are also going to die in the other world.) Thus we can also be absolutely sure of having really experienced everything that we remember.

But I'm afraid that I am again going too far into philosophy. I don't know if one can understand the last ten lines at all without having studied philosophy. N.B. Today's philosophy curriculum would also not help much in understanding such questions, since in fact 90 percent of today's philosophers see their main task [as] getting religion out of people's heads, so that their effect is similar to that of the bad churches.

6.10.61 The religious views I wrote to you about have nothing to do with occultism. Religious occultism consists of summoning the spirit of the Apostle Paul or the Archangel Michael, etc. in spiritualistic meetings, and getting information from them about religious questions. What I wrote to you was in fact no more than a vivid representation, and adaptation to our present way of thinking of certain theological doctrines, that have been preached for 2000 years—though mixed with a lot of nonsense, to be sure.

When one reads the kinds of things that in the course of time have been (and still are) claimed as dogma in the various churches, one must indeed wonder. For example, according to Catholic dogma, the all-benevolent God created most of mankind exclusively for the purpose of sending them to Hell for all eternity, that is all except the good Catholics, who constitute only a fraction of the Catholics themselves.

I don't think it is unhealthy to apply the intellect [*Verstand*] to any area [whatsoever] (as you suggest). It would also be quite unjustified to say that in just this very area nothing can be accomplished with the intellect. For who would have believed, 3000 years ago, that one would [now] be able to determine how big, how massive, how hot and how far away the most distant stars are, and that many of them are 100 times bigger than the sun? Or who would have thought that one would build television sets?

When, 2500 years ago, the doctrine that bodies consist of atoms was first put forward, this must have seemed just as fantastic and unfounded then as the religious doctrines appear to many people today. For at that time literally not a single observational fact was known, which could have instigated the development of the atomic theory; but this occurred on purely philosophical grounds. Nevertheless this theory has today brilliantly confirmed itself and has become the foundation for a very large part of modern science. Of course, one is today a long way from being able to justify the theological view of the world [*das theologische Weltbild*] scientifically, but I believe that it may also be possible today to perceive, by pure reasoning (without depending on any particular religious belief), that the theological view of the world is entirely consistent with all known facts (including the conditions present on our Earth).

The famed philosopher and mathematician Leibniz attempted to do this as long as 250 years ago, and this is also what I tried to do in my last letter. The thing that I call the theological worldview is the concept that the world and everything in it has meaning and sense [*Sinn und Vernunft*], and in particular a good and unambiguous [*zweifellosen*] meaning. From this it follows directly that our presence on Earth, because it has of itself at most a very uncertain meaning, can only be the means to the end [*Mittel zum Zweck*] for another existence. The idea that everything in the world has a meaning is, by the way, exactly analogous to the principle that everything has a cause, which is the basis of the whole of science.

3.1.3 Comments on the Letters

An attractive, plausible, and stable idea in these letters is, as Gödel once said to me more explicitly, that, as we grow older, we generally get to know better how to learn but that, unfortunately, we no longer have sufficient vigor, stamina, and time to make full use of this gradually acquired knowledge and capability. It would, therefore, be desirable to have an afterlife to continue the process of learning and to bring to fruition what our endeavors in this life have prepared us for. Since, however, the hypothesis of an afterlife, though not conclusively refutable, is hardly convincing, a more reasonable and familiar course is to concentrate on this one life, seeing it as the only one we have to work with.

I am under the impression that, in the European (or at least the Christian) tradition, you have to have an afterlife to be immortal. This is not so according to the prevalent conception of immortality in China. According to this conception, there are three forms of immortality: (1) setting a good example by your conduct; (2) doing good deeds; and (3) saying significant things of one kind or another. The idea is that these achievements will remain after we die, for they will be preserved in the memory of our community and will continue to affect others. Since they are ours, this means that parts of us will continue to live after us and we will have gained immortality by achieving (1) or (2) or (3).

I once mentioned this conception to Gödel. He seemed not to view such achievements as forms of immortality, apparently on the ground that you yourself will no longer be there to enjoy the rewards of your good deeds by seeing their positive effects on others. Whether or not one agrees with Gödel on this point, at least for those of us who have little faith in an afterlife, the Chinese conception of immortality has the advantage of capturing some of the familiar and accessible central goals of our lives. Regardless of belief in an afterlife, most of us do place great value on these goals and believe we should do our best to achieve them (or other "good" goals). I can see that, as we approach our death, belief in an afterlife can be comforting, since most of us do have certain unfinished projects. I do not see, however, that the assumption of an afterlife, just as an opportunity for further learning, should make any difference in how we plan and live our lives in this world.

The Chinese conception of immortality may resemble that of the Enlightenment. In 1765 Diderot, for example, wrote in a letter "Posterity, to the philosopher, is what the world beyond is, to the religious man." In the *Encyclopedia*, he defined a sense of immortality by saying "It is the kind of life that we acquire in the memory of men" and "If immortality considered from this aspect is a chimera, it is the chimera of great souls."

Spinoza's idea of an eternal life has some affinity with the views of Taoism, especially those of Zhuang Zi, who would have endorsed the thought expressed by Spinoza in the next to the last paragraph of *Ethics*: "Whereas the wise man is scarcely at all disturbed in spirit, but, being conscious of himself, and of God [Nature], and of things, by a certain eternal necessity, never ceases to be, but always possesses true acquiescence of his spirit." Eternal life, however, is not an afterlife: "Men are indeed conscious of the eternity of their mind, but they confuse eternity with duration, and ascribe it to the imagination or memory which they believe to remain after death" (note to Proposition 34 of Part 5 of *Ethics*). Like Confucius, Spinoza thought about life rather than death: "A free man thinks of death least of all things; and his wisdom is a meditation not of death but of life" (Proposition 67 of Part 4).

Values have much to do with the fulfillment of wishes. If you think of yourself as part of a community, small or large, then your range of wishes includes those of others in the community, and what is of value to them becomes part of your own wishes. In this way your range of values is broadened and becomes less dependent on an afterlife.

In any case, it is of interest to consider, under the reasonable assumption that we have only this life, Gödel's observation that we learn better as we grow older. This idea presents us with the practical question of how to plan our lives in such a way as to take advantage of this improved capacity in old age. A crude analogy might be the wish to travel as far as you can in your life, with the understanding that as you approach the end of your journey the same amount of physical strength will enable you to cover a longer distance than before because of your acquired ability to use your strength more effectively. The analogy is, of course, defective.

At the beginning of life we have little idea of what physical and mental resources we have been given. The environment into which we are born is another given element, independent of our own efforts. Gradually we acquire better knowledge and understanding of these given elements and their evolving states, which make up what we have at each stage. For each segment of our lives we make choices on the basis of what we see as our current situation. A whole life plan will include some obvious considerations: attention to physical and mental health; balancing immediate gratification versus preparations for the future (by acquiring good habits, meeting basic needs, and improving needed physical and mental resources); and, of course, achieving what we can at each stage without unduly exhausting the resources needed to sustain us in the future.

In practice, a life plan may be seen as a continuing preparation for death (with reference to your evolving anticipation of death). In a fundamental way, we must work with probabilities and uncertainties, for much depends on what actually happens to us and our surroundings in the future, and we can only try to make informed guesses.

Comprehensive common goals include being true to ourselves and being autonomous, goals to a large extent embodied in finding out what we want and what we are able to do, and then attempting to combine these desires and capacities in a rough project which is modified from time to time. For most people, wants are concerned, first, with human relations and, secondly, with work. Both depend a good deal on other people, but there are a few kinds of work that depend mainly on oneself. In accordance with the ideal of autonomy it is desirable to reduce the extent to which we depend on others and on circumstances. We may, for instance, try, to eliminate "false needs" and to confine our dependence on others to a small number of persons whom we can trust.

It is possible to view Gödel's life in terms of these homely observations. I shall present what I take to be a plausible account of his intellectual development, the story of a life devoted to the pursuit of philosophy, in the traditional European sense. To begin, I single out the quest for a worldview as Gödel's central goal.

Because of his concern with philosophy, he undoubtedly developed an especially articulate awareness of his own worldview, which tied together his work and his life. We may take it that his aim in life was to make the greatest possible contribution that he could to the ideal of finding and justifying the correct or true worldview. Even though it is hard, and perhaps uninformative, to be explicit about how the many aspects of Gödel's thought relate to his aim in life as I have characterized it, I see this idea as a helpful guide in my attempt to place his wide range of thoughts within a single broad framework.

As far as I know, the four letters to his mother quoted above contain Gödel's most extended statement on his views about an afterlife. In addition, I have come across some related but scattered observations in other contexts—for example, the comments on hope and occult phenomena in the letters to his mother quoted in Chapter 1 (pp. 43, 44).

During his conversations with me, Gödel also made several related statements, sometimes with explicit reference to his "rationalistic optimism," (which I consider in Chapter 9, p. 317).

In the nearly two years prior to his death in January of 1978, Gödel was almost exclusively occupied with his health problems and those of his wife. We have no way of knowing whether or how he thought about the question of an afterlife during this period; as far as I know, he made no attempt to work.—Wittgenstein, by contrast, after a diagnosis of cancer of the prostate gland in the autumn of 1949, continued to write philosophy when he was strong enough. Shortly before his death in April 1951, he told Maurice Drury: "Isn't it curious that, although I know I have not long to live, I never find myself thinking about a 'future life.' All my interest is still on this life and the writing I am still able to do" (Rhees 1984:169).

3.2 Religion and Gödel's Ontological Proof

Religions are associated with reverence and piety. In the strict sense, being religious includes believing in and worshiping a transcendent divine reality that creates and controls all things without deviation from its will. In an extended sense, a religion is any system of ideals and values such that (1) they constitute an ultimate court of appeal, (2) one can enthusiastically strive toward them, and (3) one can regulate one's conduct according to one's interpretation of them. A religion embodies a value held to be of supreme importance—a cause, principle, or system of beliefs—held with ardor, devotion, conscientiousness, and faith. In this sense, some people are said to make Marxism or democracy, or even pleasure, their religion.

Max Weber included Confucianism and Taoism in his study of the major world religions. (Indeed, an English translation of this part of his study is entitled *The Religion of China—Confucianism and Taoism*.) In contrast, Fung Yu-lan denies that Confucianism is a religion and believes that:

3.2.1   The place which philosophy has occupied in Chinese civilization has been comparable to that of religion in other civilizations.... In the world of the future, man will have philosophy in the place of religion. This is consistent with the Chinese tradition. It is not necessary that man should be religious, but it is necessary that he should be philosophical. When he is philosophical, he has the very best of the blessings of religion. (Fung 1948:1, 6).

If we identify one's philosophy with one's worldview, then religions constitute a special type of philosophy which is distinguished from other types by a heavier reliance on faith, a greater tendency toward reverence and devotion, and, ideally, a better unified system of values as a guide to conduct. Religions have taken on various different forms in the history of mankind. For instance Einstein distinguished between a cosmic religious feeling and a religion of fear blended variously with moral or social religions, each of which appeals to some anthropomorphic conception of God (Einstein 1954:36–38).

Gödel described Einstein as certainly religious in some sense, although not in that of the churches, and saw his conception as close to the ideas of Spinoza and Eastern religions. In 1975 Gödel gave his own religion as "baptized" Lutheran (though not a member of any religious congregation) and noted that his belief was *theistic*, not pantheistic, following Leibniz rather than Spinoza.

For Spinoza, God and nature, properly understood, are one and the same thing. Since we have no doubt that nature, or the world, exists, the major problem is not to prove the existence of God but to understand nature properly. Like Gödel, Spinoza believes that human reason is capable of discovering first principles and providing us with a fixed point in the universe. Indeed, Gödel's recommendation of an axiomatic theory for metaphysics bears a striking resemblance to the course taken by Spinoza in his *Ethics: Demonstrated in the Geometrical Order*. Gödel was not satisfied, however, with Spinoza's impersonal God.

One may believe that God exists without also believing it possible to find an articulate and convincing argument to prove the existence of God. For Pascal, for instance, religion is supported by faith in a transcendent and hidden principle. Gödel's mother apparently thought that the question of an afterlife could not be settled by the intellect alone.

Like Gödel, Wittgenstein thought a good deal about religion, but his views on religious matters were more tentative and changed over the years. In the summer of 1938 Wittgenstein delivered several lectures on religious belief; some of his students' notes on these lectures were published in 1966. Among other things, with respect to religion he said: "We don't talk about hypothesis, or about high probability. Nor about knowing" (1966:57). Once, near the end of his life, Drury reminded him that in one of their first conversations he had said there was no such subject as theology. He replied, "That is just the sort of stupid remark I would have made in those days [around 1930]" (Rhees 1984:98). On the matter of proving God's existence, he wrote in 1950:

3.2.2 A proof of God's existence ought really to be something by means of which one could convince oneself that God exists. But I think that what *believers* who have furnished such proofs have wanted to do is to give their 'belief' an intellectual analysis and foundation, although they themselves would never have come to believe as a result of such proofs. Perhaps one could 'convince someone that God exists' by means of a certain kind of upbringing, by shaping his life in such and such a way. (Wittgenstein 1980:85)

In 1972 Gödel told me that his study of Leibniz had had no influence on his own work except in the case of his ontological proof, of which Dana Scott had a copy. We now know that there are two pages of notes in Gödel's papers, dated 10 February 1970, and that he discussed his proof with Scott that month. The following academic year Scott presented his own notes to a seminar on entailment at Princeton University.

These notes, which began to circulate in the early 1970s, are somewhat different from Gödel's own, both in the ordering of the material and in replacing Gödel's Axiom 1 by the special case: Being God-like is a positive property. In *Reflections on Gödel* (RG:195) I reproduced a version of Scott's notes but made a mistake in copying Scott's Axiom 5 (Gödel's Axiom 1): I wrote "Being NE is God-like" instead of "Being God-like is a positive property." Both Gödel's and Scott's notes are reproduced faithfully and discussed in Sobel 1987 and Anderson 1990. I reproduce Gödel's notes here, in a less technical notation, to indicate his line of thought.

Gödel uses the notion of a positive property as primitive. He says that positive means positive in the moral aesthetic sense, independent of the accidental structure of the world, and that it may also mean pure *attribution*—that is, the disjunctive normal form in terms of elementary propositions (or properties) contains a member without negation—as opposed to *privation* (or *containing privation*).

Axiom 1 The conjunction of any number (collection) of positive properties is a positive property. For instance, if A and B are positive properties, having both of them is to have a positive property too.

Axiom 2 A property is positive if and only if its negation is not positive: every property or (exclusive) its negation is positive.

Definition 1 G(x) or an object x is God-like if and only if x possesses all positive properties: for every property A, if P(A) then A(x).

Definition 2 A property A is an essence of an object x if and only if (1) A(x) and (2) for every property B of x, necessarily every object y which has the property A has the property B too.—Any two essences of x are necessarily equivalent.

[The definition says: (1) A(x) and (2), for every B, if B(x), then, necessarily, for every y, A(y) implies B(y). Hence, if A is an essence of x, then any object which has property A necessarily has all the other properties of x too. In other words, x is, in a sense, entirely determined by A.]

Axiom 3 If a property is positive (or negative), it is necessarily positive (or negative). It follows from the nature of a property whether it is positive or negative.

Theorem 1 If x is God-like, then the property of being God-like is an essence of x: if G(x), then G is an essence of x.

[By hypothesis, G(x). Hence, by Definition 2, we have to prove only: (a) for every property B of x, necessarily for every object y, if G(y), then B(y). By Definition 1, since G(x), x possesses all positive properties. Therefore, by Axiom 2, all properties of x are positive. Hence, if B(x), then B is positive. By Axiom 3, we have: (b) if B(x), then necessarily P(B). By Definition 1, necessarily G(y) implies that P(B) implies B(y). Therefore, necessarily P(B) implies that G(y) implies B(y). By modal logic, if necessarily P(B), then necessarily for all y, G(y) implies B(y). By (b), if B(x), then necessarily for all y, G(y) implies B(y).—But this is the desired conclusion (a). Hence, G is an essence of x.]

Definition 3 Necessary existence. E(x) if and only if, for every essence A of x, there exists necessarily some object which has the property A. [An object necessarily exists if and only if every essence of it is necessarily exemplified.]

Axiom 4 P(E). The property of necessary existence is a positive property.

Theorem 2 If G(x), then necessarily there is some object y, G(y).

[By Axiom 4, E is a positive property. By Definition 1, it is a property of x, since G(x). Hence, if G(x), then E(x). By Theorem 1, if G(x), then G is an essence of x, and, therefore, by E(x) and Definition 3, there is necessarily some object y, G(y).]

From Theorem 2, it follows [by familiar logic] that, if there is some x, $G(x)$, then there is necessarily some object y, $G(y)$. [But a familiar rule of modal logic says: if p necessarily implies q and p is possible, then q is possible.] Hence, if possibly there is some x, $G(x)$, then possibly there is necessarily some object y, $G(y)$. [But there is another rule of modal logic: if it is possible that p is necessary, then p is necessary.] Therefore:

Theorem 3 If it is possible that there is some God-like object, then it is necessary that there is some God-like object.

The remaining task is to prove that possibly there is some God-like object. This means that the system of all positive properties (or their corresponding propositions) is compatible [or consistent]. This is true because of:

Axiom 5 If A is a positive property and [if] necessarily for all x, $A(x)$ necessarily implies $B(x)$, then B is a positive property.

This axiom implies that self-identity ($x = x$) is positive and self-nonidentity (the negation of $x = x$) is negative. [Since every object is necessarily self-identical, self-identity is necessarily implied by every property. Hence, since there must be some positive property (even just for the whole enterprise to make sense), self-identity is a positive property. By Axiom 1, its negation is not positive (and therefore negative).]

But if a system of positive properties were incompatible, it would mean that its sum property [the conjunction of all the properties in the system], which is positive [by Axiom 1], would be self-nonidentity, which is, however, negative. [Therefore, there is possible some God-like object. By Theorem 3, there is necessarily some God-like object. Hence, God necessarily exists.—In this argument, God's possible existence is identified with the compatibility of the system of all positive properties, which is identified with the consistency of the system of their corresponding propositions.—At the end of his notes, Gödel offers an alternative proof of the conclusion, which replaces this paragraph by a different line of thought.]

Given the fact that self-nonidentity is a negative property, it follows that, if a property A is positive, then the following is *not* the case: every object necessarily does not have the property A. Otherwise $A(x)$ would necessarily imply the negation of $x = x$. [By assumption, the negation of $A(x)$ is necessarily true for all x. Hence, $A(x)$, being false, necessarily implies everything, including the negation of $x = x$.] By Axiom 5, self-nonidentity would be positive, contrary to the just proved conclusion that it is negative. [By Definition 1 and Axiom 1, G is a positive property. Therefore, it is not the case that every object necessarily does not have the property G. Hence, using the familiar relation between possibility and necessity, we have: Theorem 4. It is possible that there is some object x, $G(x)$.—Indeed, the argument proves that, for any positive property A, possibly there is some x, $A(x)$.—Combining this with Theorem 3, we have: Theorem 5. It is necessary that there is some object x, $G(x)$. By Definition 2 and Theorem 1, this object x is uniquely determined by its property G. Consequently, God necessarily exists.]

This concludes my exposition of Gödel's notes of 10 February 1970. (I may well have missed some points and misrepresented some others.) His general line of thought is familiar from the history of philosophy. Descartes, for example, spoke of perfections instead of positive properties, but the crucial steps of his argument in the Fifth Meditation are similar to Gödel's: (a) God is the subject of all perfections, by definition and in accordance with our clear and distinct idea; and (b) existence is a perfection.

In 1676 Leibniz wrote some notes in connection with his visits and discussions with Spinoza in The Hague, and observed that Descartes had assumed the conceivability or possibility of a most perfect being, but had failed to show a way in which others could arrive for themselves at a clear and distinct experience of that concept. Leibniz then produced an argument for the same conclusion and showed it to Spinoza: "He thought it sound, for when he contradicted it at first, I put it in writing and gave him this paper," which contained the following three steps:

L1 By a *perfection* I mean every simple quality which is positive and absolute or which expresses whatever it expresses without any limits. But because a quality of this kind is simple, it is unanalyzable or indefinable, for otherwise either it will not be one simple quality but an aggregate of many or, if it is one, it will be contained within its limits and hence will be understood through negation of what is beyond these limits; which is contrary to hypothesis, since it is assumed to be purely positive.
L2 From this it is not difficult to show that *all perfections are compatible with each other*, or can occur in the same subject. [For a summary of Leibniz's argument, see below.]
L3 Therefore there is, or can be conceived, a subject of all perfections or a most perfect being. Hence it is clear that this being exists, since existence is contained in the number of perfections (Leibniz 1969:167–168).

To demonstrate L2, Leibniz illustrated the general situation of the system of all perfections by considering the special case of only two perfections, that is, the proposition: (H) A and B are incompatible. According to Leibniz, (H) cannot be proved without analyzing A or B or both; but, since they are, by hypothesis, unanalyzable (simple), (H) is not provable. Hence the proposition (H) is not necessarily true. Therefore, it is possible that (H) is false: that A and B can occur in the same subject.

This argument—and similarly Gödel's—obviously involves the difficult tasks of conceiving and envisaging a sufficiently rich (and yet pure) collection of perfections or positive properties to satisfy the conditions: (a) they are all compatible, (b) they are all actually exemplified simultaneously in some one object, and (c) they include enough of the qualities commonly associated with a significant portion of the familiar conceptions of God. For instance, even if we assume Gödel's thesis that all concepts are sharp (even though we do not perceive them clearly), there remains the problem of singling out, programmatically at least, those concepts which determine perfections or positive properties.

As we know, Kant objects to the ontological arguments on the ground that existence is not a predicate or a property. We may feel that it is a somewhat arbitrary matter to decide whether existence is a property. However, one is inclined to doubt that, merely by selecting a collection of properties, one could possibly be assured that there must actually exist some object that possesses all the properties in the collection. In Kant's words, I may have the concept of a *thaler* without actually owning a *thaler*.

Gödel's Axiom 1 states explicitly that any conjunction of positive properties is a positive property. Unlike Leibniz, he does not explicitly appeal to the concept of *simple* properties. However, at least in terms of expressing properties, his conception also points to certain positive properties which are *simple* in the sense that they are not combinations of other properties. Whatever these simple positive properties might be, we can envisage at least all Boolean combinations of them by conjunction, disjunction, and negation. As an illustration, suppose that these simple positive properties and their Boolean combinations are all the properties.

By Gödel's Axiom 2, these properties are divided into two classes: the positive ones and the negative ones, the latter being negations of the former. Gödel seems to suggest that a property is positive if and only if its disjunctive normal forms contains some member without negation, that is, some disjunct which is either a simple positive property or a conjunction of simple positive properties. For instance, being self-identical *or* self-non-identical is a positive property, and its negation—that is, being self-non-identical *and* self-identical—is a negative property. This division does satisfy Axiom 2, since every member of the disjunctive normal form of the negation of one with some member without negation is always a conjunction with some negative term.

If this is the correct interpretation of Gödel's notes, then God possesses not only all the simple positive properties but also all their Boolean combinations that are positive in the just-specified sense. Nonetheless, all the simple positive properties are compatible if and only if all the positive properties are compatible. This is so because the conjunction of all the positive properties includes the conjunction of all simple positive properties as a part; and yet it is equivalent to a disjunction which includes the conjunction of all simple positive properties as one member. Let S be the conjunction of all simple positive properties, T be the conjunction of all the other positive properties. Clearly if S and T, then S. But the disjunctive normal form of the conjunction of S and T is of the form S or U. Clearly if S, then S or U.

It is not clear that the properties commonly attributed to God, such as being omnipotent, omniscient, and omnibenevolent, are simple properties, even though we are inclined to see them as positive properties. The reduction of all positive properties to the simple ones promises to lighten the task of proving their compatibility, since we are inclined to think that simple (positive) properties are mutually independent and, consequently, mutually compatible.

The task of finding all the mutually independent simple positive properties seems to be essentially of the same type as the much-discussed ideal or assumption in the theory of Wittgenstein's *Tractatus* (1922) that there *must be* a complete collection of mutually independent elementary propositions, which may be hidden from us but which can in principle be revealed by the right sort of "ultimate analysis."

When two or more properties exclude one another, they cannot all be positive properties or all occur in elementary propositions. In such cases there is the problem of selecting one of the properties to be the positive or elementary one. For instance, an object may have any one of a group of parallel properties, such as different colors, shapes, sizes, tastes, odors, weights, and so on; it seems arbitrary to choose one property (say blue) rather than another (say yellow) as the positive or elementary one. This familiar example illustrates the difficulty involved in finding mutually compatible properties. Of course, the restriction to necessarily positive properties contracts the range of candidates from which selections can be made.

As we know, Wittgenstein, late in life, abandoned the elementary propositions of his *Tractatus*. All the same, since the *Tractatus* captures some significant features of our picture of the world, it continues to get and deserve our attention. Analogously, it is likely that Gödel's ontological proof, though it fails to provide a convincing proof of the existence of God as traditionally conceived, will surely stimulate meaningful reflection.

The text of Gödel's ontological proof of 10 February 1970 is included in the third volume of his *Collected Works*, together with an appendix of selected "Texts relating to the ontological proof." These texts include two loose sheets in longhand (one of which is dated "ca. 1941") and three excerpts from Gödel's philosophical notebooks (written in Gabelsberger shorthand): two short ones from 1944, and a long one from 1954. The texts in shorthand have been transcribed by Cheryl Dawson and then translated from German into English by Robert M. Adams, who also wrote an introductory note to both the main text and the appendix. (*CW* 3, 388–402)

Of special interest is the long excerpt from 1954 (pp. 103–108 of vol. 14 of Gödel's philosophical notebooks; CW 3, 433–437). In this excerpt, Gödel makes a number of observations on the ontological proof:

(1) The proof must be grounded on the concept of *value* and on the *axioms* for value (it can be grounded only on axioms and *not* on a definition of "positive"). (2) The positive and the true assertions are the same, for different reasons. (3) It is possible to interpret the positive as "perfective" or "purely good" (but not as "good"). (4) That the *necessity* of a positive property is itself a positive property is the essential presupposition for the ontological proof. And (5) the positive properties are precisely those which can be formed out of the elementary ones through applications of conjunction, disjunction, and implication.

The long excerpt also contains some highly suggestive general observations. One of them recommends the study of philosophy:

Engaging in philosophy is salutary [*wohltätig* (*wohltuend?*)] in any case, even when no positive results emerge from it (and I remain perplexed [*ratlos*]). It has the effect [*Wirkung*] that "the color [is] brighter," that is, *that reality* appears *more clearly* [*deutlicher*] as such.

This observation reveals that, according to Gödel's conception, the study of philosophy helps us to see reality more distinctly, even though it may happen that no (communicable) positive results come out of it to help others.

Gödel's other general observations are packed into two consecutive paragraphs, which provide a concentrated illustration of what is central to his conception of philosophy. It seems to me that the assertions in these two paragraphs can be divided into six parts for purposes of discussion.

1. The fundamental philosophical concept is cause. It involves: will, force, enjoyment, God, time, space. Will and enjoyment: Hence life and affirmation and negation. Time and space: Being near = possibility of influence.
2. The affirmation of being is the cause of the world. The first creature: to being is added the affirmation of being. From this it follows further that as many beings as possible will be produced—and this is the ultimate ground of diversity (variety delights).
3. Harmony implies more being than disharmony, for the opposition of parts cancels their being.
4. Regularity consists in agreement; for example: at the same angle, there is the same color.
5. Property = cause of the difference of things.
6. Perhaps the other Kantian categories (i.e., the logical, including necessity) can be defined in terms of causality, and the logical (set-theoretical) axioms can be derived from the axioms for causality. Moreover it should be expected that analytical mechanics would follow from such an axiom.

The inclusion of God under assertion 1 is related to the identification of the cause of the world with the affirmation of being in assertion 2. In one of the two excerpts from 1944, Gödel explicitly links the cause of the world with a "proof of the existence of an a priori proof of the existence of God": "According to the Principle of Sufficient Reason the world must have a cause. This must be necessary in itself (otherwise it would require a further cause)."

Implicit in assertions 2 and 3 is the idea that the affirmation of being is a positive value, or perhaps the only ultimate (positive) value. Gödel seems to identify the true with the good (and the beautiful). The affirmation of being is both the cause and the purpose of the world. Like God, we *will* the affirmation of being and *enjoy* it. The production of as many possible beings as possible is an explication of the Leibnizian idea of the best possible world.

In his discussions with me in the seventies, Gödel said on several occasions that he was not able to decide what the primitive concepts of philosophy are. Assertion 1 may be interpreted as an attempt to do so by reflecting on what is involved in the fundamental concept of cause. The line of thought here is related to his observation, to be considered in Chapter 9, that the meaning of the world is the separation of force and fact. In the case of conscious beings, force works together with will and enjoyment to increase the affirmation of being.

Observations 4 and 5 on regularity and property, respectively, presumably have to do with the positive value of those items: regularity gives order and contributes to harmony; property causes diversity, which is a positive value.

Conjecture 6 may depend on Gödel's association of positive value with both assertions and the affirmation of being. He once said to me that there is a sense of cause according to which axioms *cause* theorems. It seems likely that Gödel has in mind something like Aristotle's conception of cause or *aitia*, which includes both causes and reasons. In any case, if the logical categories and axioms are definable and derivable from the category of cause and its axioms, the concept of cause is no longer restricted to causality in space and time.

For those who find Spinoza's conception of God plausible and attractive, a natural question is why Leibniz or Gödel chooses not to adopt it. The familiar reply on behalf of Leibniz is that Spinoza does not allow for the notion of individuality. For Spinoza, God or Nature is the one substance of the universe, possessing the two known attributes: thought and matter. Within this unity, particular existences, whether things or poems, are not substances but *modes* of extension and thought.

It seems to me, however, that the identification of God with Nature is a valuable simplification, which helps us to focus our attention on life and the world as we know them. According to Spinoza's philosophy, the highest state of joy, the state of contentment in oneself or "the intellectual love of God", is attainable in our present life: As we learn to see the world from the natural perspective of rational thinking, we come more and more to see it "under the aspect of eternity." By offering an actual axiomatic presentation in his *Ethics*, Spinoza enables us to compare what he believes with what we believe at many points, not just to ask whether his axioms are plausible, but also to question his "propositions" (or theorems).

Gödel's bold speculations on God and an afterlife are an integral part of the European philosophical tradition. They bear more directly on familiar common concerns than do his reflections on the nature of logic and mathematics. At the same time, for people like me who come from a different cultural background, it is easier to appreciate his thoughts on more universal subjects, like mathematics and natural science, than his ideas on religion and metaphysics, which are more closely bound to a particular cultural tradition.

However, my difficulty with Gödel's speculations may have more to do with his distinctive position than with the European tradition. He himself says that his views are contrary to the spirit of the time. I find it easier, for instance, to appreciate the general outlooks of Europeans like Russell and Einstein than Gödel's views on God and the afterlife.

3.3 Worldviews: Between Philosophy and Ideology

At any moment we are explicitly or implicitly interested in reaching one kind of desirable state: to have singled out a wish and to know how to consummate it. In order to arrive at such a state, I select one of my own wishes to attend to, take its fulfillment as a goal, and look for feasible ways to reach that goal. An overarching ideal for me is to find a unifying wish or goal to serve as backbone for the structure of my various wishes and as a central guide for my action. As a member of various groups, I am also involved in the goals of these groups. And each group has its own ideal of finding a unifying goal.

One central aim of philosophy is to find such unifying goals and especially to envision a desirable state of the whole human species that could serve as a goal for all of us both individually and together. Ideally we would like to find either (1) a unifying goal for each individual that agrees with the collective unifying goal; or (2) a collective unifying goal that determines the individual's unifying goals in such a way that the collective goal becomes both just and attainable.

This abstract characterization of a central ideal of philosophy is intended to capture some basic features of widely influential religions, philosophies, and ideologies. The Christian religion, for example, proposes for every person the shared unifying goal of loving God; this goal, if adopted by everyone, promises to benefit not only each individual but mankind as well. Marxism proposes measures to attain the collective goal of a classless ideal society, which is widely desired. Those who find Marxism convincing tend to subordinate their individual unifying goals to the collective goal. Confucianism tries to combine the collective goal of a stable and contented society with the individual goal, for the select few, of *nei sheng wei wang*—to be a sage (internally) and to be able to govern justly (as an external application of one's wisdom).

There are several components of any unifying goal that forms part of an articulate worldview as a guide to action. The goal's effectiveness is a function of these components. One of them is the question of whether the goal is feasible and desirable in itself. The feasibility of a collective goal depends on the efforts of the members of the collective, which are in turn determined by the goal's desirability for the members. The question is whether a sufficient number of members desire the collective goal strongly enough to be inspired to pursue it, even though they may have to sacrifice some of their private interests.

The feasibility of a program of action to produce a desired result depends, then, on our knowledge of causal connections: whether action *A* will produce effect *B*. In practice, our beliefs about feasibility depend more on persuasion than on knowledge; persuasion is sufficient to produce action. But if the belief is not knowledge, the action usually does not produce the promised result. We are, therefore, faced with the task of bridging the gap between belief and knowledge.

In this connection a pejorative sense of the word *ideology*, which had been proposed in 1796 as a name for the philosophy of mind or the science of ideas, was introduced in 1802 by Napoleon Bonaparte. According to this new usage, which is common today, sensible people rely on experience, or have a *philosophy*; irresponsible people rely on *ideology*. Napoleon attacked the principles of the Enlightenment as an "ideology" and attributed "all the misfortunes which have befallen our beautiful France [since 1792] to this diffuse metaphysics, which in a contrived manner seeks to find the primary causes and on this foundation would erect the legislation of peoples, instead of adapting the laws to a knowledge of the human heart and of the lessons of history" (in Williams 1983:154).

An ideology in this sense is also said to be a "theory, which, resting in no respect upon the basis of self-interest, could prevail with none save hot-headed boys and crazed enthusiasts" (Sir Walter Scott, 1827). Marx and Engels criticized the ideology of their radical German contemporaries on the ground that their thought was an abstraction from the real processes of history and not based on knowledge of actual material conditions and relationships. More broadly, an ideology is an abstract, impractical or fanatical theory.

These criticisms of what is called an ideology are motivated by the rational requirement that a program of action be based on appropriate knowledge of the crucial relevant factors. It is easy to agree that the most important factors are the facts about the human heart and the lessons of history. But opinions differ as to what these facts and lessons are; for instance, it is difficult to determine the nature and the place of self-interest in the human heart or the part that material conditions have played and will play in history.

We have different interpretations of the world because there are many things about the world of which we have no real knowledge. We extrapolate from what we know in different ways according to our own different situations and perspectives. In this sense, a program to change the world certainly depends on some view of the world which is very much an interpretation of the world, since it has to make bold extrapolations from what we really know. At the same time, a carefully argued grand program of change can have a special attraction for us and can focus our attention on important aspects of the world; the appeal of such a program is especially strong if it offers a plausible way of unifying thought and action.

Historical experience tells us that there are some rough correlations between types of programs and types of followers. According to one generalization, radical programs tend to prevail with "hot-headed boys and crazed enthusiasts."—But the correlation is often much more complex than such rough generalizations would suggest. As we know, participants and sympathizers of a movement are drawn to it from diverse groups and for different reasons. (For the sources of the quotations in the preceding paragraphs, see the entry on "Ideology" in Williams 1983.)

To take a personal example, from the summer of 1972 and for several years thereafter, I was strongly interested in Marxism, and I made serious efforts to convince myself that Marxism contains the kernel of the right worldview. There was a strong will to believe at work: to believe that China was doing well and was opening up a new era in the world. Linked to this belief was the inclination to accept the official Chinese version of Marxism and of what was happening in China, according to which China was indeed at the stage of transition to communism.

From 1977 to 1979, a less distorted picture of the actual situation in China was gradually revealed to me through personal conversations and published accounts of what had happened. Slowly I began to realize that my belief about what was happening was fundamentally incorrect and that my extrapolation from this belief to my belief in the strength of what I vaguely took to be Marxism was without real foundation.

Marxism contains different components and has been given diverse interpretations. Some of its components are more plausible than others. Its implied program of action as applied to any given situation faces special problems in each case. There have been many attempts to distinguish the philosophy (the theory) of Marxism from the ideology of Marxism as a guide to practice, which depends more on what we wish to believe. Since doing the right thing usually requires knowledge that we have, it is common to appeal to what we wish to believe and to make mistakes as a result.

In China there was, from the 1950s on, largely through the influence of Mao Tse Tung, an eagerness to enter quickly the stage of "socialism"—construed primarily in terms of the formal aspect of increasing public ownership (of at least the means of production). One consequence of this preoccupation with speed and appearance was that the effects of traditional Chinese values and the weight of Chinese history on the course of events were largely interpreted in a crude and one-sided manner, especially from 1949 to 1979. The authentic forces of tradition and history were often misrepresented and exploited for the benefit of the powerful and the privileged.

It is widely accepted today, at least in China, that, conspicuously from 1957 to 1976, Mao violated the fundamental principle of Marxism: "existence determines consciousness," which implies the primary importance of the means of production. A remarkable historical fact was that, despite objections from most of his important colleagues, Mao was able to divert Chinese history into a strangely unrealistic course from 1957 to 1976—from the anti-rightist movement and the Great Leap Forward, to the Cultural Revolution.

One factor was, of course, Mao's extraordinary prestige and power. In addition, his habit of emphasizing success and downplaying failure appealed strongly to the impatience, shared by the population at large, for China to catch up and overtake the advanced countries in one way or another. By the time of Mao's death in 1976, it was clear that make-believe was predominant and that the Chinese economy was on the verge of collapse.

In 1979 the present course of *reform* and material incentive, in place of *revolution* and class struggle, had its tentative beginning. The consensus that had been reached to combine socialism with a market economy, announced dramatically in 1992, reflected a decision to put economic reform at the center, thereby obeying the fundamental Marxian empirical generalization that the material base ultimately determines the superstructure.

The governing goal of China's continuing efforts has, at least since the early 1970s, been summarized by the ambiguous word *modernization*, which includes industrialization and the quests for wealth and strength, a high standard of living, efficiency, and advanced science and technology—

in short, the transformation of China from a developing country into a developed one.

In view of the central place currently occupied by the practice of "looking toward money," what has been adopted in China appears to be more in the spirit of capitalism than in that of socialism. However, the distinction is by no means sharp; there are different shades of private and public ownership in all types of society. The Chinese experience in particular reveals the futility, and indeed the harmfulness, of arguing over the labels *socialist* and *capitalist* rather than trying to find out directly what the population at large wants.

My experience as I have reported it may perhaps be viewed as a piece of evidence against *Platonism* if Platonism is taken to imply that we should, in the first place, focus on concepts—those of capitalism and socialism in this case. It seems to me, however, that Platonism is rarely discussed explicitly in terms of its connection to such practical considerations. For instance, when Gödel argued for Platonism in mathematics, he did not discuss the relation of Platonism to political issues. In any case, we should, I believe, be careful in trying to generalize Platonism from mathematics to other areas.

Marxism offers a worldview that urges us to change the world in a revolutionary manner. Most people, however, tend to accept the society in which they live and look for guidance about how to live in society as it is. More people seek this guidance from religion or literature or popular psychology than from philosophy. In this regard, the Chinese tradition has been different from the European tradition.

In China, philosophy is traditionally concerned primarily with the problems of life. In my final examination in 1945 for a degree—with a dissertation on epistemology—Professor Shen Yuting asked me why I wanted to study philosophy. I said it was because I was interested in the problems of life. He then told me that in the West such problems were addressed by literature more than by philosophy; indeed, much of Western philosophy is oriented toward science and has little direct relevance to the problems of life.

Chinese philosophy, in contrast, has little to do with science and is rather like literature in its spirit; it is closely connected with literature, history and everyday life, whereas Western philosophy tends, more often than not, to see science, in one sense or another, as its ideal. Related to this difference is the greater inclination in the Western tradition toward system, explicitness, and separations—between subject and object, appearance and reality, abstract and concrete, knowledge and action, nature and human beings, means and ends, fact and value, formal and intuitive, and so on.

This preference for science in the European tradition has played a large part in generating much that is unique in world history: the elaborate subtleties of Plato and Aristotle, the detached system of Euclid's geometry, the systematic theology of Aquinas, the cumulative development of science and technology, the perfection of instrumental reason, the refinement of specialization and the division of labor, and so on. At the same time, the bifurcations involved have led to certain forms of fragmentation and rigidity, to a tendency toward replacing ends by means and generating meaningless wishes just to consume available means, and generally to a concentration on what can be effectively and efficiently done even if it has little to do with our fundamental, though often ill-defined, emotional needs.

We may begin with the fundamental shared interest in living a better life. For most of us, science and technology are not immediately relevant to this interest—except in the secondary sense that we make use of the products of technology. Literature is more directly relevant to it; for it teaches us about ways of life through examples. In literature the abstract and the concrete are more organically integrated than they are in science, and ambiguity is more naturally handled. At the same time, science is more objective and systematic than literature. Philosophy differs from science in that its central concepts are less precise, and from literature in that its discourse is less concrete. For each of its parts philosophy faces a choice between different ways of combining the virtues of science and literature. For that part which relates to our central interest in a better life, the more attractive choice, it seems to me, lies on the side of affinity to literature, as in Chinese philosophy.

To meet the central need of living a better life, we face, apart from particular problems special to one group or another, certain more or less universal problems shared by everyone. For example, although there are distinct requirements for different ways of earning a living, diligence and effective use of one's resources are generally desirable. The science of the physical world has little to say about such important common tasks as learning more about ourselves, our desires, and our capabilities; improving our habits and our ways of thinking; avoiding or mastering anger, greed, despair, envy, and vanity; cultivating the ability to establish and enjoy close personal relationships; finding and pursuing realizable positive ideals; aiming at wisdom rather than knowledge; and paying attention to our subjective world, both mental and moral.

On the whole, philosophy in the Chinese tradition concentrates more on such problems of life than does the western tradition; like literature, it is less specialized, more widely accessible, and bears more directly on our everyday concerns. Probably with these positive characteristics in mind, Professor Fung Yu-lan once told me that those who know both western and Chinese music prefer the former, but those who know both western and Chinese philosophy prefer the latter. At the same time, Chinese philosophy is more ambiguous, less precise, and less systematic; its teachings, to be effective, have to be complemented by certain external forces.

The relation between philosophy and its practical relevance is complex. The source of the fundamental tension between relevance and plausibility, between ideology and philosophy, is the need to judge and decide in the face of insufficient knowledge. It is hard enough to choose among alternative beliefs for use in local decision making. To judge objectively the value of a theory as a global guide to action is beyond the power of most of us. And history has taught us to be skeptical about grand theories.

The influence of a doctrine works at the level of intersubjective agreement in wish and belief. If a group shares certain beliefs and wishes over a certain historical period and if the program of action of a doctrine that endorses these beliefs addresses these wishes, the doctrine can serve as a dynamic force for the group. But the ideal of any theoretical pursuit also includes the quest for truth, to be tested by fact. In particular, it includes a component of universality which calls for intersubjective agreement beyond a particular group and historical period. This distinction between limited and universal applicability may be seen as one of the observable effects of the difference between ideology and philosophy, between influence and knowledge. If, however, a doctrine makes explicit its restriction to the concerns of a certain kind of society at a certain historical period, it can combine knowledge with influence in an attractive way. For example, the theory of justice, as it has been developed by John Rawls, seems to be a good example of choosing a fundamental, if restricted, problem and studying it impartially.

A good way to deal with a problem that we find too hard to solve is to break it into parts and deal with each part separately. In philosophy, there are many different ways of doing this, resulting in a number of parts which are commonly called "philosophical problems." Given the central concern of philosophy with the whole of life and the world and the restriction of its activity to thought rather than action in the ordinary sense, these problems tend to be remote from our everyday practical interests. This remoteness makes it harder to find the right questions to ask; and so the formulation of philosophical problems and the explanation of their relevance to practical concerns, which motivates our efforts to solve them, has become a substantive, integral part of the study of philosophy—distinguishing it from other disciplines.

Chapter 4
The Conversations and Their Background

In presenting these conversations, you should pay attention to three principles: (1) deal only with certain points; (2) separate out the important and the new; and (3) pay attention to connections.
Gödel, 5 February 1976

Know then thyself, presume not God to scan: The proper study of mankind is Man.
Alexander Pope, "The Rape of the Lock"

The conversations between Gödel and me touched on many aspects of philosophy. Given our different worldviews, based on our differences in knowledge and experience, I was not always able to appreciate the grounds or even the content, of some of his strong convictions. We did, however, share an interest in and a familiarity with issues in the foundations of mathematics. It is therefore not surprising that our discussions in this area were most extensive and so can serve as a point of reference for interpreting and understanding his other observations, which I often find cryptic and abrupt.

In this chapter I summarize my contacts with Gödel and present some of his more or less scattered observations on a variety of issues. In order to prepare a more or less coherent report of what Gödel said to me, I have split up our actual conversations into about five hundred segments, some of which contain disparate parts. These fragments form the basis of my reconstruction in this book. Since I do not have a verbatim record of Gödel's own words, there are bound to be misrepresentations. I have left out some segments that are overly technical or hard to interpret and inserted the remaining segments in different chapters according to their subject matter.

4.1 Actual and Imaginary Conversations

In November of 1971 Gödel talked about his Carnap paper and explained why he had decided not to have it published. As he saw it, he had shown in this paper that mathematics *is not* syntax of language, but he had not been able to give an account of what mathematics *is*: "The issue is not so much mathematics. You cannot understand what mathematics is without understanding knowledge in general; you cannot understand what knowledge is without understanding the world in general." He stated the matter more specifically in a letter to Schilpp, written at the beginning of 1959: he had decided not to publish his Carnap paper because he had failed to attain a complete elucidation of "the question of the objective reality of concepts and their relations."

I have encountered an analogous obstacle—a feeling of conceptual incompleteness—in working over and reflecting on my conversations with Gödel in the 1970s. I have reconstructed these conversations in several versions, based on very incomplete notes, in an effort (only partially successful) to interpret them and place them in perspective.

To convey some grasp of Gödel's general outlook and to indicate why I agree with him on some points but not on others, it seems necessary to articulate something of my own general outlook. Because there are major differences between our outlooks, my attempt to present the conversations in a public context involves me in a continual questioning about how either outlook would look from the standpoint of the other. This means that I have been contriving *imaginary conversations* between Gödel and me. Although much of one's philosophical thinking in general consists of silent or implicit discussions with other philosophers whose views one has absorbed, the talent to communicate such discussions as intelligible dialogues is rare.

Plato's dialogues are the standard model for imaginary philosophical conversations. There are also imaginary exchanges in many of Wittgenstein's later writings between a proponent of some familiar philosophical view and an interlocutor. And Leibniz adopts the dialogue form in his *New Essay* to contrast Locke's views with his own. These famous examples reveal the greater flexibility of dialogues over monologues in enabling the reader to weigh the comparative merits of alternative views and to see more directly the various interlinked components typically involved in a philosophical disagreement.

Actual conversations are usually less well structured than invented dialogues and are hard to reproduce for the benefit of others. They are haphazard and depend strongly on their contingent contexts (such as the shared background of the participants), which are hard to counterbalance by making explicit all the implicit assumptions. Accordingly, in order to reconstruct my extensive conversations with Gödel, I have had to describe much of their context, including not only knowledge presupposed by them but also certain written texts. An indication of the specific circumstances surrounding the conversations should clarify this point.

Most of my actual conversations with Gödel took place between October of 1971 and December of 1972, in regular sessions in his office; and from October of 1975 to June of 1976, usually on the telephone. They consisted primarily of my efforts to learn Gödel's views on various issues and of his comments on material written by me. Even when I did not understand what he said, or disagreed with it, I did my best to formulate definite responses to it, so as to get the points clear.

For the last decade or so I have thought a great deal about what he said to me, as well as about his relevant writings, published and unpublished. In the process I have come up with new questions and comments on what I take to be his thoughts. These new observations constitute a sort of imaginary conversation with him. His written and oral responses to various of my own writings are yet other kinds of conversations, as are his two letters of 1967 and 1968 (see Wang 1974a:8–11), which responded to a draft of my Skolem paper. From 1971 to 1972 he commented extensively on drafts of my *From Mathematics to Philosophy* (hereafter *MP*). From 1975 to 1976 he discussed with me several drafts of my paper "Large Sets." Following each of these "conversations," I wrote up his ideas in my own words, and we discussed the fragments I had thus produced.

In view of this complex background of interactions and preparations, I have concluded that the most promising way to clarify what Gödel said to me is to discuss it in the context of his work and what I take to be his general outlook. This is a formidable task. He told me he had not developed his own outlook far enough to present it systematically, but that he could apply it in commenting on my work. For the same reason he often chose to consider the views of other philosophers as a way of putting forward his own thoughts. I like to think of my extensive efforts to consider his work and his views as an attempt on my part to do the same sort of thing.

Now and then Gödel mentioned things of interest to me which seemed related to what we had discussed on some previous occasion. When I asked him why he had not said these things before, he would reply, "But you did not ask me." I interpret this response to imply that, since he had so many ideas on so many things, he preferred to limit his remarks to what was strictly relevant to the immediate context. One consequence of this was that he avoided topics and views on which he did not believe there was a shared interest, or even some empathy. In this respect he was not unlike Wittgenstein, who once said to Schick that he could talk only with someone who, so to speak, "held his hand."

I had been told that Gödel had declined Harvard's invitation to give the William James Lectures. When I asked him why, he gave me two reasons: (1) he was not willing to lecture to a hostile audience; (2) his ideas deserved further careful development but he had not developed them sufficiently to be able to answer objections. More than once he spoke of my *MP* as the "most unprejudiced" work in recent philosophy; I often wonder whether this judgment of his was unprejudiced and not just a result of his finding my views congenial, or at least unobjectionable. We probably did share a tentativeness in our views and a strong desire to understand and tolerate alternative positions, perhaps because we both, for different reasons, felt like outsiders in current philosophy. On the other hand, this attempt to be unprejudiced may also be a reason why *MP* is not a more effective work.

Gödel's desire to shun conflict also affected his published work. He would make great efforts to present his ideas in such a form that people with different perspectives could all appreciate them (in different ways). When he felt that his views would receive a largely unsympathetic response, he usually refrained from publishing them. More than once he said that the present age was not a good one for philosophy. This may explain, in part, why even though he had by his own admission expended more effort on philosophy than on mathematical logic or theoretical physics, he had published less in philosophy.

In several of our discussions he stressed the importance of theology for philosophy and, once or twice, offered to talk about Freud, saying that there is a way to present Freud's ideas more persuasively so that they can be seen to constitute a "theory." As I was not interested in either theology or Freud at the time, he did not expand on these subjects. (When I became interested in Freud in 1982, I regretted that I had not made use of my earlier opportunity to learn about Gödel's ideas on Freud.) Similarly, he would have been willing, had I taken the initiative, to discuss more extensively his theological views and his ideas on time and change. These circumstances are evidence of the fact that Gödel's conversations with me by no means covered the whole range of his philosophical interests.

4.2 *My Contacts with Gödel and His Work*

In 1939, as a college freshman in China, I audited Professor Wang Sianjun's course on symbolic logic and met Gödel's name for the first time, in connection with his completeness proof for predicate logic. In 1941, I came across a popular article in English in which Gödel's work was praised, and translated it into Chinese. But it was only in the spring of 1949, when I had an opportunity to teach Mathematics 281 at Harvard, that I decided to master Gödel's incompleteness theorems by teaching them.

At some stage I was struck by the apparently paradoxical situation connected with the relation between a system S (dealing with integers and sets of integers) and its (weak) second-order extension T. The consistency of S can be proved in T. Moreover, if S is consistent, it has, by the Löwenheim-Skolem theorem, a countable model and, therefore, a model dealing with integers only. Hence, since S also includes sets of integers, we seem to obtain a model of T in S, under the assumption that S is consistent. In other words, we get the conclusion that T is consistent if S is. Consequently, we seem to obtain in T a proof of its own consistency, contradicting Gödel's second theorem (unless T is inconsistent). Therefore, classical analysis would be inconsistent.

Primarily in order to seek clarification of this puzzling situation, I wrote to Gödel on 7 July 1949 asking to see him. I met with him for the first time a few days later in his large, rather bare office on the ground floor of Fuld Hall at Princeton. (I had spoken with him by telephone in February of that year.)

At this meeting I explained my line of thought to Gödel. He pointed out that there is an ambiguity in the notion of model in the above argument. But I did not grasp his idea and continued to try to formalize the steps involved. In January of 1950 I completed a manuscript on the subject and sent it to Paul Bernays and to Barkley Rosser for scrutiny. Bernays was convinced by the argument, but eventually Rosser noticed that the integers in S and T are defined differently. Only then did I realize that the difficulty was as Gödel had suggested. Since the components of the argument are of some interest, they were later published (Wang 1951a, 1951b, and 1952).

On the evening of 26 December 1951, I attended Gödel's Gibbs Lecture to the American Mathematical Society at Brown University. On this occasion he read his manuscript so rapidly that I could not capture much of what he was saying. He concluded the lecture by reading a fairly long quotation in French from Hermite.

In June 1952, when Gödel came to Harvard with his wife Adele to accept an honorary degree, I was present at W. V. Quine's dinner party for them. On this occasion, Adele was impressed by the friendliness of the colleagues gathered there and urged Gödel to move to Harvard. She also expressed an interest in collecting newspaper reports of the award ceremony, which I afterwards obtained and delivered to her.

In the 1950s I occasionally spoke with Gödel by telephone and saw him once or twice at his small office in Fuld Hall next to the library. It was probably in August of 1956 that Kreisel took me to the Gödels' home on Linden Lane for tea. I remember that we talked about Alan Turing's suicide. Gödel's first question was: "Was Turing married?" After receiving a negative answer to the question, he said, "Maybe Turing wanted but failed to get married." The next time I saw Gödel was, I believe, more than fifteen years later, on 13 October 1971, when we began our regular discussion sessions.

My close contact with Gödel began more or less accidentally. Around 1965 I was invited to write an introduction to Thoralf Skolem's collected papers in logic, and I decided to make a careful survey of all his work in logic. On 14 September 1967 I sent Gödel a draft of this essay and asked for his comments. The part of the paper that directly concerns Gödel's own work deals with the role of Skolem's work in arriving at the proof of the completeness of predicate logic, one of Gödel's major results.

Since about 1950 I had been struck by the fact that all the pieces in Gödel's proof had apparently been available earlier in the work of Skolem. In my draft I explained this fact and said that Gödel had discovered the theorem independently and given it an attractive treatment.

On 7 December 1967 Gödel replied, stating that his late response was due to his difficulty in finding the appropriate perspective for making clear the novelty of his own contribution. He was unhappy with my interpretation: "You say, in effect, that the completeness theorem is attributed to me only because of my attractive treatment. Perhaps it looks this way, if the situation is viewed from the present state of logic." He went on to distinguish between the mathematical and the philosophical sides of the matter and to speak more generally about the role his philosophical views played in his work in mathematical logic.

Gödel's point was that the result was rightly attributed to him because he was the one who had the "required epistemological attitude" to draw the conclusion, even though the step was, *mathematically*, "almost trivial." I was convinced by his explanation and revised my draft in the light of it. The revised version was later published in Skolem's *Selected Logical Works* (1970). In his letter, Gödel also contrasted his own and Skolem's epistemological views, with special reference to Skolem's 1929 monograph (reprinted in Skolem 1970:227–273).

4.2.1 Skolem's epistemological views were, in some sense, diametrically opposed to my own. For example, on p. 253, evidently because of the transfinite character of the completeness question, he tried to *eliminate* it, instead of answering it, using to this end a new definition of logical consequence, whose idea exactly was to *avoid* the concept of mathematical truth. Moreover he was a firm believer in set-theoretical relativism and in the sterility of transfinite reasoning for finitary questions (see p. 273).

On 19 December 1967 I wrote to Gödel to ask more questions, some of them philosophical questions of a more general character. He marked this letter "*wissenschaftlich interessant*," indicating that he was interested in discussing the questions it raised.

On 7 March 1968 Gödel sent me another letter both to elaborate and qualify some aspects of his previous letter and to reply to some questions directly relevant to it. The letter concludes with a promise: "Unfortunately I was very busy the past few weeks with rewriting one of my previous papers. But I hope to be able soon to answer the other questions raised in your letter of December 19." The rewriting he referred to was evidently his paper on finitary mathematics in Gödel 1990:271–280, 305–306, hereafter CW2).

In January of 1970 I planned to visit Gödel in Princeton but, through some confusion, the meeting did not materialize. On 25 May 1971 I wrote to ask permission to quote a portion of his letter of 7 December 1967 in what was to become my book From Mathematics to Philosophy (MP). Soon afterward, he had Stanley Tennenbaum give me his favorable response. On 9 July, he wrote to me directly: "As you probably have heard from Professor Tennenbaum already, I have no objection whatsoever to your publishing my letter of December 7, 1967. In fact, I am very much in favor of these things becoming generally known. I only have to require that you also publish my letter of March 7, 1968." This was followed by a list of detailed instructions on how the quotations were to be presented. (The main portions of the two letters are in MP:8–11, in accordance with his instructions.) Toward the end of the letter, he said: "I am sorry that, in consequence of my illness, our meeting, proposed for January 1970, never materialized. I shall be very glad to see you sometime this year at your convenience."

I then proposed that he comment on a draft of MP. After receiving it, he sent me a request "to mention to me the passages where my name occurs." I pointed to three parts which were extensively concerned with his published work: (1) Chapter VI, the concept of set; (2) Chapter II, section 3, mechanical procedures; and (3) Chapter X, section 6, mathematical arguments (on minds and machines).

He must have read these parts very closely. We did not begin to meet immediately, but once we started our regular sessions, he commented (for several months) extensively on these sections and contributed his own views to "enrich" (his word) them. He contributed (1) an alternative account of the axiom of replacement (p. 186) and five principles for setting up axioms of set theory (pp. 189–190); (2) a new section 3.1 (pp. 84–86); and (3) a new section 7 (pp. 324–326). In addition, because his two letters are included in the Introduction, he commented on that and contributed some additional observations (pp. 8–13).

Gödel preferred to present his contributions in the form of indirect quotations, although this did not prevent him from going through several stages of revision and deletion. Many of the alternative formulations, discussions, and longer explanations he provided were deleted in the published version. I restore some of them in several chapters of this book. In the following account, I organize my chronological review of the discussions around my notes of the various conversations.

Because I spent the summer of 1971 in the Boston area, my first meeting with Gödel did not take place until the autumn, on 13 October. He recalled that we had last met at his house more than ten years earlier. Between October of 1971 and December of 1972 we met quite regularly in his office next to the new library, usually on Wednesdays from 11:00 A.M. to between 1:00 and 1:30 P.M. According to my records, we had twenty such sessions (five in 1971 and fifteen in 1972). Gödel gave me permission to take notes. For the first session, because I had neglected to bring a pen or a pencil, he sharpened a pencil for me to use. Friends had suggested that I should bring a tape recorder, but at that time I did not find the idea congenial and did not propose it.

Usually both of us arrived early. While I stayed downstairs in the library Gödel went to get water to take his medicine. He usually brought slips of paper to remind himself of the things he wished to talk about, and I took down as much of the substance of his observations as I could. Often I attempted to reorganize the notes shortly afterward and prepared questions for the next session. Nonetheless, my notes remain in a very unsatisfactory state, and the best way to put them into useful form is not entirely clear.

In order to preserve as complete a record as possible, I have reconstructed as many of Gödel's observations as I could from each session. Even so, there are many observations that I am not able to accept or even understand; we undoubtedly gave different meanings to some of the crucial words, and some of his statements may be metaphorical or tentative in character. Unreliable as these records are, a sympathetic reader will, I believe, find them stimulating. They may also be useful to future scholars.

After a few meetings, Oskar Morgenstern called me to say that Gödel enjoyed these sessions very much; Oskar also asked me to try to learn more about the content of the large mass of Gödel's notes written in Gabelsberger shorthand (in German). When I asked Gödel about these notes, he said with a smile that they were only for his own use. On several occasions he proposed to let me see some of his unpublished manuscripts, but in each case he told me at the next session that he had examined the manuscript and found it not yet in a form fit to be shown. (Incidentally, at the beginning of one of the sessions, on a beautiful spring day in 1972, Morgenstern came with me to Gödel's office and took several photos of Gödel and me together.)

For the sessions up to June of 1972, the time was divided into three parts: general philosophical discussions, considerations of my manuscript, and Gödel's contributions (with repeated revisions). After the book manuscript was sent away in June, the last two parts were largely dropped. I then suggested to Gödel that he simply tell me about his philosophical views in a systematic manner. He replied, however, that he had not yet developed his philosophy to the point of being able to lecture on it. He could only apply it in more specific contexts, for instance, to make comments on views offered by others. I have been struck by this distinction that he drew and believe it is important. It may also, in part, explain why he never as far as I know prepared a systematic exposition of his philosophy.

After the summer of 1972 I spent several years trying to learn about Marxism. (At one point, my college teacher Yuting Shen urged me to drop this effort and concentrate on learning philosophy from Gödel. But I did not, at that time, follow his advice.) I also did some work related to computers in 1973–1974.

In the summer of 1975 I became a visitor (for about fifteen months) at the Institute for Advanced Study and resumed extensive contact with Gödel. Most of our conversations were by telephone because he had basically stopped going to his office. I sent him written versions of some parts of our discussions so that he could comment on them in our next telephone call. Some of my reports of his sayings in this book are, therefore in a form that he approved of; other parts he read but was not satisfied with, even though he recognized them as his own statements. (In these cases he seemed to expect, or hope, that I would come up with a clearer exposition than his own.) Still other parts were never seen by him. Therefore, he probably would not have wished to publish much of the material in the form I "quote," and it is quite possible that there are places where I am mistaken about what he actually said.

I have made no serious attempt to look into Gödel's *Nachlass*, which, on many points, may contain better presentations than mine or provide more extended contexts which may even prove some of my reports, cum interpretation, to be mistaken. In addition, compared with most people, Gödel seems to have made a much greater separation between what he was willing to say in conversation and what he was willing to publish— thinking in terms of both the quality of the content and the necessary qualifications and receptivity of his readers. So what I report in this book must be understood *cum grano salis*. While I find Gödel's strong preference for brevity admirable, I do not think it advisable for others to imitate his style in this respect. Particularly in this attempt to report his views fully, I do not strive for brevity, and often include several of Gödel's slightly different formulations of one point, in hopes of reducing the danger of gross misrepresentation.

4.3 Chronology and Miscellany: 1971 to 1972

Gödel's discussions with me included both scattered observations and continued elaborations of several aspects of his basic philosophical viewpoint. It is, not surprisingly, difficult to draw a sharp boundary between the two categories. I present in this section both the somewhat isolated observations and an outline of the chronological evolution of the more intricate considerations elaborated in separate other chapters.

As I said before, the early discussions were based on several parts of a book manuscript I later published as *From Mathematics to Philosophy* (*MP*). Clearly, it is more convenient to refer to the published text than to the original manuscript, and I have followed this practice.

13.10.71 Gödel began the discussions by considering my examination of the formalization or analysis or explication or understanding or perception of the intuitive concept of *mechanical procedure*—or of what we mean by the word *mechanical* or *computable* (compare *MP*:81–102). The examination was centered on Turing's definition of mechanical procedures. Gödel wanted to use this example to support his Platonism (in mathematics), that is, his belief that concepts are sharp and that we are capable of perceiving them more and more clearly. In addition, he began to argue for his thesis that mind or spirit is not (equivalent to) matter and is superior to computers.

These are two of the main topics of our continued discussions. What Gödel said about them will be reported in detail in Chapters 6 and 7. Here I present only the incidental observations.

With regard to my remarks on *speed functions* and *ordinal recursions* (*MP*:98), Gödel commented:

4.3.1 The speed and the ordinal approaches should come out the same. Faster and faster increasing functions help to define distinguished ordinal notations. Self-reference and "catching points" are relevant here.

Gödel was in favor of metaphysics and opposed to positivism. When I asked him about the work of Saul Kripke, he said:

4.3.2 Kripke is, though not a positivist, still doing linguistic philosophy.

27.10.71 In this session Gödel discussed my questions about the distinction between mechanical and material and about his statement that physics is finitary. he approved and extended my criticisms of positivism (compare *MP*:7), distinguished semantic from intensional paradoxes, talked about the axiom of replacement, and defended the appeal to intuition. He also made a number of incidental observations, mostly in answer to my questions.

4.3.3 Charles Hartshorne is an example of a contemporary metaphysician.

When I asked whether we can compare the evolution of mathematical concepts with the development of fictional characters in the mind of a novelist, Gödel observed:

4.3.4 Fictional characters are empirical. In contrast, the concept of set, for instance, is not obtained by abstraction from experience. Kant was right: our experience presupposes certain concepts, which do not come from experience. We arrive at such concepts—cause and effect, for instance—only on the occasion of experience. The parallel between this and coming from experience often leads to a wrong inference.

4.3.5 Category theory is built up for the purpose of proving set theory inadequate. It is more interested in feasible formulations of certain mathematical arguments which apparently use self-reference. Set theory approaches contradictions to get its strength.

A colleague of mine had suggested that I ask Gödel about his reaction to the "Polya-Weyl wager." This wager was set in 1918 (see *MP*:248); in Morris Schreiber's English translation, it goes as follows:

Between G. Polya and H. Weyl a bet is hereby made, according to the specifications below. Concerning both the following theorems of contemporary mathematics

(1) Every bounded set of numbers has a least upper bound.

(2) Every infinite set of numbers has a countable subset.

Weyl prophesies:

A. Within 20 years (that is, by the end of 1937), Polya himself, or a majority of the leading mathematicians, will admit that the concepts of number, set, and countability, which are involved in these theorems and upon which we today commonly depend, are completely vague; and that there is no more use in asking after the truth or falsity of there theorems in their currently accepted sense than there is in considering the truth of the main assertions of Hegel's physics.
B. It will be recognized by Polya himself, or by a majority of the leading mathematicians, that, in any wording, theorems (1) and (2) are false, according to any rationally possible clear interpretation (either distinct such interpretations will be under discussion, or agreement will already have been reached); or that if it comes to pass within the allotted time than a clear interpretation of these theorems in found such that at least one of them is true, then there will have been a creative achievement through which the foundation of mathematics will have taken a new and original turn, and the concepts of number and set will have acquired meanings which we today cannot imagine.

Weyl wins if the prophecy is fulfilled; otherwise, Polya wins. If at the end of the allotted time they cannot agree who has won, then the professors of mathematics (excluding the bettors) at the E.T.H and at the Universities of Zurich, Göttingen, and Berlin, will be called to sit in judgement; which judgement is to be reached by majority; and in case of a tie, the bet is to be regarded as undecided.

The losing party takes it upon himself to publish, in the *Jahresberichten der Deutschen Mathematiker-Vereinigung*, at his own expense, the conditions of the bet, and the fact that he lost.

Zurich, February 9, 1918.
[H. Weyl]   [G. Polya]
The consummation of the bet is hereby attested:
Zurich, February 9, 1918.
(Witnesses)

When the bet was called in 1940, everyone, with Gödel as the sole exception, declared Polya the winner. Weyl's prophesy was not fulfilled. Gödel explained his dissenting vote, with the qualification that Weyl had overstated the implied position:

4.3.6   I take the issue to be: Whether in 1938 a leading mathematician would think that the concept of set can be made sufficiently clear, not [whether he or she would think] that the concept of set is an adequate foundation of mathematics. I believe that mathematicians are wavering between the two points of view on the issue and, therefore, very few of them have a strong opinion one way or the other.

10.11.71   Gödel continued the discussion on minds and machines, on the perception of concepts, and on the epistemology of set theory. He also began to talk about phenomenology.

24.11.71   Gödel continued with comments on the draft of the introduction to MP. He said more about Husserl and talked about the nature of logic, the paradoxes introspection, and the relation of language to philosophy.

Gödel told me that Oskar Morgenstern wanted a copy of my draft of From Mathematics to Philosophy. I later sent Morgenstern a copy, and he called me on 6 December and 13 December to tell me several things: Gödel enjoyed his discussions with me; Gödel and he were old friends from Vienna who saw each other often; Gödel had a great deal of philosophical writings in a German shorthand; and Gödel had an English translation of his Bernays paper with a long new footnote.

6.12.71   In reply to a question of mine, Gödel talked about his views on the nature of logic. He discussed Kant and Husserl, his own rationalistic optimism, and some differences between minds and machines.

In reply to my question about his shorthand notes, Gödel said:

4.3.7   They are for my own use only and not for circulation; they are like Wittgenstein's Zettel.

At the end of the session we agreed to meet again on 20 December. On the evening of 19 December, however, Gödel telephoned me to postpone the meeting to 5 January.

5.1.72   Gödel talked about Husserl, set theory, positivism and objectivism, the concept of creation, and the philosophical implications of his inexhaustibility theorems. In addition, he commented on my incidental question: whether model theory has some broader philosophical interest:

4.3.8   We have to consider for this purpose a general theory of representations in mathematics, a complete representation of some category, such as finite groups by matrices, or Boolean algebras. Representations are very important mathematically from the point of [view of] solving problems. For example, whether a theorem follows from the axioms in number theory or analysis is a question of the representation of all models of the axioms. If we get the representation of all their models, we can decide derivability by models. Beginning with a given axiom system, we can also add new axioms. More systematic methods [of adding axioms] than those available so far will be found in this way [by finding the representation of all models?]. From the standpoint of idealistic philosophy, such representations are very important. For instance, Hegel began with the opposition of something and nothing. [I wonder whether Gödel had in mind the idea of beginning with something and nothing as the extreme cases of representations of a tautology and a contradiction, from which we get other systems by adding and taking away axioms.]

4.3.9   The axioms correspond to the concepts, and the models which satisfy them correspond to the objects. The representations give the relation between concepts and objects. For Spinoza the connection of things are the connections of ideas. Two representations of the same thing are conformal. For example, we have a correlation in the geometry of 3-space between points and planes. They are so related that we can take points as objects and planes as concepts, or the other way round. We have here a general proportionality of the membership relation (the concept) and the sets (the objects). The original difference is that concepts are abstract and objects are concrete. In the case of set theory, both the membership relation and the sets are abstract, but sets are more concrete. Numbers appear less concrete than sets. They have different representations [by sets] and are what is common to all representations. But we operate with numbers in concrete ways: [for example, we add or multiply by thinking of] a collection of two indeterminate things. With large numbers we use idealization and extrapolation.

19.1.72   Gödel mainly commented on the draft of the introduction to *MP*. The two substantive questions he raised (to be discussed in Chapters 5 and 8) have to do with positivism: its relation to the special theory of relativity and to Hilbert's proposed proof of the continuum hypothesis. He also commented on "Wittgenstein's two philosophies" (*MP*:13; discussed in Chapter 5).

I asked Gödel to name some recent philosophers whom he found congenial. In reply, he said:

4.3.10   William Henry Sheldon at Yale, who was still alive a few years back, C. Hartshorne, and Josiah Royce. But the followers of Sheldon are not so good; they tend to be more positivistic. Sheldon wanted to revive idealistic philosophy. Hartshorne is in the tradition of the scholastics; he must add what has been done by the followers of Leibniz.

I then asked him about Brand Blanshard and A. N. Whitehead, and he said:

4.3.11   Blanshard is not as good as Sheldon, being more positivistic; Whitehead's theories are far-fetched and too complicated.

Gödel commented on my discussion of the "big book" idea (*MP*:357–358). (This idea had been suggested by Wittgenstein in his lecture on ethics.) In connection with my phrase "the peculiar place of ethics relative to our possible knowledge," Gödel stressed that something has value *for somebody*. He said that "The line between value and fact is not sharp" does not follow form "Determining basic aspirations would seem to relate facts to values."

Gödel had recommended Husserl's *Ideas* to me, and I tried to read it. Not being sufficiently motivated, I found it too long-winded. Gödel thought that the difficult style was deliberate—in order to prevent the reader from getting the illusion of understanding the text.

2.2.72   This session was devoted to set theory, Jacques Herbrand's definitions of computable functions, and Hilbert's ideas on the continuum hypothesis. At the end of the session Gödel said we would meet again in three, rather than two weeks.

I asked about Gödel's open question on Herbrand's second definition of recursiveness (see Gödel 1986:368, n. 34 and *MP*:87–88). In reply he said:

4.3.12   We should distinguish intuitionistic general recursiveness (R), intuitionistic computability (C), and intuitionistic computability from some finite set of equations (F). R is included in F, and F is included in C. The open question is whether R is identical with F. A slightly more general question is whether R is identical with C.

About this time Gödel received an invitation from the Rockefeller University to accept an honorary doctorate in June. He asked me to send him some information about the university. I proposed to send him, in addition, some material about Wittgenstein's later work. The letter I sent him on 9 February illustrates the pattern of our communication between sessions:

After our meeting on February 2, I have sent you some published information about this university and also a copy of Moore's report on Wittgenstein's lectures of 1930–1933.

I have further revised the chapter on sets and the section on mechanical procedures. I enclose herewith a set of these revisions. I feel particularly uncertain about the revisions made on the material about sets. They may easily contain inaccuracies and mistakes. I have tried to indicate on the covering sheet the places which contain references to you, as well as the places where I feel insecure.

Within the next few days, I hope to return to the revision of the introduction. Looking forward to the meeting on February 23.

23.2.72   Gödel talked about the axioms of set theory and the coincidence of formal systems with many-valued Turing machines. Much of the session was devoted to religion, his rationalistic optimism, and some personal items about himself.

He began the session by asking me about religion in China after 1949. There is no record of my replies in my notes. (Looking back with hindsight to the years from 1949 to 1972, I now think that, for the majority of the Chinese population in those days, Maoism was very much like a fundamentalist religion.) Gödel then went on to express some of his ideas about the afterlife and rationalistic optimism.

Gödel also mentioned various facts about his personal life. His wife was much older than he. They had made some extensions to their house. His brother was a radiologist. Einstein and Morgenstern served as witnesses for his application for American citizenship, for which he had studied how the Indians came to America.

The next session came three—rather than two—weeks later.

15.3.72 Gödel talked mainly about Husserl and his relation to Kant. In addition he made some general observations.

4.3.13 See 6.3.16.

To my observation that Marxist philosophy is thought to reveal certain gross facts about human nature (*MP*:2), Gödel said that it has influenced human nature [presumably rather than described it faithfully].

In my draft I had objected to Husserl on the ground that philosophy as a superscience is not feasible in the foreseeable future. Gödel, however, demurred:

4.3.14 It is not appropriate to say that philosophy as rigorous science is not realizable in the foreseeable future. Time is not the main fact [factor]; it can happen anytime when the right idea appears.

The next session was scheduled for 29 March, but on 28 March Gödel telephoned to postpone it for one week.

5.4.72 Gödel and I agreed that he prefers Husserl and I prefer Kant. He then expressed some atypically vehement objections to Wittgenstein's views. (See Chapter 5 below.) (I now realize that his unrestrained criticism was occasioned by a letter of 17 January 1972 from Menger asking Gödel to evaluate Wittgenstein's remarks on his famous theorem.) He continued with some observations on the nature of philosophical thinking (see 9.2.4).

Gödel telephoned me on 7 April to suggest a number of changes to my manuscript, chiefly revisions in the versions I had worked out for some of the paragraphs attributed to him.

19.4.72 Gödel offered detailed comments on the section on mechanical procedures (*MP*:81–99). In addition, he made several fragmentary remarks related to Einstein's theory of relativity and quoted Josiah Royce as saying that reason means communication with the divine mind.

3.5.72 This session was largely devoted to detailed comments on the chapter about the concept of set (*MP*:187–209).

By this time Gödel had decided to accept the honorary doctorate from Rockefeller, in a ceremony scheduled for 1 June. He began the session by asking me to get exact details about the convocation. He then raised the question of copyright in reference to his explicit contributions to *MP*. The idea was that he would have the right to republish them although, he added, he had no present intention of doing so. (This request was afterwards accepted by the publisher.)

Gödel commented on the question of *determining* arbitrary sets (*MP*:197). For him, completeness means that every consistent set exists. For him, arbitrary sets are determined: it is not a question of determination. The most general concept of arbitrary set is also a determination for him. "Arbitrary" in this case can go together with "precise".

In my draft I had spoken of "errors coming from approximating the intuitive concept of largeness." Gödel said that (1) only approximating is not a serious source of error, and that (2) a pre-set-theoretical concept may be wrong, an example being the belief that a proper subset is always smaller. He compared the constructible sets with nonstandard models in which we can have the axiom "All sets are finite" even though infinite sets occur. The question of whether measurable cardinals occur in the universe of constructible sets has more to do with nonstandard models than with the question of mere largeness.

Gödel talked more about the relation between axioms of infinity and the constructible universe (*MP*:204). What is justified in this is: if you call all ordinals constructible, it is really artificial. Later on it turned out that only a countable section of ordinals matters in what counts in the constructible. He then outlined a proof of this result and observed that every subset [of the countable model] is definable. Preliminary concepts such as that of constructible sets are necessary to arrive at the natural concept, such as that of set.

In regard to counterintuitive, unlikely, implausible, or unreasonable consequences of the continuum hypothesis, Gödel referred to the consequence he had listed as point 3 (Gödel 1990:264) or point 4 (ibid.:186) as the most unreasonable. He mentioned the example of squaring the circle by ruler and compass in connection with my suggestion that maybe no plausible axioms can decide the continuum hypothesis (ibid.:198).

Gödel said that two more sessions would be devoted to my manuscript and that he would complete his revisions within four weeks. The next meeting was scheduled for 17 May, but on 16 May Gödel called to postpone it until 24 May.

24.5.72   Gödel made several comments on the preface and introduction of *MP*. (Originally the book was to be entitled *Knowledge and Logic*. I had decided before this session to rename it *From Mathematics to Philosophy*.)

Gödel asked some questions about the forthcoming ceremony for his honorary degree. Would he sit or stand while the citation was read? [Sit.] Would he have to make a speech? [No.] Would he be the first or the second of the two recipients? [Second.] He preferred to be the second.

In my draft I had used the term *structural factualism*. Gödel suggested that, in view of the emphasis on *substantial facts*, it was more appropriate to say *substantial factualism*.

In my draft I had urged paying attention also to "facts of intention" and "intentional objects." Gödel commented that one has to cultivate the capacity for introspection, *Empfindung* (as feeling or perception), and conceptual thinking. He distinguished the syntactical (or formalistic) from the constructive by pointing out that neither Kronecker nor Brouwer (nor Karl Menger) was interested in the syntactical.

On 1 June Gödel traveled from Princeton to the Rockefeller University to receive his honorary doctorate. I offered to fetch him at the train station, but he protested that he knew perfectly well how to get about in New York City.

14.6.72 Gödel made some additional observations on the introduction. He described the honorary-degree ceremony and noted that there had been no religious service and no publicity related to it.

On my idea of "Newtonian worlds" (*MP*:26), he said that it is too much to claim that Newtonian physics is forced on us like arithmetic. He agreed that the attitude in traditional mathematics was more inclined to the constructive (ibid.:27). He stressed that logic is not on the same plane as other knowledge (as a comment on p. 28). In reference to my plea to "correct the all too human tendency to assimilate differences" in philosophy (ibid.:6), he said that he favored assimilation.

On 20 June I talked with Gödel by telephone, and a short time later I went away for about seven weeks. When I returned to New York, we agreed to resume the sessions on 9 August. On 7 August he tried unsuccessfully to reach me to postpone the meeting.

9.8.72 This was an abbreviated session. Gödel remarked on the elegant printing of the postcard I had sent him from China. We discussed his question on religions in China and the relation between China and Russia. I took no notes, but remember that we disagreed both on what we took to be the facts and on the conclusions we drew from them.

13.9.72 Gödel talked about various things, including the concept of concept and the concept of absolute proof, evidence, Ideas (in the Kantian sense), fallibility, and his rationalistic optimism. He made a number of scattered observations about the Vietnam war, the American bombing, China, Russia, Thieu, Hanoi, fascism, the protests, communism, and so on. Among other things, he said that Russia had delivered a lot of oil to China and that Hanoi had secretly helped the Thieu government.

Gödel also mentioned his Gibbs lecture and his paper on Kant and relativity theory. The former is a lively presentation: about half of it considers Platonism and "actually proves that Platonism is correct," mentioning only in passing the disjunction that either mind is superior to all computers or there are number-theoretical questions undecidable by the mind. The latter article deals with Kant's transcendental aesthetic. He promised to show me one of the two papers soon.

Gödel asked: "Isn't it strange that the great philosophers of twenty years ago—Ducasse, Sheldon, Blanshard, Hartshorne—have no successors?" [He recommended, in these philosophers and in philosophers generally, the audacity to] "generalize things without any inhibition."

4.10.72 Gödel talked about Hegel's logic and about "bions" (see Chapter 9). He said that he was not yet ready to show me either his Kant paper or his Gibbs lecture. He divided the population into two classes, workers and intellectuals:

4.3.15 The rulers find it hard to manipulate the population: so they use materialism to manipulate the intellectuals and use religion to manipulate the workers. Before the communists can conquer the world, they will have to have some rational religion. The present ideal is not a sufficiently strong motive. Can't reform the world with a wrong philosophy. The founders of science were not atheists or materialists. Materialists began to appear only in the second half of the eighteenth century.

I brought up the Chinese teaching of three kinds of immortality based on moral or practical or intellectual achievements. Gödel said that these can provide only much weaker motives than religion. He then mentioned the religion of Spinoza and Einstein, which posits a desirable state of unity with nature as God and makes one unafraid of death. He also mentioned Nirvana and nonexistence.

18.10.72 Gödel made observations (to be considered later) on Wittgenstein, the relation between logic and philosophy, with special reference to Husserl and Hegel, and the intensional (in contrast to the semantic) paradoxes. At the end of this session Gödel and I agreed that at the next session we would discuss Husserl's 1910 essay "Philosophy as Rigorous Science."

8.11.72 Apart from making a number of comments on the English translation of Husserl's essay, Gödel devoted this session to expounding his own philosophical views (to be discussed in Chapter 9.)

The text for discussion was the English translation of Husserl's essay in *Phenomenology and the Crisis of Philosophy* (Lauer 1965). Gödel began by observing that the translation is, on the whole, good.

29.11.72 Gödel discussed explicitness and the axiomatic method, Carnap and Wittgenstein, his own working hypothesis, strict ethics, and the infinitude of integers.

4.3.16 Hartshorne has no idea of mathematical logic, and his ontological argument is wrong. This is an example of the negative effect of not knowing logic. Ninety percent of the intellectuals think that religion is terribly harmful; metaphysicians also want to conceal religious truth. The discovery of metaphysical truth will benefit mankind.

15.12.72 Apart from some general remarks at the beginning of the session, Gödel devoted the time to hinting at some of his basic philosophical ideas: on absolute knowledge and the Newtonian scheme, Husserl and the concept of time, monadology, the theory of concepts, and Platonism.

He also talked about the contract for the book [*MP*] and suggested that I consult a lawyer about it. [I did not do so.] He found it inexplicable that, without a declaration of war, Haiphong city and harbor had been destroyed by U.S. bombing. He believed that Hanoi supported Thieu rather than Ming. He found it difficult to believe that Lin Biao had tried to kill Mao. He wished to determine whether China or Russia was more rational and asked me to find a book in English on the Russian condition that took a neutral position.

Gödel said: "Russia has come to the conclusion that one should make use of the bad capitalist mode of competition and its motives too, such as employing material rewards legally." He believed that there are two philosophies in Russia, one exoteric and one esoteric. The esoteric philosophy is a unique system from which all true consequences are derived. Karl Michelet had, he said, attempted this with an improved version of Hegel's philosophy.

The session on 15 December 1972 was the last of the regularly scheduled sessions between Gödel and me. For the next two-and-a-half years I was occupied with other things and spoke with Gödel only occasionally by telephone. I have no record of these conversations and can now remember only a few scattered occasions.

After my visit to China in the summer of 1972, I had become interested in Marxism and, derivatively, in Hegel's philosophy. In September 1972 I was invited to present a paper at a conference on western and eastern logic, to take place in June of 1973 at the University of Hawaii. I decided to write an essay "Concerning the Materialist Dialectic," with the intention of forcing myself to be explicit about some of my vague and superficial impressions of the subject. I worked on the essay from the autumn of 1972 on and presented it on 29 June 1973. After some further revisions, the paper was published in *Philosophy East and West* in 1974.

Starting in July of 1973 I worked for a year on computer-related topics at the IBM Research Laboratories. On 3 November 1973 Gödel asked me what I was working on and I said "character recognition." He then said that he too was interested in that problem. I felt sure that there was a misunderstanding and explained that I was merely trying to see how computers can be made to recognize the characters of the Chinese written language. He then dropped the topic.

On the same occasion Gödel observed that imperialism benefits only a small privileged class in an imperialist country. Napoleon, he said, stood for an idea, whereas Hitler was defensive. In addition, he made some observations on knowledge, China, and Russia, the content of which I unfortunately no longer remember.

4.4 Continuation: 1975 to 1977

In 1975 I was asked to speak on the concept of set at the International Congress on Logic and the Methodology of Science, held in London, Ontario, that summer. I read a paper on "Large Sets," which was published, after revision, in 1977. Meanwhile, Gödel had arranged for me to be a visitor at the Institute for Advanced Study for the year beginning in July of 1975 and to occupy a house on Einstein Drive. That autumn I resumed my discussions with Gödel, using the revision of my talk on large sets as the initial frame of reference. Up to January of 1976, the discussions centered largely on objectivism with regard to sets and concepts (mostly reported in Chapter 8).

By this time Gödel had largely ceased to go to his study at the Institute, so our discussions were held sporadically and by telephone. I also kept less careful records than I had for our regular sessions. I include in this chapter only those of Gödel's observations which I find hard to classify under the main topics considered elsewhere in this book.

19.10.75 Gödel spoke about secret theories. As an example, he conjectured that there is a secret philosophy in Russia which is fruitful for doing science and mathematics, but that the general principles of this philosophy are kept secret.

25.10.75 Gödel said that he disliked the whole field of set theory in its present state: the task was to create a certain plausibility. (I take him to mean that there was too much technical mathematical work, not enough philosophical or conceptual thinking.) He was not in favor of the temporal or the fluid. He found the talk about *possible* sets objectionable only because of their fluidity; he would not mind if they were fixed.

9.11.75 Gödel told me he valued formal analogies and gave as an example the analogy between Euclidean space and an electric circuit. He said that falling in love at first sight is not attractive because it is far-fetched and unclear.

I reproduce below some of the general observations Gödel made between 16 November and 7 December 1975.

4.4.1 Sets are the limiting case of objects. All objects are in space or related to space. Sets play for mathematics the same role as physical objects for physics. The laws of nature are independent of nature. It is analytic that they do not change. If nature changes, they determine the change.

4.4.2 [On a common friend:] He is the only person who is a good mathematician, has broad interests, and [is] a criminal; power or money will straighten out his difficulties.

4.4.3 I like Islam: it is a consistent [or consequential] idea of religion and open-minded.

4.4.4 See 7.3.11.

4.4.5 I distrust the "history of historians." History is the greatest lie. Only the bare facts are true, the interactions are usually wrong [wrongly reported]. I am also not interested in history that discusses ideas. Many things are wrong [wrongly reported]. For instance, for Leibniz monads did not interact, but [Christian] Wolff and others attribute to him the view that they interact.

4.4.6   Mathematical objects are not so directly given [as physical objects]. They are something between the ideal world and the empirical world, a limiting case and abstract.

4.4.7   Concepts are there but not in any definite place. They are related each in the other and form the "conceptual space." Concepts are not the moving force of the world but may act on the mind in some way.

4.4.8   We have no way of knowing what the transcendental and the a priori are.

4.4.9   We have means of knowing something about the spiritual world. The meaning of the world would be part of what is given outside of sensations. Hegelian synthesis is concerned also with higher levels and higher forms of wish which are directly given outside of sensations.

4.4.10   For Kant, the mind is the transcendental ego which is subjective and separate from the outside world. [The] outer world is unknowable for Kant. But the unconscious accompanies sense perceptions: the ideas we form of sensations refer to the object itself.

4.4.11   Inborn [eingeboren] ideas are finished [as they are] but there may be something more general which comes from [the] outside psychologically but not physically. This third thing besides thinking and sense perception suggests something like an objective mind. This something does represent an aspect of, and may be a plan of, objective reality.

From early November to the middle of December 1975, I wrote four fragments reporting and discussing Gödel's ideas on sets and concepts. On 18 November I sent him thirteen pages entitled "Sets and Concepts" (fragment M); he commented carefully on this document from 24 November on. This was soon followed by fragments N (eight pages, see below) and C (six pages), reporting on what he said about concepts. Later I used fragment C as the basis for my lecture to the Association for Symbolic Logic in March of 1979. The most ambitious fragment, Q, consisted of eighteen pages and was entitled "Quotations from Gödel on Objectivism of Sets and Concepts," which I sent to him on 15 December 1975. Gödel liked M better than Q, on which he commented extensively on 4 January 1976.

As I said before, by the autumn of 1975 Gödel had largely ceased going to his study at the Institute. At the beginning of December, however, he suggested that I meet him there at four o'clock on Tuesday the 9th. Since we both arrived early in the midst of a heavy rain, the session began at quarter of four. It was largely devoted to the fragments M and C about sets and concepts which I had recently sent him. He also made a number of more general observations, probably indirect comments on another fragment, marked N, in which I tried to combine some of Gödel's ideas with my own current interest in Marxism.

4.4.12   The notion of existence is one of the primitive concepts with which we must begin as given. It is the clearest concept we have. Even "all," as studied in predicate logic, is less clear, since we don't have an overview of the whole world. We are here thinking of the weakest and the broadest sense of existence. For example, things which act are different from things which don't. They all have existence proper to them.

4.4.13   Existence: we know all about it, there is nothing concealed. The concept of existence helps us to form a good picture of reality. It is important for supporting a strong philosophical view and for being open-minded in reaching it.

In fragment N, I had tried to relate the considerations about sets and concepts to Gödel's suggestion that we could discern the meaning of the world in the gap between wish and fact. Apparently as a comment on this attempt, Gödel brought up what he called "the sociological" and said that concern with the sociological leads to religion and to power:

4.4.14   Power is a quality that enables one to reach one's goals. Generalities contain the laws which enable you to reach your goals. Yet a preoccupation with power distracts us from paying attention to what is at the foundation of the world, and it fights against the basis of rationality.

4.4.15   The world tends to deteriorate: the principle of entropy. Good things appear from time to time in single persons and events. But the general development tends to be negative. New extraordinary characters emerge to prevent the downward movement. Christianity was best at the beginning. Saints slow down the downward movement. In science, you may say, it is different. But progress occurs not in the sense of understanding the world, only in the sense of dominating the world, for which the means remains, once it is there. Also general knowledge, though not in the deeper sense of first principles, has moved upwards. Specifically, philosophy tends to go down.

4.4.16   The view that existence is useful but not true is widely held, not only in mathematics but also in physics, where it takes the form of regarding only the directly observable [by sense perception] as what exists. This is a prejudice of the time. The psychology behind it is not the implicit association of existence with time, action, and so on. Rather the association is with the phenomenon that consistent but wrong assumptions are useful sometimes. Falsity is in itself something evil but often serves as a tool for finding truth. Unlike objectivism, however, the false assumptions are useful only temporarily and intermediately.

Gödel was in the Princeton Hospital for several days in the beginning of April of 1976. From then on extended theoretical discussions virtually stopped. In June of 1976 he began to talk about his personal problems and told me a good deal about his intellectual development. (I report these observations in Chapters 1 and 2).

On 19 April 1976 he talked about the circumstances surrounding his communication to several individuals, in early 1970, of a manuscript entitled "Some Considerations Leading to the Probable Conclusion that the True Power of the Continuum is Aleph-two." This paper contained serious mistakes (see Gödel 1990:173–175 and Gödel 1995):

4.4.17 Taking certain pills for three months had damaged my mathematical and philosophical abilities. When I wrote the paper I was under the illusion that my ability had been restored. Can't expect wrong sayings from one of the greatest logicians. The pills had also affected my practical ability in everyday behaviors and, for a period, I had done "things which were not so beautiful."

On 23 April 1976 Gödel told me he was going to Philadelphia for a checkup on Monday [the 26th].

10.5.76 He mentioned that he had not been well the night before. Psychiatrists, he said, are prone to make mistakes in their calculations and overlook certain consequences. Antibiotics are bad for the heart. E. E. Kummer was bad in large calculations.

28.5.76 Gödel asked me whether Wittgenstein had lost his reason (when he was writing his remarks on the foundations of mathematics).

1.6.76 In reply to my question about his current work on the continuum problem, Gödel said that he had written up some material about the relation between the problem and some other propositions. Originally, he had thought he had settled the problem, but there was a lacuna in the proof. He still believed the proposition [his new axiom] to be true; even the continuum hypothesis may be true.

4.4.18 In principle, we can know all of mathematics. It is given to us in its entirety and does not change—unlike the Milky Way. That part of it of which we have a perfect view seems beautiful, suggesting harmony; that is, that all the parts fit together although we see fragments of them only. Inductive inference is not like mathematical reasoning: it is based on equality or uniformity. But mathematics is applied to the real world and has proved fruitful. This suggests that the mathematical and the empirical parts are in harmony and the real world is also beautiful. Otherwise mathematics would be just an ornament and the real world would be like an ugly body in beautiful clothing.

4.4.19 In my later years [apparently after 1943] I had merely "followed up with work in logic."

On 5 June 1976 Gödel spoke to me about "an interesting theological theory of history, analogous to antihistory":

4.4.20 There is a pair of sequences of four stages: (1) Judaic, (2) Babylonian, (3) Persian, (4) Greek; (a) early Christianity (Roman), (b) Middle Ages, (c) capitalism, (d) communism. There is a surprising analogy between the two sequences, even in dates, and so on. The ages in the second sequence are three times longer than those in the first. In addition, we can compare England and France with Persia, Germany with Greece. The origin of the idea is theological. But the similarity is much closer than can be expected. There are structural laws in the world which can't be explained causally. They have something to do with the initial condition of the world. I had not spent much time on these ideas about history.

Gödel said that he had neglected to publish things and went on to list some of his unpublished work:

4.4.21   I was always out for important results and found it better to think than to publish.

4.4.22   There is an intuitive picture of the whole thing about intuitionistic demonstrability. Take nonmathematical sequences (galaxies, etc.) and consider them only up to finite limits, only countable. The real world is the model. It is essential that no new ordinals arise. A double construction: (1) use empirical sequences and add independent new sets to continue them; (2) then construct a countable (or even nonstandard) model.

4.4.23   Einstein's religion is more abstract, like that of Spinoza and Indian philosophy. My own religion is more similar to the religion of the churches. Spinoza's God is less than a person. Mine is more than a person, because God can't be less than a person. He can play the role of a person. There are spirits which have no body but can communicate with and influence the world. They keep [themselves] in the background today and are not known. It was different in antiquity and in the Middle Ages, when there were miracles. Think about *déjà vu* and thought transference. The nuclear processes, unlike the chemical, are irrelevant to the brain.

Chapter 5
Philosophies and Philosophers

The possible worldviews [can be divided] into two groups [conceptions]: skepticism, materialism and positivism stand on one [the left] side; spiritualism, idealism and theology on the other [the right]. The truth lies in the middle, or consists in a combination of these two conceptions.
Gödel, ca. 1962

There are two fundamental difficulties in doing philosophy. In the first place, what we know is inadequate to the task of answering the questions we naturally and reasonable ask. It is hard to find the boundary between what we know and what we do not know, to take into consideration our partial knowledge in the relevant areas in an appropriate manner, and to fit all the different parts together into an organic whole. It is not even easy to find a good starting point. We can, however, view this task as a cooperative goal to which we can, perhaps, make a noteworthy contribution, whether by adhering only to what is clear or by offering a tentative broad survey of the world.

In the second place, philosophy aims to involve one's whole person. For example, Wittgenstein said to Drury in 1949: "It is impossible for me to say in my book [*Philosophical Investigations*] one word about all that music has meant in my life. How then can I hope to be understood?" Again, in the same conversation, Wittgenstein said: "I am not a religious man but I cannot help seeing every problem from a religious point of view" (in Rhees 1984:160, 79). One's temperament, upbringing, and experience condition one's style of thinking and one's attitude toward many issues in philosophy. For example, the attitudes of Gödel and of Wittgenstein toward the concrete and the abstract, the relation between science and philosophy, the place of science and everyday experience in philosophy, the nature and the value of metaphysics, and the importance of language for philosophy are all quite different. This example suggests some of the reasons why there are so many different philosophies.

Each of us has various emotional needs and is exposed to many different outlooks, pieces of knowledge and information, communities of ideas, human relations, and so on. To articulate a philosophy that does justice to all these factors is obviously a tremendously difficult task. Most of us do not succeed in attaining this impossible goal, nor do we even attempt it. Instead, we select one aspect or a few aspects of philosophy which we have encountered and absorbed, and we concentrate on doing justice to them.

As we know, there are many different philosophies and schools of philosophy. Indeed, there are different conceptions of what philosophy is and different things that people want—and believe that it is possible to get—from philosophy. These conceptions vary from culture to culture. They also change with time and with experience—both historically and personally.

Around 1933 Wittgenstein came upon a conception or method of philosophy which aims to counteract "the misleading effect of certain analogies." Although most people would view this task as no more than a subsidiary part of philosophy, Wittgenstein observed: "If, for example, we call our investigations 'philosophy,' this title, on the one hand, seems appropriate, on the other hand it certainly has misled people. (One might say that the subject we are dealing with is one of the heirs of the subject which used to be called 'philosophy.')" (Wittgenstein 1975:28). Those of us who are not satisfied with such a conception may still see this type of philosophy as a kind—different from the ordinary kind—of specialization within philosophy which is useful as an antidote and a reminder to discipline our speculation.

The more familiar kind of specialization divides a subject into different parts according to their subject matter. Within philosophy we typically have metaphysics, logic, moral philosophy, epistemology, political philosophy, philosophy of language, philosophy of mind, philosophy of science, philosophy of mathematics, philosophy of law, and so on. In addition, we have the history of philosophy—which can be subdivided according to periods, types of philosophy, individual philosophers, and so on. Specialists in one branch may either regard that branch as central to all of philosophy or choose it because it is well suited to their individual interests and abilities. Wittgenstein, for example, views the philosophy of language as central, and Gödel sees the philosophy of mathematics as the sure path to fundamental philosophy. In contrast, Rawls confines his attention to political philosophy but does not take it to be central to philosophy as a whole.

In his discussions with me, Gödel frequently commented, on the one hand, on the philosophies of Kant and Husserl, and, on the other hand, on positivism and empiricism, with special attention to the views of Carnap. He also made occasional observations on the views of Wittgenstein. It is clear to me that his sympathies were with Husserl and that he opposed the logical positivists, the leaders of whom had been his teachers in Vienna. His attitude toward Kant's philosophy is ambivalent: he studied it carefully and liked some of its ideas, but he disliked its overall perspective, for he saw it as opening the door to much bad philosophy.

My main purpose in this chapter is to report and discuss Gödel's observations on Kant, Husserl, Carnap, and Wittgenstein. Since, however, Gödel's oral remarks were fragmentary and since I may, in some cases, have recorded them incorrectly, I begin with a written text, apparently the text for a lecture he planned to give around 1963. This text provides a schema for classifying alternative philosophies and illustrates his distinctive approach and his sympathies in philosophy. One remarkable feature of Gödel's own work is his ability to achieve philosophically significant, precise results, combined with a tendency to begin with some solid facts—such as his own famous theorem and the success of physics or mathematical logic—and then to make uninhibited generalizations and analogies. At the same time, this forcefully affirmative attitude is moderated by an open-minded tolerance and a willingness to take into consideration the strength of views opposed to his own.

5.1 How Gödel Relates Philosophy to the Foundations of Mathematics

Around 1962 Gödel wrote in Gabelsberger shorthand a manuscript entitled "The Modern Development of the Foundations of Mathematics in the Light of Philosophy." It was found in his papers with a letter and an envelope from the American Philosophical Society dated 13.12.61. Gödel had marked it "*Vortrag*" (lecture). The letter from the society states that Gödel may wish, as a newly elected member (in April 1961), to follow the custom of giving a talk on a topic of his own choosing—in either April or November of 1963. Gödel probably wrote the manuscript with such a lecture in mind but decided not to deliver it.

In 1986 the text was transcribed by Cheryl Dawson and distributed to a few colleagues. Shortly afterward I made, for my own use, a crude English translation, which has since been corrected by Eckehart Köhler, John Dawson, and Charles Parsons. Both the transcribed text and the English translation are published in Gödel's *Collected Works* (*CW*3).

This wide-ranging text is of special interest because it illustrates how Gödel viewed the interaction between the philosophy of mathematics and philosophy as a whole. It puts at the center of philosophical conflicts the attitude of the philosopher—either optimism and apriorism on the one hand or pessimism and empiricism on the other—toward the power of reason to ascertain that there is, indeed, order in the universe. Since "mathematics, by its nature as an a priori science, always has, in and of itself, an inclination toward" order and universality, it is, Gödel believes, the stronghold of our optimism toward reason.

Gödel sees his own inexhaustibility theorem and the related quest for new axioms as evidence in favor of Husserl's belief in our capacity for *categorial intuitions*. He concludes by recommending Husserl's phenomenology—seen as a development of the core of Kantian philosophy—as the best approach to philosophy, to be combined with a new science of concepts which Gödel proposed in analogy to the spectacularly successful science of the modern world. Accordingly, we are led from the study of the foundations of mathematics, to a new fruitful outlook on philosophy, which promises to change our knowledge—and therewith our worldview—in a fundamental way. Let me now give a more extended summary of the text.

The text begins with a schema of alternative philosophical worldviews, using the "distance" from theology as a sort of coordinate system. In this schema, skepticism, materialism, and positivism stand on the "left" side; spiritualism, idealism, and theology stand on the "right" side. Roughly speaking, faith, order, and optimism increase as we move from the left (the "negative") to the right (the "positive"). "The development of philosophy since the Renaissance has, by and large, gone from right to left." In physics in particular, this leftward swing reached its peak with the now-prevalent interpretation of quantum theory.

Mathematics has always had an inclination toward the right. For instance, "the empirical theory of mathematics, such as the one set up by Mill, has not been well received." Indeed, mathematics has evolved into ever-higher abstractions and ever-greater clarity in its foundations. Since around the turn of the century, however, the antinomies of set theory have been seized upon as the pretext for a leftward upheaval—as the spirit of the time extends its dominance to mathematics. Yet the resulting skeptical view of mathematics goes against the nature of mathematics, which Hilbert tried to reconcile with the spirit of the time by the remarkable androgyne (*Zwitterding*) of his formalist program.

It turns out, however, that it is impossible to reconcile these two things in this manner. Gödel's own theorem shows that "it is impossible to carry out a proof of consistency merely by reflecting on the concrete combination of symbols, without introducing more abstract elements." One must, therefore, "either give up the old rightward aspects of mathematics or attempt to uphold them in contradiction to the spirit of the time."

It cannot be denied that in our own time great advances in many respects owe a great deal to precisely this leftward shift in philosophy and worldview. But Gödel believes that the correct attitude is to combine the leftward and the rightward directions. In mathematics, he recommends the path of cultivating (deepening) our knowledge of the abstract concepts themselves.

The way to do this, Gödel asserts, is through Husserl's phenomenology—a "technique that should bring forth in us a new state of consciousness in which we see distinctly the basic concepts." This approach takes our experience (including introspection) seriously; so it should be seen as part of a liberal empiricism.

In support of this approach, Gödel considers the intellectual development of a child, which he sees as being extended in adulthood in two directions. The extension of a child's experimentation with external objects and its own sensory and motor organs leads to science as we know it. An analogous extension of a child's increasing understanding of language and concepts is, in Gödel's view, the task of Husserl's phenomenology and may lead to something like a new science or philosophy (of the mind). Moreover, "even without applying a systematic and conscious procedure," new axioms become evident as we look for the axioms of mathematics, and our capacity to axiomatize may be seen as an example of movement in this direction.

This intuitive grasping of ever newer axioms agrees with the Kantian conception of mathematics. Indeed, the whole phenomenological method is, according to Gödel, a precise formulation of the core of Kantian thought. The idea of phenomenology—though "in not an entirely clear way"—is for Gödel the really important new thing in Kant's philosophy. It avoids "both the fatal leap of idealism into a new metaphysics as well as the positivistic rejection of every metaphysics.... But now, if the misunderstood Kant has already led to so much that is interesting, how much more can we expect from the correctly understood Kant?"

Before turning to a general discussion of Gödel's division of philosophy into the left and the right, I select a few passages from his text for comment.

5.1.1   Thus one would for example, say that apriorism belongs in principle on the right and empiricism on the left side. Furthermore, one sees also that optimism belongs in principle toward the right and pessimism toward the left. Moreover, materialism is inclined to regard the world as an unordered and therefore meaningless heap of atoms. In addition, death appears to it [materialism] to be final and complete annihilation, while, on the other hand, theology and idealism see sense, purpose, and reason in everything. Another example of a theory evidently on the right is that of objective law and objective esthetic values; whereas the interpretation of ethics and esthetics on the basis of custom, upbringing, and so on belongs toward the left.

Comment.   These observations help to clarify Gödel's distinction between views on the right and on the left. The problem is, of course, to look for reasonable combinations of them—as Gödel himself asserts later in the text.

5.1.2 Now one can of course by no means close one's eyes to the great advances
which our time exhibits in many respects, and one can with a certain justice make
plausible that these advances are due just to this leftward spirit in philosophy and
worldview. But, on the other hand, if one considers the matter in proper historical
perspective, one must say that the fruitfulness of materialism is based in part only
on the excesses and the wrong direction of the preceding rightward philosophy.
As far as the rightness and wrongness, or, respectively, truth and falsity, of these
two directions is concerned, the correct attitude appears to me to be that (the)
truth lies in the middle or in a combination of the two conceptions. Now, in the
case of mathematics, Hilbert had of course attempted just such a combination, but
one obviously too primitive and tending too strongly in one direction.

Comment. Gödel does not deny that the mechanical systems of combinations of symbols are more transparent than (say) set theory. But he
suggests that this is because these systems are set up using relatively simple abstract concepts, and that the task is to try to see less simple abstract
concepts more clearly as well. The combination he has in mind appears to
be a recognition of different degrees of certainty and clarity with a recommendation to look more closely at the evidence for different levels of
idealization in their distinctness and interrelations. His own sympathy is
clearly with the right in accepting the high levels of idealization. His idea
is a combination only in the sense of admitting, in favor of the left, that
we do have a firmer grasp of those abstract concepts which are involved
in the more concrete and mechanical situations. He denies, however, that
we can give an account of any reasonably adequate part of science in
"material terms." We are free, he says to stop at different levels of idealization; yet he believes that there is no good reason for stopping at or
before any one of the familiar levels, from small integers up to full set
theory (of course short of contradictions, which would in fact help to
reveal hidden distinctions).

5.1.3 In what manner, however, is it possible to extend our knowledge of those
abstract concepts, that is, to make these concepts themselves precise and to gain
comprehensive and secure insight about the fundamental relations that are present
among them, that is, the axioms that hold for them? The procedure must thus
consist, at least to a large extent, in a clarification of meaning that does not consist
in defining. Now in fact, there exists today the beginnings of a science which
claims to possess a systematic method for such a clarification of meaning, and that
is the phenomenology founded by Husserl. Here clarification of meaning consists
in concentrating more intensely on the concepts in question by directing our
attention in a certain way, namely, onto our own acts in the use of those concepts,
onto our powers in carrying out those acts, and so on. In so doing, one must keep
clearly in mind that this phenomenology is not a science in the same sense as the
other sciences. Rather it is (or in any case should be) a procedure or technique that
should bring forth in us a new state of consciousness in which we see distinctly
the basic concepts we use in our thought, or grasp other basic concepts, hitherto

unknown to us. I believe there is no reason at all to reject such a procedure as hopeless at the outset. Empiricists, of course, have the least reason of all to do so, for that would mean that their empiricism is, in truth, an apriorism with its sign reversed.

Comment.   Gödel seems to suggest (as an ideal) that we should aim to use the phenomenological method to discover the axioms for the primitive concepts of philosophy (and of more restricted fields). But I am not aware of any conspicuous successful examples of definite axioms arrived at in this manner. Neither the axiom of choice, the axiom of replacement, the "axiom" of constructibility, the "axiom" of determinacy, nor even Dedekind's axioms for arithmetic were obtained by going back to the ultimate acts and contents of our consciousness in the manner recommended by phenomenology (see Wang 1987a, section 7.3, hereafter *RG*). Nor is it clear to me how complete a Husserlian justification of (say) Dedekind's axioms can be found—although I regard this example as a fruitful test case for phenomenology. Gödel's belief (and perhaps Husserl's also) is probably that such radical introspections are possible and that only such introspections can render our quest systematic and our result secure. I have seen no persuasive argument, empirical or otherwise, for this possibility.

I can only guess what is meant by the sentence about empiricism. Husserl and others have spoken of phenomenology as a thoroughgoing empiricism. Empiricism would be an apriorism if it denied that additional attention to the acts and the contents of our consciousness would make a difference. If the mind were entirely blank, there would have to be a powerful mechanism associated with the mind to give us all we know on the basis of the data of experience. The mind, as we see from its observable operations, is both more and less than a camera or a mirror. In particular, to expect that neurophysiology will fully explain our knowledge would seem to require a highly competent internal mechanism. Maybe the "inverted sign (or direction)" refers to the contrast between the mind's contributing everything and its contributing nothing. In the latter case, we may speak of an "inverted apriorism" in the sense of taking it for granted that *all* the information comes from outside. In any case, since the concept of experience can and has been understood in so may ways, it seems necessary to look closely at what a specific form of *empiricism* understands by experience and how it deals with it. In particular, phenomenology may be said to be paying more rather than less attention to experience than other doctrines that go more familiarly by the name "empiricism."

5.1.4   But not only is there no objective reason for the rejection [of phenomenology], one can on the contrary even present reasons in its favor. If one considers the development of a child, one notices that it proceeds in two directions: on the one hand, it consists in experimenting with the objects of the external world and with its [own] sensory and motor organs; on the other hand, in coming to a better and better understanding of language, and that means, as soon as the child has gotten beyond the most primitive form of designation, of the basic concepts on which it [language] rests. With respect to the development in this second direction, one can justifiably say that the child passes through states of consciousness of various heights; for example, one can say that a higher state of consciousness is attained when the child first learns the use of words, and similarly at the moment when it for the first time understands a logical inference. Indeed, one may now view the whole development of empirical science as a systematic and conscious extension of what the child does when it develops in the first direction. The success of this procedure is, however, an astonishing thing, and is far greater than one would expect a priori: it leads after all to the great technological development of recent times. That makes it thus appear quite possible that a systematic and conscious advance in the second direction will also [lead to results that] far exceed the expectations one may have a priori.

Comment. Gödel sees a parallel between the two directions in child development and their extensions. The suggestion seems to be that phenomenology is to the second direction (the "mental" world) as empirical science is to the first (the material world). The first direction is not self-contained, since language and concepts are crucial to its systematic extension. The primary data of the second direction are the acts and contents of our consciousness, which are private and unstable. Moreover, they have acquired "hidden meanings" through childhood experiences and historical heritage, which are, to a large extent, no longer accessible.

Gödel speaks of systematic and conscious extensions. He implies that we have acquired, and applied in the development of empirical science, a systematic (and conscious) extension in the first direction, and he seems to assert that phenomenology promises a similar systematic procedure for extension in the second direction. But the "systematic" procedure of empirical science has evolved and is passed on more through praxis than through talk or abstract thinking. The development of phenomenology has been quite different: Husserl has said a good deal about his method, but there are few successful, relatively conclusive, and unambiguous applications of the method.

The phrase "systematic and conscious" has quite different meanings and functions as applied to the two directions. Husserl characterized the method used in the actual practice of empirical science as "naive" and recommended a different ("truly scientific") attitude. From this perspective, it is questionable whether the procedure of extensions along the first direction is either systematic or conscious. Indeed, I believe that much of the strength of scientific procedure is derived from its "impurity," that is, its inclusion of unconscious and unsystematic components. (A major obstacle to the development of artificial intelligence is precisely the problem of making these unconscious components explicit.)

It is possible to extract from Husserl's writing a plausible sense in which he is indeed striving for a systematic and conscious procedure in the second direction. But the distance between method and application is much greater in philosophy than it is in technology. The method becomes clear (or clearer) only when it is demonstrated in operation. It seems to me that neither Husserl nor Gödel has produced any convincing examples. In my opinion, the role of the unconscious presents a more fundamental obstacle than the occasional failure to fully communicate our conscious thoughts. Graham Wallas (1925) and Jacques Hadamard (1945) consider some aspects of this problem. Wallas in particular speaks of a period of "incubation" before reaching "illumination", in his consideration of Henri Poincaré's account of his discovery of a new theorem (p. 80). The unconscious or subconscious, it is supposed, was doing the work during the period of incubation, when mental acts and contents arose which were, almost by definition, largely unrecoverable. Even though the "illumination" reached in such cases can sometimes be "verified," the reason is, I believe, that the verification does not require the sort of radical rootedness that Husserl seems to demand.

It is, however, possible, and reasonable, to dissociate Gödel's suggestions from the more radical requirements and more comprehensive claims made by Husserl for his approach. Instead of questioning whether the actual impure procedures in empirical science can be said to be systematic and conscious, we may, on the contrary, accept them as a sort of model for systematic and conscious procedures. In other words, even while borrowing some of Husserl's ideas, we can leave room for adding more mixed and less pure considerations to take care of, for example, intersubjectivity and the external world. In addition, I see no reason why one should concentrate, as Gödel seems to suggest, on primitive concepts and the axioms for them. In the case of axioms, Dedekind's work on the natural numbers offers, in my opinion, a clearer model of conceptual analysis and a reliable starting point for further refinements.

Gödel's thoughts about child development are attractive quite apart from any strict adherence to Husserl's phenomenology. They can and should, I think, be seen as ideas directed at the task of founding a "science of the mind." Seen in this light, the ideas do not commit us to an exclusively phenomenological approach. Nor do they exclude appropriate attention to the role of the biological, historical, genetic, and social factors in our development and cognitive activity. Indeed, studies looking in such directions are not unfamiliar in the literature.

5.2 Some General Comments

Gödel's general schema of dividing worldviews into the right and the left is reminiscent of a familiar contrast introduced by William James at the beginning of his *Pragmatism* (1907:9–13). James identifies a person's philosophy with his or her "view of the universe" (or worldview). "The history of philosophy," he says, "is to a great extent that of a certain clash of human temperaments [between the] tender-minded [rationalist] and the tough-minded [empiricist]." Since temperament is not a recognized aspect of reason, a professional philosopher will urge only impersonal reasons for the (desired) conclusions. (F. H. Bradley once defined metaphysics as an attempt to give bad reasons for one's prejudices.) James characterizes the tender-minded person as rationalistic (going by principles), intellectualistic, idealistic, optimistic, religious, monistic, dogmatical, and a believer in free will; the tough-minded person as empiricist (going by facts), sensationalistic, materialistic, pessimistic, irreligious, pluralistic, skeptical, and fatalistic.

According to James, neither type of philosophy fully satisfies the needs of our nature, even though he himself favors empiricism. His own solution is *pragmatism*, as he understood it, a view which "can remain religious like the rationalisms, but at the same time, like the empiricisms, it can preserve the richest intimacy with facts" (1907:23). The "religion" James recommends is a "meliorism" that treats the "salvation of the world" as a possibility, which becomes more and more a probability as more agents do their "level best" (pp. 137, 139). This is a plausible and attractive belief, but it is not religion in the theological sense as, say, Gödel understands it.

There is also a problem with the range of what James takes to be facts. A familiar debate concerns whether to recognize, beyond empirical facts, also conceptual, and, in particular, mathematical facts. Terminology aside, it seems possible to modify the familiar criticisms of empiricism so as to show that pragmatism similarly fails to give an adequate account of mathematics as we know it, especially of its "useless parts," its autonomy, and its internal cohesiveness.

Like James, Gödel also asserts that "truth lies in the middle or in a combination of the two conceptions." His proposed solution appears to be Husserl's phenomenology, and he says nothing explicitly about its relation to religious concepts. Unlike James, who spells out his pragmatism, Gödel leaves his proposal in the state of a brief observation within the context of his essay. Elsewhere he suggests that Husserl's method may be applicable to metaphysical or religious concepts as well.

A close association of metaphysics with religion, by way of theology, has a long tradition. It began with the introduction of the world *metaphysics* to label Aristotle's work on First Philosophy, which may be seen as a mixture of theology and the philosophy of logic. Theology offers a path from the philosophy of knowledge to the philosophy of value. This is clear in the work of Aquinas. If it is possible to arrive at fundamental theological knowledge, including the existence of God, then the first principles of the philosophy of value are accessible to rational thinking. Gödel seems to me to believe that this is possible. He seems to believe that by using Husserl's method the program can be executed more convincingly than similar attempts by Plato and Leibniz.

In Chapter 3 I consider some of Gödel's tentative thoughts about religious metaphysics, which did not, I am sure, make much use of Husserl's method. His discussions with me were primarily concerned with Platonism or objectivism in mathematics, minds and machines, the concepts of set and concept, and the nature of logic—all of which I deal with in separate chapters. In addition, he made scattered observations on the views of a number of philosophers, notably Kant, Husserl, Wittgenstein, and Carnap.

From 1924 to 1939 Gödel was studying at the University of Vienna and, for much of that time, was closely associated with the principal members of the Vienna Circle, then the center of the school of logical positivism (RG:48–52). Gödel was familiar with their views, but did not find them congenial. He participated in the Circle's intensive study of Wittgenstein's Tractatus from the autumn of 1926 until the early months of 1928; but said afterwards that he had never studied Wittgenstein's work thoroughly—"only very superficially,"—and had not been influenced by it (RG:17, 19, 20).

In his correspondence and conversations with Carnap between 1931 and 1935 (RG:51–52), Gödel implicitly criticized Carnap's general philosophical viewpoint by pointing out the inadequacy of Carnap's definition of analytic truth. Not until the 1950s, however, did Gödel write an elaborate criticism of the philosophy of mathematics of Carnap, Hahn, and Schlick—in the six versions of his Carnap paper, "Is Mathematics Syntax of Language?" The spirit of this essay is similar to that of my own 1985 paper, "Two Commandments of Analytic Empiricism" (a slightly different version appears in Wang 1985a).

In February of 1959 Gödel wrote a letter to Schilpp, the editor of the volume that was to include the Carnap essay, to say that he was not satisfied with it and had, therefore, decided not to publish it. According to his own account, he began his study of Husserl in 1959. It seems to me that the two decisions may have been related. He had, he told me once, proved conclusively in this essay that mathematics *is not* syntax of language but said little about what mathematics *is*. At the time he probably felt that Husserl's work promised to yield convincing reasons for his own beliefs about what mathematics is.

It is, therefore, not surprising that, when he commented on various philosophers during his discussions with me, he had more to say about the views of Husserl than about the positivists or empiricists. Indeed, his own criticisms of the empiricists tend to be similar to Husserl's. I myself agree with these criticisms, as far as I am able to understand them. I am not, however, able to accept, or even evaluate, the strong positive theses on the power of reason favored by Gödel—such as Husserl's project of "philosophy as a rigorous science" and Gödel's own belief that "Philosophy as an exact theory should do for metaphysics as much as Newton did for physics" (in Wang 1974a, hereafter *MP*:85).

5.3 For Husserl—With Digressions on Kant

Available evidence indicates that from 1959 on Gödel studied Husserl's work carefully for a number of years. His library includes all of Husserl's major writings, many marked with underlinings and marginal comments, and accompanied by inserted pages written mostly in Gabelsberger shorthand. These comments are now being transcribed, and a selection of them will be published in a future volume of Gödel's *Collected Works*. In the 1960s he recommended to some logicians that they should study the sixth investigation in *Logical Investigations* for its treatment of *categorial intuition*. In his discussions with me in the 1970s he repeatedly urged me to study Husserl's later work.

Gödel told me that the most important of Husserl's published works are *Ideas* and *Cartesian Meditations* (the Paris lectures): "The latter is closest to real phenomenology—investigating how we arrive at the idea of self." According to Gödel, Husserl just provides a program to be carried out; his *Logical Investigations* is a better example of the execution of this program than is his later work, but it has no correct technique because it still adopts the "natural" attitude.

I once asked Gödel about Husserl's *Formal and Transcendental Logic*, because I thought it might be more accessible to me than some of the other books. Gödel said that "it is only programmatic: it is suggested that formal logic is objective and transcendental logic is subjective, but the transcendental part—which is meant to give justifications—is rudimentary." Gödel did not, I believe, much like *The Crisis of European Science*.

Before 1959 Gödel had studied Plato, Leibniz, and Kant with care; his sympathies were with Plato and Leibniz. Yet he felt he needed to take Kant's critique of Leibniz seriously and find a way to meet Kant's objections to rationalism. He was not satisfied with Kant's dualism or with his restriction of intuition to sense intuition, which ruled out the possibility of intellectual or categorial intuition. It seems likely that, in the process of working on his Carnap paper in the 1950s, Gödel had realized that his realism about the conceptual world called for a more solid foundation than he then possessed. At this juncture it was not surprising for him to turn to Husserl's phenomenology, which promises a general framework for justifying certain fundamental beliefs that Gödel shared: realism about the conceptual world, the analogy of concepts and mathematical objects to physical objects, the possibility and importance of categorial intuition or immediate conceptual knowledge, and the one-sidedness of what Husserl calls "the naive or natural standpoint."

Gödel mentioned phenomenology for the first time in our discussions on 10 November 1971 in the context of pointing out the limitations of my proposed *factualism*, which urges philosophers to do justice to what we know, for instance, in mathematics. On another occasion he said that he had formerly been a factualist but had at some stage realized that philosophy requires a new method. It is tempting to believe that this realization occurred in the 1950s and that he found in phenomenology the new method he had been looking for.

In any case, Gödel was sympathetic to factualism as an antidote and a limited method, even though not as the whole or basic method. In my opinion, two of the components in Kant's philosophy are: the transcendental method, which tries to capture that part of our thought which is potentially shared by all minds, and a factualism which takes existing knowledge in mathematics and physics as a given datum and asks how it is possible. For Gödel, the appeal of Husserlian phenomenology was, I think, that it developed the transcendental method in a way that accommodated his own beliefs in intellectual intuition and the reality of concepts.

In the rest of this section, I quote and organize Gödel's scattered observations on Husserl (and Kant) in what I see as a reasonable order. Because so much of the discussion overlaps the general considerations of Chapter 9, I make numerous cross-references, to avoid repetitions. (The reader will gain the most complete understanding of Gödel's view's on these philosophers, therefore, by switching back and forth between this section and the relevant quotes in Chapter 9.) As I said, he introduced the topic of phenomenology in connection with the limitations of the idea of doing justice to what we know.

5.3.1   See 9.3.23.

5.3.2   See 9.3.24.

For Gödel, factualism for everyday knowledge was more important than factualism for exact science. Even though what we know of his philosophical work is intimately linked to science, especially mathematics, he himself suggests that science or the study of scientific thinking, in contrast to everyday thinking, has little to offer to fundamental philosophy:

5.3.3   Husserl is a factualist not for the exact sciences but for everyday knowledge. Everyday knowledge is prescientific and much more hidden than science. We do not say why we believe it, how we arrive at it, or what we mean by it. But it is a scientific task to examine and talk about everyday knowledge, to study these questions of why, how and what. To deny that we can do this is an irrational attitude: it means that there are meaningful scientific problems that we can never solve. Whether Husserl got the right method is another question.

5.3.4   Studying scientific thinking would not get to as much depth as studying everyday thinking. Science is not deeper. There is nothing new in scientific discoveries; they are all explained in everyday thinking. One must not expect much from science [in doing philosophy]; for instance, it will not help [in learning] how to perceive concepts.

5.3.5   In principle Kant also started from everyday knowledge, and he privately arrived at superscience. Everyday knowledge, when analyzed into its components, is more relevant in giving data for philosophy. Science alone won't give philosophy; it is noncommittal regarding what really is there. A little bit of science is necessary for philosophy. For instance, Plato stipulates that no one unacquainted with geometry is to enter the academy. To that extent the requirement is certainly justified.

5.3.6   Husserl's is a very important method as an entrance into philosophy, so as finally to arrive at some metaphysics. Transcendental phenomenology with *epoché* as its methodology is the investigation (without knowledge of scientific facts) of the cognitive process, so as to find out what really appears to be—to find the objective concepts. No bright mind would say that material objects are nothing else but what we imagine them to be.

[This last observation probably refers to the complex content involved in (say) seeing a tree, as elaborated by Husserl, for whom this region (of seeing a physical object) is to serve as "a guiding clue in phenomenological inquiries" (*Ideas*, Section 150).]

Gödel's own main aim in philosophy was to develop metaphysics—specifically, something like the monadology of Leibniz transformed into an exact theory—with the help of phenomenology.

5.3.7   Phenomenology is not the only approach. Another approach is to find a list of the main categories (e.g., causation, substance, action) and their interrelations, which, however, are to be arrived at phenomenologically. The task must be done in the right manner.

5.3.8   Husserl used Kant's terminology to reach, for now, the foundations and, afterwards, used Leibniz to get the world picture. Husserl reached the end, arrived at the science of metaphysics. [This is different from what Gödel said on other occasions.] Husserl had to conceal his great discovery. Philosophy is a persecuted science. Without concealment, the structure of the world might have killed him.

5.3.9   Husserl developed a general method and applied it to metaphysics as well as to the foundations of everyday knowledge (e.g., the phenomenology of time) before applying it to other sciences. These are the right subjects. *Epoché* cannot be applied anywhere else. Heidegger published Husserl's lectures [*The Phenomenology of Internal Time-Consciousness*, 1928], but they are far from what Husserl had said. Heidegger applied the method to our will (emotions, etc.); so he did not really apply Husserl's method.

Gödel usually did not say that phenomenology includes a metaphysics as a theory, even though he might have thought that Husserl did go on to obtain, privately, a metaphysics. He formulated his own ideal thus: "Philosophy as exact theory should do for metaphysics as much as Newton did for physics" (*MP*:85).

5.3.10   See 9.3.10.

5.3.11   The beginning of physics was Newton's work of 1687, which needs only very simple primitives: force, mass, law. I look for a similar theory for philosophy or metaphysics. Metaphysicians believe it possible to find out what the objective reality is; there are only a few primitive entities causing the existence of other entities. Form (*So-Sein*) should be distinguished from existence (*Da-Sein*): the forms—though not the existence—of the objects were, in the middle ages, thought to be within us.

On different occasions Gödel made scattered observations on phenomenology and Husserl's work.

5.3.12   General philosophy is a conceptual study, for which the method is important. (Phenomenology is a conceptual study, for which the method is important.) Phenomenology strives to understand what is going on in our mind. Relationships must be seen. Plato's study of the definition of concepts was the beginning of philosophy.

5.3.13   By using his phenomenological viewpoint, Husserl sees many things more clearly in a different light. This is different from doing scientific work. It involves a change of personality.

5.3.14   Both Husserl and Freud considered—in different ways—subconscious thinking.

5.3.15   Some reductionism is right: reduce to concepts and truths, but not to sense perceptions. Really it should be the other way around: Platonic ideas [what Husserl calls "essences" and Gödel calls "concepts"] are what things are to be reduced to. Phenomenology makes them [the ideas] clear.

5.3.16   Phenomenology goes back to the foundations of our knowledge, to the process of how we form the knowledge, and to uncovering what is given to us from inside. It wants exactly to transcend [what is taken as] knowledge and get superknowledge. It has a basic belief that others will agree inwardly: they would come to the same conclusions.

5.3.17   The basis of everything is meaningful predication, such as Px, x belongs to A, xRy, and so on. Husserl had this. Hegel did not have this; that is why his philosophy lacks clarity. Idealistic philosophers are not able to make good ideas precise and into a science.

5.3.18   Husserl introduced a method: clearly every mathematician had that in his head before mathematical logic was formulated. It is just the axiomatic method.

5.3.19   Leibniz believed in the ideal of seeing the primitive concepts clearly and distinctly. When Husserl affirmed our ability to "intuit essences," he had in mind something like what Leibniz believed. Even Schelling adhered to this ideal, but Hegel moved away from this. True metaphysics is constantly going away. Kant was a skeptic, or at least believed that skepticism is necessary for the transition to true philosophy.

5.3.20   I don't particularly like Husserl's way—long and difficult. He tells us no detailed way about how to do it. His work on time is lost from the manuscripts.

Gödel made this statement last in March of 1976 in reply to my request for some successful cases of applying the method of phenomenology which would teach me by examples. The reference to Husserl's work on time suggests that Gödel believed Husserl to have done instructive work on our idea of time but that, unfortunately, it had been lost (compare 9.5.11). It is clear to me that Gödel regarded it as very difficult, and of central importance to philosophy, to understand our idea of time. For instance, he made, on different occasions, the following observations on the importance and difficulty of this topic, which I discuss in Chapter 9.

5.3.21   See 9.5.4.

5.3.22   See 9.5.1.

5.3.23   As we present time to ourselves, it simply does not agree with fact. To call time subjective is just a euphemism. Problems remain. One problem is to describe how we arrive at time. Another problem is the relation of our concept of time to real time. The real idea behind time is causation.

5.3.24   See 9.5.8.

There is widespread skepticism about an appeal to intuition and introspection (or self-observation). Even though Husserl did not hesitate to talk about intuitions, he did discuss the difficulties of self-observation and try to distance phenomenology from introspectionist (empirical) psychology (*Ideas*, Section 79). Gödel had no hesitation, however, in using the concept of introspection—undoubtedly having in mind something different from the forms of introspection associated with empirical psychology. After contrasting language and symbols with concepts and saying that we have no primitive intuitions about language, he proceeded to make several observations on introspection, phenomenology, and psychology.

5.3.25 Phenomenology is necessary in order to distinguish between knowing a proposition to be true by understanding it [by attaining an intuitive grasp of a proof of it] and by remembering that you have proved it. [A proposition or a proof is] a net of symbols associated with a net of concepts. To understand something requires introspection; for instance, the abstract idea of a proof must be seen [the idea "behind" a proof can only be understood] by introspection.

5.3.26 Long before mathematical logic was discovered, one had been applying [in everyday life] the rules of logic (e.g., the distributive law and more generally the rules of computation) with understanding; now it is no longer necessary. [I take this to mean that we can now apply these rules mechanically, or blindly, thereby achieving an economy of thought.] Mechanical rules of computation had also been applied in mathematics; for example, Euclid applied the distributive law in making inferences.

5.3.27 Introspection is an important component of thinking; today it has a bad reputation. Introspective psychology is completely overlooked today. *Epoché* concerns how introspection should be used, for example, to detach oneself from influences of external stimuli (such as the fashions of the day). Even the scientists (fashions of the day). Even the scientists [sometimes] do not agree because they are not [detached true] *subjects* [in this sense].

5.3.28 One fundamental discovery of introspection marks the true beginning of psychology. This discovery is that the basic form of consciousness distinguishes between an intentional object and our being pointed (*gerichtet*) toward it in some way (feeling, willing, cognizing). There are various kinds of intentional object. There is nothing analogous in physics. This discovery marks the first division of phenomena between the psychological and the physical. Introspection calls for learning how to direct attention in an unnatural way. To apply it in everyday life would only be harmful.

5.3.29 When we understand or find the correct analysis of a concept, the belief is that psychological study comes to the same conclusion. This science of intuition is not yet precise, and people cannot learn it yet. At present, mathematicians are prejudiced against intuition. Set theory is along the line of correct analysis.

One of Gödel's recurrent themes was the importance of experiencing a sudden illumination—like a religious conversion—in philosophy. (This theme, by the way, reminds me of the teachings of Hui Neng's "sudden school" of Zen (Chan) Buddhism in China.) In particular, Gödel believed that Husserl had such an experience at some point during the transition between his early and later philosophy (compare 9.1.13 to 9.1.15).

5.3.30 At some time between 1906 and 1910 Husserl had a psychological crisis. He doubted whether he had accomplished anything, and his wife was very sick. At some point in this period, everything suddenly became clear to Husserl, and he did arrive at some absolute knowledge. But one cannot transfer absolute knowledge to somebody else; therefore, one cannot publish it. A lecture on the nature of time also came from this period, when Husserl's experience of seeing absolute knowledge took place. I myself have never had such an experience. For me there is no absolute knowledge: everything goes only by probability. Both Descartes and Schelling explicitly reported an experience of sudden illumination when they began to see everything in a different light.

5.3.31   Husserl could not communicate his ideas. He knew much more. This is not surprising: generally in psychoanalysis and other fields, many things—drives, will, decisions, and so on—are hidden. But we can only judge on the basis of what has been communicated.

5.3.32   Around 1910 Husserl made a change in his philosophy—as can be seen from his article "Philosophy as a Rigorous Science." Intentionally his style also changed around this time—in conformity with his changed method. An example is his use of long sentences after the change. It was a way to make the reader pay attention to the subtleties of his thoughts.

5.3.33   Metaphysics in the form of something like the Leibnizian monadology came at one time closest to Husserl's ideal. Baumgarten [1714–1762] is better than Wolff [1679–1754], and also better than Fichte and Hegel.

With regard to Husserl's "transcendental turn," Richard Tieszen told me, in correspondence, that Husserl lectured on Kant's philosophy every day of the week except Sunday during the winter semester of 1905–1906. Subsequently, in his five lectures in 1907—later published as *The Idea of Phenomenology*—he first made public his change of approach to philosophy. In Tieszen's opinion, Husserl's radical shift at this time came from a combination of two factors: (a) he had become aware of apparently insurmountable problems in his naturalistic framework; and (b) he then began to study Kant and thought that those problems could be resolved by a thoroughgoing transcendental approach. Perhaps one could say that the "sudden illumination" occurred when Husserl saw—or at least thought he saw—that the new approach was all-powerful.

Gödel's observation 5.3.30 seems to suggest that—as I also used to believe—Husserl was an absolutist (or "foundationalist" in its strongest sense). However, even though he did speak in an absolutist way from time to time, there are various passages in his writings which deny that we can attain any infallible, absolutely certain insights. (Examples of both types are given in Follesdal 1988; for Husserl's own criticism of what he calls "absolutist" theories of truth, compare Tieszen 1989:181–182.)

In my draft of *MP*, I wrote: "According to Husserl, ideal objects such as emotions, values, prices and Riemann manifolds have as much reality as physical objects and are as much suitable subjects for the development of autonomous conceptual sciences." Gödel commented:

5.3.34   This statement is not to be taken seriously—one is not to make a metaphysics of it. Emotions are occurrences in space-time; they are not ideal objects.

Rather, one should say, the concepts of emotions such as anger. The value of something may mean either that it is a value or that it has value. It's better to say that emotions have—rather than are—value(s).

A digression on Kant. In discussing Husserl, Gödel often compared his work with Kant's. He knew Kant's work very well and spoke highly of his ideas elsewhere (see 5.1 above). But in these conversations he spoke more often of what he regarded as the negative aspects of Kant's philosophy. In the 1970s I found Kant's philosophy more attractive than Husserl's, and Gödel tried to change my preference.

For instance, when I expressed my admiration for Kant's architectonic, Gödel replied: "A thorough and systematic beginning is better than a sloppy architectonic." When I observed that Kant went beyond the purely intellectual, he mentioned Max Scheler's development of a phenomenology of the will. I thought that this comment contradicted his observation, quoted in 5.3.9, against Heidegger. When I remarked that, contrary to Husserl's claim that his phenomenology was a science, there had been no conspicuous cooperative progress in its development, Gödel replied:

5.3.35   Husserl only showed the way; he never published what he had arrived at during thirty years of work, but only published the method he used. He requires very gifted followers: as good as he or better.

5.3.36   Kant and Husserl are close in terminology; for example, both speak of "transcendentalism." Husserl does what Kant did, only more systematically. Kant and Leibniz were also absolutists; of the three, only Husserl admits this explicitly. Both Husserl and Kant begin with everyday knowledge. Husserl sets down the beginnings of a systematic philosophy. Kant recognizes that all categories should be reduced to something more fundamental. Husserl tries to find that more fundamental idea which is behind all these categories. Kant's axioms about the categories say very little. The true axioms should imply all a priori science.

5.3.37   It is not meant to be a criticism of what Husserl has done to point out that he wants to teach not some kind of propositional knowledge, but an attitude of mind which enables one to direct one's attention rightly, to strain one's attention in a certain direction. Kant's philosophy of arithmetic and geometry comprises assertions without proof. For Husserl, the general idea of space is a priori to some extent: things are as they appear (not always objects, also other aspects).

5.3.38   According to Kant, we are morally obliged to assume something even though it may be meaningless. What is subjective, even with agreement, is different from what is objective, in the sense that there is an outside reality corresponding to it. One should distinguish questions of principle from questions of practice: for the former, agreement is of no importance.

5.3.39   Kant also makes self-observation of everyday life. Kant is inconsistent. His epistemology proves that God, and so on, have no objective meaning; they are purely subjective, and to interpret them as objective is wrong. Yet he says that we are obliged to assume them because they induce us to do our duty to our fellow human beings. It is, however, also one's duty not to assume things that are purely subjective.

5.3.40 Kant notices only an ambiguous and uncertain psychological fact which is not necessary. His insights are different from those in the book [presumably the first *Critique*].

5.4 *Against (Logical) Positivism*

Positivism, including logical positivism, is closely related to certain forms of empiricism, naturalism, and scientism. Gödel developed intellectually in the midst of the leading logical positivists—Hahn, Schlick, and Carnap. But he found their philosophical outlook unsatisfactory, both generally and, especially, in connection with their account of mathematics, which fails to do justice to what we know and makes it hard to do certain mathematical work related to the philosophy of mathematics.

According to Gödel's own account, he had been a Platonist or objectivist or realist in mathematics since about 1925 (*RG*:20). But he began to make his views public only in the 1940s; some of the things he said in the 1930s suggest a more ambivalent attitude. For example, he expressed skepticism toward set theory in his lecture "The Present Situation in the Foundations of Mathematics," delivered to the American Mathematical Society on 30 December 1933 (to be published in *CW* 3). Later, through his study of Husserl's work from 1959 on, he seems to have come to believe that he had found an epistemological foundation for his objectivistic position.

In the section "Against Positivism" (*MP*:7–13), I summarize parts of what Gödel said to me about positivism in correspondence and in conversation. That discussion consists of four parts: (1) general observations; (2) two letters to me explaining the importance of his objectivistic conception for his own work in logic; (3) a comparison between Hilbert's approach and his own approach to Cantor's continuum hypothesis, illustrating the negative effect of a positivistic conception; and (4) the relation of positivism to physics. It is hard to draw a line between his observations negating the value of positivism and those favoring objectivism. In this chapter, I confine my attention to (1) and (4) and leave the ideas related to (2) and (3) to chapters 7 and 8.

Gödel's negative feeling toward positivism results to some extent from his belief that the positivistic attitude has had negative effects on the pursuit of philosophy and science. On the one hand, he believes it directs the attention of philosophers away from more fruitful types of work in philosophy. On the other hand, he believes it prevents us from effectively pursuing certain areas of fundamental physics and mathematics. In general, he believes that the positivistic attitude imposes an arbitrary restriction on the possibilities of fully exercising our mental power to understand and, thereby, improve the world in a fundamental way.

Gödel made a number of overlapping remarks on different occasions about the general outlook of positivism.

5.4.1   The purpose of philosophy is not to prove everything from nothing, but to assume as given all—including conceptual relations—that we see as clearly as shapes and colors, which come from sensations but cannot be *derived* from sensations. The positivists attempt to prove everything from nothing. People claim that positivism follows from science. This is in some sense true. As a result, observations play a disproportionally large part. [Compare 9.3.6]

5.4.2   Exactly as in learning the [experiential] primitives like the sensations about color and shape, one cannot prove [the primitive concepts of philosophy]. If in philosophy one cannot assume what can only be seen, then one is, like the positivists, left only with the sensations. [Compare 9.2.]

5.4.3   Even if we adopt positivism, it seems to me that the assumption of such entities as concepts is quite [as] legitimate as the assumption of physical objects and that there is quite as much reason to believe in their existence. They are necessary for obtaining a satisfactory system of mathematics in the same sense as physical objects are necessary for a satisfactory theory of our actually occurring sense perceptions. [For related observations, see 7.2.18 and 7.4.6.]

5.4.4   Positivists (1) decline to acknowledge our having a priori knowledge; (2) reduce everything to sense perceptions, or at least, while assuming physical objects, connect everything to sense perceptions; (3) contradict themselves when it comes to introspection, which they do not recognize as experience. They have too narrow a notion of experience, and the foundations of their philosophy are arbitrary. Russell makes even more drastic mistakes: as if sense experience were the only experience we can find by introspection.

5.4.5   Positivists decline to acknowledge any a priori knowledge. They wish to reduce everything to sense perceptions. Generally they contradict themselves in that they deny introspection as experience, referring to higher mental phenomena as "judgments." They use too narrow a notion of experience and introduce an arbitrary bound on what experience is, excluding phenomenological experience. Russell (in his 1940 [*Inquiry into Meaning and Truth*]) made a more drastic mistake in speaking as if sense experience were the only experience we can find by introspection.

5.4.6   The spirit of time always goes to positivism and materialism; for instance, Plato was followed by Aristotle. Positivism and materialism have similar consequences.

5.4.7   One bad effect of logical positivism is its claim of being intimately associated with mathematical logic. As a result, other philosophers tend to distance themselves from mathematical logic and therewith deprive themselves of the benefits of a way of precise thinking. Mathematical logic makes it easier to avoid mistakes—even for one who is not a genius.

5.4.8   Mathematical logic should be used more by nonpositivistic philosophers. The positivists have a tendency to represent their philosophy as a consequence of logic—to give it scientific dignity. Other philosophers think that positivism is identical with mathematical logic, which they consequently avoid.

5.4.9   Those philosophers who are not positivists are surprisingly ignorant of mathematical logic. Because the positivists identify it with positivism, naturally other philosophers object to the claimed support for a philosophy they dislike, and, consequently, pay little attention to it. The point is not so much explicit use of logic, but rather the way of thinking and also so to think that the fruits can be put into the terms of logic.

Remarks Related to Carnap

5.4.10   Wittgenstein's negative attitude toward symbolic language is a step backward. Those who, like Carnap, misuse symbolic language want to discredit mathematical logic; they want to prevent the appearance of philosophy. The whole movement of the positivists wants to destroy philosophy; for this purpose they need to destroy mathematical logic as a tool. There is an inner logic in this, which may even be a conscious one in some of the positivists. The belief is that truth—including what is true in religion—is harmful. Another idea at work in Carnap is this: the concealment of truth in positivism will only work for the lower intelligence; for the more intelligent, positivism encourages them to think the opposite. Carnap believes that for the present stage—also especially for science— positivism is more useful [than other philosophical positions]. Carnap believes that at present philosophy is beyond the reach of knowledge. [For the context of this observation, see the passage that introduces 5.5.6 in the next section.]

5.4.11   I agree that—as Einstein said to Carnap [quoted in *MP*:381]—there is a tendency to water down positivism to the extent of no longer meaning anything distinctive.

5.4.12   Carnap assumes infinitely many expressions, which are *idealized* physical objects. Finitary results are given a physical interpretation, which is taken to follow as an empirical fact. This is close to Mill's point of view.

5.4.13   Carnap takes mathematics as linguistic conventions. But objectivity and perceptibility are connected: We can see [the correctness of] the correct definitions; for instance, the definition of measurable sets [of real numbers] is true. [My work on] the Carnap paper caused me tremendous trouble.

5.4.14   My Carnap paper proved that mathematics is *not* syntax of language. But it failed to prove the positive statement of what mathematics is.

5.4.15   Carnap's work on the nature of mathematics was remote from actual mathematics; he later came closer to actual science in his book on probability.

Carnap had a book on Leibniz around 1947 [I wonder whether this remark by Gödel is based on reliable information].

Positivism and Physics

It is a well-known fact that the success of Einstein's special theory of relativity was a major inspiration for the central thesis of logical positivism that the criterion for a statement to be meaningful is its verifiability—ultimately by sense experience. Indeed, in connection with the discovery of his special theory, Einstein himself mentions the decisive influence of Hume and Mach: "The type of critical reasoning which was required for the discovery ... was decisively furnished, in my case, especially by the reading of David Hume's and Ernst Mach's philosophical writings" (in Schilpp 1949:53).

At the same time, Einstein's attitude toward quantum theory is, in his own words, opposed to "the positivistically inclined modern physicist" (ibid.:667). As a scientist, "the facts of experience do not permit him to let himself be too much restricted in the construction of his conceptual world by the adherence to an epistemological system. He therefore must appear to the systematic epistemologist as a type of unscrupulous opportunist" (ibid.:684). Gödel contrasted Einstein's position with that of Bohr (compare *MP*:7):

5.4.16   The heuristics of Einstein and Bohr are stated in their correspondence. Cantor might also be classified together with Einstein and me. Heisenberg and Bohr are on the other side. Bohr [even] drew metaphysical conclusions from the uncertainty principle.

In his discussions with me, Gödel made a number of comments on the relation between positivism and physics, with special emphasis on the special theory of relativity. In May 1972 he wrote a passage to summarize these views, which I reproduced in *From Mathematics to Philosophy* (*MP*:12–13).

5.4.17   It must be admitted that the positivistic position also has turned out to be fruitful on certain occasions. An example often mentioned is the special theory of relativity. The fruitfulness of the positivistic point of view in this case is due to a very exceptional circumstance, namely the fact that the basic concept to be clarified, i.e., simultaneity, is directly observable, while generally basic entities (such as elementary particles, the forces between them, etc.) are not. Hence, the positivistic requirement that everything has to be reduced to observations is justified in this sense. That, generally speaking, positivism is not fruitful even in physics seems to follow from the fact that, since it has been adopted in quantum physics (i.e., about 40 years ago) no substantial progress has been achieved in the basic laws of physics, even though the "two-level" theory (with its "quantization" of a "classical system," and its divergent series) is admittedly unsatisfactory. Perhaps, what ought to be done is to separate the subjective and objective elements in

Schrödinger's wave function, which so far has by no means been proved impossible. But exactly this question is "meaningless" from the positivistic point of view.

Gödel made several related observations on positivism more informally in the course of the discussions.

5.4.18   Under exceptional circumstances, positivism is fruitful. For example, simultaneity is directly observable, and so reducing everything to observations is justified. Generally speaking, quantum mechanics is positivistic. The two-level theory is not satisfactory. We should perhaps distinguish the subjective and the objective elements. But exactly this question is positivistically meaningless.

5.4.19   Positivism is generally not fruitful in scientific research, although it may have been valuable in the discovery of the special theory of relativity. Generally speaking, the right ideas are fruitful. Positivism is pedagogically better for the special theory of relativity.

As first, Gödel wished to point out that, even for the discovery of the special theory of relativity, the positivistic outlook is unnecessary. But he then decided to leave out the following passage:

5.4.20   The positivistic attitude is not necessary for arriving at the special theory of relativity. It is a mathematical fact that the Maxwell equations are invariant under Lorentz transformations. In view of the wide applicability of the Maxwell equations, one may be inclined to assume that all physical phenomena can be explained by the Maxwell equations, or at least that additional physical laws are like the Maxwell equations in the single respect of being invariant under Lorentz transformations. From either assumption it follows that a physical body (in particular, a clock and, therewith, time) proceeding on a moving body will slow down.

This passage, written out by Gödel, was a reformulation of what he had said earlier in the discussions:

5.4.21   Consider the special theory of relativity from the absolutist view. It is a mathematical fact that the Maxwell equations are invariant with respect to the Lorentz transformations. Further, assume that all phenomena can be explained by the Maxwell equations. It follows that a physical body proceeding on a moving body will slow down, also a clock, also time. The positivist attitude is not necessary at all. The assumption that everything is explained by the Maxwell equations is too strong. Replace it by a weaker assumption: It is to be expected that what is to be added [to the Maxwell equations] is also compatible with the invariance. Therefore, we have the statement: Every physical law is invariant under the Lorentz transformations. In terms of the conception of absolute time and space, we may say that the time measurement is distorted when moving. Physically [this alternative formulation makes] no difference, but it is not acceptable to the positivists. Nonpositivistically one would draw the conclusion that it is physically indeterminable, which is the real thing. Einstein's genius suggests the question whether it is necessary not to be a complete positivist.

The following observation seems to be related to Gödel's own rotating universes as solutions to Einstein's field equations of gravitation (compare Section 9.5):

5.4.22 Lorentz space is not realized in the world. What is realized is seen from cosmology: Riemann space and even absolute space [are] less relativistic. If the universe rotates, then the whole world moves with uniform motion. That would be the most striking confirmation of the absolutist view one can think of.

As I mentioned at the beginning of this section, the discussions against positivism included a comparison between Hilbert's and Gödel's works on the continuum hypothesis (summarized in *MP*:11–12). The idea is that Hilbert had an attractive approach to the problem, but, because of his "quasi-positivistic attitude," he made an unjustifiably strong claim for it and failed to appreciate what could have been achieved from his approach—with the right attitude. Therefore, we have here a striking example of how a positivistic leaning may hamper one's research in mathematics. I turn to detailed observations on this point in Chapter 8.

5.5 Gödel and Wittgenstein

Like many philosophers of my generation, I had periodically struggled with the philosophical writings of Wittgenstein. Given my deep involvement in Gödel's views, it was natural for me to try to come to terms with the apparent incompatibility between their outlooks. After a preliminary attempt in *RG* (pp. 58–67), I continued the effort in several essays: a lecture (1987b) in August 1986 at the Wittgenstein Symposium; an article in *Synthese* (1991); and a lecture to the Gödel Society in August 1991 (1992). Since my main purpose in the present context is to consider Gödel's observations, I include here only a brief summary of my own impressions, derived from an attempt to compare the two philosophers.

Whereas Gödel emphasizes the abstract and the universal, Wittgenstein pays more attention to the concrete and the particular. Gödel is particularly interested in the relation between philosophy and science. For Wittgenstein, "the difficulty in philosophy is to say no more than we know"; he is for *showing* our views by our work rather than *saying* what we wish to accomplish through a philosophical program—such as Husserl's of philosophy as rigorous science or Gödel's of doing for philosophy what Newton did for physics. In contrast to Wittgenstein, Gödel considers language unimportant for the study of serious philosophical issues. Both of them believe that everyday thinking is of more fundamental relevance to philosophy, but in practice Gödel has appealed more to science. Both consider philosophy to comprise conceptual investigations, but their conceptions of *concept* are radically different. Both occupied much of their time with the philosophy of mathematics, but their perspectives and conclusions often run in contrary directions. Finally, while they both find that science as it is commonly done adopts a one-sided perspective, Gödel wishes to improve science while Wittgenstein tries to demystify it.

As a student in the University of Vienna, Gödel studied with several teachers (notably Schlick, Hahn, and Carnap) who were greatly influenced by Wittgenstein. From 1926 to 1927, at the age of 20, he attended an extended, continuous discussion of the *Tractatus* in the Vienna Circle. One would, therefore, expect him to have a strong response, positive or negative, to Wittgenstein's work. As far as I know, however, there is no record of Gödel's response at that time.

In 1975, Gödel drafted several replies to an inquiry, which gave some relevant information: he first studied Wittgenstein's work around 1927, but, he said "never thoroughly" (*RG*:17) or "only very superficially" (*RG*:19): "Wittgenstein's views on the philosophy of mathematics had no influence on my work, nor did the interest of the Vienna Circle in that subject start with Wittgenstein (but rather went back to Professor Hans Hahn)" (*RG*:20).

It is likely that Gödel found Wittgenstein's work too imprecise to discuss. In his conversations with me in 1972, however, he did comment on Wittgenstein's work several times. In January, Gödel made some observations in connection with my brief discussions of Wittgenstein's "two philosophies" (*MP*:13–14):

5.5.1 The *Tractatus* gives a well-rounded picture. The first philosophy is a system, the second a method. It is hard to speak of the second philosophy. The only thing in common is the rejection of metaphysics. In a stronger sense Wittgenstein refuted metaphysics. The main points are the refutation of metaphysics and the centrality of language.

In October, Gödel made another observation on the *Tractatus* and also commented on Wittgenstein's defense of Schopenhauer against Schlick's criticism (quoted in *MP*:380):

5.5.2 Is the *Tractatus* compatible with basic stuff of the conceptual sort? Probably not. If so, we must take it as a matter of counter-proof of the system. [In 1930 or 1931 Wittgenstein did say that the objects (entities, things, etc.) in the *Tractatus* include both particulars and universals (Lee 1980:120). However, it is not so easy to accommodate the universals in his system. (Compare Wang 1985a: 76.)]

5.5.3 Maybe Schopenhauer's philosophy was helpful to Wittgenstein in the sense of a ladder. In the *Tractatus* period, that would be the only reasonable interpretation.

Gödel's main comments on Wittgenstein were made on 5 April 1972. Karl Menger had written to Gödel in January asking him to comment on Wittgenstein's discussion of his (Gödel's) theorem in *Remarks on the Foundations of Mathematics* (1967; hereafter *RFM*). At the time, I too was interested in discussing Wittgenstein's work with Gödel and sent him some material in early February. In particular, I called Gödel's attention to Wittgenstein's later (around 1932) criticism of the underlying principles of *atomicity* and *finiteness* used in his own early work (reported by G. E. Moore 1955:1−4 and considered at length in Wang 1985a:95−99). When I met him in his office on 5 April, Gödel asked me: What was Wittgenstein doing all these years? Undoubtedly he had in mind the long lapse between the completion of the *Tractatus* in 1918 and the correction of his mistakes in 1932.

Between receiving Menger's letter in January and meeting with me in April, Gödel had evidently looked at *RFM* and the material I had sent. He was quite ready to express his impressions on this occasion. His habitual calmness was absent in his comments:

5.5.4 Has Wittgenstein lost his mind? Does he mean it seriously? He intentionally utters trivially nonsensical statements. What he says about the set of all cardinal numbers reveals a perfectly naive view. [Possibly the reference is to *RFM*:132 and the surrounding observations.] He has to take a position when he has no business to do so. For example, "you can't derive everything from a contradiction." He should try to develop a system of logic in which that is true. It's amazing that Turing could get anything out of discussions with somebody like Wittgenstein.

5.5.5a He has given up the objective goal of making concepts and proofs precise. It is one thing to say that we can't make precise philosophical concepts (such as apriority, causality, substance, the general concept of proof, etc.). But to go further and say we can't even make mathematical concepts precise is much more. In the *Tractatus* it is said that philosophy can't be made into a science. His later philosophy is to eliminate also science. It is a natural development. To decline philosophy is an irrationalistic attitude. Then he declines all rationality—declining even science.

On 20 April 1972 Gödel wrote his reply to Menger's January letter, commenting on some of Wittgenstein's discussions of his own famous theorem (compare *RG*:49):

5.5.5b It is indeed clear from the passages you cite [*RFM*:117−123, 385−389] that Wittgenstein did *not* understand it (or pretended not to understand it). He interpreted it as a kind of logical paradox, while in fact it is just the opposite, namely a mathematical theorem within an absolutely uncontroversial part of mathematics (finitary number theory or combinatorics). Incidentally, the whole passage you cite seems nonsense to me. See, for example, the "superstitious fear of mathematicians of contradictions."

Wittgenstein had made various comments on Gödel's theorem between 1935 and 1944, including extensive discussions in 1937 and 1944. From these observations—mostly published by now—it is clear that he had given much thought to the matter and considered Gödel's proof philosophically important. However, even though many philosophers have puzzled over them, we still have no satisfactory understanding of several parts of his comments on Gödel's theorem.

On 29 November 1972 Gödel commented on the following quotation from Carnap in my typescript (*MP*:380): "When we found in Wittgenstein's book [the *Tractatus*] statements about 'the language', we interpreted them as referring to an ideal language; and this means for us a formalized symbolic language. Later Wittgenstein explicitly rejected this view. He had a skeptical and sometimes even a negative view of the importance of symbolic language for [philosophy]." —I quote Gödel's comment on this passage in 5.4.10 above. On another occasion, in the context of his observation 5.5.1, Gödel made a related remark which also seems appropriate as a comment on this quotation:

5.5.6 To use the *Tractatus* the way Carnap does has some value. There is, however, no ideal language. In what way could one even conceive of an ideal language?

Earlier in this section I quoted Gödel's observation (5.5.1) which mentions the "centrality of language" in both of Wittgenstein's "two philosophies." In general, Gödel deplored the overestimation of the importance of language for philosophy. Specifically, he blamed this overestimation for the widespread failure to distinguish the intensional from the semantic paradoxes (a topic to be discussed later in Chapter 8). In the context of emphasizing the importance of this distinction, Gödel stated at some length his negative attitude toward an excessive reliance on language:

5.5.7 We do not have any primitive intuitions about language. Language is nothing but a one-one correspondence between abstract objects and concrete objects [namely the linguistic symbols]. Everything has to be proved [when we are dealing with language]. The overestimation of language is deplorable.

5.5.8 Language is useful and even necessary for fixing our ideas. But this is a purely practical affair. Our mind is more inclined to sensual objects, which help to fix our attention on abstract objects. This is the only importance of language. It is ridiculous [to expect] that we should have any primitive intuitions about language, which is just an association of symbols with concepts and other entities.

5.5.9 If you use language to define combinations of concepts replaced by combinations of symbols, the latter are completely unimportant. Symbols only help us to fix and remember abstract things: in order to identify concepts, we associate them with certain symbols. All primitive evidence of logic is, when you investigate it, always of concepts; symbols have nothing to do with it. Seeing complicated symbols is easier; they are easier to handle. One can overview more symbols. We remember a complicated concept by means of a symbol denoting it. If it is a natural concept, then we can understand it.

Undoubtedly Wittgenstein and Gödel differ in their conceptions of language and their experience with it. In any case, the relation of mathematics to language seems to exhibit certain striking peculiarities. On the one hand, language (including symbols and diagrams) is of great practical importance to a mathematician, packing much information into an economical reminder. On the other hand, in comparison with other human enterprises, mathematics is less likely to be distorted or confused by language. In studying mathematics, a (foreign) student is less handicapped by deficiencies in the natural language of the text or the teacher. Communication of mathematical ideas depends less on facility in writing or speaking a natural language. It is often possible, for example, to find an accurate long proof from very fragmentary hints, such as a diagram or a few crucial words. One of my college teachers once told me that he had been advised to study English but decided instead to study "the universal language"—meaning mathematics. Something of this sort may be part of what Brouwer has in mind when he speaks (somewhat misleadingly perhaps) of mathematics as language-independent, or "an essentially languageless activity of the mind."

The effects of the different attitudes of Gödel and Wittgenstein toward language and its relation to philosophy are most striking in their philosophies of mathematics—especially of set theory. Whereas Gödel made significant contributions to set theory and saw the quest for new axioms in set theory as a good illustration of our mind's powers, Wittgenstein persistently attempted to "show how very misleading the expressions of Cantor are." Indeed, Wittgenstein wrote in 1929: "There is no religious denomination in which the use of metaphorical [not metaphysical] expressions has been responsible for so much sin as it has in mathematics" (Wittgenstein 1980:1). [In a letter of 19 September 1991 G. H. von Wright informed me that the word *metaphysischer* in the printed text had been a misreading of the original manuscript.] We encounter here a remarkable conflict of views which may serve as a stimulating datum for the study of the nature of philosophical disagreements and of plausible ways to decompose them—so that, perhaps, constructive dialogue may become possible between proponents of two philosophical positions.

In terms of the division of philosophical worldviews mentioned at the beginning of this chapter, we could say that Gödel leans toward the right and the tender-minded and Wittgenstein toward the left and the tough-minded. Wittgenstein once made a related contrast: "No, I don't think I would get on with Hegel. Hegel seems to me to be always wanting to say

[that] things which look different are really the same. Whereas my interest is in showing that things which look the same are really different" (in Rhees 1984:157). Kant also speaks of the different manifestations of reason's "twofold, self-conflicting interest" in universality and determinateness: some people are almost "hostile to heterogeneity"; some almost "extinguish the hope of ever being able to determine" things in universal terms (Kant 19:540).

Chapter 6

Minds and Machines: On Computabilism

It is conceivable (although far outside the limits of present-day science) that brain physiology would advance so far that it would be known with empirical certainty (1) that the brain suffices for the explanation of all mental phenomena and is a machine in the sense of Turing; (2) that such and such is the precise material structure and physiological functioning of the part of the brain which performs mathematical thinking.
Gödel, Gibbs Lecture, 1951 note 17

Computabilism is the thesis that the brain and the mind function basically like a computer; *neuralism* is the thesis that the brain suffices for the explanation of mental phenomena. During his discussions with me in the 1970s, Gödel argued for his strong conviction that neither computabilism nor neuralism is true—a position which excludes the possibility that additional knowledge will yield the outcome envisaged in point (1) above.

If we do not assume neuralism, then the issue of computabilism is split into two subproblems: one dealing with neural phenomena and the other with mental phenomena. In addition, since we possess a well-developed physics, it is common to identify the relation between mind and body with that between mind and matter, and so neuralism is replaced by *physicalism*. If, however, we try to make the assumptions explicit, we may distinguish, in an obvious manner, (a) on the one hand, physicalism with respect to biological, neural, and mental phenomena; and (b) on the other hand, computabilism with respect to physical, biological, neural, and mental phenomena.

Of these seven distinct problems, the central one that Gödel discussed with me was computabilism as an explanation of mental processes, that is, the issue of whether all thinking is computational—with special emphasis on mathematical thinking. Gödel's main concern was to demonstrate that not all mathematical thinking is computational.

The actual discussions began with my consideration of *mechanical procedure* as an example of a fairly successful characterization of general mathematical concepts. Specifically, Gödel commented (1) on my observation that Turing computability is not an entirely sharp concept (Wang 1974a, hereafter *MP*:81–83); and (2) on my formulation of the argument for the adequacy of Turing's definition of mechanical procedure (ibid.:90–95). These formulations led to Gödel's responses (ibid.:84–85, 102 n. 30, 326), which included, as an afterthought: (3) a conjectured disproof of the common belief that there is no mind separate from matter. Gödel also commented (4) on my review of attempts to employ his incompleteness theorem to disprove computerism for mental phenomena (ibid.:315–320). These comments led to the two paragraphs in *MP* that begin at the middle of p. 324. In this chapter, in order to begin with the more familiar material, I consider (4) and (3) first, and then turn to (2) and (1).

Apart from a number of incidental observations, I examine successively Gödel's ideas on the following topics: (a) the relation between mental computabilism and Gödel's incompleteness theorem on the computational inexhaustibility of mathematics; (b) the lack of solid evidence for the widespread belief in physicalism (or parallelism between the physical and the mental); (c) the strength and weakness of Turing's formulation and justification of his definition of *computer* and *computation*; and (d) physical and neural computabilism. Gödel's consideration of topic (a), in particular, continues the thoughts he expressed in his Gibbs lecture, which was written and delivered in 1951 (in Gödel 1995, hereafter *CW3*).

6.1 Mental Computabilism—Gödel's Theorem and Other Suggestions

One line of thought much pursued in trying to refute mental computabilism uses Gödel's inexhaustibility theorem. The theorem implies that, for every computer that generates theorems, there is some truth which we can see to be true but which cannot be generated by the computer. It appears, therefore, that our mental power surpasses any computer in proving theorems. When we try to make this argument precise, however, it turns out that there are subtle loopholes in it.

One form of Gödel's theorem says that, if a reasonably strong theorem-proving computer or program is sound or consistent, then it cannot prove the truth that expresses its own consistency. In his Gibbs Lecture, Gödel uses this form to draw several consequences. In 1972 he wrote up two of these consequences as follows:

6.1.1 The human mind is incapable of formulating (or mechanizing) all its mathematical intuitions. That is, if it has succeeded in formulating some of them, this very fact yields new intuitive knowledge, for example the consistency of this formalism. This fact may be called the "incompletability" of mathematics. On the other hand, on the basis of what has been proved so far, it remains possible that there may exist (and even be empirically discoverable) a theorem-proving machine which in fact *is* equivalent to mathematical intuition, but cannot be *proved* to be so, nor even be proved to yield only *correct* theorems of finitary number theory. [See *MP*:324.]

6.1.2   Either the human mind surpasses all machines (to be more precise: it can decide more number-theoretical questions than any machine), or else there exist number-theoretical questions undecidable for the human mind. [It is not excluded that both alternatives may be true.]

In the text written in 1972, Gödel went on—going beyond his Gibbs lecture—to reject the second alternative by arguing for a "rationalistic optimism" (*MP*:324–325). (See section 9.4, together with related observations on this argument.) Clearly he himself realized that such a refutation of mental computabilism is not convincing, as we can infer from his continued efforts to find other ways to achieve the desired refutation.

In the Gibbs lecture, Gödel continued with a different line of thought. In one direction, he elaborated on the possibility, asserted in 6.1.1 above, that there might exist a theorem-proving computer *in fact* equivalent to mathematical intuition.

6.1.3   It is not precluded that there should exist a finite rule [a computer] producing all its evident axioms. However, if such a rule exists, we with our human understanding could certainly never know it to be such; that is, we could never know with mathematical certainty that all propositions it produces are correct; or, in other terms, we could perceive to be true only one proposition after the other, for any finite number of them. The assertion, however, that they are all true could at most be known with empirical certainty, on the basis of a sufficient number of instances or by other inductive references. [Gödel appended to the end of this statement the note quoted at the beginning of this chapter.]

Since every "finite rule" is characterized by a finite set of axioms and rules of inference, it is, as far as we know, possible for us to know of any finite rule that it is correct. In that case, no finite rule could fully capture our mathematical intuition—because, if it did, we would know its consistency as well, which goes beyond the rule. The point of 6.1.3 is: *if* there were a finite rule equivalent to our mathematical intuition, *then* we would never know it to be such; otherwise we would also know the consistency of the finite rule, and so it would *not* be equivalent to our mathematical intuition.

If we reflect on the character and development of mathematical intuition as revealed by the practice of the community of mathematicians, we may be able to examine more closely the likelihood of the possibility that mathematical intuition is (or is not) in fact equivalent in power to some computer. The relevant phenomena are, however, so complex and indefinite that I, for one, am reluctant to face this formidable task.

In the Gibbs lecture Gödel also introduced a distinction between mathematics in the *subjective* sense—as the system of all demonstrable propositions—and mathematics in the *objective* sense—as the system of all true mathematical propositions. Using this distinction, he could reformulate 6.1.2 as follows:

6.1.4   Either subjective mathematics surpasses the capability of all computers, or else objective mathematics surpasses subjective mathematics, or both alternatives may be true.

Gödel then drew some tentative, and debatable, conclusions:

6.1.5   If the first alternative holds, this seems to imply that the working of the human mind cannot be reduced to the working of the brain, which to all appearance is a finite machine with a finite number of parts, namely, the neurons and their connections.

6.1.6   [The second alternative] seems to disprove the view that mathematics is only our own creation; for the creator necessarily knows all properties of his creatures, because they can't have any others except those he has given to them. So this alternative seems to imply that mathematical objects and facts (or at least *something* in them) exist objectively and independently of our mental acts and decisions, that is to say, some form or other of Platonism or "realism" as to the mathematical objects [holds].

If we accept the inferences and assertions in these two paragraphs, we also have a variant of 6.1.5: either physicalism is false or else Platonism in mathematics is true, or both. In fact, the rest of Gödel's Gibbs lecture was devoted to an attempt to argue in favor of Platonism in mathematics—a topic which he also discussed extensively in his conversations with me and which will be the subject matter of Chapter 7.

Gödel's thoughts about the nature and definition of *creation* and about the proposition that the brain is like a computer are among his favorite ideas. He elaborated on them in our discussions, and I consider them later, in the appropriate contexts. For the present, I limit myself to those of Gödel's observations which are directly relevant to the implications of his theorem. Not surprisingly, some of these observations are similar to those in his Gibbs lecture:

6.1.7   The incompleteness results do not rule out the possibility that there is a theorem-proving computer which is in fact equivalent to mathematical intuition. But they imply that, in such a—highly unlikely for other reasons—case, either we do not know the exact specification of the computer or we do not know that it works correctly.

6.1.8   My incompleteness theorem makes it likely that mind is not mechanical, or else mind cannot understand its own mechanism. If my result is taken together with the rationalistic attitude which Hilbert had and which was not refuted by my results, then [we can infer] the sharp result that mind is not mechanical. This is so, because, if the mind were a machine, there would, contrary to this rationalistic attitude, exist number-theoretic questions undecidable for the human mind.

6.1.9   There is a vague idea that we can find a set of axioms such that (1) all these axioms are evident to us; (2) the set yields all of mathematics. It follows from my incompleteness theorem that it is impossible to set up an axiom system satisfying (1) and (2), because, by (1), the statement expressing the consistency of the system should also be evident to me.—All this is explicitly in my Gibbs lecture.

6.1.10   Another consequence of my theorem is a disjunction of two propositions: (a) Mathematics is incompletable in the sense that its evident axioms cannot be embodied in a finite rule and, therefore, the human mind surpasses finite machines, or else (b) there exist absolutely undecidable Diophantine problems for the human mind. This consequence of my theorem, like the preceding one, is sharp.—Either alternative is opposed to the materialist philosophy. Alternative (a) is against the identification of the brain with mind. Alternative (b) disproves the view that mathematical objects are our creation.

Given Gödel's result that a formal system or a theorem-proving computer cannot prove its own consistency, an obvious idea for refuting computabilism is to try to argue that mind can prove its own consistency. In *MP* I considered this attempt at length (*MP*:317–321). In the course of discussing my manuscript, Gödel made several observations on this line of thought. Later he wrote a one-sentence summary of them (*MP*:328 n. 14):

6.1.11   Because of the unsolved intensional paradoxes for concepts like *concept, proposition, proof*, and so on, in their most general sense, no proof using the self-reflexivity of these concepts can be regarded as conclusive in the present stage of development of logic, although, after a satisfactory solution of these paradoxes, such [an] argument may turn out to be conclusive.

The intensional paradoxes certainly include that of the concept: being a concept that does not apply (meaningfully) to itself. I am not sure what other examples Gödel had in mind. An example about the general [or absolute] concept of proof might be: this proposition is not provable. But I am merely conjecturing: I wish I had asked him. As I said before, Gödel finds the intensional paradoxes an important open problem and distinguishes them from the semantic paradoxes which, he says, are trivial and have been solved.

6.1.12   If one could clear up the intensional paradoxes somehow, one would get a clear proof that mind is not [a] machine. The situation of the general concept of *proof* is similar to that with the general concept of *concept*. Both belong to the field of *bankruptcy* [an implicit reference to the discussion in *MP*:190], because we have not cleared up the contradictions surrounding these general concepts. Otherwise a proof: once we understand the general concept of proof, we have also a proof by the mind of its own consistency. As it is, we can actually derive contradictions from the general concept of proof, including the self-application of proof. On the basis of our defective understanding of the general concept of proof, we can potentially arrive at the conclusion that evidence is simply inconsistent. This shows that something is wrong with our logical ideas, which should be completely evident.

6.1.13   The concept of *concept* and the concept of *absolute proof* [briefly, AP] may be mutually definable. What is evident about AP leads to contradictions which are not much different from Russell's paradox. Intuitionism is inconsistent if one adds AP to it. AP may be an *idea* [in the Kantian sense]: but as soon as one can state and prove things in a systematic way, we no longer have an idea [but have then a concept]. It is not satisfactory to concede [before further investigation] that AP or the general concept of concept is an idea. The paradoxes involving AP are intensional—not semantic—paradoxes. I have discussed AP in my Princeton bicentennial lecture [reprinted in Gödel 1990, hereafter *CW2*:150–153].

6.1.14   It is possible that a clarification of AP could be found so that, by applying it, mathematical intuition would be able to prove its own consistency, thereby showing that it differs from a machine. Since, however, we are not clear about AP, it remains possible that either the consistency of mathematical intuition is not a proposition or at least it is not evident. The argument [against computabilism, by proving the consistency of our mathematical intuition] may be correct, if we find the solution to the paradoxes involving AP, because the proof [of consistency] might belong to the domain that is retained.

6.1.15   Brouwer objects to speaking of all proofs or all constructible objects. Hence the extensional and the intensional paradoxes do not appear in intuitionism according to his interpretation. But I think that this exclusion of *all*, like the appeal to type theory in the theory of concepts, is arbitrary [from the intuitionistic standpoint].

6.1.16   It is immediately evident that I am consistent, if you accept AP as a concept. There is an apparent contradiction in my own use of the *human mind* also as a concept. What is to be avoided is to use this concept in a self-referential manner. We don't know how to do it. But I make no self-referential use of the concept of human mind.

The main point of Gödel's observations 6.1.11 to 6.1.16 for the present context is, as I see it, the idea that if we come to a better understanding of the general concept of proof, we may be able to see in a direct manner that the whole range of what we are able to prove mathematically is indeed consistent. If so, mathematical intuition is, unlike a computer, capable of seeing and proving its own consistency. Gödel's adaptation of the Kantian distinction between ideas and concepts seems to suggest that, even though absolute proof looks like an idea to us in our present state of ignorance, it may turn out to be a concept upon further investigation. If we can see absolute proof as a concept, we shall be able to state and prove things about it in a systematic way. In particular, it is possible that we shall be able to apply our improved mathematical intuition to prove its own consistency.

Some of Gödel's brief observations on related points follow.

6.1.17   When one speaks of *mind* one does *not* mean a machine (in any general sense) but a machine that recognizes itself as right.

In June 1972, at a meeting to honor John von Neumann, Gödel asked the following question:

6.1.18   Is there anything paradoxical in the idea of a machine that knows its own program completely?

6.1.19   The brain is a computing machine connected with a spirit. [Compare 6.2.14.]

6.1.20   The machine always knows the reasons. We can know or strongly conjecture a statement without being able to offer a proof. In terms of self-analysis, we are not aware of everything in us; of much in our minds we are simply unconscious. We are imprecise and often waver between different alternatives. Consciousness is the main difference.

6.1.21   Consciousness is connected with one unity. A machine is composed of parts. [Compare 9.4.13.]

6.1.22   The active intellect works on the passive intellect which somehow shadows what the former is doing and helps us as a medium. [Compare 7.3.14.]

There is a terminological complication in Gödel's use of the terms *human mind* and *mathematical intuition*. I tend to think in terms of the collective experience of the human species, and so I asked him once about his usage. His reply suggests to me a simplifying idealization:

6.1.23   By *mind* I mean an individual mind of unlimited life span. This is still different from the collective mind of the species. Imagine a person engaged in solving a whole set of problems: this is close to reality; people constantly introduce new axioms.

On 5.6.76 Gödel told me about a conjecture which he believed would, if true, prove mind's superiority over computers (misstated in *RG*:197):

6.1.24   It would be a result of great interest to prove that the shortest decision procedure requires a long time to decide comparatively short propositions. More specifically, it may be possible to prove: For every decidable system and every decision procedure for it, there exists some proposition of length less than 200 whose shortest proof is longer than 10^{20}. Such a result would actually mean that computers cannot replace the human mind, which can give short proofs by giving a new idea.

6.2 Mind and Matter: On Physicalism and Parallelism

The problem of mind and matter is notoriously elusive. Once we distinguish mind from matter, we seem to be committed to a fundamental dualism. Yet it is then hard to come up with any reasonable account of how the interaction between mind and matter works. At the same time, we are also accustomed to such a distinction in our everyday thinking.

One familiar formulation of the central question about the relation between mind and matter is to ask whether, as Gödel puts it, "the brain suffices for the explanation of all mental phenomena." One simple test for the existence of any such explanation is to ask whether there are a sufficient number of brain operations to *represent* the mental operations so that every mental operation corresponds to one or more neural operations. In other words, regardless of how mind and matter interact, we may ask the less elusive—one might say *quantitative*—question whether there exists some one-to-one or many-to-one correlation between neural and mental phenomena.

A convenient term for the belief that there indeed exists some such correlation is *psychoneural parallelism*. If we assume that all neural operations are physical operations of a special type, we may also identify this position as *psychophysical parallelism*, which may be viewed as a definite component—or even a precise formulation—of the somewhat vague position of *physicalism*. In this context, I identify physicalism with parallelism, and, for the moment, do not distinguish between the different forms of parallelism, which correlate the physical with the biological, then the neural, and then the mental.

Instead of psychoneural or psychophysical parallelism, Gödel uses the formulation: (1) There is no mind separate from matter. Since his conjectured refutation of (1) also refutes parallelism, I shall, for the moment—instead of trying to find a faithful interpretation of (1)—simply identify it with parallelism. Using this simplification, two of Gödel's assertions (*MP*:326) can be reformulated thus:

6.2.1   Parallelism is a prejudice of our time.

6.2.2   Parallelism will be disproved scientifically (perhaps by the fact that there aren't enough nerve cells to perform the observable operations of the mind).

A prejudice is not necessarily false. Rather it is just a strongly held belief not warranted by the available evidence—its intensity being disproportionate to the solidity of evidence for it. The widespread belief in parallelism today is one aspect of the prevalence of scientism, which, as we know, is largely a consequence of the spectacular success and, therewith, the dominant position of science and technology in our time.

By the way, Wittgenstein makes similar observations in his *Zettel* (notably in the paragraphs 605 to 612). For instance: "The prejudice in favor of psychophysical parallelism is a fruit of primitive interpretation of our concepts." He imagines someone who makes rough jottings—as a text is recited—that are sufficient to enable the person to reproduce the text later, and then says: "The text would not be *stored up* in the jottings. Why should it be stored up in our nervous system?" (Wittgenstein 1981).

Regardless of whether Gödel's conjecture 6.2.2 could be confirmed, it is remarkable as an illustration of the significant idea that the philosophical issue of parallelism is (also) a scientific and empirical problem. This is a point Gödel emphasized several times in his discussions with me.

6.2.3   It is a logical possibility that the existence of mind [separate from matter] is an empirically decidable question. This possibility is *not* a conjecture. They don't even realize that there is an empirical question behind it. They begin with an assumption that no [separate] mind exists. It is a reasonable assumption that in some sense one can recall every experience in one's life in every detail: if this assumption is true, the existence of mind may already be provable from it.

6.2.4   Logic deals with more general concepts; monadology, which contains general laws of biology, is more specific. The limits of science: Is it possible that all mind activities—infinite, for example, always changing, and so on—are brain activities? There can be a factual answer to this question. Saying no to thinking as a property of a specific nature calls for saying no also to elementary particles. Matter and mind are two different things.

6.2.5   The mere possibility that there may not be enough nerve cells to perform the function of the mind introduces an empirical component into the problem of mind and matter. For example, according to some psychologists, the mind is capable of recalling all details it ever experienced. It seems plausible that there are not enough nerve cells to accomplish this if the empirical storage mechanism would, as seems likely, be far from using the full storage capacity. Of course other possibilities of an empirical disproof are conceivable, while the whole question is usually disregarded in philosophical discussions about mind and matter.

In connection with the broad issue of the nature of philosophy and its relation to science, Gödel used, when commenting on my discussion of "the divorce of philosophy from science and life" (*MP*:376), the issue of mind and matter as an example:

6.2.6   Many so-called philosophical problems are scientific problems, only not yet treated by scientists. One example is whether mind is separate from matter. Such problems should be discussed by philosophers before scientists are ready to discuss them, so that philosophy has as one of its functions to guide scientific research. Another function of philosophy is to study what the meaning of the world is. [Compare Section 9.4 below.]

At different times, Gödel made scattered observations relevant to parallelism and the contrast between mind and matter.

6.2.7   It is a weaker presupposition to say that the mind and the brain are not the same—than [to say] that the mind and the brain are the same.

6.2.8   The fundamental discovery of introspection marks the beginning of psychology. [For further elaboration, see 5.3.28.]

6.2.9   Mind is separate from matter: it is a separate object. In the case of matter, for something to be whole, it has to have an additional object. [Compare 9.4.12.]

In June 1972, Gödel asked at a public meeting:

6.2.10   Is there enough specificity in the enzymes to allow for a mechanical interpretation of all functions of the mind?

It is common to distinguish the emergence of life from the emergence of mind. In this sense, the distinction between mind and matter assimilates biological and neural phenomena to physical phenomena. If we do not assume this assimilation, then psychophysical parallelism includes as components biophysical, neurobiological, and psychoneural parallelisms. For instance, some biologists affirm that, whether or not computabilism holds for the physical, it does not hold for the biological—in particular, because of the importance of the historical dimension in life.

In his summary, prepared in 1972, of the early discussions, Gödel adds, after giving his conjecture about a scientific refutation of psychoneural parallelism, some of his other opinions:

6.2.11   More generally, I believe that mechanism in biology is a prejudice of our time which will be disproved. In this case, one disproof, in my opinion, will consist in a mathematical theorem to the effect that the formation within geological times of a human body by the laws of physics (or any other laws of a similar nature), starting from a random distribution of the elementary particles and the field, is as unlikely as the separation by chance of the atmosphere into its components.

This complex statement calls for some interpretative comment. From Gödel's other observations (see below), it seems clear that by *mechanism* in this context, he means, Darwinism, which he apparently sees as a set of algorithmic laws (of evolution). Even though he seems to believe that the brain—and presumably also the human body—functions like a computer (see below), he appears to be saying here that the human body is so complex that the laws of physics and of evolution are insufficient to account for its formation within the commonly estimated period of time.

In his discussions with me, Gödel made some related remarks.

6.2.12   I don't think the brain came in the Darwinian manner. In fact, it is disprovable. Simple mechanism can't yield the brain. I think the basic elements of the universe are simple. Life force is a primitive element of the universe and it obeys certain laws of action. These laws are not simple, and they are not mechanical.

6.2.13   Darwinism does not envisage holistic laws but proceeds in terms of simple machines with few particles. The complexity of living bodies has to be present either in the material or in the laws. The materials which form the organs, if they are governed by mechanical laws, have to be of the same order of complexity as the living body.

Gödel seems to believe both that the mind is more complex than the brain and that the brain and the human body could not have been formed as a matter of fact entirely by the action of the forces stipulated by such laws as those of physics and evolution. Of course, the desire to find "holistic laws" has been repeatedly expressed by many people. As we know, however, no definite advance has been achieved so far in this quest.

If the brain is just an ordinary physical object, then neural computabilism is a consequence of physical computabilism. But Gödel seems to make a surprising turn, which I missed for a long time. It depends on his belief that there is mind (or spirit) separate from matter. He seems to say that the brain is in itself just a physical object, except for the fact that it is connected to a mind.

6.2.14   Even if the finite brain cannot store an infinite amount of information, the spirit may be able to. The brain is a computing machine connected with a spirit. If the brain is taken to be physical and as [to be] a digital computer, from quantum mechanics [it follows that] there are then only a finite number of states. Only by connecting it [the brain] to a spirit might it work in some other way.

It seems to follow from this remark that the brain is a special and exceptional computer and physical object, because we have no way to *connect* an ordinary computer or physical object to a spirit in such an intimate manner. The complexity of the human body asserted in 6.2.11 may, therefore, have to do with Gödel's belief that it is, through the brain, connected to a mind. According to 6.2.12, life force is a primitive element of the universe. Indeed, Gödel's inclination toward monadology seems to suggest that the life force is more basic than the accompanying physical embodiment that develops with it.

6.3 Turing Machines or Gödelian Minds?

As I mentioned before, in the summer of 1971 Gödel agreed to hold regular sessions with me to discuss a manuscript of mine, which was subsequently published in 1974 as *From Mathematics to Philosophy* (*MP*). In the very first session, on 13 October 1971, he made extensive comments on the section on mechanical procedures (especially *MP*:81–83, 90–95).

Specifically, he concentrated on my discussion of the precision and justification of Turing's definition of mechanical procedures.

The main points Gödel introduced in this session, and continued to elaborate on in later sessions, are three: (1) Turing machines fully capture the intuitive concept of mechanical (or computational) procedures—and, equivalently that of formal system—in a precise definition, thereby revealing the full generality of Gödel's own incompleteness theorems; (2) Turing machines are an important piece of evidence for Gödel's belief that sharp concepts exist and that we are capable of perceiving them clearly; (3) Turing's argument for the adequacy of his definition includes an erroneous proof of the stronger conclusion that minds and machines are equivalent.

As an issue relevant to both (1) and (2), Gödel introduced and then repeatedly reconsidered a technical point about Turing's definition. I had construed Turing's definition as dealing with total functions and had argued that the definition "is actually not as sharp as it appears at first sight" because it includes the condition that the computation always terminates: "It is only required that this condition be true, the method to be used in establishing its truth is left open" (MP:83). Both for the purpose of supporting his belief in sharp concepts and in order to link up mechanical procedures with formal systems, Gödel chose to construe Turing's definition as dealing with partial functions. There were repeated discussions on this point, to which I return in Section 6.4 (below).

In connection with point (2), Gödel immediately began to elaborate his own Platonism in mathematics and to give other examples of our ability to perceive sharp concepts clearly. I leave this aspect of the discussion for the next chapter, and concentrate here primarily on Point (3), which is concerned with one of Gödel's attempts to prove mind's superiority over computers.

In connection with (1), Gödel often emphasized the importance of Turing's definition. In his Princeton lecture of 1946, he attributed the importance of the concept of general recursiveness (or Turing computability) to the fact that it succeeds "in giving an absolute definition of an interesting epistemological notion" (Gödel 1990, hereafter *CW2*:150). In the 1960s he singled out Turing's work as the decisive advance in this regard and added two notes to his own earlier work to say so (Gödel 1986, hereafter *CW1*:195, 369). In the second note, written in 1964, he added some observations in the direction of Point (3):

6.3.1 Note that the question of whether there exist finite *non-mechanical* procedures (such as those involving the use of abstract terms on the basis of their meaning), not equivalent with any algorithm, has nothing whatsoever to do with the adequacy of the definition of "formal system" and of "mechanical procedure." ... Note that the results mentioned in this postscript do not establish any bounds for the powers of human reason, but rather for the potentiality of pure formalism in mathematics [CW1:370].

Around 1970 Gödel wrote a paragraph entitled "A Philosophical Error in Turing's Work" CW2:306), intended as a footnote after the word *mathematics* in the above quotation. The version in *MP* (pp. 325–326), which is under discussion in this chapter, is a revision, written in 1972, of the "error" paragraph. Before discussing Gödel's complex comments on this "error," let me digress long enough to give some indication of Turing's ideas.

Turing passes from the abstract use of the word *mechanical* ("performed without the exercise of thought or volition") to a concrete use ("performable by a machine") and considers the actions of a "computer" (i.e., an abstract human being who is making a calculation). The computer is pictured as working on squared paper as in "a child's arithmetic book." Turing then proceeds to introduce several simplifications, arguing in each case that nothing essential is lost thereby. For instance, we may suppose that the computation is carried out on a potentially infinite tape divided into squares or cells, the two-dimensional character of paper being non-essential. The main idea is that computation proceeds by discrete steps and that each step is local and locally determined, according to a finite table of instructions.

Ordinarily we store the instructions in our mind as "states of mind" which, together with the symbols under observation, determine what we are to do at each stage, such as changing the content of some cells, moving some distance to observe other cells, and changing the state of mind. Without loss of generality, Turing assumes that the computer observes only one cell at a time, in which only one symbol (including "blank") is written. Moreover, he assumes only three basic acts: changing the content of the cell under observation; shifting attention to the next cell (to the left or to the right); and changing the "state of mind."

In my draft of *MP*, I tried to justify the adequacy of Turing's definition of mechanical procedure by speaking of the mind and the brain interchangeably-thereby implicitly assuming neural parallelism (see *MP*:91–95). In particular, I stated and formulated a "principle of finiteness": "The mind is only capable of storing and perceiving a finite number of items at each moment; in fact, there is some fixed finite upper bound on the number of such items" (p. 92). Among the applications of this principle, I mentioned the issue of storage:

[FSM] [that is, Finitely many States of Mind] Moreover, the number of states of mind which need be taken into account is also finite, because these states must be somehow stored in the mind, in order that they can all be ready to be entered upon. An alternative way of defending this application of the principle of finiteness is to remark that since the brain as a physical object is finite, to store infinitely many different states, some of the physical phenomena which represent them must be "arbitrarily" close to each other and similar to each other in structure. These items would require an infinite discerning power, contrary to the fundamental physical principles of today. A closely related fact is that there is a limit to the amount of information that can be recovered from any physical system of finite size (*MP*:92–93).

It was in commenting on this paragraph that Gödel first stated, on 13 October 1971, his idea that the brain is a computer connected to a mind (see 62.14 above). He went on to say:

6.3.2   It is by no means obvious that a finite mind is capable of only a finite number of distinguishable states. This thesis presupposes: (1) spirit is matter; (2) either physics is finitary or the brain is a computing machine with neurons. I have a typed page relevant to this thesis which is forthcoming in *Dialectica* [undoubtedly a reference to the note later published in Gödel 1990:306].

On 10 November 1971 Gödel gave an improved formulation of the two presuppositions:

6.3.3   The thesis of finitely many states presupposes: (a) no mind separate from matter; (b) the brain functions according to quantum mechanics or like a computer with neurons. A weaker condition is: physics remains of the same kind as today, that is, of limited precision. The limited precision may be magnified, but it will not be different in kind.

It was only much later, probably in May of 1972, that Gödel gave me several typed pages for inclusion in *MP*, which included (a) a reformulation of his note of Turing's philosophical error; (b) a reformulation of 6.3.3 as footnote 30 attached to my [FSM] paragraph; and (c) a further elaboration of 6.3.3. Item (b) reads as follows:

6.3.4   [Gödel points out that] the argument in this paragraph, like the related arguments of Turing, depends on certain assumptions which bear directly on the broader question as to whether minds can do more than machines. The assumptions are: (1) there is no mind or spirit separate from matter; (2) physics will always remain of the same kind in that it will always be one of limited precision (*MP*:102).

The typed pages for (a) and (c) are highly complex (printed in *MP*:325–326). Instead of reproducing the passage in full, I propose to break it into several parts and comment on them as I continue. Roughly speaking, (a) is devoted to proposing a possible line of approach to prove the superiority of mind over computers, and (c) is devoted to an additional analysis, possibly stimulated by my formulation of [FSM], to consider the conditions under which what Gödel calls "Turing's argument" becomes valid. The complexity of (c) stems from both the inference from the conditions and

Gödel's positive and negative comments on the plausibility of each of the several conditions.

6.3.5   Attempted proofs for the equivalence of minds and machines are fallacious. One example is Turing's alleged proof that every mental procedure for producing an infinite series of integers is equivalent to a mechanical procedure.

6.3.6   Turing, in his 1937, p. 250 [Davis 1965:136], gives an argument which is supposed to show that mental procedures cannot carry farther than mechanical procedures. However, this argument is inconclusive, because it depends on the supposition that a finite mind is capable of only a finite number of distinguishable states.

Interpretation.   One problem is to identify from 6.3.6 the Turing argument being considered. Before doing that, however, one has to interpret the phrase "proofs for the equivalence of mind and machines." For a long time I assumed that it refers to proofs for the full thesis of equivalence: the thesis of mental computabilism, the thesis that minds can do no more than computers. As a result of this assumption, I puzzled over the matter and wrote the following two paragraphs:

I have certainly never interpreted this particular reasoning by Turing in such a manner. Nor do I believe that Turing himself intended to draw such a strong consequence from it. Even though he often tried to argue in favor of mental computabilism, I am not aware that he had ever claimed to appeal to this particular argument of his as a proof of the conclusion attributed to him by Gödel.

Moreover, Gödel implies that what Turing allegedly proved is sufficient to establish computabilism for the mental. In other words, he suggests that, in order to refute mental computabilism, it is necessary that there are mental *procedures* which are systematic but cannot be carried out by any computer. It seems to me sufficient to refute mental computabilism by finding certain tasks which minds can do but computers cannot—without necessarily resorting to a systematic mental *procedure*. In any case, it seems to me desirable to distinguish the thesis of mind's superiority from the specific requirement of there being some noncomputational systematic mental procedure. If one believes that the two theses are equivalent, then an explicit argument to show the equivalence seems to me to be needed.

Recently, however, I have decided that my previous interpretation of the phrase "proofs for the equivalence" had been too literal and had not captured Gödel's intention. My present interpretation of the phrase is to take "proofs for the equivalence" to mean, in this context, just proofs aimed in the general direction of, or *toward*, establishing the equivalence of mind and machines. Under this interpretation, Gödel's choice of the Turing argument as his target of attack was motivated by his desire to find some sharp issue to consider within the murky area of trying to prove or disprove the equivalence of minds and computers. Furthermore, under Gödel's interpretation of the Turing argument, although that argument, even if it is sound, fails to prove mental computabilism fully, nonetheless, a refutation of it along the line of Gödel's proposal would succeed in refuting mental computabilism fully.

At the same time, Gödel expresses strong views on several familiar beliefs which are of independent interest, quite apart from their relation to the Turing argument and Gödel's proposed line of refutation. Indeed, I myself find these views more stimulating and less elusive than their connection to the Turing argument. The first full paragraph of p. 326 in *MP* can be summarized in four assertions:

6.3.7   It is a prejudice of our time to believe that (1) there is no mind separate from matter; indeed, (1) will be disproved scientifically.

6.3.8   It is very likely that (2) the brain functions basically like a digital computer.

6.3.9   It is practically certain that (2') the physical laws, in their observable consequences, have a finite limit of precision.

6.3.10   If we accept (1), together with either (2) or (2'), then Turing's argument becomes valid.

I consider 6.3.7 at length in Section 6.2 above and discuss 6.3.8 and 6.3.9 in section 6.5 below. The difficult task is the interpretation and evaluation of 6.3.10. Since, as I explain in section 6.5, it is reasonable to accept 6.3.9, the content of 6.3.10 is, essentially, that if we accept either (1) or parallelism, then Turing's argument is valid, which, according to Gödel, shows that mental procedures cannot accomplish more than mechanical procedures.

Most of us today are accustomed to thinking of the functions of the brain and the mind interchangeably. For instance, in my formulation of [FSM], quoted above, the appeal to the correlation is quite explicit. In Turing's own formulation of his argument, the situation is not so obvious. In any case, it seems necessary first to understand what Gödel means by Turing's argument.

From 6.3.6, it seems possible to see Gödel as making the following assertions:

6.3.11   If (i) a finite mind is capable only of a finite number of distinguishable states, then (ii) mental procedures cannot carry any farther than mechanical procedures.

6.3.12   Turing's argument (iii) for the condition (i) is his idea which centers on the following sentences: "We will also suppose that the number of states of mind which need be taken into account is finite. The reasons for this are of the same character as those which restricted the number of symbols. If we admit an infinity of states of mind, some of them will be 'arbitrarily close' and will be confused" [Davis 1965:136].

Gödel does not question the inference from (i) to (ii). But, in order to infer (i) from (iii), he believes it necessary to use some additional assumptions which he cannot accept. Indeed, Gödel's own proposal is to find a way to disprove both (i) and (ii). At the same time, he observes in 6.3.10 that if we assume (1) and (2) or (2'), then we can infer (i) from Turing's argument (iii). From this perspective, my formulation of [FSM], quoted above, may be seen as a sketch of such an argument.

Alternatively, we may try to prove Gödel's 6.3.10 as follows. By (1), there is no mind separate from the brain. Therefore, in order to prove (i), it is sufficient to prove that the brain is capable of only finitely many distinguishable states. The finite limit of precision recognized in (2') implies that within a finite volume we can distinguish only finitely many points. Therefore, since the brain is finite, when we observe it as a physical object, we can distinguish only finitely many states of it. Since the states have to be represented by observably distinguishable brain states, the brain, observing itself "from inside," can have no special advantage. Otherwise the brain would be able to distinguish more states than are allowed by the finite limit of precision.

There remains the question whether it is necessary for Turing to appeal to such additional assumptions in order to complete his argument (iii) for the conclusion (i). At the beginning of his essay, Turing summarizes in advance his justification of his definition of "calculable by finite means"—therewith of (i) as a part of the definition—in one sentence: "For the present I shall only say that the justification lies in the fact that the human memory is necessarily limited" (Davis 1965:117). One would be inclined to acknowledge such a limitation, however, whether one is thinking of the brain's memory or the mind's.

In trying to indicate the adequacy of his "atomic operations," Turing does bring in the notion of physical system. "Every such operation consists of some change of the physical system consisting of the [human] computer and his tape. We know the state of the system if we know the sequence of symbols on the tape, which of these are observed by the computer (possibly with a special order), and the state of mind of the computer" (Davis 1965:136). If we believe that there is mind separate from matter, we may feel also that there are distinguishable states of mind which are not adequately represented in the *physical* system. In other words, there may be distinguishable states of mind which are not distinguishable in their physical representation in the brain.

Gödel's own attempt to refute mental computerism includes the following statements (*MP*:325):

6.3.13   *Mind, in its use, is not static, but constantly developing.*

6.3.14   Although at each stage of the mind's development the number of its possible states is finite, there is no reason why this number should not converge to infinity in the course of its development.

6.3.15   Now there may exist systematic methods of accelerating, specializing, and uniquely determining this development, for example, by asking the right questions on the basis of a mechanical procedure. But it must be admitted that the precise definition of a procedure of this kind would require a substantial deepening of our understanding of the basic operations of the mind. Vaguely defined procedures of this kind, however, are known, for example, the process of defining recursive well-orderings of integers representing larger and larger ordinals or the process of forming stronger and stronger axioms of infinity.

The example about defining larger and larger ordinals is, by the way, an implicit reference to Turing's 1939 Princeton doctoral dissertation, in which he tried to find a sequence of ordinal logics by continually adding at each stage new true propositions of the type which are, by Gödel's theorem, undecidable within the preceding ordinal logics in the sequence. Turing's idea was to confine the nonmechanical—intuitive—steps entirely to the verification that certain relations between integers do define larger and larger ordinals.

Assertion 6.3.13 seems to be confirmed by our experience with the workings our own minds. In contrast, 6.3.14 and 6.3.15 are conjectures, and it is not clear what would constitute a confirmation or disproof of either of them.

When we think about our mental states, we are struck by the feeling that they and the succession of them from one state to the next are not so precise as those of Turing machines or computers generally. Moreover, we develop over time, both individually and collectively; and so, for instance, what appeared to be complex becomes simple, and we understand things we did not understand before. Here again, we feel that the process of development is somewhat indefinite and not mechanical. Yet we do not see how we can capture these vaguely felt differences in formulations that are sufficiently explicit to secure a rigorous proof that we can indeed do more than computers can in certain specific ways. Gödel's choice of conjecture (6.3.14) gives the impression of providing us with an exact perspective for clarifying the differences, since the distinction between the finite and the infinite is one of the clearest differences we know, especially from our experience in mathematics.

But the relation between the contrast of the finite versus the infinite and that of the mechanical versus the nonmechanical is not simple. Typically computers, which each have only a fixed (finite) number of machine states, can in principle add and multiply any of the infinitely many numbers. A mind or a computer need not be in distinct states in order deal with distinct numbers. Gödel's notion of "the number of mind's states converging to infinity" is, I think, a complicated requirement, since there are states of different degrees of complexity. We seem to need a criterion to determine what sort of thing constitutes a state, in order to be able to count the number of states in any situation. For instance, we may try to specify a measure of simplicity such that what we think of as possible states of computers are exactly the simple ones according to the measure. It is not clear to me what a natural and adequate measure might be, except, perhaps, that it must imply the condition that the simple states be physically realizable.

Assume for the moment that some such criterion is given. How do we go about determining whether or not the number of the states of the mind converges to infinity? It would be hard to break up all mental states into such simple states. An easier approach might be this: select certain things that minds can do and show that they require more and more simple states in the agreed sense. Ideally, of course, we would have a proof of mind's superiority over computers if we could find something which minds can do but which cannot be done by using no matter how many *simple* states. If, however, we do not have such a strong result, but have only proved 6.3.14 in terms of simple states (in the agreed sense), it does not follow that we would have attained a proof of mind's superiority.

Suppose we have found a proof of 6.3.14. Converging to infinity in this case means just that, for every n, there is some stage in the development of a mind such that the number of the mind's states is greater than n. Since the states are, by hypothesis, of the kind that is appropriate to computers, there is, for each stage in the mind's development, some computer that has the same states the mind has at that stage. It remains possible that the different stages of the mind's development are related in a computable manner, so that there is a sort of supercomputer which modifies itself in such a way that, at each stage of the mind's development, the supercomputer functions like the computer that has the same states the mind has at that stage. Hence, it seems to me that the crucial issue is not whether the number of mind's states converges to infinity, but rather whether it develops in a computable manner.

Gödel's own statement, 6.3.15, seems to indicate the ambiguity of the conjecture that there may be some mental procedure that can go beyond any mechanical procedure. For instance, Gödel's own definition of constructible sets gives a systematic procedure by which, given any ordinal number a, we can define all constructible sets of order a or less. The procedure is not mechanical, since it is demonstrable that we cannot give all ordinal numbers by a mechanical procedure. At the same time, we ourselves cannot, at any stage of our development, give all ordinal numbers either.

Gödel's quest for nonmechanical systematic procedures seems to bear some resemblance to the Leibnizian idea of a universal characteristic. In fact, what Gödel said on two occasions about the Leibnizian idea gives some indication of the goal of his own quest:

6.3.16 [Conversation on 15.3.72.] In 1678 Leibniz made a claim of the universal characteristic. In essence it does not exist: any systematic procedure for solving problems of all kinds must be nonmechanical.

6.3.17 But there is no need to give up hope. Leibniz did not, in his writings about the *Characteristica universalis*, speak of a utopian project. If we are to believe his words, he had developed this calculus of reasoning to a large extent, but was waiting with its publication till the seed could fall on fertile ground. [See Russell paper, *CW*2:140].

With respect to the central issue of mind's superiority over computers, Gödel's note on Turing's philosophical error, we may observe, singles out three properties for comparing minds with computers: (a) mind's constant development in contrast with the predetermined character of a computer (6.3.13); (b) the possible convergence to infinity of the states of the mind, in contrast with the finiteness of the states of every computer (6.3.14); and (c) the possibility that there are nonmechanical mental procedures (6.3.15). Of these three contrasts, (a) is a fundamental fact that opens up different directions for further exploration. Conjectures (b) and (c) are two examples of such directions.

In particular, direction (c) looks for an extension of the concept of *mechanical* procedure to some suitable concept of *systematic* procedure with the following property: that it is precise enough and defined precisely enough to enable us to prove that it can accomplish more than can be accomplished by any mechanical procedure. In order, however, to define such a concept or such a procedure, we have to find some criterion of precision that is broader than that of being mechanical. Seen from this perspective, what Gödel is after here resembles his quest for a general definition of provability or definability (discussed in his 1946 Princeton lecture, *CW*2:150–153). In both cases, he is looking for "an absolute definition of an interesting epistemological notion."

There are various systematic procedures which improve our mental powers but which either are not mechanical or at least were not initially introduced as mechanical: the decimal notation, logarithms, algebra and analytic geometry as they are taught in secondary schools, and so on. Along a different direction, we can also view certain research programs as systematic procedures. With regard to many of these fruits of the mind's power, we may ask whether computers are capable of producing such procedures. Indeed, in some cases, we can show that the vaguely defined procedures can be replaced by mechanical procedures; in other cases we do not have precise enough formulations to determine whether they are or are not so replaceable.

6.4 Formal Systems and Computable Partial Functions

One of the points that Gödel and I discussed repeatedly was the question whether mechanical procedures are embodied in total or partial functions computable by Turing machines.

In defining a *computable* total function f, by a machine F, it is required that for every input m, there exists a number n such that a definite relation R holds between m and n. The relation R embodies the computation of the machine F to arrive at n as the value of $f(m)$, by beginning with m as input. The condition is of the form: for each m, there is an n, $R(m,n)$. It requires that the computation terminate (successfully) for each input m. There is an open question as to how this condition of general success is proved. (For an extended consideration of this question, see Wang 1990a, Chapter 2.)

On this point Gödel observed:

6.4.1   The precise concept of mechanical procedures does not require this condition of universal success. A mechanical procedure may or may not terminate. Turing's solution (analysis) is correct and unique. For this sharp concept there is not a problem of proof (of the condition of universal success). The unqualified concept is the same for the intuitionists and the classicists.

Later Gödel wrote an elaboration of this remark:

6.4.2   The precise notion of mechanical procedures is brought out clearly by Turing machines producing partial rather than general recursive functions. In other words, the intuitive notion does not require that a mechanical procedure should always terminate or succeed. A sometimes unsuccessful procedure, if sharply defined, still is a procedure, that is, a well-determined manner of proceeding. Hence we have an excellent example here of a concept which did not appear sharp to us but has become so as a result of a careful reflection. The resulting definition of the concept of mechanical by the sharp concept of "performable by a Turing machine" is both correct and unique. Unlike the more complex concept of always-terminating mechanical procedures, the unqualified concept, seen clearly now, has the same meaning for the intuitionists as for the classicists. Moreover it is absolutely impossible that anybody who understands the question and knows Turing's definition should decide for a different concept (*MP*:84).

To my suggestion that these partial procedures may be thought to be artificial and not mathematically interesting, Gödel responded:

6.4.3   At least one interesting concept, viz., that of a formal system, is made perfectly clear in a uniquely determined manner. There is no requirement of being successful [in trying to prove a statement] in a formal system. The concept was not clear to me in 1930 (or even in 1934); otherwise I would have proved my incompleteness results in the general form for all formal systems.

6.4.4 Formal systems coincide with many-valued Turing machines. The one who works the Turing machine can set a level at each time by his choice. This is exactly what one does in applying a formal system.

Gödel later wrote up these two observations for *From Mathematics to Philosophy*:

6.4.5 It may be argued that the procedures not requiring general success are mathematically uninteresting and therefore artificial. There is, I would like to emphasize, at least one highly interesting concept which is made precise by the unqualified notion of a Turing machine. Namely, a formal system is nothing but a mechanical procedure for producing theorems. The concept of formal system requires that reasoning be completely replaced by "mechanical operations" on formulas in just the sense made clear by Turing machines. More exactly, a formal system is nothing but a many-valued Turing machine which permits a predetermined range of choices at certain steps. The one who works the Turing machine can, by his choice, set a lever at certain stages. This is precisely what one does in proving theorems within a formal system. In fact, the concept of formal systems was not clear at all in 1930. Otherwise I would have then proved my incompleteness results in a more general form. Note that the introduction of many-valued Turing machines is necessary only for establishing agreement with what mathematicians in fact do. Single-valued Turing machines yield an exactly equivalent concept of formal system (*MP*:84).

Interpretation.   If one wishes to prove q in a formal system F, we can think of q as the input. If q is an axiom, it can be recognized as such and the proof is complete. Otherwise the next stage consists of all the alternative premises from which q follows by some rule of inference. For instance, if the only rule is modus ponens, the next stage consists of p and "q if p," for every proposition p in F. If, for some p, both p and "q if p" are axioms, then we have a proof q in F. Otherwise, we repeat the process for the propositions that are not axioms. In this way we have a tree structure. The one who works the machine makes choices or "sets a level" at certain stages. In this sense, a formal system is representable by a "many-valued Turing machine." We may also introduce a linear order of all alternative premises at different stages (say by the length of p) by an enumeration of all the nodes of the tree. In this way we get back to single-valued Turing machines.

With regard to Turing's definition of successful computational (or general recursive) procedures, Gödel made two observations:

6.4.6 It is imprecise in one and only one way, while originally the concept was not at all precise. The imprecision relates to the question whether the procedure is absolutely or demonstrably computable; in other words, whether the condition of universal success is merely true or demonstrable (say, intuitionistically).

6.4.7 The definition of total computable functions (in terms of Turing machines) is also precise from the objectivistic viewpoint, since the condition is either true or false, and the method of proving it is a separate issue not affecting the precision of the concept.

I used the concept of *mechanical procedure* in *MP* as an example to discuss tentatively the general question, "If we begin with a vague intuitive concept, how can we find a sharper concept to correspond to it faithfully?" (*MP*:81). Gödel replaced the word "sharper" by "sharp" and answered the question categorically by asserting that

The sharp concept is there all along, only we did not perceive it clearly at first. This is similar to our perception of an animal far away and then nearby. We had not perceived the sharp concept of mechanical procedures sharply before Turing, who brought us to the right perspective. And then we do perceive clearly the sharp concept (*MP*:84–85).

He went on to say more about the perception of concepts, linking it to "philosophy as an exact theory" and offering several examples of our successful perception of sharp concepts. As this part of the discussion has more to do with Platonism, I deal with it in the next chapter.

6.5 Neural and Physical Computabilism

The thesis of physical computabilism intends to assert that the physical world is like a computer or that physical processes are all algorithmic. Given, however, the limitations of our capacity to observe the world as it is, we have to approach the thesis by asking only—initially at least—whether physical laws based on our observations and our reflections on them are, and will continue to be, algorithmic. Similarly, instead of asking whether the brain *is* a computer, it is more suitable in our present state of knowledge to ask whether the brain functions basically *like* a computer.

On the issue of neural computabilism, Gödel seems to give an affirmative answer (quoted above as 6.3.8):

6.5.1   It is very likely that (a) the brain functions basically like a digital computer (*MP*:326).

This conjecture is stated in a context in which (a) is a companion of assumption (b): that there is no mind separate from matter. Since, however, Gödel believes (b) to be false and sees, as quoted above in 6.2.14, the brain as a computer connected to a mind, there is the problem of whether he is asserting 6.5.1 under the assumption (b) or not. Given the fact that he evidently believes that the mind does not function like a computer, he may be merely saying that, for those who believe (b), 6.5.1 is true.

In relation to physical computabilism, Gödel gives explicitly only a partial answer (quoted above as 6.3.9):

6.5.2   It is practically certain that (c) the physical laws, in their observable consequences, have a finite limit of precision [*MP*:326].

A comparison of statements 6.3.2 and 6.3.3, quoted above, indicates that Gödel considers (c) to be weaker than the assertion (d) that physics is finitary.

Since our observation of such physical properties as length, weight, temperature, and so on cannot yield completely accurate numerical values, in comparing the precise consequences of physical laws with our observations, we have to make allowance for certain minor differences, say, with respect to what we call "insignificant digits." If we take this familiar observation as the interpretation of (c), then we can, I believe, agree with Gödel that 6.5.2 is true. It follows that the numerical values we obtain by measurement and direct observation are all rational—or finite—numbers.

The formulation and testing of physical laws are ultimately based on a comparison of their consequences with the results—of limited precision—of our observations. There is a sense in which every (real) number and every function can be closely approximated, arbitrarily, by computable ones. The relations determined by physical laws which are only between results of observations can, therefore, all be seen as computable relations. From this perspective, we may see the use of noncomputable real numbers and functions as just a convenient way of summarizing and generalizing the observed data about physical properties and relations.

However, as we know, even though physical laws have to agree with data from observations, they are obtained through a great deal of reflection and construction on the basis of such data. It does not, therefore, follow from (c) that physical laws must be finitary or algorithmic. That is, I think, why Gödel said that (c) is a weaker condition than assertion (d).

In our discussions, I was puzzled by Godel's tendency to identify materialism with mechanism (in the sense of computabilism), because, for all we know, physical theory may or may not be and remain algorithmic. He seems to suggest that (c) will continue to hold and that, if there is no mind separate from matter, there is no difference in the observable consequences of materialism and mechanism.

Since I often failed to understand what Gödel said, sometimes I could not even formulate my questions well enough to communicate to him what I wanted to know. As a result, I was, on some occasions, not even able to see whether he was answering my questions. Let me, however, try to reconstruct some of the exchanges as clearly as I can.

When I asked him the reason for his belief that the brain as a physical object is capable only of finitely many distinguishable states, he replied:

6.5.3   Quantum mechanics is only finitary: this is certainly the case with chemical processes; we do not know the nuclear processes—which probably are not essential to neural activities.

I asked Gödel whether it is possible for there to be a physical box whose outputs are not a computable function of its inputs. I also asked whether, even if the physical world proceeds in a computable manner, it is possible that we do not know the initial conditions because there has been, in some sense, an infinite past. Earthquakes above a fixed lower bound, for example, may begin at instants that form a noncomputable sequence. To both questions, Gödel answered that we can find out that such a proposition is true only if we get a different kind of physics. Presumably, he meant by that: only if we develop some physical theory for which (c) is no longer true.

I asked about the possibility that in the future physics may use more mathematics, so that, in particular, mechanically unsolvable problems may become solvable in the physical world and physical computabilism may be disproved. Gödel's reply seems to shift the question to one about our mental powers:

6.5.4   In physics, we are not likely to go beyond real numbers, even less to go beyond set theory. Rationalistic optimism includes also the expectation that we can solve interesting problems in all areas of mathematics. It is not plausible that physics will use all of mathematics in its full intended richness. Moreover, at each stage, physics, if it is to be true once and for all, is to be presented on a given level, and therefore cannot use all of mathematics. [Gödel seems to consider it possible that we will at some stage arrive at definitive physical laws, and to contrast this with the open-endedness of mathematics. Elsewhere, he said:] Nuclear forces might require all of mathematics; the recondite parts of mathematics would then be brought back to the mainstream of scientific studies.

In connection with Gödel's idealization of mind as one individual's mind (6.1.23), I observed that it is easier to think of the human species continuing forever than of a single human mind doing so, and that we can also think of bigger and bigger machines being made; it then appears possible that the whole machine race could do more than any single machine. Gödel commented:

6.5.5   Such a state of affairs would show that there is something nonmechanical in the sense that the overall plan for the historical development of machines is not mechanical. If the general plan is mechanical, then the whole race can be summarized in one machine.

I also asked the familiar question whether robots may be able to operate in a noncomputable way as a result of growth through interactions with one another and with the environment. In reply, Gödel said:

6.5.6   A physical machine of limited size can never do anything noncomputable; it is not even excluded that it can grow bigger and bigger. This is because a machine is something we build and fully understand—including its manner of growth.

It seems to me that this answer depends on Gödel's belief in (c) of 6.5.2, or perhaps even on the assumption that physics is and will remain algorithmic. Otherwise, a robot may operate noncomputably through its interaction with its physical environment, and we may be able to know this with the help of suitable nonalgorithmic physical laws. In view of these observations, and Gödel's assertion about the brain functioning like a computer, I was and remain puzzled by the following statement:

6.5.7   To disturb Turing's conclusion we need no separate mind if we allow that the individual brain grows bigger and bigger.

One interpretation depends on the ambiguity of the phrase "separate mind." As I have quoted before, the brain, for Gödel, is a computer connected to a mind. If the combination is such that the mind is not *separate* in some suitable sense, then, as the brain grows bigger, it may derive powers through its connection to a mind so that, unlike a growing physical machine, it may operate noncomputably. On the other hand, it is likely that by "Turing's conclusion" Gödel means the proposition that a mind or brain can only have finitely many distinguishable states. If this is the case, it seems that if a brain or any physical object grows bigger indefinitely, then there is room for a continued increase of the number of its distinguishable states beyond any finite upper bound.

The major part of this chapter is concerned with the issue of mental computabilism—especially attempts to prove the mind's superiority over computers. Most discussions in the literature, because they implicitly assume psychoneural parallelism, make no distinction between mental and neural computabilism, so that one can switch back and forth between them.

I have given more details on many of the points touched on in this chapter in Wang 1993.

Chapter 7
Platonism or Objectivism in Mathematics

It is by viewing together a number of relevant facts that we come to believe in objectivism [in mathematics]. Philosophy consists of pointing things out rather than arguments.
Gödel, 25 November 1975

In his discussions with me in the 1970s, Gödel used the words *Platonism* and *objectivism* interchangeably. The two terms usually evoke different associations. Platonism implies the belief in a knowable objective reality of mathematical objects and concepts, while objectivism emphasizes the thesis that propositions about them are either true or false. There is, however, no doubt that our intuition of (the objectivity of) the truth or falsity of propositions explicates the content of our belief that the things they are about are objectively real. For this reason the crucial point is, as I believe and as Gödel agrees, the fact that we do have objectivity in mathematics.

Many people are put off by Gödel's seemingly mystical language of *perceiving* concepts and mathematical objects. But if we recall his derivation of this manner of speaking from the recognized fact of mathematical objectivity, then we have a common starting point. For example, in the Cantor paper (Gödel 1990, hereafter *CW2*:268) he says:

7.0.1   We do have something like a perception also of the objects of set theory, as is seen from the fact that the axioms force themselves upon us as being true.

Among the relevant facts mentioned by Gödel in support of objectivism are the following. (1) Facts are independent of arbitrary conventions. (2) Correct number-theoretical theorems reveal objective facts about integers. (3) These facts must have a content, because the consistency of number theory is not trivial but is derived from higher facts. (4) We can't assume sets arbitrarily because if we did we would get contradictions. (5) Objectivism is fruitful; it was fundamental to Gödel's own work in logic (Wang 1974a, hereafter *MP*:9); and the generic sets in Paul Cohen's work always require a realism about real numbers.

Platonism in mathematics occupies a central place in Gödel's philosophy and in his conversations with me. As a result, this chapter is closely related to the next two chapters, and it was often difficult to decide how best to distribute the material among them. I have tried to avoid duplication and, where I can, to use cross reference. My general idea is to put the material on sets and pure concepts in Chapter 8 and to relegate general methodological considerations to Chapter 9.

What Gödel said during our conversations reveals a more flexible and accommodating outlook than the view commonly attributed to him on the basis of his published statements. Specifically, he emphasizes (1) the fallibility of our knowledge; (2) the epistemological priority of objectivity over objects; (3) the primary importance of number theory—rather than set theory—for the position of objectivism; and (4) our relative freedom to choose between constructive and classical mathematics, with their different degrees of clarity and certainty.

The degrees of clarity and certainty of different parts of mathematics tend to decrease as we move from simple numerical computations to constructive and classical number theory, then to classical analysis and full set theory. At the same time, this movement in the direction of decreased certainty and clarity accompanies the historical and conceptual process of enlarging the realm of objectivity in mathematics. The main task of foundational studies is to reflect on this process by studying what I would like to call the *dialectic* of intuition and idealization, which is a kind of dialectic of the intuitive and the formal, the subjective and the objective. I discuss this dialectic in the first section of this chapter.

In section 7.2, I give an account of Gödel's contrast between *creation* and *discovery*, as well as his proposed arguments for extending the range of the discovered in mathematics from a minimum to some maximum. The remarkable extent of the intersubjective agreement of our mathematical intuition is the fundamental empirical datum for the formulation and the evaluation of every account of the nature of mathematics. The continued extension of the range of our intersubjective agreement tends to favor the discovery view of mathematics over the creation view, and the belief in an objective mathematical reality helps to explain the lack of arbitrariness and the restrictions on our freedom in mathematical thinking.

One idea central to the distinctly optimistic component of Gödel's objectivism is his belief that we are able to *perceive* concepts more and more clearly, not only in mathematics but also in fundamental philosophy. (For a brief summary of this position, see *MP*:84–86.) Whereas it is comparatively easy to share this belief in the case of mathematical concepts, Gödel's extrapolation from basic science to exact philosophy in this regard is contrary to our experience with the history of philosophy. In particular, as philosophers of this century have often emphasized, the essential immunity of mathematics to the contingent vicissitudes of language cannot be shared by philosophy. Section 7.3 is devoted to a report and a discussion of Gödel's observations on our capacity to perceive concepts.

In section 7.4 I summarize what Gödel takes to be the relevant facts in support of objectivism in mathematics, some of which will be elaborated in the next chapter. Finally, in the last section, I consider some apparent ambiguities in Gödel's position.

Near the end of his Gibbs lecture of 1951, Gödel distinguishes Platonism from a broader conception of objectivism:

7.0.2 [By the Platonistic view I mean the view that] mathematics describes a nonsensual reality, which exists independently both of the acts and the dispositions of the human mind and is only perceived, and probably perceived very incompletely, by the human mind (Gödel 1995, hereafter *CW3*).

7.0.3 Mathematical objects and facts (or at least *something* in them) exist objectively and independently of our mental acts and decisions [original manuscript, p. 16].

Even though Gödel made an admittedly inconclusive attempt to prove the thesis of 7.0.2 in his Gibbs lecture, his discussions with me emphasized instead the thesis of 7.0.3. On the one hand, it is easier to establish 7.0.3 than 7.0.2. On the other hand, once we accept 7.0.3, we may look to 7.0.2 for additional reasons to strengthen it.

7.1 The Dialectic of Intuition and Idealization

Natural numbers are central to objectivism. Gödel's published papers have more to do with sets and concepts than with numbers. (Compare Wang 1987a, hereafter *RG*:283–319.) In contrast, in his conversations with me on objectivism in mathematics Gödel stressed the central place of number theory—an area that has the advantage of being comparatively simple and stable, relative to the increase of our knowledge.

7.1.1 Just for the justification of the general position of objectivism, it is sufficient to confine one's attention to natural numbers [without bringing in sets and concepts, at least initially]. Objectivism agrees with Plato.

7.1.2 The real argument for objectivism is the following. We know many general propositions about natural numbers to be true (2 plus 2 is 4, there are infinitely many prime numbers, etc.) and, for example, we believe that Goldbach's conjecture makes sense, must be either true or false, without there being any room for arbitrary convention. Hence, there must be objective facts about natural numbers. But these objective facts must refer to objects that are different from physical objects because, among other things, they are unchangeable in time.

7.1.3 Logic and mathematics—like physics—are built up on axioms with a real content and cannot be explained away. The presence of this real content is seen by studying number theory. We encounter facts which are independent of arbitrary conventions. These facts must have a content because the consistency of number theory cannot be based on trivial facts, since it is not even known in the strong sense of knowing.

7.1.4   As far as sets are concerned, set theory is not generally accepted—as number theory is. The real argument has to be modified: For those mathematicians who believe in the truth of the familiar axioms of set theory or for the majority of those who think about set theory, there must be objective facts about sets.

7.1.5   There is a weak kind of Platonism which cannot be denied by anybody. Even for one who accepts the general position of Platonism, concepts may be [as unacceptable as a] square circle. There are four hundred possibilities: e.g., Platonism for integers only, also for the continuum, also for sets, and also for concepts. If we compare Goldbach's conjecture with the continuum hypothesis, we are more certain that the former must be either true or false.

Statement 7.1.5 is one example of Gödel's idea that we have a choice in deciding how strong an objectivism we are willing to accept in mathematics. His strategy is, I believe, to begin with some weak form of objectivism which nobody can deny, and then try to indicate how we are naturally led to stronger and stronger forms.

What is this weak kind of undeniable objectivism? Sometimes Gödel seems to mean by this simply the recognition that there is something general in the world—and whatever inevitably follows from this recognition. One possibility is the statement attributed by him to Bernays: It is just as much an objective fact that the flower has *five* petals as that its color is *red*. Since the idea is not to determine fully a unique weak objectivism but to indicate a weak *kind*, any natural, simple example can be chosen as an illustration.

According to Gödel, it might be that there are only finitely many integers and: If 10^{10} is already inconsistent, then there is no theoretical science. Elsewhere he said:

7.1.6   Nothing remains if one drives to the ultimate intuition or to what is completely evident. But to destroy science altogether, serves no positive purpose. Our real intuition is finite, and, in fact, limited to something small. The physical world, the integers and the continuum all have objective existence. There are degrees of certainty. The continuum is not seen as clearly [as the physical world and the integers].

These observations suggest both that we may start with numerical computations over small numbers and that there are forceful reasons why we do not choose to stop with them. Since *small* is an ambiguous word, it is hard to determine a unique collection of such correct assertions and their negations. But we may imagine some reasonable collection of this kind, such that each assertion in it is either true or false and we can find out which. To this extent, we may say that we all believe in a form of Platonism: something like this vague and neutral formulation could be said to define an "inevitable" or "universal" Platonism. We are inclined to say, in addition, that every correct assertion in this collection is an unconditional mathematical truth. And that this limited collection of objective truths can serve as a natural starting point to review how it leads to familiar enlargements.

One who would admit to be true only the members of this restricted range might be called a "strict finitist." One apparent reason for this radical position is adherence to what is *really* intuitive or perspicuous. For instance, we know, or expect, that we become fatigued and confused before we get definite results in complex computations with large numbers. George Miller's magic number 7 says that we are able to grasp at the same time 7 items, plus or minus 1 or 2. (Compare 8.2.9 below.)

We have, however, no available way of distinguishing in a uniform manner, between small (or feasible) and large numbers. We find it hard to locate any stable stopping place, either conceptually or relative to our experience. Historically, we have continually increased the range of feasible numbers, by improved notation, by the abacus, by computers, and so on. Conceptually, it is impossible to find an n such that n is small but n plus 1 is large. To deny this leads to the familiar *paradox of small numbers*: 1 is small, n plus 1 is small if n is; therefore, all (the infinitely many positive) integers are small. Indeed, the very act of singling out the operation of adding 1 as a clear basis for getting larger and larger numbers is itself an act of abstraction, to give form to a range of nebulous relations of order.

In other words, if we begin with small numbers, we are not able to find a natural stopping place until all the (finite) numbers are exhausted. If we try to find the totality of all feasible numbers, our failure inevitably leads us to the infinite totality of all (finite) numbers. This seems to be the first totality that satisfies both of two attractive requirements: (1) it includes all feasible numbers, and (2) we can work with it (as a stable limit or unit). Both historically and conceptually, these considerations are apparently inescapable. But to accept them is to make what Gödel called the "big jump." However, most discussions on the foundations of mathematics are concerned with issues that arise only after we have made this big jump.

It is well known, for instance, that both Hilbert's finitism and Brouwer's intuitionism take this big jump for granted. Indeed, it is only after the big jump has been made that familiar issues over potential and actual infinity, construction and description, predicative and impredicative definitions, countable and uncountable sets, strong axioms of infinity, and so on arise in their current form.

Once we make the big jump and recognize infinitely many numbers, we face immediately the essential part of the debates between Hilbert's finitism (the half of it that stipulates what has a "real content," disregarding the disproved other half that was to justify classicism on the basis of it), Brouwer's intuitionism (as restricted to natural numbers), and classical number theory. The next enlargement is to see how much can be done by handling sets like numbers (semi-intuitionism or predicativism). To envisage arbitrary (uncountably many) sets of numbers gets us to classical analysis. To consider also sets of these sets, their sets, and so on, leads to arbitrary sets. This quick summary may be seen as an account of the main features of the existing familiar distinctions of the varying ranges.

In the 1950s I was struck by the impression that what the different schools on the philosophy of mathematics take to be the range of mathematical truths form a spectrum, ordered more or less by a linear relation of containment that exhibits a step-by-step expansion. Instead of viewing the schools as contending and conflicting nonoverlapping paths, it is possible to take a more detached position and examine more closely the step-by-step expansion from one stage to the next. Indeed, I found that much of what had gone (for nearly eighty years) under the name of "foundational studies" could be seen from a neutral viewpoint as productive work directed to the more exact determination of the ranges and their interrelations.

At that time, I gave an extended description of this impression and presented the familiar alternative views (on the foundations of mathematics) under the following headings: (ii) anthropologism; (iii) finitism; (iv) intuitionism; (v) predicativism (number as being); (vi) extended predicativism (predicative analysis and beyond); (vii) Platonism (Wang 1958). I also considered (i) logic in the narrower sense (primarily predicate logic). [Strictly speaking, not every heading is contained in every later one. In particular, (ii) and (iv) both have special features that somewhat disrupt the linear order. But these refinements need not be considered in the present context.]

I found it reassuring when Gödel expressed similar ideas on several occasions in the 1970s. It turns out that something like this outlook had been a favorite of his since around 1930, even though he did not mention it in his published work. Allow me to quote his formulation of it in footnote 30 of the third version (written in the 1950s) of his Carnap paper (CW3):

7.1.7 Some body of unconditional mathematical truth must be acknowledged, because, even if mathematics is interpreted to be a hypothetico-deductive system [i.e., if the most restricted standpoint (implicationism) is taken], still the propositions which state that the axioms imply the theorems must be unconditionally true. The field of unconditional mathematical truth is delimited very differently by different mathematicians. At least eight standpoints can be distinguished. They may be characterized by the following catchwords: 1. Classical mathematics in the broad sense (i.e., set theory included), 2. Classical mathematics in the strict sense, 3. Semi-intuitionism, 4. Intuitionism, 5. Constructivism, 6. Finitism, 7. Restricted Finitism, 8. Implicationism.

Roughly speaking, 1 and 2 correspond to my (vii); 3 to (iv) and (v); 4 and 5 (differing, I believe, in that 4 adds to 5 free choice or lawless sequences to deal with the continuum) correspond to (iv); 6 to (iii); 7 to (ii) (though with differences); with 8 corresponding to taking (i) as the body of unconditioned truths.

For the purpose of sorting out alternative philosophies, it is sufficient to confine our attention to the essentials. Hence, we may appropriately overlook some of the fine points and consider a simplified list, limiting our attention to natural numbers and sets: (a) strict (or restricted) finitism as applied to numbers, (b) finitism (as applied to numbers), (c) intuitionist number theory, (d) classical number theory, (e) predicative analysis, (f) classical analysis, and (g) set theory.

Speaking loosely, we move from small numbers (in a) to (arbitrary) large numbers and thereby slip into the potentially infinite (in b and c). The next stage (d) is concerned with the actual infinite totality of numbers, whereas (e), a sort of "countabilism," begins to introduce sets, but only to the extent that they can be handled more or less like numbers. Arbitrary sets of numbers come in with (f), which may be taken to be concerned only with small sets, and we move from them to large sets, in (g).

Conceptually and developmentally, the transition from each stage to the next seems quite natural. In the first place, it seems arbitrary to take any number as the largest. Next, when we deal with infinitely many numbers, we are led to the principle of mathematical induction, which calls for some way of dealing with sets of numbers. Once we envisage such sets, we are led, by idealization, to the idea of arbitrary sets of natural numbers. But then sets of sets, and so on also come to mind.

Our historical experience shows that such extensions have not produced irresolvable contradictions or even lesser difficulties. On the contrary, on the whole and in the long run, strong agreement tends to prevail among practising mathematicians, if not always over the issue of importance, at least over that of correctness. A major concern of the philosophy of mathematics is evidently to study the justification of this agreement and to determine what it is that is agreed upon. The separation of the ordered stages is one way to reduce the difficulty of this task.

It is a familiar idea that infinity is at the heart of mathematics. Moreover, one feels that once the "jump" to infinity is made (from a to b or c or d), the additional extensions are not as remote from each other or from the "simplest" infinity as the infinite is from the finite. Indeed, Gödel once conjectured:

7.1.8 If set theory is inconsistent, then elementary number theory is already inconsistent.

This conjecture says that if the latter is consistent, so is the former. Such a conclusion certainly cannot be proved in set theory if set theory is consistent, since if it could, set theory would prove its own consistency and, therefore, by Gödel's incompleteness theorem, would be inconsistent.

Probably the idea behind the conjecture is our feeling that the extensions beyond the "simplest" infinity are so closely linked from one stage to the next that a serious weakness at one point would bring down the whole edifice. It is not excluded, although it is not likely, given our accumulated experience, that some new paradoxes will be found in set theory or even in classical analysis. If that should happen, there would be alternative possibilities: we might either find some convincing local explanation or trace the trouble back to the initial big jump to the infinite.

Once the wide disagreement between strict finitism and Platonism is decomposed along this line, we have—Gödel observed—more choices:

7.1.9   There is a choice of how much clarity and certainty you want in deciding which part of classical mathematics is regarded as satisfactory: this choice is connected to one's general philosophy.

The decomposition is characterized by what I propose to call a dialectic of intuition and idealization. On the one hand, Gödel emphasizes that our real intuition is limited to small sets and numbers. On the other hand, he finds, for instance, the Kantian notion of intuition too restrictive and has faith in the power of our intellectual—or categorial or conceptual or essential—intuition to accomplish such difficult tasks as finding the right axioms of set theory and generally clarifying basic concepts. The bridge— which I detected from his observations—between these two contrary components of his view is, to speak vaguely but suggestively, a sort of *dialectic*. By this I mean to point to our experience of the way our mathematical knowledge is increased and consolidated through the interplay of the enlargements of our intuition and our idealization.

Idealization is a constrained and testable way of extending or generalizing our beliefs by analogy or extrapolation or projection. It aims at extending both the range of the subject matter and the power of intuition of the subject or agent. With respect to mathematical knowledge, we seem to be justified, on empirical grounds, in believing that idealization has been successful so far and will continue to be so. Of course, we have sometimes run into difficulties and even onto wrong tracks and shall undoubtedly continue to do so. But this phenomenon is also familiar in (say) physics and biology—indeed to a greater extent than in the pursuit of mathematics.

I consider Gödel's general observations on the concepts of idealization and intuition in Chapter 9; here I mention only those which are directly relevant.

7.1.10   Strictly speaking we only have clear propositions about physically given sets and then only about simple examples of them. If you give up idealization, then mathematics disappears. Consequently it is a subjective matter where you want to stop on the ladder of idealization.

7.1.11   Without idealizations nothing remains: there would be no mathematics at all, except the part about small numbers. It is arbitrary to stop anywhere along the path of more and more idealizations. We move from intuitionistic to classical mathematics and then to set theory, with decreasing certainty. The increasing degree of uncertainty begins [at the region] between classical mathematics and set theory. Only as mathematics is developed more and more, the overall certainty goes up. The relative degrees remain the same.

I have mentioned the natural inclination that leads us to take the big jump from the finite to the infinite. This big jump, like the law of excluded middle, is an idealization. Once we are willing to take this jump, it becomes difficult to argue against taking other jumps or making other idealizations. In order to justify accepting the big jump but rejecting other jumps, it is necessary to find a notion of the intuitive that applies to the fruit of the big jump but not to additional jumps.

Kant's concept of intuition seems to satisfy this requirement to some extent. There are, however, as Gödel points out, difficulties in applying the concept in a way that does justice to our arithmetical intuition.

7.1.12   A good English rendering of Kant's term *Anschauung* is Kantian intuition or concrete intuition. Kant's considerations of pure intuition fail to produce a well-grounded belief in the consistency of arithmetic. This is a ground for rejecting Kant. Our intuition tells us the truth of not only 7 plus 5 being 12 but also [that] there are infinitely many prime numbers and [that] arithmetic is consistent. How could the Kantian intuition be all? There are objective facts about intuition.

7.1.13   Our real intuition is finite, and, in fact, limited to something small. Kantian intuition is too weak a concept of idealization of our real intuition. I prefer a strong concept of idealization of it. Number theory needs concrete intuition, but elementary logic does not need it. Non-elementary logic involves the concept of set, which also needs concrete intuition. Understanding a primitive concept is by abstract intuition.

It is well known that Hilbert sees Kantian intuition as a basis of his belief that the real content of mathematics lies in his *finitary* mathematics. Gödel himself points out this relation in the Bernays paper (*CW2:272*, n.b):

7.1.14   What Hilbert means by *Anschauung* is substantially Kant's space-time intuition confined, however, to configurations of a finite number of discrete objects. Note that it is Hilbert's insistence on *concrete* knowledge that makes finitary mathematics so surprisingly weak and exclude[s] many things that are just as incontrovertibly evident as finitary number theory.

Even though Gödel believes that the real content of mathematics goes far beyond its finitary part, he still finds significant the restricted concept of intuition of a finitary mathematician. In this connection, Sue Toledo has reported some observations by Gödel:

7.1.15   In this context, Gödel noted, it would be important to distinguish between the concepts of evidence intuitive *for us* and *idealized* intuitive evidence, the latter being the evidence which would be intuitive to an idealized finitary mathematician, who could survey completely finitary processes of arbitrary complexity. *Our* need for an abstract concept might be due to our inability to understand subject matter that is too complicated combinatorially. By ignoring this, we might be able to obtain an adequate characterization of idealized intuitive evidence. This would not help with Hilbert's program, of course, where we have to use the means at our disposal, but would nevertheless be extremely interesting both mathematically and philosophically. (Toledo 1975:10).

In this connection Gödel is pointing out that, even in the limited domain of finitary mathematics, we do not yet possess an adequate characterization of idealized intuition. In practice, of course, this fact has not prevented us from idealizing beyond this realm and acquiring intuitions about broader idealized structures. We have here one example of the advantages of a liberal position of objectivism: it finds within itself suitable places for restricted perspectives, such as the finitary one, and leaves room for doing justice to their special concerns as well.

The extensions of finitary number theory to the intuitionistic and then to the classical are good examples of the dialectic between intuition and idealization.

Roughly speaking, finitary number theory restricts its attention to decidable or computable properties. One natural idea is to include all and only properties that involve addition, multiplication, and operations *like* them. The familiar idea of *potential infinity* suggests that we refrain from talking directly about the totality of numbers and limit ourselves to pointing to it by using only "free variables." In this way, we arrive at the formal system F—sometimes called *quantifier-free primitive recursive arithmetic*— *which codifies, as is now generally agreed, Hilbert's finitary number theory.*

The commonly accepted formal system H for intuitionistic number theory goes beyond the system F in permitting certain uses of quantifiers over all numbers (including iterated mentions of the totality of all numbers), but restricts itself to employing them only in combination with intuitionistic logic. The familiar formal system N for classical number theory results from the system H by substituting classical logic for intuitionistic logic.

The process by which we arrive at the formal systems F, H, and N from our intuitive understanding of finitary, intuitionistic and classical number theory obviously involves the dialectic of the intuitive and the formal, of intuition and idealization. What is more remarkable is that, once we have the formal systems, we are able to see precise relations between them which enable us to gain a clear intuitive grasp of some of the relations between the original concepts. It so happens that the most informative results along this direction originated with Gödel: his interpretation of the system H by way of a natural extension of the system F (in the Bernays paper) helps to clarify the content of both systems, as well as their interrelationship; his translation of the system N into the system H (Gödel 1933) proves the relative consistency of the former to the latter, and localizes their differences at their different interpretations of existence and disjunction.

The investigations of predicative analysis—and also predicative set theory—may be seen as a natural extension of the formal system N for classical number theory. By restricting our attention to sets that are, like the set of natural numbers, countable, it is possible to obtain from this line of work comparatively transparent analogues of many concepts and theorems in classical analysis and classical set theory.

The most surprising result in this direction also came from Gödel, who, by choosing a suitable mixture of constructive and classical notions, was able to arrive at an informative model of classical set theory which possesses a number of attractive properties (Gödel 1939). In this case, the dialectic of the intuitive and the formal, and of the constructive and the nonconstructive, is striking: the intuitive concepts of predicativity and classical ordinal numbers are codified within a formal system of set theory to produce both an intuitive model of the system itself and a precise formal result of the relative consistency of the continuum hypothesis. Indeed, Gödel himself sees the work as a remarkable illustration of the fruitfulness of his objectivism (*MP*:10).

7.1.16 However, as far as, in particular, the continuum hypothesis is concerned, there was a special obstacle which *really* made it *practically impossible* for constructivists to discover my consistency proof. It is the fact that the ramified [predicative] hierarchy, which had been invented *expressly for constructivistic purposes*, has been used in an *entirely nonconstructive way*.

The most serious and extensive applications of the dialectic of intuition and idealization in Gödel's discussions with me were in connection with my attempt to justify the axioms of set theory (see *MP*:181–190). Gödel found my attempt congenial and, although I do not remember clearly, probably suggested, as a way to characterize my approach, the term "intuitive range of variability". (See the first two lines of the paragraph beginning at the middle of p. 182 of *MP*.—By the way, as Charles Parsons first pointed out, the word 'only' in the first line should be deleted.) In other words, Gödel saw my way of justifying the familiar axioms of set theory as one of showing in each case that the multitudes introduced by each axiom do constitute intuitive ranges of variability which we can *overview*. He also contrasts this principle with other principles that have been used for setting up axioms (*MP*:189–190).

I leave most of the detailed discussions of this subject for the section on set theory in Chapter 8, and confine myself here to some of Gödel's general observations. For example, immediately after saying that he preferred a stronger concept of intuition than Kant's (7.1.13), Gödel said:

7.1.17   It is a strong idealization of the concept of our real intuition to speak of sets as given by an overview. The idealized time concept in the concept of overview has something to do with Kantian intuition. Impredicative definitions have nothing to do with whether a set is given by an overview [which deals with extensions]. An intuitive range is contrasted with sets given by concepts [only] and more generally with something of which we have no overview: for example, the totality of all sets obtainable by the iterative concept of set. There is a huge difference between it and the power set of the set of finite ordinal numbers.

As I mentioned before, Gödel considers the step from our experience with individual natural numbers to the acknowledgment of all of them the big jump. He sees the recognition of the power set of a given set as the second jump in the formation of sets:

7.1.18   To arrive at the totality of integers involves a jump. Overviewing it presupposes an [idealized] infinite intuition. In the second jump we consider not only the integers as given but also the process of selecting integers as given in intuition. "Given in intuition" here means [an idealization of] concrete intuition. Each selection gives a subset as an object. Taking all possible ways of leaving elements out [of the totality of integers] may be thought of as a *method* for producing these objects. What is given is a psychological analysis, the point is whether it produces objective conviction. This is the beginning of analysis [of the concept of set].

7.1.19   We idealize the integers (a) to the possibility of an infinite totality, and (b) with omissions. In this way we get a new concretely intuitive idea, and then one goes on. There is no doubt in the mind that this idealization—to any extent whatsoever—is at the bottom of classical mathematics. This is even true of Brouwer. Frege and Russell tried to replace this idealization by simpler (logical) idealizations, which, however, are destroyed by the paradoxes. What this idealization—realization of a possibility—means is that we conceive and realize the possibility of a mind which can do it. We recognize possibilities in our minds in the same way as we see objects with our senses.

7.2 Discovery and Creation: Expansion through Idealization

In connection with the position of objectivism, Gödel makes various observations about the contrast between creation and discovery, as well as between the subjective and the objective. By adhering to the concept of creation as the making of something out of nothing, he sees severe limitations on the human capacity to create. For the purpose of securing a solid ground for our mathematical knowledge, he judges the familiar strategy of taking intersubjective agreement as the ultimate criterion of truth to be an inconsistent half-measure. In particular, his belief in our capacity to know objective reality as it is is at the center of his dissatisfaction with Kant's philosophy.

From the Gibbs Lecture to the Conversations in the 1970s

In the writings published during his lifetime, Gödel rarely discusses explicitly the familiar and elusive issue of whether mathematics is discovered (found) or created (made) by us. He did, however, consider this issue during his conversations with me, and, as I now know, in preparing his Gibbs lecture in 1951. Given his conception of creation, it is easy to conclude that mathematics must depend on *something* not created by us. Sometimes he traces this something back to rather intangible beginnings. It then seems hard to show how we can make so much out of so little. From his various interconnected observations, I detect a trend in his thoughts: once we grant that *something* is given objectively, it is relatively easy to see that the continued enrichment of mathematics demands, for the same reason, that we also grant a certain richness to what is objectively given.

In his Gibbs lecture, Gödel attempts to prove Platonism by arguing against "the view that mathematics is only our own creation." In addition, he makes some suggestions to exclude other positions which recognize the objectivity of mathematics in the sense of 7.0.3 but fall short of Platonism as defined by 7.0.2. Once he said to me:

7.2.1   My Gibbs lecture gives a lively presentation. It proves Platonism.

Nonetheless, although he proposed more than once to show me the text of his lecture, he decided in the end that it was not in a sufficiently finished form to be shown to me. When, eventually, I had the opportunity to read the text of the lecture, I noticed that, contrary to the impression conveyed by 7.2.1, he was quite tentative in his conclusions.

In any case, it is reasonable to see the main purpose of the Gibbs lecture as a preliminary attempt to prove Platonism in mathematics. Even though he introduces the issue of Platonism under the assumption that "there exist absolutely undecidable mathematical propositions"—a hypothesis he later claimed to be refutable by his rationalistic optimism

(*MP*:324–325)—he announces that he will discuss the issue independently of that assumption (original manuscript, p. 21).

In arguing against the creation view of mathematics, Gödel makes several assertions which were later more or less repeated in his conversations with me:

7.2.2 The creator necessarily knows all properties of his creatures, because they can't have any others except those he has given to them (p. 16).

7.2.3 One might object that the constructor need not necessarily know *every* property of what he constructs. For example, we build machines and still cannot predict their behavior in every detail. But this objection is very poor. For we don't create the machines out of nothing, but build them out of some given material. If the situation were similar in mathematics, then this material or basis for our constructions would be something objective and would force some realistic viewpoint upon us even if certain other ingredients of mathematics were our own creation. The same would be true if in our creations we were to use some instrument in us different from our ego (such as "reason" interpreted as something like a thinking machine). For mathematical facts would then (at least in part) express properties of this instrument, which would have an objective existence [ibid.:18].

7.2.4 First of all, if mathematics were our free creation, ignorance as to the objects we created, it is true, might still occur, but only through lack of a clear realization as to what we really have created (or, perhaps, due to the practical difficulty of too complicated computations). Therefore, it would have to disappear (at least in principle, although perhaps not in practice) as soon as we attain perfect clearness. However, modern developments in the foundations of mathematics have accomplished an insurmountable [unsurpassable?] degree of exactness, but this has helped practically nothing for the solution of mathematical problems [ibid.:21–22].

7.2.5 Secondly, the activity of the mathematicians shows very little of the freedom a creator should enjoy. Even if, for example, the axioms of integers were a free invention, still it must be admitted that the mathematician, after he has imagined the first few properties of his objects, is at the end of his creative activity, and he is not in a position also to create the validity of the theorems at his will. If anything like creation exists at all in mathematics, then what any theorem does is exactly to restrict the freedom of creation. That, however, which restricts it must evidently exist independently of the creation [ibid.:22].

7.2.6 Thirdly: If mathematical objects are our creations, then evidently integers and sets of integers will have to be two different creations, the first of which does not necessitate the second. However, in order to prove certain propositions about integers, the concept of set of integers is necessary. So here, in order to find out what properties *we* have given to certain objects of our imagination, [we] must first create certain other objects—a very strange situation indeed!

At this point, Gödel points out that he had formulated his critique in terms of the rather vague concept of free creation or free invention—

evidently implying that, as a result, neither the position nor his proposed refutation of it could be precise and conclusive. He goes on to say that there were attempts to provide a more precise meaning of the concept of creation, which would have the effect of making its disproof more precise and cogent also (ibid.:23).

7.2.7 I would like to show this in detail for the most precise, and at the same time the most radical formulation that has been given so far. It is that which asserts mathematical propositions to be true solely due to certain arbitrary rules about the use of symbols. It is that which interprets mathematical propositions as expressing solely certain aspects of syntactical (or linguistic) conventions, that is, they simply repeat parts of these conventions. According to this view, mathematical propositions, duly analyzed, must turn out to be as void of content as, for example, the statement "All stallions are male horses." Everybody will agree that this proposition does not express any zoological or other objective fact, but its truth is due solely to the circumstance that we choose to use the term *stallion* as an abbreviation for *male horse*.

Gödel continues with many pages of arguments against this syntactical—or verbal or abbreviational or notational—conventionalism. He then concludes the lecture with some tentative observations in opposition to what he called "psychologism" and "Aristotelian realism," which he regards as the main alternatives to the creation view and to his own Platonist position (as defined above in 7.0.2). He declares his faith that "after sufficient clarification of the concepts in question" it would be possible to prove Platonism "with mathematical rigor."

In the 1950s, Gödel spent many years, probably from 1953 to 1959, working on his Carnap paper, "Is Mathematics Syntax of Language?" for the purpose of refuting the position of syntactical conventionalism in mathematics, which had been held by his Vienna teachers Carnap, Schlick, and Hahn. Historically, this conventionalism is of great significance. Because of its striking simplicity and apparent transparency it constitutes the main novel attraction of the powerful movement of logical positivism. It "completes" the sketch of a philosophy in Wittgenstein's *Tractatus* by an eager extrapolation based on an equivocation (see Carnap 1936:47, discussed in Wang 1985a:15). The awareness of its inadequacy had led Wittgenstein and Quine to look for modifications of it that would preserve its preference for adherence to the concrete. Given the fact that Gödel had developed his own opposing outlook while he was in Vienna at the center of the logical positivist movement, it is not surprising that he felt it important to refute conventionalism. Nonetheless, he eventually decided not to publish his Carnap paper. He once gave me as his reason for that decision his judgment that, even though the paper had demonstrated that mathematics is *not* syntax of language, it had not made clear what mathematics *is*.

During one of our discussions, Gödel made the following observation on conventionalism:

7.2.8 Conventionalism confuses two different senses of convention: arbitrary ones which have no content and serious ones with an objective base. We are not creating mathematical objects by introducing conventions. In order to introduce conventions, we have to know the concepts. In order to work with the conventions, one needs all of mathematics already, for instance, to prove that they are consistent, that is, that they are admissible conventions.

As I said before, in our discussions Gödel was emphatic in his adherence to a traditional concept of creation:

7.2.9 To create is to make something out of nothing and we give what we create all their properties. This is different from making something out of something else. For example, we make automobiles but do not know all their properties.

Originally the word *create* was used mainly in the precise context of the original divine creation of the world. Augustine, for instance, insisted that creatures cannot create. According to Dr. Johnson's dictionary, *to create* (as said of God) is "to form out of nothing." If we follow this tradition, we (human beings) can create only in a deviant extended sense, as in the quotation from H. L. Mansen cited in the Oxford English Dictionary: "We can think of creation only as a change of the condition of that which already exists."

At the same time, even if we begin with a broad nontraditional conception of creation, the experience of the rich stability of mathematics may lead us to the discovery view. Einstein, analogously, said about theoretical physics: "To him who is a discoverer in this field, the products of his imagination appear so necessary and natural that he regards them, and would like to have them regarded by others, not as creations of thought but as given realities" (Einstein 1954:270).

In our discussions, I called Gödel's attention to the fact that Riemann and Brouwer sometimes speak of creations in mathematics. In particular, I mentioned two of Brouwer's statements: (1) "Man always and everywhere creates order in nature"; (2) "This intuition of two-oneness, the basal intuition [*Urintuition*] of mathematics, creates not only the numbers one and two, but also all finite numbers" (Brouwer 1975:123, 126). When I asked Gödel whether we can speak of a continuous creation, he replied:

7.2.10 When Riemann and Brouwer speak of creating objects in our mind, they mean doing this according to certain principles, which depend on our intuition. In the case of Brouwer, the lack of arbitrariness means that he does not create arbitrarily out of that which is shown in our intuition. For Brouwer, mathematics expresses the essence of the human mind. If we use *create* in place of *make* for automobiles and do so similarly in the conceptual world, then Brouwer's concept of creation is of this kind. Using this concept, we may speak of a faculty of what we can create. We have not determined or decided what to create. The notion of continuous creation can apply to set theory, but not to number theory. By creating the integers we have determined Goldbach's conjecture; that is, we recognize the propositions about numbers as meaningful. In set theory, every proposition need not be meaningful. It is indefinite to say that we have created sets. Creating mathematical objects in this sense does not mean that there are no objects not created by us. Creation in this sense does not exclude Platonism. It is not important which mathematical objects exist but that some of them do exist. Objects and concepts, or at least something in them, exist objectively and independently of the acts of human mind.

7.2.11 Brouwer is not talking about creation in his assertion (2), he was merely saying that we get numbers out of the *Urintuition*. It is a good example of constructing something out of something given. The word *construct* here is analogous to physical construction. The two-oneness contains the material from which we combine and iterate to get numbers. This *Urintuition* is quite intangible. But this is all right, because something which is very simple always appears as almost nothing. For example, Hegel identifies the mere something with nothing.

"Data of the Second Kind"
I now believe that Brouwer's *Urintuition* of two-oneness or "twoity" illustrates the *sort* of thing that points quite directly to what Gödel, in the Cantor paper, takes to be "the given underlying mathematics" (*CW*2:268).

7.2.12 That something besides the sensations actually is immediately given follows (independently of mathematics) from the fact that even our ideas referring to physical objects contain constituents qualitatively different from sensations or mere combinations of sensations, for example, the idea of [physical] object itself; whereas, on the other hand, by our thinking we cannot create any qualitatively new elements, but only reproduce and combine those that are given. Evidently the "given" underlying mathematics is closely related to the abstract elements contained in our empirical ideas.[40] [See 7.2.14 for footnote.]

7.2.13 It by no means follows, however, that the data of this second kind, because they cannot be associated with actions of cartain things upon our sense organs, are something purely subjective, as Kant asserted. Rather they, too, may represent an aspect of objective reality, but, as opposed to the sensations, their presence in us may be due to another kind of relationship between ourselves and reality.

7.2.14 [Footnote 40] Note that there is a close relationship between the concept of set and the categories of pure understanding in Kant's sense. Namely, the function of both is "synthesis," that is, the generating of unities out of manifolds (e.g., in Kant of the idea of *one* object out of its various aspects).

Clearly the restriction of the power of our thinking to reproducing and combining given elements is in conformity with Gödel's conception of creation. Mind's power of synthesis must be a component of its ability to combine. Combining, presumably, also includes selecting, and it includes as well the interaction between conscious thinking and unconscious thinking, which is a familiar experience. For example, many of us are aware of the benefits derivable from periods of incubation in undertaking a complex piece of intellectual work. When we are fatigued or stuck, a night's rest or an extended abstention from conscious engagement with the task at hand often results in unexpected advances.

What is done in the unconscious is also thinking, in the sense of combining and reproducing given elements. Mind's power lies in the manner in which the given is processed and, in particular, analyzed and synthesized. Since it is generally agreed that computers also can combine and reproduce, it follows that, if we are to prove mind's superiority to computers we must clarify and substantiate our belief that by thinking a mind can do more than a computer can, by virtue of the mind's ability to deal more flexibly with subtler data. Given our well-tested belief that objective reality is richly and subtly complex, it seems reasonable to conclude that objectivism in mathematics allows more room than does the creation view for our mind to carry out its mathematical thinking in a way that surpasses the capability of computers.

In order to explicate the complex passage in 7.2.12, we must first consider what Gödel wrote immediately before it in the Cantor paper:

7.2.15 But despite their remoteness from sense experience, we do have something like a perception also of the objects of set theory, as is seen from the fact that the axioms force themselves upon us as being true. I don't see any reason why we should have less confidence in this kind of perception, and more generally, in mathematical intuition [a correction proposed by Gödel himself to replace "i.e., in mathematical intuition"] than in sense perception ["taken in a more general sense, including, for instance, looking at a city from an airplane"—phrase added by Gödel November 1975].

7.2.16 It should be noted that mathematical intuition need not be conceived of as a faculty giving an *immediate* knowledge of the objects concerned. Rather it seems that, as in the case of physical experience, we *form* our ideas also of those objects on the basis of something else which *is* immediately given. Only this something else is *not*, or not primarily, the sensations (*CW2:268*).

At least in his discussions with me, Gödel did not identify mathematical intuition with something like the perception of sets. That may be why he told me specifically that it was a mistake in the original text to say "in this perception, i.e., in mathematical intuition," pointing out that such perception is but a special type of mathematical intuition. In fact, my impression is that mathematical intuition for him is primarily our intuition that certain propositions are true—such as modus ponens, mathematical induction, 4 is an even number, some of the axioms of set theory, and so on. Only derivatively may we also speak of the perception of sets and concepts as mathematical intuition.

Implicit in 7.2.16 is the familiar truth that the "something else which *is* immediately given"—in the case of physical experience—is, in the first place, the sensations. The continuation of 7.2.16 in 7.2.12 points out that, even in physical experience, something beside sensations is actually immediately given, as is seen from the fact that qualitatively different ideas like that of (physical) *object* itself are involved.... This line of thought is undoubtedly related to Kant's observation that in physical experience we apply the categories of pure understanding, which are qualitatively different from sensations.... Consequently, our physical knowledge, in particular our sense perception, is based on, besides sensations, some other type of datum as well, that is, data of the second kind (the term introduced in 7.2.13).

Gödel's discussion of "the 'given' underlying mathematics" is less explicit. Since mathematics is obviously "qualitatively different from" nothing (and its combinations), it must be based on something that is immediately given: this seems to me the basic argument that is hardest to question. Our mathematical experience shows that we may also be said to have something like a perception of mathematical objects and concepts. Since sense perception is, as we all agree, based (primarily) on the sensations, which are immediately given, the mathematical analogue of perception must also be based on something immediately given because it cannot come from nothing (seeing that "by thinking we cannot create any qualitatively new elements").

A strikingly similar point is made by Frege in a remarkably different manner. Frege wishes to argue for the possibility of "the presentation of a thought that does not belong to the inner world." For this purpose, he first observes, "the visual impressions we have are not only not the same, but markedly different from each other. And yet we move about in the same external world. Having visual impressions is certainly necessary for seeing things, but not sufficient. What must still be added is not anything sensible. And yet this is just what opens up the external world for us; for without this non-sensible something everyone would remain shut up in his inner world." Frege then adds tentatively, "So perhaps, since the decisive factor lies in the non-sensible, something non-sensible, even without the cooperation of sense-impressions, could also lead us out of the inner world and enable us to grasp thoughts" (Frege 1918:26–27).

Frege does not pause to give his reason for believing that there is or must be this desired other type of "something non-sensible." Rather he goes on to say: "Outside our inner world we should have to distinguish the external world proper of sensible, perceptible things and the realm of what is non-sensibly perceptible. We should need something non-sensible for the recognition of both realms."

Presumably Frege believes that, since we do "grasp" or "perceive" thoughts (nonsensibly), there must be an objective realm of thoughts. It seems that Frege's "something non-sensible" corresponds to Gödel's "data of the second kind," which are elusive and likely to be misleading if we "reify" them. That may be why neither Frege nor Gödel says much that is specific about them. (See Yourgrau 1989, pp. 339–403, on this and other similarities between the views of Frege and Gödel.)

Many philosophers are put off by Gödel's language of mathematical (or conceptual) perception and intuition. But it seems to me that what is at stake can also be expressed in other terms. Our elementary mathematical experience shows that we are certain of many mathematical propositions: for example, 2^{10} times 2^{10} is 2^{20}, the billionth digit of the decimal expansion of the irrational number e is either 0 or greater than 0. What is the ground for such strong beliefs as these? If it is said that the ground is nothing besides our training, then one could ask how training alone could possibly secure so much for us.

Most of us would agree that empirical propositions such as "I have two hands" or "the earth already existed ten days ago," are believed at least in part because there have been certain sensations, certain immediately given data due to our relation to reality. The arguments of Gödel and Frege point strongly to the presence of another kind of experience as well. It certainly seems plausible to admit that, apart from training, our mathematical beliefs are similarly based at least in part on certain immediately given data which are, however, "due to another kind to relationship between ourselves and reality."

It seems to me hard to deny, given our mathematical experience, that there must be some data underlying our faith in certain mathematical propositions. Gödel's (and Frege's related) assertions about ideas such as the idea of a physical object are meant to show that even our physical ideas require certain immediately given data that are not sensations. This is an additional argument, introduced for the purpose of reducing the doubt that there could possibly by any data other than sensations.

In short, Gödel asks us to acknowledge two kinds of datum: (a) sensations, the primary data for our ideas referring to physical objects; and (b) data of the second kind, which include (b1) those immediately given data, other than the sensations, on the basis of which we *form* our physical ideas (what Gödel calls "the abstract elements contained in our empirical ideas"), and (b2) "the 'given' underlying mathematics." Gödel observes that (b2) "is closely related to" (b1). The data of the second kind in both cases enable us, as explicated in the footnote cited in 7.2.14, to form concepts whose function is *synthesis*.

In other words, the data of the second kind are the basis on which we *form* both Kant's categories of pure understanding and mathematical concepts such as those of set and number. Gödel offers no direct characterization of the data of the second kind. But Brouwer's *Urintuition* of two-oneness may, I think, be seen as a more direct image of the given underlying mathematics than the concepts of set and number. The fact that we have ideas of these Kantian categories and also mathematical concepts points to certain features of reality which in their relation to us enable us to have such ideas, on the basis, or through the mediation, of the data of the second kind. It is natural to presume that these features of objective reality are just the concepts our ideas aim at capturing.

Consider now Gödel's fundamental disagreement with Kant, as tentatively asserted in passage 7.2.13: the data of the second kind "may represent an aspect of objective reality." As we know, according to Kant, even though the categories of pure understanding play a central role in determining what is objective in our experience, they are not objective in the sense of representing an aspect of the things in themselves. Rather they are, in this sense, purely subjective, though perhaps conditioned in some impenetrable way by the things in themselves.

Since, however, we can begin only with what we believe we know, it is more natural to dispense with the additional, and largely inaccessible, realm of the things in themselves and say, for instance, that our idea of physical object is based on some data of the second kind which represent an aspect of reality. As a matter of fact, we do believe that there are physical objects in the real world. But in any case I do not think this issue about our idea of physical object is directly relevant to the question of a mathematical world. Therefore we may concentrate on the data of the second kind "underlying mathematics"—briefly, "mathematical data."

As I said before, it is hard to deny that there are such mathematical data. But just granting this does not seem to get us very far. For all we know, it might give us only something like (say) 1, 2, and many. The reasoning that leads to the conclusion that there are some mathematical data is, however, quite general. Over the years, the domain of mathematics has been extended, and in the process obscurities and crises (the irrational numbers, the infinitesimals, the complex numbers, the divergent series, the parallel axiom, the paradoxes of set theory) have been clarified and overcome. As we gain increasing confidence in more and more of mathematics, or as the range of our mathematical intuition increases, we believe we know more and more new things. Since, however, "by our thinking we cannot create any qualitatively new elements," there must have been (or we must have seen) more and more new given elements, that is, additional mathematical data.

We start with the empirical fact of our believing what we know to be so, and we go on to examine the validity of what we suppose we know. This examination of the foundations of mathematics has in this century produced the familiar schools of strict finitism, formalism (or finitism), intuitionism, semi-intuitionism, and logicism. From a less engaged perspective, these schools may be seen as alternative delimitations of the range of mathematical truth, roughly in the order, not historically but conceptually, of moving from the narrower to the broader. Our interest is then shifted to a study of what is involved in going from one stage to the next.

A brief sketch of some of the main features of such a study was given in the last section—construed as a *dialectic* of the criterion of *intuition* as a way of characterizing our strong and stable beliefs and the procedure of *idealization* to purify and extend our conceptions. Such an approach is thought to be instructive, because the interaction of intuition and idealization, vague though they are as concepts, has worked so well so far, and we have every reason to believe that it will continue to work well.

It is my impression that Gödel would assent to the belief—although he does not seem to say so explicitly—that each extension calls for some qualitatively new elements as additional mathematical data. Such postulated data are meant to link up our conceptions with objective reality, or the mathematical world. The postulation of such data is, I think, a way of explicating our belief that the edifice of mathematics, surprisingly rich and stable, must have some objective basis. With or without such data, the main point is that just as the success of physics has led us to accept more and more elaborate theories about the physical world, the advances in mathematics should induce us to accept a richer and richer theory of the mathematical world. But the analogy contains various facets. For example, relative to our present knowledge, the connections between the different parts of mathematics (and those between certain parts of them—say, number theory and set theory—and physics) are not nearly as close as those between different parts of physics.

According to Gödel in the Cantor paper:

7.2.17   The question of the objective existence of the mathematical world is an exact replica of the objective existence of the outer world (*CW*2:268).

In the same context (two paragraphs back) he makes strong use of his analogy of "something like a perception" of sets to "sense perception, which induces us to build up physical theories and to expect that future sense perceptions will agree with them." I would rather speak in terms of a comparison, as a start, (say) between our seeing our beliefs about small integers as true and our seeing our beliefs about medium-sized physical objects as true. In other words, if one wishes to speak in terms of perceiving mathematical objects, what is meant is, in the first place, that we see as true the strong and stable beliefs we have which are ordinarily said to be about such objects. In this way, I hope to avoid or postpone the complex issue about the nature of mathematical objects and their differences from physical objects. In view of Gödel's observations on the epistemological priority of objectivity over objects, I am inclined to think that he would be sympathetic to this (tactical?) procedure.

A related earlier discussion is Gödel's famous analogy between physics and mathematics in the Russell paper, which, according to what he told me about the passage, may be reformulated slightly differently:

7.2.18 Even if we adopt positivism, it seems to me that the assumption of such entities [sets and concepts as existing independently of our definitions and constructions] is quite as legitimate as the assumption of physical objects, and there is quite as much reason to believe in their existence. They are in the same sense necessary to obtain a satisfactory system of mathematics as physical objects are necessary for a satisfactory theory of our sense perceptions, and in both cases it is impossible to interpret the propositions one wants to assert about these entities as propositions about the "data," that is, in the latter case the actually occurring sense perceptions ["and in the former case actual simple computations with integers."—added by Gödel in 1975] (CW2:128).

By the way, the addition is more specific than the specification—elsewhere in the Russell paper—of his mathematical analogue of sense perceptions: "arithmetic, i.e., the domain of the kind of elementary indubitable evidence that must be most fittingly compared with sense perception (ibid.:121). In the 1970s Gödel characterized 7.2.18 as an ad hominem argument, in the sense that it resorts to what the positivists (also) believe, and uses their language (of *assumption, data,* etc.).

How this comparison between mathematical and physical knowledge is to be extended seems to be a secondary issue which neither is important in the present context nor promises any kind of uniquely satisfactory solution. Perhaps we can compare number theory with Newtonian physics, since these are probably the most decisive parts of mathematics and physics with regard to the generation in us of a strong belief in an objective mathematical world and a strong belief in the fruitfulness of physical theory. There is also some similarity between the unending quest for new axioms of set theory and the quest for a unified theory in physics. But the place of set theory in the minds of pure mathematicians is, certainly at present, less central than that of the goal of a unified theory in the minds of theoretical physicists.

Gödel's suggested refutation of subjectivism in mathematics appeals to the fact that we believe we have mathematical knowledge. Once we accept certain simple mathematics, we tend to go from one extension to another, with some decrease in degree of certainty and with occasional setbacks (confusions and cotradictions). From our experience, however, we have acquired the belief that robust expansions, in general and in the long run, become more certain, stable, and useful. Such confidence, founded on our gross experience, is undoubtedly the ultimate justification of our belief in a mathematical world, which, moreover, is fruitful in doing some types of mathematical work (as illustrated by Gödel's letters (*MP*:8–11), which I consider in section 7.4 below).

In my opinion, the objective existence of a world can mean for us only our experience of the successful accumulation of convergently stable beliefs about its subject matter, beliefs that hold fast in the light created by all our attempts to be unprejudiced. There is nothing in our concept of objective existence that requires causal effects on our sense organs. The familiar and natural distinction is expressed by saying that the physical world is not only objective but also *actual*. Actual existence is an extra dimension added to objective existence. If we do not question the objective existence of the physical world, it is hard to find reasons to doubt that of the mathematical world. That is why a comparison of mathematics with physics is of crucial relevance.

7.3 The Perception of Concepts

In my discussion of mathematical concepts, I spoke of sharpening or formalizing a vague intuitive concept and asked the question (*MP*:81): If we begin with a vague intuitive concept, how can we find a sharper concept to correspond to it faithfully? Gödel objected to this formulation and said that the task is to try to see or understand a concept more clearly. In addition he proposed to replace the word *sharper* by *sharp*, because he evidently wanted a fixed target that in itself admits of no degrees.

I eventually summarized Gödel's scattered observations on our capacity to perceive or understand concepts, in his own words, in less than two printed pages in *From Mathematics to Philosophy* (*MP*:84–86). For the purpose of understanding his line of thought, I begin this section by discussing the parts of this summary.

In the first place, there are concepts, and we are able to perceive them as we are able to perceive physical objects.

7.3.1 If we begin with a vague intuitive concept, how can we find a sharp concept to correspond to it faithfully? The answer is that the sharp concept is there all along, only we did not perceive it clearly at first. This is similar to our perception of an animal first far away and then nearby. We had not perceived the sharp concept of mechanical procedures before Turing, who brought us to the right perspective. And then we do perceive clearly the sharp concept.

7.3.2 There are more similarities than differences between sense perceptions and the perceptions of concepts. In fact, physical objects are perceived more indirectly than concepts. The analog of perceiving sense objects from different angles is the perception of different logically equivalent concepts.

7.3.3   If there is nothing sharp to begin with, it is hard to understand how, in many cases, a vague concept can uniquely determine a sharp one without even the *slightest* freedom of choice.

7.3.4   "Trying to see (i.e. understand) a concept more clearly" is the correct way of expressing the phenomenon vaguely described as "examining what we mean by a word."

At this juncture, Gödel proposed a conjecture that there is some special physical organ to enable us to handle abstract impressions as well as we do:

7.3.5   I conjecture that some physical organ is necessary to make the handling of abstract impressions (as opposed to sense impressions) possible, because we have some weakness in the handling of abstract impressions which is remedied by viewing them in comparison with or on the occasion of sense impressions. Such a sensory organ must be closely related to the neural center for language. But we simply do not know enough now, and the primitive theory on such questions at the present stage is likely to be comparable to the atomic theory as formulated by Democritus.

An important reason for Gödel's strong interest in objectivism in mathematics and in our capacity to perceive concepts clearly in many cases, is, I think, his extrapolated belief or uninhibited generalization that we can see the fundamental concepts as clearly in philosophy as in mathematics and physics. Otherwise, it would be difficult to understand why he introduces the following remarkable recommendation and prediction in this context:

7.3.6   Philosophy as an exact theory should do to physics as much as Newton did to physics. I think it is perfectly possible that the development of such a philosophical theory will take place within the next hundred years or even sooner.

As examples of our ability to perceive concepts clearly Gödel mentions two cases and, in describing them, links the definition of a concept to the axioms that concern it:

7.3.7   The precise concept meant by the intuitive idea of velocity clearly is ds/dt, and the precise concept meant by "size" (as opposed to "shape"), e.g. of a lot, clearly is equivalent with Peano measure in the cases where either concept is applicable. In these cases the solutions again are *unquestionably* unique, which here is due to the fact that only they satisfy certain axioms which, on closer inspection, we find to be undeniably implied in the concept we had. For example, congruent figures have the same area, a part has no larger size than the whole, etc.

Gödel evidently believes that, for many important fundamental concepts, we are capable of seeing clearly the axioms implied by our intuitive ideas of them. A natural question is how to deal with ambiguous concepts, which, as we know, include most fundamental philosophical concepts. Presumably in order to anticipate this question, Gödel seems to suggest that we have ambiguous concepts only where we mix two or more exact concepts in one intuitive concept.—Our experience shows, however, that ambiguities in many central concepts cannot be resolved in this manner.—In any case, Gödel offers a clarification of two ambiguous concepts: continuity and point. Even though I do not think that these two examples are useful evidence in favor of his strong assertion in 7.3.6, they are of interest in themselves:

7.3.8   There are cases where we mix two or more exact concepts in one intuitive concept and then we seem to arrive at paradoxical results. One example is the concept of continuity. Our prior intuition contains an ambiguity between smooth curves and continuous movements. We are not committed to the one or the other in our prior intuition. In the sense of continuous movements a curve remains continuous when it includes vibrations in every interval of time, however small, provided only that their amplitudes tend toward 0 if the time interval does. But such a curve is no longer smooth. The concept of smooth curves is seen sharply through the exact concept of differentiability. We find the example of space-filling continuous curves disturbing because we feel intuitively that a continuous curve, in the sense of being a smooth one, cannot fill the space. When we realize that there are two different sharp concepts mixed together in the intuitive concept, the paradox disappears. Here the analogy with sense perception is close. We cannot distinguish two neighboring stars a long distance away. But by using a telescope we can see that there are indeed two stars.

7.3.9   Another example along the same line is our intuitive concept of points. In set theory we think of points as parts of the continuum in the sense that the line is the set of the points on it (call this the "set-theoretical concept"). In space intuition we think of space as a fine matter so that each point has zero weight and is not part of matter (but only a limit between parts). Note that it is not possible to cut a material line segment or a rod in two ways at the same point or surface P, once with P on the left part, once on the right, because there is nothing in between the two completely symmetrical parts. According to this intuitive concept, summing up all the points, we still do not get the line, rather the points form some kind of scaffold on the line, We can easily think of intervals as parts of the line and assign lengths to them, and, by combining intervals, to measurable sets, where we have to consider two measurable sets which differ only by sets of measure zero as representing the same part of the continuum. But when we use the set-theoretical concept and try to assign a length to any arbitrary set of points on the line, we lose touch with the intuitive concept. This also solves the paradox that set-theoretically one can decompose a globe into a finite number of parts and fit them together to form exactly a smaller globe. In the light of what has been said this only means that one can split the scaffold consisting of the points into several parts and then shift these parts together so that they will all be within a smaller space without overlapping. The result holds only for the set-theoretical concept, while it is counterintuitive only for the intuitive concept.

The above nine entries reproduce Gödel's own text, as published in *From Mathematics to Philosophy* (MP:84–86) but broken into appropriate parts. In our conversations, Gödel made several related observations which occasionally add something to his written formulations.

In place of 7.3.1, he said:

7.3.10   I am for the Platonic view. If there is nothing precise to begin with, it is unintelligible to say that we somehow arrive at a precise concept. Rather we begin with vague perceptions of a concept, as we see an animal from far away or take two stars for one before using the telescope. For example, we had the precise concept of mechanical procedure in mind, but had not perceived it clearly before we knew of Turing's work.

7.3.11   The ego may lose reason just as it may lose sense perception. Sense perception is also not immediate. In mathematics there is something objective. [After saying something like 7.3.2, Gödel added:] The Platonic view helps in understanding things; this fact illustrates the possibilities of verifying a philosophical theory.

In connection with his language of perceiving concepts, he said,

7.3.12   Sets are objects but concepts are not objects. We perceive objects and understand concepts. Understanding is a different kind of perception: it is a step in the direction of reduction to the last cause.

Gödel made several remarks related to 7.3.5:

7.3.13   The perception of concepts may either be done by some internal organ or just by an inner perception—our own experience—using no special organ. I conjecture that some physical organ is necessary for this.

7.3.14   I believe there is a causal connection in the perception of concepts. But at present the theory is like the theory of atoms at the time of Democritus. Already *noûs* in Aristotle is a causal affair: the active intellect works on the passive intellect. [Compare 6.1.22.] The active intellect is, I believe, located in some physical organ. It might even have images.—I am cautious and only make public the less controversial parts of my philosophy.

7.3.15   Some physical organ is necessary to make the handling of abstract impressions possible. Nobody is able to deal effectively with them, except in comparison with or on the occasion of sense impressions. This sensory organ must be closely related to the center for language.

In the manuscript of my book I stated: "Historically, many interesting questions were answered, or at least clarified, only after the crucial concepts—such as continuity, area, construction by ruler and compass, theorem, set, etc.—had been formalized. For example, there are continuous functions which have no derivative." (*MP*:82). As comments on this statement, Gödel made several observations similar to 7.3.7 and 7.3.8:

7.3.16   There is no doubt at all that ds/dt is the only way to make clear the concept of velocity. This unique determination is surprising. It is another verification of rationalism. On the concept of area, Lebesgue's analysis is undoubtedly correct in the cases where both the analysis and the concept are applicable: only they satisfy the axioms we want; for instance, a proper subset must have a smaller area, congruent surfaces have the same area.

7.3.17   In contrast, continuity cannot be made precise in a unique way, because it involves two different concepts not distinguished in the ordinary perception—as two stars are seen as one without the telescope. What is involved here is an ambiguity, not an unavoidable vagueness. In our prior intuition we are not committed to the one or the other: namely, *continuous* movement or *smooth* curve. A continuous movement remains continuous—but is no longer smooth—if it includes infinite vibrations in its smallest parts. A smooth curve must be differentiable and can no longer fill the space.

The observation in 7.3.9 was probably a response to the following statements of mine: "Rigidity of the formalized concept leads to decisions in cases where mere use of the intuitive notion was insufficient. For instance, the existence of a space-filling curve can only be established after the exact definition of curve is introduced" (*MP*:81–82).

Other comments of Gödel's, related to 7.3.9 are:

7.3.18   The existence of a decomposition of a space means: one can split the scaffold consisting of the limits into several parts and then shift these parts together so that they will fill a smaller or bigger space.

7.3.19   In space intuition, a point is not a part of the continuum but a limit between two parts. If we think of space as fine matter, then a point has weight zero and is not a part of matter. According to this concept, all the points do not add up to the line but only make up a scaffold (*Gerüsst*) or a collection of points of view. Then it is not surprising that one can shift them around. When we turn to the mathematical or set-theoretical concept of points, or rather when we look at parts of the continuum and assign a length to each part, we begin with intervals and arrive at measurable sets. We come to view the continuum as a system of parts or a Boolean algebra without indivisible elements. Instead of thinking of the continuum as consisting of points, we think of it as a union of certain measurable sets such that two sets differing by a zero set are taken to be equivalent. It is then not surprising that we can split the scaffold into appropriate parts and shift them together in a suitable way to fill a smaller or larger space. In the process we no longer adhere to the intuitive concept of points as limits but rather work with sums of limits as parts of the continuum.

Another favorite example of our ability to perceive concepts for Gödel is Turing's analysis of the concept of mechanical procedure, which I discuss in Chapter 6. Instead of the perception of concepts, Gödel also speaks of the *analysis* of concepts, which he sees as the central task of philosophy. In this connection, he distinguishes science from philosophy and envisages an eventual convergence of the two:

7.3.20   The analysis of concepts is central to philosophy. Science only combines concepts and does not analyze concepts. It contributes to the analysis of concepts by being stimulating for real analysis. Einstein's theory is itself not an analysis of concepts (and does not penetrate into the last analysis); its metaphysics (with its four-dimensional frame) deals with observations which are the given for science. Physical theories change quickly or slowly; they are stimulating to investigate but are not the correct metaphysics. Exact reasoning, positive integers, and real numbers all occur in metaphysics. (It is not so sure that topology also does.) For example, natural objects differ more or less, and metric space is concerned with how much they differ. Abstract structures are naturally chosen. Analysis is to arrive at what thinking is based on: the inborn intuitions.

7.3.21   The epistemological problem is to set the primitive concepts of our thinking right. For example, even if the concept of set becomes clear, even after satisfactory axioms of infinity are found, there would remain more technical (i.e., mathematical) questions of deciding the continuum hypothesis from the axioms. This is because epistemology and science (in particular, mathematics) are far apart at present. It need not necessarily remain so. True science in the Leibnizian sense would overcome this apartness. In other words, there may be another way of analyzing concepts (e.g., like Hegel's) so that true analysis will lead to the solution of the problem.

7.3.22   At present we possess only subjective analyses of concepts. The fact that such analyses do not yield decisions of scientific problems is a proof against the subjectivist view of concepts and mathematics.

7.3.23   See 9.4.15.

7.4 Facts or Arguments for Objectivism in Mathematics

It seems to me that Gödel based his belief in objectivism in mathematics on a procedure of viewing together relevant facts on several different levels. On the most fundamental level, as elaborated in 7.2, there must be *something* objective in mathematics: there must be some datum of the second kind which represents an aspect of objective reality. Its presence in us is due to another kind of relationship between ourselves and reality, which is different from the corresponding relationship underlying the presence of the data of the first kind.

The dialectic of intuition and idealization, considered in 7.1, indicates the natural process by which the realm of the objective in mathematics is extended step by step. At the same time, within each realm of objectivity we also notice certain facts which support our belief in its objectivity. The examples of our ability to perceive concepts—discussed in 7.3—are facts that support our belief that mathematical concepts have an objective basis.

Among the relevant facts which may be seen as direct evidence for the objectivity of numbers and sets, we may mention the following. In connection with Gödel's "real argument" for objectivism in mathematics, he makes two observations related to those in 7.1:

7.4.1 For example, we believe that Fermat's conjecture makes sense: it must be either true or false. Hence, there must be objective facts about natural numbers. But these objective facts must refer to objects which are different from physical objects, because they are, among other things, unchangeable in time.

7.4.2 Number theory—the fact that it doesn't lead to contradictions—is simply there, though we can decide only some of the problems in it. [Compare 7.1.3.]

I consider at length Gödel's views on the concepts of pure set and pure concept in the next chapter. Some of his general arguments may, however, be stated here. For example, he elaborates his comparison of paradoxes with sense deceptions—originally mentioned in passing in his Cantor paper (CW2:268).

7.4.3 The set-theoretical paradoxes are hardly any more troublesome for the objectivistic view of concepts than deceptions of the senses are for the objectivistic view of the physical world. The iterative concept of set, which is nothing but the clarification of the naive—or simply the correct—concept of set, resolves these extensional paradoxes exactly as physics resolves the optical paradoxes by the laws of optics.

7.4.4 The argument that concepts are unreal because of the unresolved logical (intensional) paradoxes is like the argument that the outer world does not exist because there are sense deceptions.

7.4.5 With regard to the unresolved intensional paradoxes about the concept of concept, the comparison with deceptions of the senses is an adequate argument against the weak argument for the strong conclusion that, since there are these paradoxes, concepts cannot exist—so that it is impossible to arrive at a serious theory of concepts because existing things cannot have self-contradictory properties. The paradoxes can only show the inadequacy of our perception—that is, understanding—of the concepts (such as the concept of concept) rather than throw doubt on the subject matter. On the contrary, they reveal something which is not arbitrary and can, therefore, also *suggest* that we are indeed dealing with something real. *Subjective* means that we can form concepts arbitrarily by correct principles of formations of thought. Since the principles leading to the paradoxes seem to be quite correct in this sense, the paradoxes prove that subjectivism is mistaken.

In other words, reality offers resistance and constraints to our subjective inclinations. The unresolved paradoxes do not prove the impossibility of a serious theory of concepts. At the same time, unless we assume Gödel's rationalistic optimism, it is also not excluded that unresolved paradoxes may turn out to be unresolvable. It seems desirable to distinguish those beliefs which depend on such convictions from others which do not.

The fundamental fact is that we do understand mathematical concepts— or, rather, that we see that certain propositions about them are true. This fact must have some objective basis, and so there must be some mathematical data of the second kind, as defined in 7.2. We are not able to specify these data exactly, but we do know that, for instance, simple computations about integers are as certain as almost anything we know. From this starting point, we are naturally led, as indicated in 7.1, to arbitrary natural numbers and sets. Moreover, I have just stated certain facts which directly support our belief in the objectivity of numbers, pure sets, and pure concepts.

In addition, Gödel proposes another kind of argument, which appeals immediately to beliefs that opponents of objectivism also share. Positivism or any form of anti-objectivism restricts the data to sense experience and what people generally agree on, such as what constitutes success. Gödel labels as ad hominem the type of argument that goes directly back to such facts. In particular, he sees his analogy between mathematics and physics—quoted above in 7.2.18—as an ad hominem argument.

Gödel's two letters—considered below—are what he calls an argument from success. He saw this as an ad hominem argument too and proposed on 4 January 1976 to add the following passage to the letters:

7.4.6   It is an assumption even made by the positivists that if a hypothesis leads to verifiable consequences which could be reached in another way or to theorems provable without this hypothesis, such a state of affairs makes the truth of the hypothesis likely. However, mathematicians like to take the opposite position: it is correct to take objectivism to be fruitful, but it need not be true. This position is opposite to the nature of truth—or even science and the positivists.

Regarding this last position, Gödel had said earlier, in January 1972:

7.4.7   Even recognizing the fruitfulness of my objectivism for my work, people might choose not to adopt the objectivistic position but merely to do their work *as if* the position were true—provided they are able to produce such an attitude. But then they only take this as-if point of view toward this position after it has been shown to be fruitful. Moreover, it is doubtful whether one can pretend so well as to yield the desired effect of getting good scientific results.

In one of the several fragments I prepared in 1975 for the purpose of discussing them with Gödel, I wrote, "Looking more closely at the place of Gödel's objectivism in his mathematical practice, we see then that it is, among other things, a useful heuristic picture; in fact, his mathematical

work has influenced some people to entertain the same sort of picture."
Gödel commented:

7.4.8 Abraham Robinson is a representative of an as-if position, according to
which it is fruitful to behave as if there were mathematical objects and in this way
you achieve success by a false picture. This requires a special art of pretending
well. But such pretending can never reach the same degreee of imagination as one
who believes objectivism to be true. The success in the application of a belief in the
existence of something is the usual and most effective way of proving existence.

The argument from success in favor of objectivism in mathematics differs from the argument from our mathematical intuition in that it goes
through conspicuous consequences of a thesis which are universally acceptable instead of trying to prove the thesis by a direct appeal to our
shared intuition. On the one hand, it is easier to agree that the results are
impressive than to agree that we do see, by the other argument, the truth
of the thesis of objectivism. On the other hand, it is not so easy to determine whether some weaker thesis cannot produce the same effect.

Gödel's central argument from success in his letter to me of 7 December 1967 is supplemented by the letter of 7 March 1968. It was stimulated
by a draft of my Skolem paper, in which I suggested that, since Skolem
had given the mathematical core of Gödel's proof of the completeness of
predicate logic in 1922, Gödel's proof did not add much to Skolem's
work.

In his carefully prepared reply to my request to comment on the draft,
Gödel pointed out that in the intellectual climate of the 1920s, the apparently easy inference from Skolem's work to his own theorem of completeness was conceptually or philosophically a very difficult step. He also
offered an explanation for this surprising blindness or prejudice.

At that time, the dominant trend in mathematical logic, represented
by Hilbert, Skolem, and Herbrand, was to regard as reliable only finitary
reasoning. Therefore metamathematics, which had been introduced by
Hilbert for the declared purpose of providing the foundations for mathematics, had to restrict itself to using only finitary reasoning. However,
the easy inference from Skolem's work to the completeness theorem is
definitely non-finitary. That was why no one for so many years, before
Gödel's work in 1929, had been able to notice the easy inference.

As Gödel himself put it (MP:8–9):

7.4.9 This blindness (or prejudice, or whatever you may call it) of logicians is
indeed surprising. But I think the explanation is not hard to find. It lies in a widespread lack, at that time, of the required epistemological attitude toward metamathematics and toward non-finitary reasoning (MP:8–9).

7.4.10 Non-finitary reasoning in mathematics was widely considered to be meaningful only to the extent to which it can be "interpreted" or "justified" in terms of

a finitary metamathematics. (Note that this, for the most part, has turned out to be impossible in consequence of my results and subsequent work.) This view, almost unavoidably, leads to an exclusion of non-finitary reasoning from metamathematics. For such reasoning, in order to be permissible, would require a finitary metamathematics. But this seems to be a confusing and unnecessary duplication.

7.4.11   Moreover, admitting "meaningless" transfinite elements into metamathematics is inconsistent with the very idea of this science prevalent at that time. For according to this idea metamathematics is *the* meaningful part of mathematics, through which the mathematical symbols (meaningless in themselves) acquire some substitute of meaning, namely rules of use. Of course, the essence of this viewpoint is a rejection of all kinds of abstract or infinite objects, of which the prima facie meanings of mathematical symbols are instances. That is, meaning is attributed solely to propositions which speak of *concrete and finite objects*, such as combinations of symbols.

7.4.12   But now the aforementioned easy inference from Skolem 1922 is definitely non-finitary, and so is any other completeness proof for the predicate calculus. Therefore these things escaped notice or were disregarded.

Apparently in considering how to clarify the importance of his easy inference from existing work, Gödel was led to reflect on the general relation between his philosophical outlook and his major work in logic. Or perhaps he wanted, as he said later in a letter in 1971, to make these ideas of his generally known. In any case, he went beyond commenting on my draft to expound on this significant broad issue:

7.4.13   I may add that my objectivistic conception of mathematics and metamathematics in general, and of transfinite reasoning in particular, was fundamental also to my other work in logic.

Among his other work in logic, Gödel concentrated on two items: his proof of the consistency of the continuum hypothesis by his transfinite model of constructible sets, and his incompleteness theorems. He observed that, in both cases, he used transfinite concepts which yielded either a finitary *relative* consistency proof or finitarily provable results such as the existence of undecidable propositions. I consider his results in set theory in Chapter 8 and confine my attention here to the incompleteness work.

In the first place, Gödel remarked that his device of "Gödel numbering," is unnatural from the perspective of the formalistic conception of mathematics.

7.4.14   How indeed could one think of *expressing* metamathematics *in* the mathematical systems themselves if the latter are considered to consist of meaningless symbols which acquire some substitute of meaning only *through* metamathematics?

In his second letter, Gödel added another observation (*MP*:10):

7.4.15   I would like to add that there was another reason which hampered logicians in the application to metamathematics, not only of transfinite reasoning, but of mathematical reasoning in general—and, most of all, in expressing metamathematics in mathematics itself. It consists in the fact that, largely, metamathematics was not considered as a science describing objective mathematical states of affairs, but rather as a theory of the human activity of handling symbols.

His two other observations on the dependence of his discovery of the incompleteness theorem on his objectivism follow several similar remarks on his consistency results in set theory (*MP*:9,10):

7.4.16   Finally it should be noted that the heuristic principle of my construction of undecidable number-theoretical propositions in the formal systems of mathematics is the highly transfinite concept of "objective mathematical truth," as *opposed* to that of "demonstrability," with which it was generally confused before my own and Tarski's work. Again, the use of this transfinite concept eventually leads to finitarily provable results, for example, the general theorems about the existence of undecidable propositions in consistent formal systems.

7.4.17   A similar remark applies to the concept of mathematical truth, where formalists considered formal demonstrability to be an *analysis* of the concept of mathematical truth and, therefore, were of course not in a position to *distinguish* the two.

7.5 Conceptions of Objectivism and the Axiomatic Method

There appear to be some ambiguities in Gödel's characterizations of his conceptions of objectivism and the axiomatic method. I myself am in favor of construing them in a liberal manner that would allow us to improve our knowledge by taking advantage of our intuitions on all levels of generality and certainty. What I mean by this vague statement should become clear at the end of this section.

To begin, let us consider what Gödel says in the last two paragraphs of his expanded Cantor paper. There he appears to distinguish three different criteria of truth. First, he contrasts truth-by-correspondence with truth by our expectation that we can see more and more axioms (*CW*2:268):

7.5.1   However, the question of the objective existence of the objects of mathematical intuition (which, incidentally, is an exact replica of the question of the objective existence of the outer world) is not decisive for the problem under consideration.

7.5.2   The mere psychological fact of the existence of an intuition which is sufficiently clear to produce the axioms of set theory and an open series of extensions of them suffices to give meaning to the question of the truth or falsity of propositions like Cantor's continuum hypothesis.

In addition, he says:

7.5.3   Besides mathematical intuition, there exists another (though only probable) criterion of the truth of mathematical axioms, namely their fruitfulness [a notion explained by him on p. 261] in mathematics and, one may add, possibly also in physics (CW2:269).

In November of 1975, I characterized his statement 75.2 as asserting the possibility of recognizing meaningfulness without realism; Gödel then changed it to: "He himself suggests an alternative to realism as ground for believing that undecided propositions in set theory are either true or false."

In connection with 7.5.1, it is clear that, if the objects of mathematical intuition do exist, every proposition about them is either true or false. However, as Gödel himself emphasized in his conversations, objectivity is better defined for us than objects: "Out of objectivity we define objects in different ways" (compare Chapter 9). In set theory, or also in number theory, we have many undecided propositions. The essence of objectivism in a domain is the belief that every proposition in it is either true or false. One difference between set theory and number theory is that, even though we do not know all the axioms in either case, we know, in the case of number theory, a general form of all the axioms yet to be found—namely as new cases of the principle of mathematical induction.

It seems to me that when Gödel calls 7.5.2 an alternative to realism, he is restricting realism to the sense of asserting the objective existence of the objects of mathematical intuition. In the central sense—as just suggested—of realism or objectivism, 7.5.2 illustrates the typical ground for our belief in objectivism. As a "criterion of truth in set theory" or elsewhere, the kind of psychological fact described in 7.5.2 is the primary on—or indeed the only one available to us. It is on the basis of such facts that we believe in the objective existence of the objects. In this sense, correspondence to reality as the criterion of truth is derived from this criterion.

Whether or not one believes in objectivism in a domain is a psychological fact based on one's experience. We may consider five possible components of this belief: (a) the objects of the domain have objective existence; (b) all the propositions about it are either true or false; (c) we know that every such proposition can be decided; (d) we expect to be able to decide eventually every (significant) proposition about it; and (e) belief (c) will never be refuted.

Belief (c) implies (b), (d) and (e). Neither (c) nor (b) necessarily implies (a). For instance, with regard to a domain introduced by abbreviational conventions, we believe (b) and (c) but not (a). In the case of number theory and set theory, which are our main concern here, we know that there are undecided propositions, but there can be disagreements over the five beliefs.

The belief in objectivism can be and has been construed in different ways. One possibility is to require not only (b) but also (a): I am in favor of equating (a) and (b). In any case, with regard to domains with undecided propositions, we do not know either (a) or (b) in a strong sense of knowing, but have to appeal to (c) or (d) or (e). Belief (c) implies (d) and (e). I would like to construe objectivism in the broad sense of identifying (e) with belief in objectivism, so that, if one accepts (e), one is already accepting not only (b) but also (a) in the weak sense of its not being refutable in fact. It seems to me hard to refute (b) or (a) in a conclusive manner without being able to refute (e) first.

In my opinion, the widely accepted belief in the priority of objectivity over objects implies the belief that the issue of objectivism in mathematics is, in the first place, belief (b); belief (a) is of importance primarily because of its intimate relation with (b). Gödel's statement 7.5.2 is, I think, an example of trying to infer (d) from our experience of being able to find— and to anticipate more of—stable axioms of set theory.

Statement 7.5.3 is an example of Gödel's tendency to focus his attention on the axioms, since he seems to imply in 7.5.3 that mathematical intuition is concerned only with the axioms and is contrasted with success or fruitfulness (CW2:261): "Success here means fruitful in consequences, in particular in 'verifiable' consequences, i.e. consequences demonstrable without the new axiom." The truth of these consequences, however, had also been seen by mathematical intuition, and we see certain mathematical propositions, such as numerical computations, to be true directly, without going through the axioms. Indeed, we apply our intuition at all levels of generality.

In other words, even though positivists tend to doubt that we have direct access to propositions other than the "verifiable" ones, I see no reason why an objectivist has to deny that we do appeal to, and have intuition of, such verifiable propositions.

In his discussions with me, Gödel stressed the central importance of the axiomatic method for philosophy. He did not elaborate his conception of the method, except that he often gave the impression that the task is to find the primitive concepts and then try to see the true axioms for them directly by our intuition. In practice, of course, he recognizes that considerations on many levels are involved when we try to find the axioms or the principles of an area. Nonetheless, he seems to have, or assume, a notion of intrinsic necessity as the attainable ideal.

In connection with the fruitfulness of axioms, Gödel suggests, without giving examples, the following possibility:

7.5.4   There might exist axioms so abundant in their verifiable consequences, shedding so much light on a whole field, and yielding such powerful methods for solving problems (and even solving them constructively, so far as that is possible) that, no matter whether they are intrinsically necessary they would have to be accepted at least in the same sense as any well-established physical theory (CW2:261).

It is implicitly assumed here that such axioms do not contradict any of our firmer beliefs. The striking examples of Gödel's own axiom of constructibility and the currently much-studied axiom of determinacy have conspicuously all the qualities specified in 7.5.4. However, we do not accept them as among the (ultimate) axioms of set theory, because the axiom of determinacy contradicts the axiom of choice and the axiom of constructibility is contradicted by certain plausible axioms of large cardinals, which, however, we do not clearly see to be intrinsically necessary either. It seems, therefore, that intrinsic necessity is an ideal which, in practice, we may or may not attain in choosing axioms.

Even though Gödel strove to find axioms with intrinsic necessity directly by intuition, he was willing to endorse alternative approaches. One striking example was his endorsement of Russell's analogy between logic and zoology, which was followed by an approving description of Russell's 1906 proposal.

7.5.5 The analogy between mathematics and a natural science is enlarged by Russell also in another respect (in one of his earlier writings). He compares the axioms of logic and mathematics with the laws of nature and logical evidence with sense perception, so that the axioms need not be evident in themselves, but rather their justification lies (exactly as in physics) in the fact that they make it possible for these "sense perceptions" to be deduced; which of course would not preclude that they also have a kind of intrinsic plausibility similar to that in physics (CW2:121).

The reference is, I believe, to the following paragraph in a paper by Russell first published in 1906 in French (see Wang 1987a:314):

7.5.6 The method of logistic is fundamentally the same as that of every other science. There is the same fallibility, the same uncertainty, the same mixture of induction and deduction, and the same necessity of appealing, in confirmation of principles, to the diffused agreement of calculated results with observation. The object is not to banish "intuition," but to test and systematise its employment to eliminate the errors to which its ungoverned use gives rise, and to discover general laws from which, by deduction, we can obtain true results never contradicted, and in crucial instances confirmed, by intuition. In all this, logistic is exactly on a level with (say) astronomy, except that, in astronomy, verification is effected not by intuition but by the senses. The "primitive propositions," with which the deductions of logistic begin, should, if possible, be evident to intuition; but that is not indispensable, nor is it, in any case, the whole reason for their acceptance. This reason is inductive, namely that, among their known consequences (including themselves), many appear to intuition to be true, none appear to intuition to be false, and those that appear to intuition to be true are not, so far as can be seen, deducible from any system of indemonstrable propositions inconsistent with the system in question (quoted in Wang 1987a:314).

In this paragraph, the "method of logistic" is undoubtedly what is commonly called the "axiomatic method" today. I am in favor of adopting this liberal conception of the axiomatic method and do not think that Gödel would reject it. His apparently exclusive concern with finding axioms directly by intuition may be just a consequence of his belief that such a use of the axiomatic method is the most fruitful choice. If this conjecture is true, then disagreement with his position in this connection would be over one's estimation of the comparative fruitfulness of alternative approaches.

In any case, I am in favor of construing the axiomatic method along the liberal line of Russell's argument in 7.5.6. Indeed, it is not clear to me why the axiomatic method should occupy as central place in philosophy as Gödel seems to assign to it. For instance, Rawls's method of "reflective equilibrium," which is related to but possibly broader than the method described in 7.5.6, seems to be appropriate to philosophy. I consider Rawls's method at length in section 10.3 below.

Chapter 8
Set Theory and Logic as Concept Theory

Logic is the theory of the formal. It consists of set theory and the theory of concepts. . . . Set is a formal concept. If we replace the concept of set by the concept of concept, we get logic. The concept of concept is certainly formal and, therefore, a logical concept. . . . A plausible conjecture is: Every set is the extension of some concept. . . . The subject matter of logic is intensions (concepts); that of mathematics is extensions (sets).
Gödel, ca. 1976

For someone who considers mathematical objects to exist independently of our constructions and of our having an intuition of them individually, and who requires only that the general mathematical concepts must be sufficiently clear for us to be able to recognize their soundness and the truth of the axioms concerning them, there exists, I believe, a satisfactory foundation of Cantor's set theory in its whole original extent and meaning.
Gödel, The Cantor Paper, 1964

It is clear that Gödel saw concept theory as the central part of logic and set theory as a part of logic. It is unclear whether he saw set theory as belonging to logic only because it is, as he believed, part of concept theory, which is yet to be developed. For present purposes, I take as a given his categorical statement that logic consists of set theory and concept theory. I have attempted to clarify this conception of logic in *Recollections of Kurt Gödel* (Wang 1987a, hereafter *RG*:309–310); this chapter is mainly a report of Gödel's own fragmentary observations on this issue.

In my opinion, Gödel's conception of logic is a natural development of what Frege wanted logic to be. I developed this idea earlier (1990a, 1994) in the context of a framework for classifying alternative conceptions of logic. I do not, however, say much about this topic in the present work.

Between October of 1971 and May of 1972, Gödel and I discussed a draft of my chapter on the concept of set for *From Mathematics to Philosophy* (hereafter *MP*:181–223). These discussions were, he said, intended to "enrich" this chapter. On points on which we agreed, I made no specific attributions to him, even where his suggestions had led to reformulations.

In conformity with his wishes, I acknowledged his contributions in the following contexts: (1) his justification of the axiom of replacement (*MP*:186), in contrast to my own; (2) his five principles by which axioms of set theory are set up (189–190); (3) his distinction between logic and mathematics in their relation to the paradoxes (187–188); (4) one of his explications of the phrase "give meaning to the question of the truth or falsity of propositions like the continuum hypothesis" (199); and (5) a comparison of the axiom of measurable cardinals with certain physical hypotheses (25, 208, 223n. 23). I shall consider here the details of these contributions.

Work by Charles Parsons (1983:268–297) and Michael Hallett (1984) is of special relevance to the discussions of the iterative concept of set in *From Mathematics to Philosophy* and should be compared with Gödel's concept as reported here.

From 18 October 1975 until 4 January 1976, we had extensive discussions on set theory and logic as concept theory, first in connection with a draft of my essay "Large Sets" (Wang 1977) and then through the interplay between his observations and four fragments I had produced for purposes of discussion. This material has not been published to date, except for one remark that I reported in "Large Sets" (Wang 1977:310, 325, 327). In this chapter I formulate and organize his remarks of this period in combination with relevant observations he made before then.

The topics we discussed include: the scope and the function of logic; the nature of sets, concepts, and classes; logic as concept theory; the concept of set and the axioms of set theory; and Cantor's continuum problem and Cantor's hypothesis. I shall follow Gödel's strategy of using Cantor's continuum problem as a focal point in considering the nature of set theory.

8.1 Cantor's Continuum Problem and His Hypothesis

The most famous problem in set theory is Cantor's continuum problem, which asks what appears to be an elementary question: How many points are there on (a segment of) the line? How many real numbers or sets of natural numbers? A natural and obvious reply is that there are infinitely many points or real numbers or number sets. This answer is correct, as far as it goes, but it ceased to be completely satisfactory after Cantor introduced a precise distinction, within the infinite, between the countable and the uncountable, and then proved that the set of real numbers, unlike the set of integers which is countable, is uncountable. Moreover, Cantor was able to define the sizes, or the *cardinalities* of infinite sets in such a way that there are many distinct uncountable cardinalities.

In 1874 Cantor announced for the first time his conjecture that the cardinality of the continuum, that is, the set of real numbers, is the smallest uncountable cardinal number (Cantor 1932:132). This conjecture is what is known in the literature as the *continuum hypothesis*. It remains unsettled today: we have neither a proof nor a disproof of it. However, according to the objective picture of sets, it is either true or false, however difficult it may be for us to know which is the case. If and when the conjecture is settled, this success—that is, the fact that it is settled—would be a crucial piece of evidence in favor of the objective picture of sets.

The most important result on the continuum hypothesis so far is that it can neither be proved nor disproved on the basis of the familiar axioms of set theory currently in use. Gödel sees this conclusion as a significant and lively incentive to search for new axioms. Moreover, he views the fact of our being able to reach such a remarkable proof as strong evidence for the objective picture: it is, he believes, only by a serious application of the objective picture that we have been able to establish the consistency and independence of the hypothesis relative to the known axioms of set theory.

It is well known that there is a one-one correlation between real numbers and sets of positive integers. The continuum hypothesis says that there is also a one-one correlation between these sets and the countable ordinal numbers, which correspond to the ordinal types of the well-ordered sets of positive integers. In order to prove or disprove the hypothesis, it is necessary to find sufficiently explicit characterizations of the countable sets and the countable ordinals, so that one can try to determine whether there is a one-one correlation between them.

On 4 June 1925 in Münster Hilbert delivered an address "On the Infinite," in which he outlined an attempted proof of the continuum hypothesis from the familiar axioms of set theory. As we now know, the outline cannot lead to a correct proof, since the conclusion to be reached is false. However, the underlying idea is plausible and suggestive. In 1930 Gödel became acquainted with Hilbert's outline and began to reflect on the continuum problem. In 1938 he reached a proof of the weaker conclusion that the continuum hypothesis (CH) is consistent with the familiar axioms of set theory and wrote it up: CH is not, he concluded, refutable by those axioms.

In 1939 he published his proof (Gödel 1990, hereafter *CW*2:28–32). Shortly afterward Bernays said in his review: "The whole Gödel reasoning may also be considered as a way of modifying the Hilbert project for a proof of the Cantor continuum hypothesis, as described in Hilbert 1925, so as to make it practicable and at the same time generalizable to higher powers" (Bernays 1940:118).

In January 1972 I asked Gödel about this observation in which Bernays compared Gödel's proof with Hilbert's outline. Gödel replied immediately, and, on two later occasions, returned to the comparison:

8.1.1   For Hilbert the absolute consistency of CH is not stronger than its relative consistency, because he claimed to have proved also the consistency of the axioms of set theory [as part of his claimed proof of CH]. In outer structure my proof is more similar to Hilbert's outline: both use ordinals and functionals of ordinals, and nothing else; both define, in terms of ordinal numbers, a system of functions (or sets) for which CH is true. In details, however, there are two differences. (1) While Hilbert considers only recursively defined functions or sets, I admit also nonconstructive definitions (by quantification). (2) While I take the ordinals as given, Hilbert attempts to construct them. This case is a classical example of using the same approach but attaining different successes.

8.1.2   Hilbert believed that CH is true in constructive mathematics and that nothing true in constructive mathematics can ever be wrong in classical mathematics—since the latter, due to its consistency, is only a supplement and completion to the former. Moreover, Hilbert was not interested in constructive mathematics [in itself, being just a ladder to get classical mathematics by providing a consistency proof for it]. Brouwer was completely different. According to Hilbert, a real correct consistency proof of set theory contains CH.

8.1.3   Hilbert thinks that if one proves the consistency of set theory in the natural way, then the consistency of CH is a corollary of the proof—though not of just the theorem. This is true and realized by my own proof: the consistency of the power-set axiom reveals the consistency of CH [and of the generalized CH too]. It is strange that Hilbert presents the idea in such a way that one does not see this point [immediately].

In revising my summary of these observations for *From Mathematics to Philosophy* (*MP*:11–12), Gödel added some additional remarks:

8.1.4   Hilbert was not a constructivist in the sense of totally rejecting nonconstructive proofs. His error consists in his view that nonconstructive *metamathematics* is of no use. Hence he expected that his constructive metamathematics would lead to the solution of the problem.

8.1.5   Hilbert believed that (1) the continuum hypothesis is true (and provable by his outline) in constructive mathematics, (2) nothing true in constructive mathematics can ever be wrong in classical mathematics, since the role of the latter is solely to *supplement* the former (3) so as to obtain a complete system in which every proposition is decided. Hilbert's Lemma II (1925:391) was supposed to prove (1), and his Lemma I (385) was supposed to prove *mathematically* the part of (2) relevant to CH—that is, to prove that any refutation of CH from classical axioms could be replaced by a constructive refutation. The assertion (2) is another philosophical error (stemming from the same quasi-positivistic attitude).

8.1.6   If the term *constructive* is—as Hilbert had in mind—identified with *finitary*, Hilbert's proof scheme is not feasible. Otherwise it might be. But it would at any rate be an enormous detour if one only aims at a consistency proof for CH. On the other hand, it would solve the much deeper, but entirely different problem of a constructive consistency proof of Zermelo's axioms of set theory.

Gödel had already stated, in his letter to me of 7 March 1968, that it would be impossible for a constructivist to discover his proof (see MP:10, quoted above in 7.1.16).

In Chapter 7 I considered the argument from success which Gödel set out in the letters to me, regarding his completeness and incompleteness theorems. Parts of those letters are also relevant to his work in set theory, as well as to his observations on Paul Cohen's forcing method for proving independent results in set theory.

In his letter of 7 December 1967, he explained the fundamental place of objectivism in the discovery of his model L of constructible sets for set theory:

8.1.7   [H]ow could one give a consistency proof for the continuum hypothesis by means of my transfinite model L if consistency proofs have to be finitary? (Not to mention that from the finitary point of view an interpretation of set theory in terms of L seems preposterous from the beginning, because it is an "interpretation" in terms of something which itself has no meaning.) The fact that such an interpretation (as well as any non-finitary consistency proof) yields a finitary *relative* consistency proof apparently escaped notice (MP:9).

On 7 March 1968 he wrote another letter, qualifying and elaborating on the above paragraph:

8.1.8   On rereading my letter of December 7, I find the phrasing in the above paragraph is perhaps a little too drastic. It must be understood cum grano salis. Of course, the formalistic point of view did not make *impossible* consistency proofs by means of transfinite models. It only made them much harder to discover, because they are somehow not congenial to this attitude of mind (ibid.:9–10). [Followed by the passage quoted above in 7.1.16.]

In my letter of 18 November 1975, attached to fragment M, I raised the following question in connection with Gödel's argument from success: "What can we say about Cohen's work [1966]? Would it be right to say that he needed a realistic view of real numbers—the continuum—at least?" Gödel replied by discussing M and also commented later on my reconstruction of his reply. Let me try to reproduce what he said on these two occasions:

8.1.9   Cohen's work, as he developed it, was based on my constructible sets, [an idea] which is based on a realist position. This is only one way of carrying out independence proofs. In fact, I had previously developed a part of a related method—not from constructible sets but from some idea stimulated by reading some work of Brouwer's—and proved the independence of the axiom of choice.

In Cohen's proofs one makes generality or impossibility statements about what one does not know. Nobody can understand this. This would be nonsense if sets were not—physically so to say—real but were only as one constructs them oneself. The easiest way to understand Cohen's idea is to imagine sets to be physical sets. This is not the only way. As a heuristic, if sets are real, you can make definite statements about them, even though you only know them to a small extent; such as no prime numbers occur in them. Generality becomes equivalent to impossibility: a property is true of all if there is no possibility of exhibiting—not demonstrable, really from the real world—a counterexample. The following fact is clear in these proofs: If an arbitrary physical set is envisaged, empirical knowledge cannot define a definite limit; but Cohen nonetheless teaches us how generic statements could be made about it. It is impossible to understand what is behind this. One doesn't see how Cohen's proofs work; but one can see how my proofs work, if they are carried out in light of what we know after Cohen's work.

On another occasion, Gödel said about Cohen's idea of forcing:

8.1.10   Forcing is a method to make true statements about something of which we know nothing.

Given the fact that the continuum hypothesis is not decidable on the basis of the familiar axioms of set theory, it is natural to look for other plausible axioms that would settle the issue. Gödel himself tried for a number of years, after 1963, to find such axioms. It is known that in 1970 he wrote three manuscripts on this quest: (1) Some considerations leading to the probable conclusion that the true power of the continuum is aleph-two; (2) A proof of Cantor's continuum hypothesis from a higher plausible axiom about orders of growth; and (3) an unsent letter to Tarski. (All three pieces are included in Gödel's *Collected Works*, volume 3, with an introductory note by Robert M. Solovay.)

In 1972 Oskar Morgenstern told me that Gödel was working on a big paper on the continuum problem. In November of 1975, in the context of relating the introduction of new axioms to the task of making them plausible, Gödel mentioned what is now known as his *square axiom*: There is a set S, of cardinality aleph-one, of functions of positive integers, such that, for every function f of positive integers, there is some majorizing function g in S; that is, there is some m, such that, for all n greater than m, $g(n)$ is greater than $f(n)$.

By this time, Gödel had been convinced by several logicians that the square axiom by itself sets no upper bound on the size of the continuum. But he seems to find the axiom plausible and to think that it may, in conjunction with some other true or plausible property of the continuum, determine the size of the continuum. In any case, he told me in 1976 that he believed that the size of the continuum is no greater than aleph-two and that even the continuum hypothesis may be true, although the generalized continuum hypothesis is definitely false.

Even though we still do not know whether Cantor's continuum hypothesis is true or false, it has certainly stimulated a good deal of significant work in set theory, which can justifiably be said to support the objective view of sets. We do not know, in a strong sense of knowing, that set theory, even as restricted to Zermelo's system ZF, is consistent. Nonetheless, there is a significant body of work in set theory by now, and among those who study the subject there is unanimous agreement as to which proofs are correct and which proofs are mistaken. Even though we do not have a precise formulation of the objective picture of sets, it is hard to see how any other picture could provide as satisfactory an account of our cumulative experience as that acquired through the study of set theory from Cantor to the practitioners of today.

The search for new axioms going far beyond those of the system ZF is an active component of current work in set theory. This search has a special charm as a way of broadening our vistas by pure intellect. At the same time, we rarely need the full power of ZF in mathematics. We never use all the ranks. Even the need for omega-one (the first uncountable ordinal number) ranks in proving Borel determinacy is exceptional. Roughly speaking, Harvey Friedman (1971) proved that no proof of Borel determinacy can be carried out with fewer ranks than omega-one, and D. A. Martin (1975) gave a proof of the theorem, using omega-one ranks.

In connection with the relation of set theory to the common practice of mathematicians, Gödel observed:

8.1.11 Even though the rank hierarchy in set theory is rich, ordinary mathematics stays in much lower than most of the possible stages, with really feasible iterations of the formation of power set: to omega-one or to the limit of some sequence r_n (with omega as r_1, omega-x as r_{n+1} if x is r_n). Ordinary mathematics never needs unbounded quantifiers (which range over all sets).

8.1.12 My Cantor paper was written to drive from mathematicians the fear of doing set theory because of the paradoxes. It is fruitful for mathematicians to be interested in foundations: for example, systematic methods for solving certain problems have been developed. Mathematicians are only interested in extensions: after forming concepts they do not investigate generally how concepts are formed.

8.2 Set Theory and the Concept of Set

At the beginning of this chapter I quoted Gödel's declaration that objectivism provides a satisfactory foundation for Cantor's set theory. Roughly speaking, it says that, if we accept objectivism, the concept of set is sufficiently clear for us to recognize the soundness and the truth of the axioms of set theory. The main task, therefore, is to see that the concept of set is indeed clear enough for us to accept its axioms on the basis of objectivism.

8.2.1   The distinction between many and one cannot be further reduced. It is a basic feature of reality that it has many things. It is a primitive idea of our thinking to think of many objects as one object. We have such ones in our mind and combine them to form new ones.

8.2.2   A set is a unity of which its elements are the constituents. It is a fundamental property of the mind to comprehend multitudes into unities. Sets are multitudes which are also unities. A multitude is the opposite of a unity. How can anything be both a multitude and unity? Yet a set is just that. It is a seemingly contradictory fact that sets exist. It is surprising that the fact that multitudes are also unities leads to no contradictions: this is the main fact of mathematics. Thinking [a plurality] together seems like a triviality: and this appears to explain why we have no contradiction. But "many things for one" is far from trivial.

8.2.3   This [fact]—that sets exist—is the main objective fact of mathematics which we have not made in some sense: it is only the evolution of mathematics which has led us to see this important fact. In the general matter of universals and particulars, we do not have the merger of the two things, many and one, to the extent that multitudes are themselves unities. Thinking [a plurality] together may seem like a triviality. Yet some pluralities can be thought together as unities, some cannot. Hence, there must be something objective in the forming of unities. Otherwise we would be able to think together in all cases.

8.2.4   Mathematical objects are not so directly given as physical objects. They are something between the ideal world and the empirical world, a limiting case and abstract. Objects are in space or close to space. Sets are the limit case of spatiotemporal objects—either as an analogue of construing a whole physical body as determined entirely by its parts (so that the interconnections of the parts play no role) or as an analogue of synthesizing various aspects to get one object, with the difference that the interconnections of the aspects are disregarded. Sets are quasi-spatial. They have an analogy to one and many, as well as to a whole and its parts.

The last observation is related to the comparison with Kant's idea of synthesis quoted above in Chapter 7.

In that chapter I discussed the dialectic of intuition and idealization, beginning with natural numbers because they are generally familiar and therefore also significant for those who are not interested in set theory. As far as the essential transition—from small to large, finite to infinite and beyond—is concerned, we may also confine our attention just to sets. We may go from small sets to large sets by the dialectic of intuition and idealization, intuitive overview and thought, the subjective and the objective, knowledge and existence.

Gödel compared sets and numbers in these words:

8.2.5   Numbers appear less concrete than sets. They have different representations and are what is common to all representations. For example, we add or multiply by dealing with a collection of two indeterminate things.

Before turning to the clarification and application of these different forms of dialectic, I consider some familiar peripheral issues about the objectivistic conception of axiomatic set theory.

Since there are mathematical and physical objects, there are also pure sets and empirical sets, such as the set of people currently residing in Beijing, and so on. In order that there be sets, there must be nonsets—individuals—which are the constituents of some of the sets; the existence of sets presupposes their existence; they are conceptually the original objects or elements. Typically, in a philosophical conception of set theory, there are *Urelements*, which correspond to the individuals or nonsets. Usually, the empty set is also taken to be a sort of individual, because, like individuals, it (has the empty extension or) has no members.

As we know, set theory—when studied mathematically—usually confines its attention to pure sets and includes the empty set as the only *Urelement* or the initial object from which (other) sets are formed. We can formulate this familiar idea as follows:

8.2.6 *Individual* is a difficult concept in philosophy. But the idea of *Urelement* is not difficult for set theory, because we are in this context not interested in what an individual is but rather leave the question open. We do not attempt to determine what the correct *Urelements* are (MP:181–182).

The iterative concept of set sees sets as determined, in the first place, by their extensions. According to Russell (1919:183), we cannot take sets "in the *pure* extensional way as simply heaps or conglomerations": the empty set has no members at all and cannot be regarded as a "heap"; it is also hard to understand how it comes about that a set with only one member is not identical with its one member. Hence, if there are such things as heaps, we cannot identify them with the sets composed of their constituents.

Gödel sees this line of thought as adducing reasons against the extensional view of sets, and replies, in the Russell paper:

8.2.7   But it seems to me that these arguments could, if anything, at most prove that the empty set and the unit sets (as distinct from their only element) are fictions (introduced to simplify the calculus, like the point at infinity in geometry), not that all sets are fictions (Gödel 1944 in CW2:131).

Whereas I agree with Gödel's observation as a defense of the extensional view of sets, I am inclined to think that the iterative concept, although an extensional view, does not take sets "in the *pure* extensional way as simply heaps." It seems to me that a set as a unity is something more than just a heap of items. But I do not know how to explicate this vaguely felt something more.

In generating one object out of its various aspects, if we abstract from the interrelations or interconnections of the aspects, the one object generated would be the set of which the aspects are constituents, provided we think of these aspects as objects. We can likewise synthesize a small number of physical objects into one object, a set, by disregarding all the interrelations among these objects. As we come to large, though finite, and infinite manifolds, idealizations—what Husserl calls "constitutions of mathematical objects"—which go beyond the immediately given are needed. Gödel said in this connection:

8.2.8 Husserl speaks of constituting mathematical objects but what is contained in his published work on this matter is merely programmatic. Phenomenological investigations of the constitution of mathematical objects is of fundamental importance for the foundations of mathematics.

Conceptually, the finite sets built up from the empty set behave essentially like the natural numbers. For instance, sometimes one takes the natural numbers—instead of the empty set—as the Urelements. Just as we go from small numbers to large ones and then to their infinite whole, we do the same with finite sets:

8.2.9 By our native intuition we only see clear propositions about physically given sets and then merely simple examples of them. All we know about sets of integers or of finite sets is only what we know about physically existing sets; we only know small finite segments. If you given up idealization, then mathematics disappears. (Compare 7.1.10.)

According to George Miller (1956), we are psychologically capable of taking in with one glimpse only a collection of about seven items.

8.2.10 Could it be the case that there are only finitely many integers? We can't imagine such a situation. Our primitive concepts would be wrong. Number is based on the concept of different things. The concept of difference is precise. If it is not precise, then we can't iterate indefinitely. If one denies difference, one also denies iteration.

As I said before, going from the finite to the infinite involves the big jump. In particular, in order to *overview* (or run through) an infinite set, it is necessary to resort to an extension of intuition in the Kantian sense—to some sort of infinite intuition.

8.2.11 To arrive at the totality of integers involves a jump. Overviewing it presupposes an infinite intuition. What is given is a psychological analysis. The point is whether it produces objective conviction. This is the beginning of analysis. (Compare 7.1.18.)

I discuss the move from integers to the totality of integers in Chapter 7. Once we recognize that there are infinite sets, we see that the axiom of infinity is true for the concept of sets: there exists some infinite set. The other important standard axioms of set theory are, for restriction: extensionality and foundation; for getting more sets: subset formation, power set, and replacement.

The *axiom of extensionality* may be viewed as a defining characteristic of sets—in contrast to concepts or properties. In order to see that the axiom of foundation holds, we recall briefly some elementary facts:

Cantor's set theory calls our attention to the right perspective for perceiving fairly clearly the concept of set. According to this perspective, which has so far stood the test of time, there is a rank or type hierarchy of sets, which consists of what can be conceived through iterated application of the operation of collecting given objects into sets.

If we try to visualize the universe of all sets and choose to leave out the objects that are not sets, we have a peculiar tree (or rather a mess of many trees) with the empty set as the root, so that each set is a node and two sets are joined by a branch if one belongs to the other.

To get some order out of this chaos, one uses the power-set operation. Clearly, the empty set must be at the bottom. If we consider the power set of the empty set, we get all possible subsets of the empty set, and so on. In the original mess of trees representing all sets, every node except the root has some branch going downwards. Hence, every node must eventually lead back to the empty set. But if we use a power set at each successor stage and take union at every limit stage, we should be able to exhaust all possible sets on the way up, so that each node will be included in this one-dimensional hierarchy.

It seems surprising that arbitrary collections of objects into wholes should form such a neat order. Yet it is not easy to think of any non-artificial situation that would defeat this order.

The *axiom of foundation* is a generalization of the characteristic of sets that no set can belong to itself. It says that every set can be obtained at some stage, or that every collection of sets has a minimal member in the rank hierarchy as just described. Given the way the hierarchy is conceived, it is clear that, within every nonempty collection of sets, there must be some set that is of no higher rank than any set in the collection, so that no set in the collection can be a member of it.

The axiom of *subset formation* (or of "comprehension") says that if a collection (of objects or just of sets) is included in a set, then it is also a set:

8.2.12   Originally we understand sets by defining properties. Then we extensionalize and conceive of a set as a unity of which the elements are its constituents. Certainly if we can overview or run through the members of a collection, we can overview any part of the collection obtained by omitting certain members of it. (Compare *MP*:184.)

The *axiom of power set* says that all subsets of a set can be collected into a set (Compare *MP*:184):

8.2.13   The power-set operation involves a jump. In this second jump we consider not only the members of a set as given but also the process of selecting members from the set. Taking all possible ways of leaving out members of the set is a kind of "method" for producing all its subsets. We then feel that we can overview the collection of all these subsets as well. We idealize, for instance, the integers or the finite sets (a) to the possibility of an infinite totality, and (b) with omissions. So we get a concretely intuitive idea and then one goes on. There is no doubt in the mind that this idealization—to any extent whatsoever—is at the bottom of classical mathematics. (Compare 7.1.18 and 7.1.19.)

In the jump from an infinite set to its power set, we have a dialectic of the subjective and the objective, of knowledge and existence, much more than in idealizing the integers to the possibility of an infinite totality. Unlike the totality of integers, the totality of all subsets of an infinite set is not even countable. It is hard to imagine how we can know or have an intuitive acquaintance with every one of these subsets. If, therefore, knowing a set presupposes knowing all its members, it is hard to believe that we can know the power set of an infinite set.

In my opinion, this familiar obstacle can be overcome by an appeal to objectivism in set theory. According to the objectivistic concept of set, I believe, a set presupposes for its existence (the existence of) all its elements but does not presuppose for its knowability (the knowledge of) all its elements individually. The point of this distinction is, I think, related to that of Gödel's similar distinction in connection with the vicious-circle principle in the form of: no totality can contain members presupposing this totality (the Russell paper, CW2:128). The step from the existence of all subsets of an infinite set to the overviewability of its power set clearly involves a strong idealization of our intuition. This matter of presupposition, so far as existence is concerned, is not a question of temporal priority. The point is, rather, that, conceptually, objects have to exist in order for the set of them—as their unity—to exist.

The *axiom of replacement* says that, if there is a one-one correlation between a collection and a set, then the collection is also a set. For instance, if we begin with an infinite set and apply the power-set operation repeatedly, then we get an infinite collection consisting of the original set, its power set, and so on, up to every finite iteration. Since there is a one-one correlation between this collection and the set of natural numbers, it is, by the axiom of replacement, also a set. The strength of this axiom lies in the fact that, given a totality of sets built up from the empty set or other *Urelements*, we can obtain new sets by collecting together sets from the different levels, which are not included in any of the original levels.

I had given an obvious justification of this axiom by applying the idealized sense of overviewing together or running through all members of a given set. Suppose we are given a set and a one-one correlation between the members of the set and certain other given sets. If we put, for each element of the set, its corresponding set in its place, we are able to run through the resulting collection as well. In this manner, we are justified in forming sets by arbitrary replacements (*MP*:186). Gödel, however, chose to use a seemingly more complex approach which reveals more clearly the place of the axiom in the expansion of a range of given sets. (Compare the paragraph attributed to him in *MP*:186.)

8.2.14   The axiom of replacement is a deeper axiom. It does not have the same kind of *immediate* evidence—previous to any closer analysis of the iterative concept of set—which the other familiar axioms have. It is not quite evident at the beginning. This is seen from the fact that it was not included in Zermelo's original system of axioms and Fraenkel initially gave a wrong formulation. Heuristically, the best way of arriving at it is the following:

8.2.15   From the very idea of the iterative concept of set it follows that, if an ordinal number a has been obtained, the operation P of power set iterated a times from any set y leads to a set $P^a(y)$. But, for the same reason, it would seem to follow that, if instead of P, one takes some larger jump in the hierarchy of types, for example, the transition Q from x to the set obtained from x by iterating as many times as the smallest ordinal a of the well-orderings of x, $Q^a(y)$ likewise is a set. Now, to assume this for any conceivable jump operation—even for those that are defined by reference to the universe of all sets or by use of the choice operation— is equivalent to the axiom of replacement.

8.2.16   The iteration is always by ordinal numbers which have already been obtained: given any ordinal a, we can invent any jumps from sets to sets and iterate them a times. In each case we get an operation which iterates a jump an ordinal number of times. Then we get a universe closed with respect to this operation. In this way we justify the axiom of replacement and the rank or type hierarchy of sets. You can well-order any set, and then any jump can be iterated as many times as the ordinal number of its well-ordering to go from any given set to another— possibly new—set.

Here is a general observation by Gödel:

8.2.17   The axiom of subset formation comes before the axiom of power set. We can form the power set of a set, because we understand the selection process (of singling out any subset from the given set) intuitively, not blindly. By the axiom of replacement we reach higher and higher types by defining faster and faster growing functions to produce types. We then want a domain closed with respect to the procedure and, with the help of extensionalization, we arrive at the inaccessible numbers. Intuitionistic set theory stays with the intensional.

8.3   *The Cantor-Neumann Axiom: The Subjective and the Objective*

Apart from these familiar axioms of set theory, Gödel repeatedly relates objectivism in set theory to the axiom that a collection of sets is a set if and only if it is not as large as the universe V of all sets. Before turning to a consideration of this axiom, however, I would like to discuss Gödel's contrast between the subjective and the objective, which I do not clearly understand.

Within objective reality, certain multitudes are also unities; we believe this to be a fact because we are able to overview many multitudes and thereby see them as unities—sets. But already in the case of overviewing the power set of an infinite set, we have to project to the objective realm of existence the idealized possibility of forming—by omission—arbitrary subsets of the given set. What can be thought together can go beyond what can be overviewed, just as, generally, thought can go beyond intuition. Idealization is one way of extending the range of intuition with the help of thought.

8.3.1   This significant property of certain multitudes—that they are unities—must come from some more solid foundation than the apparently trivial and arbitrary phenomenon that we can overview the objects in each of these multitudes. Without the objective picture, we do not seem able to exclude complete arbitrariness in determining when [the elements of] a multitude can be thought together (broader than can be overviewed) and when not. Indeed, without the objective picture, nothing seems to prevent us from believing that every multitude can be thought together. Yet, as we know, when we do this, we get into contradictions. Some pluralities can be thought together as unities, some cannot. Hence, there must be something objective in the forming of unities.

8.3.2   In some sense, the subjective view leads to the objective view. Subjectively a set is something which we can overview in one thought. If we overview a multitude of objects in one thought in our mind, then this whole, the one thought, contains also as a part the objective unity of the multitude of objects, as well as its relation to our thought. Different persons can, we believe, each view the same multitude in one thought. Hence, it is natural to assume a common nucleus which is the objective unity. It is indeed a unity, since it is contained in another unity. Idealization is decisive in both cases [the subjective and the objective unity].

8.3.3   Even though for our knowledge we do bring in considerations of a more or less subjective nature, the range of possible knowledge is wider than the range of existence that can be justified from the subjective viewpoint. The psychological act of thinking together all objects of a multitude in one thought yields more sets from the objective viewpoint because stronger idealizations are appropriate [than from the subjective viewpoint]. From the idealized subjective view, we can get the power set. But the indefinability of the universe V of all sets can't be got by the subjective view at all. The difference in strength becomes clear only when you introduce new principles which make no sense at all in the subjective view. [Compare the Cantor-Neumann axiom, considered below.] For every set there is some mind which can overview it in the strictest sense.

8.3.4   To say that the universe of all sets is an unfinishable totality does not mean objective indeterminedness, but merely a subjective inability to finish it.

8.3.5   The proposition that all sets are constructible is a natural completion of subjective set theory for human beings. Ronald Jensen has shown that it leads to unnatural consequences such as Souslin's hypothesis. [(1972); compare *CW*2:17.] The "axiom" of determinacy is another example [which in its general form contradicts the axiom of choice].

A multitude of objects having the property that the unity of the objects in the multitude exists is a set. The multitude V of all sets does not have this property. The concept of set contains the component that sets are unities each with its elements as constituents, and it therefore rules out the possibility of a set belonging to itself, because if it did belong to itself it would be its own constituent. This has the consequence that the multitude V of all sets, being on a higher level than every set, cannot be a unity. It presupposes for its existence (the existence of) all sets and, therefore, cannot itself be a set, because if it were it would be one of its own constituents (and belong to itself).

Of course, it follows that no multitude can be a set if its being a set would, by justifiable axioms of set theory, compel V to be a set also. One might compare this situation with the nonexistence of a largest finite ordinal or a largest countable ordinal. Since, relying on familiar definitions in set theory, the smallest infinite ordinal is the set of all finite ordinals, it cannot be one of them, since no set can belong to itself. Similarly for the smallest uncountable ordinal and countable ordinals. They differ from V in that they are sets. The universe of all sets is the range of the concept of set and is a multitude (many) and not a unity (one).

By appealing to generally accepted principles of set theory, we can also provide auxiliary arguments to show that V cannot be a set. For example, the multitude of all subsets of a set is again a set and a larger set. If V were a set, the multitude of all its subsets would be a larger set, contradicting the fact that no multitude of sets could be larger than V.

In a letter to Dedekind dated Halle, 28 July 1899, Cantor called multitudes "like" V *inconsistent multitudes*, and introduced a general principle to distinguish them from sets (Cantor 1932:443):

8.3.6   If we start from the notion of a definite multitude [*Vielheit*] (a system, a totality) of things, it is necessary, as I discovered, to distinguish two kinds of multitudes (by this I always mean *definite* multitudes). For on the one hand a multitude can be such that the assumption that *all* of its elements "are together" leads to a contradiction, so that it is impossible to conceive of the multitude as a unity, as "one finished thing." Such multitudes I call *absolutely infinite* or *inconsistent multitudes*. When on the other hand the totality of the elements of the multitude can be thought without contradiction as "being together," so that their collection into "*one* thing" is possible, I call it a *consistent multitude* or a "set" [*Menge*]. Two equivalent multitudes either are both "sets" or both inconsistent.

In the last statement, two multitudes are equivalent if and only if there is a one-to-one correlation between their elements. In particular, a multitude is *like* V if and only if it is equivalent to V. In contemporary terminology, Cantor was distinguishing *proper classes* of sets from those classes which are themselves sets. We may also restate his assertion as an axiom: A proper class is a set if and only if it is not equivalent to V.

In 1925 von Neumann rediscovered this axiom and fully explored its implications in his axiom IV2 (1961:41); so it became known as "von Neumann's axiom." In November of 1975, Gödel used this axiom as evidence for the objective character of the concept of set:

8.3.7   As has been shown by von Neumann, a multitude is a set if and only if it is smaller than the universe of all sets. This is understandable from the objective viewpoint, since one object in the whole universe must be small compared with the universe and small multitudes of objects should form unities because being small is an intrinsic property of such multitudes. From the subjective viewpoint, there is no reason why only small multitudes form unities: there is little connection between the size of the multitude and thinking together the objects of the multitude in one thought, since the elements of a large but homogeneous multitude may hang together in our thought more easily than those of a small but heterogeneous multitude. For example, from the subjective viewpoint, it is hard to find a good reason to correct Frege's mistaken belief that every concept determines a set. [Subjectively, the Russell set does not appear complicated.]

Gödel is interested in this axiom for another reason as well: he considers it a *maximum principle*. In the 1950s he had commented on it in a letter to Stanislaw Ulam:

8.3.8   The great interest which this axiom has lies in the fact that it is a maximum principle, somewhat similar to Hilbert's axiom of completeness in geometry. For, roughly speaking, it says that any set which does not, in a certain well defined way, imply an inconsistency exists. Its being a maximum principle also explains the fact that this axiom implies the axiom of choice. I believe that the basic problems of set theory, such as Cantor's continuum problem, will be solved satisfactorily only with the help of stronger axioms of *this* kind, which in a sense are opposite or complementary to the constructivistic interpretation of mathematics (quoted in Ulam 1958:13).

In discussing Cantor's continuum problem, Gödel conjectures that the problem "may be solvable with the help of some new axiom which would state or imply something about the definability of sets." He mentions, in this regard, his own consistency proof of the continuum hypothesis by the "axiom" A, that every set is constructible, as a partial confirmation of this conjecture (the Cantor paper, *CW*2:183–184, 262). In the original 1947 version he added a footnote: "On the other hand, from an axiom in some sense directly opposite to this one the negation of Cantor's conjecture could perhaps be derived" (CW2:184 n. 22). In the revised version, written in 1963, he further elaborates on this observation (CW2:262–263 n. 23):

8.3.9   I am thinking of an axiom which (similar to Hilbert's completeness axiom in geometry) would state some maximum property of the system of all sets, whereas axiom A states a minimum property. Note that only a maximum property would seem to harmonize with the iterative concept of set [as we understand it, which admits arbitrary sets "regardless of if, or how, they can be defined"].

In the process of commenting on my manuscript in 1972, Gödel proposed certain revisions of my remarks on measurable cardinals, which I incorporated in the text without making the changes explicit:

8.3.10   The relation of the axiom of measurable cardinals to the usual axioms of set theory is one comparable to that between the law of gravitation and the laws of classical physics; in both cases the axiom and the law are not derivable from the other principles but extend them without contradicting them (MP:25).

8.3.11   There used to be a confused belief that axioms of infinity cannot refute the constructibility hypothesis (and therefore even less the continuum hypothesis) since L contains by definition all ordinals. For example, if there are measurable cardinals, they must be in L. However, in L they do not satisfy the condition of being measurable. This is no defect of these cardinals, unless one were of the opinion that L is the true universe. As is well known, all kinds of strange phenomena appear in nonstandard models (MP:204).

8.3.12   However, there does remain a feeling that the property of being a measurable cardinal says more than just largeness, although it implies largeness (MP:204). [This feeling has to do with the fact that it was introduced at first by the principle of uniformity of the universe of sets, which is different in character from the other principles.]

In his Cantor paper (CW2:261, 269), Gödel had discussed the criterion of fruitfulness in consequences. Once he elaborated on a similar point in connection with measurable cardinals:

8.3.13   The hypothesis of measurable cardinals may imply more interesting (positive in some yet to be analyzed sense) universal number-theoretical statements beyond propositions such as the ordinary consistency statements: for instance, the equality of p_n (the function whose value at n is the nth prime number) with some easily computable function. Such consequences can be rendered probable by verifying large numbers of numerical instances. Hence, the difference with the hypothesis of expanding universe is not as great as we may think at first (MP:223 n. 23).

The reference to "the hypothesis of expanding universe" was related to a suggestion in my original manuscript—later deleted—to compare it with the continuum hypothesis.

In our discussions, Gödel also considered extensively the principles by which we introduce the axioms of set theory. Since, however, many of his observations—especially those pertaining to Ackermann's system and the principle that the universe of all sets is not definable—are quite technical, I leave that material for the last section of this chapter.

8.4 The Function and Scope of Logic

It is hard to classify or develop many of Gödel's occasional observations on logic. One definite point, however, is that concept theory is for him the center of logic. Many of his other remarks are rather fragmentary, and sometimes he seems to say somewhat different things in different contexts. Because I did not always fully understand him and because I have no complete record of what he said, the reconstruction below must be taken cum grano salis.

The following eight paragraphs concern the function of logic in making things explicit and brief:

8.4.1   See 5.3.26.

8.4.2   In the eighteenth century mathematical logic was still a secret science. After the Cauchy type of work mathematical logic emerged. Mathematical logic makes clear what clear thinking is, but only in the foundations: there are very important things beyond. What is made explicit is usually more effective. We make jumps in the thought process. In mathematics inventions play a large part; in philosophy analysis plays a major role. Mathematical logic is trivial in mathematics, but not trivial in philosophy. It serves to abbreviate things: one hundred pages could be reduced to five pages; things are said more clearly if said with more brevity. It makes much clearer what the primitive terms are which one has in mind, and how to define other things. Positivists do apply this, but not to simplify matters, rather to complicate them.

8.4.3   One philosophical significance of mathematical logic is its explicitness and its explicit axiomatic method.

8.4.4   Mathematics often uses implicit assumptions. It is necessary to have an explicit formulation. The axioms of order on the line are not among Euclid's axioms for geometry but were first brought out explicitly by [Moritz] Pasch only in the nineteenth century. If Euclid had known logic, he would have realized that there is simply no way to complete his proposed proofs by making explicit the missing steps. In contrast, it would be possible for Pasch to leave out steps and still have correct proofs.

In this connection, it is of interest that Pasch explicitly required the removability of gaps in genuine deduction (see 84.5 below). (Compare also an analogous observation at the beginning of Frege 1884.)

8.4.5   Indeed, if geometry is to be genuinely deductive, then the process of inferring must always be independent of the *meaning* [*Sinn*] of geometrical concepts, just as it must be independent of diagrams. Only the *relations* between the geometrical concepts are to be taken into account in the propositions and definitions under consideration. It is, in the course of the deduction, certainly legitimate and useful, though *by no means necessary*, to think of the reference [*Bedeutung*] of the concepts which are involved. In fact, if it is necessary to do so, then the inadequacy of the deduction—even the insufficiency of the proof method—is revealed; if the gaps cannot be removed through a modification of the deduction (Pasch 1882:98).

8.4.6   Mathematical logic makes explicit the central place of predication in the philosophical foundation of rational thought. The axioms of order separate logic from intuition in geometry. This is of course of philosophical importance. We have an intuition of ordering which is much clearer than our metric intuition, but it is concealed in Euclid and mixed up with logic reasoning. Our topological intuition goes beyond the metric intuition; statements about topological ordering are more stable and more often true.

8.4.7   Euclid's mistakes would occur again and again, for example in physics and sociology. If we axiomatize in these areas, we again need mathematical logic. The meaning of the wave function was first clarified by von Neumann by using the axiomatic method. Mathematical logic makes it easier to avoid mistakes, even for one who is not a genius.

8.4.8   Husserl also thinks that mathematical logic should not be made the basis of philosophical thinking. It is not the chief tool but the basic tool: the foundation of all conceptual thinking that reveals the fundamental structure of rational speech. The basis of every thing is meaningful predication: something has some property, some object belongs to a set or a class, some relation holds between two things, and so on. Husserl had this; Hegel did not have it. Mathematical logic is important for carrying out ideas, not for finding the right ideas. [This passage is followed by 5.3.18.]

The above eight paragraphs relate mathematical logic to the axiomatic method, which was important for Gödel, not only in mathematics, but also in science and philosophy, for the purpose of developing theories. In the next chapter I shall return to his emphasis on the importance of the axiomatic method and of his ideal of axiomatic theories in philosophy. It should be noted that he did not restrict axiomatic theories to those embodied explicitly in formal systems: for instance, he regarded Newton's physics as a model of axiomatic theories.

It is clear from the last quotation that Gödel considered mathematical logic to be important for philosophy—more important than it is for mathematics, where it is usually trivial. Aside from his ideal of an axiomatic theory, he saw mathematical logic as helpful in doing philosophy because it enables us to be explicit and brief. His contrast between Husserl

and Hegel points to this belief in the importance of logic for a fundamental clarity in the pursuit of philosophy. The idea is, I believe, roughly
this: A significant application of logic in philosophy uses it not explicitly
but implicitly, as a way of acquiring the habit of precise thinking. In this
sense, it is likely that an intimate familiarity with some precise subject
other than logic would have more or less the same effect.

Gödel also considered the relation of logic to reason and to rationalism:

8.4.9   Reason and understanding concern two levels of concept. Dialectics and
feelings are involved in reason. We have also intuition of higher concepts. Christian Wolff confuses understanding with reason and uses only logical inferences.

8.4.10   Religion may also be developed as a philosophical system built on
axioms. In our time, *rationalism* is used in an absurdly narrow sense: sometimes
even confined to first-order logic! Rationalism involves not only logical concepts.
Churches deviated from religion which had been founded by rational men. The
rational principle behind the world is higher than people.

With regard to the scope of logic, there is controversy over whether to
identify logic with predicate (or first-order or elementary) logic or to
include set theory in it as well. Gödel called predicate logic "the logic of
the finite mind." For him, logic includes not only set theory but also—
indeed more centrally—concept theory.

On 6 June 1971 I asked Gödel about the scope of logic and, specifically,
about the view that logic should be identified with predicate logic. He had
told me earlier that, for him, logic included set theory and concept theory.
On this occasion, however, he expanded on the relation between logic
and predicate logic:

8.4.11   The propositional calculus is about language or deals with the original
notion of language: truth, falsity, inference. We include the quantifiers because
language is about something—we take propositions as talking about objects.
They would not be necessary if we did not talk about objects; but we cannot
imagine this. Even though predicate logic is "distinguished," there are also other
notions, such as *many, most, some* (in the sense of plurality), and *necessity.*

8.4.12   One idea is to say that the function of logic is to allow us to draw inferences. If we define logic by formal evidence directly concerning inference for the
finite mind, then there is only one natural choice and it is not natural to treat the
infinite as a part of logic. The part of formal inference or formal theory for the finite
mind incorporates inferences. The completeness proof of predicate logic confirms
its adequacy to this conception of logic. For Aristotle, to be valid is to have deri-
vations and not to be valid is to have counterexamples.

8.4.13   If, however, the concern is with inference, why not look for a general
theory of inference which includes every rule whose consequence necessarily
follows its premise? Since we also have intuitions about probability relations, we
should include rules governing probability inferences.

8.4.14   In contrast to set theory, predicate logic is mainly a matter of rules of inference. It is unnatural to use axioms in it. For the infinite mind, the axioms of set theory are also rules of inference. The whole of set theory is within the purely *formal* domain. We have a distinction of two kinds of higher functional calculus [higher-order logic]: in terms of inferences and in terms of concepts. According to Bernays, mathematics is more abstract—in the sense of having no concepts with content—than logic. Abstract structures like groups and fields are purely formal.

Gödel's suggestion to include in logic rules governing probability inferences seems to point to what is commonly called *inductive logic*. He said specifically that the calculus of probability, as a familiar branch of mathematics, was inadequate and not what he had in mind. The suggestion reminds me of the distinction F. P. Ramsey draws between the logic of consistency—"the most generally accepted parts of logic, namely, formal logic, mathematics and the calculus of probabilities"—and the logic of truth—inductive or human logic: "Its business is to consider methods of thought, and discover what degrees of confidence should be placed in them, i.e. in what proportion of cases they lead to truth" (Ramsey 1931:191, 198). The quest for such an inductive or human logic is certainly an important and difficult enterprise. Unfortunately, however, Gödel did not further elaborate on his suggestion in his conversations with me.

On 22 March 1976 Gödel made some remarks that overlap with these earlier observations:

8.4.15   Lower functional calculus [predicate logic] consists of rules of inference. It is not natural to use axioms. It is logic for the finite mind. But we can also add logical constants such as *many, most, some* (in the sense of plurality), *necessarily,* and so on. For the infinite mind, axioms of set theory are also rules of inference.

8.4.16   For the empiricist, the function of logic is to allow us to draw inferences. It is not to state propositions, but to go over from some propositions to some other propositions. For a theoretical thinker, the propositions embodying such inferences (or implications) are also of interest in themselves.

For Gödel, logic deals with *formal*—in the sense of universally applicable—concepts. From this perspective, the concepts of *number, set* and *concept* are all formal concepts. Consequently, even though he sometimes seems to identify logic with concept theory, I assume that the scope of logic consists, for him, of concept theory, set theory, and number theory. The following is my reconstruction of some of his observations on these ideas:

8.4.17   Set is a formal concept. If we replace the concept of *set* by the concept of *concept*, we get logic. The concept of concept is certainly formal and, therefore, a logical concept. But no intuition of *this* concept, in contrast to that of set, has been developed.

8.4.18   Logic is the theory of the formal. It consists of set theory and the theory of concepts. The distinction between elementary (or predicate) logic, nonelementary logic, and set theory is a subjective distinction. Subjective distinctions are dependent on particular forms of the mind. What is formal has nothing to do with the mind. Hence, what logic is is an objective issue. Objective logical implication is categorical. Elementary logic is the logic for finite minds. If you have an infinite mind, you have set theory. For example, set theory for a finite universe of ten thousand elements is part of elementary logic; compare my Russell paper (probably CW2:134).

According to Gödel, his Russell paper, in contrast to his Cantor paper (which deals with mathematics and set theory), deals with logic and concept theory. We have a fairly well developed set theory; we understand the concept of *set* well enough to have a satisfactory resolution of the extensional paradoxes. In contrast, we are far from having a satisfactory concept theory as yet; so, in particular, we still do not know how to resolve the intensional paradoxes. The following observation harks back to the Russell paper:

8.4.19   If you introduce the concept of *concept*, the result is still logic. But going "higher" [than the concept of *concept*] would be too abstract and no longer logic. The concept of *concept* calls for only the lowest level of abstract intuition. Whether the concept of *concept* is a formal concept is not in question. The older search for a satisfactory set theory gives way to a similar search for a satisfactory theory of concepts that will, among other things, resolve the intensional paradoxes. For this purpose, Quine's idea of stratification is arbitrary, and Church's idea along the line of limited ranges of significance is inconsistent in its original form and has not been worked out. [Compare CW2:125, 137, 138.]

Sometimes Gödel hinted at a distinction between *concepts* and *ideas* along Kantian lines. On different occasions he spoke of the concepts of *concept, absolute proof,* and *absolute definability* as ideas rather than concepts:

8.4.20   The general concept of *concept* is an *Idea* [in the Kantian sense]. The intensional paradoxes are related to questions about Ideas. Ideas are more fundamental than concepts. The theory of types is only natural between the first and the second level; it is not natural at higher levels. Laying the foundations deep cannot be extensive.

Once I asked Gödel about his Princeton lecture of 1946, in which he had discussed the task of extending the success of defining the concept of *computability* independently of any given language to "other cases (such as *demonstrability* and *definability*)" (CW2:150–153). He replied:

8.4.21   Absolute demonstrability and definability are not concepts but inexhaustible [Kantian] Ideas. We can never describe an Idea in words exhaustively or completely clearly. But we also perceive it, more and more clearly. This process may be uniquely determined—ruling out branchings. The Idea of proof may be nonconstructively equivalent to the concept of *set*: axioms of infinity and absolute proofs are more or less the same thing.

8.4.22   Ideas cannot be used in precise inferences: they lead to the theory of types. It is a kind of defeatism to think that we have this vague idea which is the very basis of our precise idea. We understand the special concept only because we previously had the general idea. We restrict the general idea to individuals to get the concept of the first type. The general idea of concept is just generality.

8.4.23   Kant's distinction between ideas and concepts is not clear. But it is helpful in trying to define precise concepts.

Gödel said more about the concept or idea of absolute proof in connection with mind's superiority over computers (see 61.11 to 61.14 above): if this can be clarified, then we can resolve the intensional paradoxes and, thereby, prove the superiority of mind.

Gödel expected that logic would be much enriched once we have a satisfactory theory of concepts. For instance, he once made the following observation about Skolem's result that every theory of natural numbers admits some nonstandard model:

8.4.24   It is a wrong interpretation of Skolem's theorem to say that it makes the characterization of integers by logic impossible, because one can use the theory of concepts.

8.5 The Paradoxes and the Theory of Concepts

Gödel was emphatic that the intensional paradoxes should be distinguished from the semantic paradoxes and the extensional paradoxes. For him, unlike the semantic paradoxes, the extensional and the intensional paradoxes are not related to a given language. The sharp distinction between *sets* (as extensions) and *concepts* (as intensions) makes it clear that intensional paradoxes such as that of the concept of all concepts not applying to themselves are not trivial variants of extensional paradoxes such as that of the set of all sets not belonging to themselves.

In his Russell paper and his Cantor paper Gödel had not made these distinctions explicit. As a result, it had been puzzling to many readers that his attitudes toward the paradoxes in the two papers appear to be incompatible. Specifically, the following two statements seem in conflict:

8.5.1   By analyzing the paradoxes to which Cantor's set theory had led, he [Russell] freed them from all mathematical technicalities, thus bringing to light the amazing fact that our logical intuitions (i.e., intuitions concerning such notions as: truth, concept, being, class, etc.) are self-contradictory (*CW2*:124).

8.5.2   They [the set-theoretical paradoxes] are a very serious problem, but not for Cantor's set theory (*CW2*:180).

In the second version of the Cantor paper, this statement was revised to read:

8.5.3   They are a very serious problem, not for mathematics, however, but rather for logic and epistemology (*CW*2:258).

I asked Gödel about this apparent discrepancy in 1971. In *From Mathematics to Philosophy*, I summarized his reply in a form revised and approved by him, as follows:

8.5.4   The difference in emphasis is due to a difference in the subject matter, because the whole paper on Russell is concerned with logic rather than mathematics. The full concept of *class* (truth, concept, being, etc.) is not used in mathematics, and the iterative concept, which is sufficient for mathematics, may or may not be the full concept of class. Therefore, the difficulties in these logical concepts do not contradict the fact that we have a satisfactory foundation of mathematics in terms of the iterative concept of set (*MP*:187−188, 221).

8.5.5   In relation to logic as opposed to mathematics, I believe that the unsolved difficulties are mainly in connection with the intensional paradoxes (such as the concept of not applying to itself) rather than with either the extensional or the semantic paradoxes. In terms of the contrast between bankruptcy and misunderstanding [*MP*:190−193], my view is that the paradoxes in mathematics, which I identify with set theory, are due to misunderstanding, while logic, as far as its true principles are concerned, is bankrupt on account of the intensional paradoxes. This observation by no means intends to deny the fact that *some* of the principles of logic have been *formulated* quite satisfactorily, in particular all those which are used in the application of logic to the sciences including mathematics as it has just been defined.

8.5.6   For sets, the paradoxes are misunderstandings, even though sets as extensions of concepts are in logic and epistemology. Sets are quasi-physical. That is why there is no self-reference. Set theory approaches contradiction to get its strength.

8.5.7   The bankruptcy view only applies to general concepts such as *proof* and *concept*. But it does not apply to certain approximations where we do have something to lean back on. In particular, the concept of *set* is an absolute concept [that is not bankrupt], and provable in set theory by axioms of infinity is a limited concept of *proof* [which is not bankrupt].

Of course, our actual conversations included less concise statements and more ramifications than the above.

Gödel repeatedly emphasizes that he himself had long ago resolved the semantic paradoxes and that it is important to distinguish semantic paradoxes, which have to do with language, from intensional paradoxes, which have to do with concepts. The confusion between concept and language, intensional and semantical, is prevalent and harmful, and is, he believes, a result of the widespread prejudice in favor of nominalism and positivism.

Gödel observed that the general tendency to confuse semantic with intensional paradoxes stems from a preoccupation with language. We understand the semantic paradoxes because, for a given language in which they can be formulated, we see that they mean nothing. For instance, in Gödel's own work on the incompletability of number theory, he first solved the semantic paradox "this is not true" (relative to a given formal language) by concluding that truth is not definable in the same language. He then went on to solve the semantic paradox "this is not provable (in the given system)" by concluding that it is a true statement, though not provable in the system.

In a draft reply to a letter of 27 May 1970 from Yossef Balas, then a student at the University of Northern Iowa, Gödel spoke of his incompletability theorem as showing that truth could not be equated with provability (in the formal system). He continued: "Long before, I had found the *correct* solution of the semantic paradoxes in the fact that truth in a language cannot be defined in itself."

In addition to the paradox of the concept of not applying to itself, Gödel once mentioned another paradox—that of the concept of not being *meaningfully* applicable to itself.

8.5.8   No language is known that semantic paradoxes come in without intensional paradoxes. Meaningful and precise concepts mean this: sentences composed from them in grammatical form have content and truth value. There is also a paradox of the concept of all concepts not meaningfully applicable to themselves. Meaningfulness is much clearer for logical concepts than for empirical concepts. But this may be just my personal habit.

8.5.9   The semantic paradoxes have to do with language and are understood. In contrast, the intensional paradoxes remain a serious problem of logic, of which concept theory is the major component. The two kinds of paradox are often mixed together because without Platonism concepts appear more like language.

8.5.10   The difference between semantical and conceptual paradoxes tends to be obliterated by nominalism. Without objectivism, concepts become closely related to language. That is why semantic and intensional paradoxes are often thought to be the same. But conceptual paradoxes can be formulated without reference to language at all.

8.5.11   Language plays no part in the intensional paradoxes, since they are concerned with concepts as properties and relations of things which exist independently of our definitions and constructions.

8.5.12   The intensional paradoxes involve only logical concepts, while the semantic paradoxes involve empirical concepts too. We see the solution of the semantic paradoxes in that they say nothing. With the intensional paradoxes, however, we don't see the solution and it is not clear that "it says nothing" is the right direction to look for it. Language plays no part in the intensional paradox. Even though we use symbols to state it, that still does not make it into a linguistic paradox. With semantic paradoxes, we are always in a definite language, which always has countably many symbols. We can never have *true* in the same language. Ordinary English is not a precise language, so the question of semantic paradoxes does not apply to it. The semantic paradoxes have no content, because they use *empirical* self-reference. With *logical* self-reference, the lack of content does not occur. For example, not-applying-to-itself is a perfectly reasonable concept; we see no reason why it should not be. It could be proved that applying-to-itself applies to itself.

8.5.13   Even though we do not understand the intensional paradoxes and have not yet found the right axioms for the theory of concepts, we know what the primitives of the theory are which cannot be reduced to anything more primitive. The semantic paradoxes are different: we have no primitive intuitions about language.

On the occasion of this discussion Gödel talked extensively about his dissatisfaction with the excessive emphasis on language in philosophy (quoted in section 5.5; see especially 5.5.7 to 5.5.9). The primitives of concept theory are, he believes, analogous to those of set theory. As I understand it, paragraph 8.5.13 says that the challenge of developing concept theory comes partly from the fact that we do have certain intuitions about the concept of *concept*, but that we do not yet perceive that important concept clearly.

To clarify the contrast between semantic and intensional paradoxes, on 18 October 1972 Gödel cited the following familiar examples:

8.5.14   Consider the sentence "I am not provable" or

(1)   (1) is not provable.

Language comes in here. But about what language is he speaking? It is impossible to define a language for which you can draw the [familiar contradictory] conclusion. The issue only becomes problematic if you have developed a language. But there would already be simpler intensional paradoxes such as:

(2)   What I am saying is not provable.

8.5.15   The self-reference in (2) is by a pronoun, and pronouns are ambiguous. But this can be corrected, following Ackermann's device. The elimination of pronouns is an important step:

(3)   What Mr. A says on 18 October 1972 between noon and a minute later cannot be proved—this being the only sentence uttered by Mr. A within that minute.

One can also write a similar sentence on a blackboard that refers to itself by time and place. Given these revisions [of (1)], you have intensional paradoxes anyway: semantic paradoxes are unimportant.

For Gödel, the importance of the distinction between extensional and intensional paradoxes has much to do with the fact that we already have a fairly satisfactory set theory which resolves the extensional paradoxes, while the unresolved intensional paradoxes provide a useful focus; they constitute a conspicuous obstacle to be overcome in the major task of developing a satisfactory concept theory. Moreover, he sees the paradoxes as evidence for objectivism, both in that they reveal a constraint imposed by objective reality on our freedom to form sets and concepts, and in that, by perceiving the concept of set more clearly, we have resolved the extensional paradoxes.

Gödel was interested in the distinction between the bankruptcy and the misunderstanding views about the relation between set theory and the paradoxes (*MP*: 190–193):

8.5.16   For concepts the paradoxes point to bankruptcy, but for sets they are misunderstandings.

8.5.17   Is the word "misunderstanding" appropriate for the characterization of the extensional paradoxes? Maybe we should call them *oversight* and *mistaken application*. *Oversight* is a more definite concept, but it is too light. Perhaps we should say *persistent* or *serious oversight*.

8.5.18   There are no conclusive arguments for the bankruptcy view of set theory. To use concepts which have led to contradictions in their most primitive evidence proves nothing. It is not only in set theory [that] we use idealizations; even finite number theory up to 10^{100} is also a wild idealization.

8.5.19   The argument that concepts are unreal because of the logical-intensional paradoxes is like the argument that the outer world does not exist because there are sense deceptions.

8.5.20   The intensional paradoxes can be used to prove that concepts exist. They prove that we are not free to introduce any concepts, because, by definition, if we were really completely free, they [the new concepts] would not lead to contradictions. It is perfectly all right to form concepts in the familiar manner: we have evidence that these are meaningful and correct ways of forming concepts. What is wrong is not the particular ways of formation, but the idea that we can form concepts arbitrarily by correct principles. These principles are unavoidable: no theory of concepts can avoid them. Every concept is precisely defined, exactly and uniquely everywhere: true, false, or meaningless. It remains precisely defined if we replace meaningless by false. We don't make concepts, they are there. Being subjective means that we can form them arbitrarily by correct principles of formation.

8.6 Sets and Concepts: The Quest for Concept Theory

Gödel associates *sets* with extension and mathematics, *concepts* with intension and logic. Sets are objects. Indeed, he identifies mathematical objects with sets and suggests that objects are physical and mathematical objects. He is not explicit on the question whether numbers are also (mathematical) objects. I prefer to regard numbers as objects too, but for most of our considerations here, it is convenient to leave numbers out. To avoid the familiar ambiguity of the word *object*, I shall take both objects and concepts to be *entities* or *things* or *beings*.

Classes are neither concepts nor objects. They are an analogue and a generalization of sets. The *range* of every concept is, by definition, a class. If the range happens to be a set, then the set is also the *extension* of the concept, because only an object can be an extension.

8.6.1   The subject matter of logic is intensions (concepts); that of mathematics is extensions (sets). Predicate logic can be taken either as logic or as mathematics: it is usually taken as logic. The general concepts of logic occur in every subject. A formal science applies to every concept and every object. There are extensional and intensional formal theories.

8.6.2   Mathematicians are primarily interested in extensions and we have a systematic study of extensions in set theory, which remains a mathematical subject except in its foundations. Mathematicians form and use concepts, but they do not investigate generally how concepts are formed, as is to be done in logic. We do not have an equally well-developed theory of concepts comparable to set theory. At least at the present stage of development, a theory of concepts does not promise to be a mathematical subject as much as set theory is one.

8.6.3   Sets and concepts are introduced differently: their connections are only outward. (If we take sets as the only objects, we get the mathematical sets—a limiting case of sets in general—which are really the world of mathematical objects.) For instance, while no set can belong to itself, some concepts can apply to themselves: the concept of *concept*, the concept of being applicable to only one thing (or one object), the concept of being distinct from the set of all finite mathematical sets, the concept of being a concept with an infinite range, and so on. It is erroneous to think that to each concept there corresponds a set.

8.6.4   It is not in the ideas (of *set* and *concept*) themselves that every set is the extension of a concept. Sets might exist which correspond to no concepts. The proposition "for every set, there is a [defining] concept" requires a proof. But I conjecture that it is true. If so, everything (in logic and mathematics) is a concept: a set, if extensional; and a concept (only) otherwise.

8.6.5   Generally the range of applicability of a concept need not form a set. An obvious example is the concept of set, whose range consists of all sets. A familiar and convenient practice is to take the range of any concept as a *class*. When the range of a concept is a set, the set is its *extension*. Since, strictly speaking, an extension should be one object but a class which is not a set is not one object, we can generally speak of the "extension" of a concept only as a *façon de parler*. Bearing this in mind, we can also think of classes as "extensions" of concepts.

8.6.6   Classes are introduced by contextual definitions—definitions in use—construed in an objective sense. [For instance, something x belongs to a class K if there is a concept C such that K is the range of C and C applies to x.] They are nothing in themselves, and we do not understand what are introduced only by contextual definitions, which merely tell us how to deal with them according to certain rules. Classes appear so much like sets that we tend to forget the line of thought which leads from concepts to classes. If, however, we leave out such considerations, the talk about classes becomes a matter of make-believe, arbitrarily treating classes as if they were sets again.

8.6.7   Classes are only a derivative hybrid convenience, introduced as a way of speaking about some aspects of concepts. A (proper) class is an *uneigentlich Gegenstand*, it is nothing in itself. In a strict sense one should not speak of *a* class: it is only a way of talking about concepts which apply to the same range of things. We tend to speak of classes as if they were single objects; but they are like fractions taken as pairs of integers. All concepts defined extensionally are classes.

8.6.8   Leibniz developed classes on the lowest level. But logically one cannot stop with the lowest classes. It is natural to extend further, because the general concept of concept is prior to the lowest classes.

8.6.9   Of course the axiom of "extensionality" holds for classes, because the *façon de parler* has been introduced for this purpose. [In other words, two classes with the same members are identical.] In contrast, two concepts which apply to the same things are often different. Only concepts having the same meaning [intension] would be identical.

8.6.10   The following sentence should be deleted from my Russell paper: "It might even be true that the axiom of extensionality (i.e., that no two different properties belong to exactly the same things, which, in a sense, is a counterpart to Leibniz's *Principium identitatis indiscernibilium*, which says no two different things have exactly the same properties) or at least something near to it holds for concepts." This statement is the assertion of a very unlikely possibility of the structure of the world which includes concepts. Such principles can only be true if difference is defined properly. I do not [no longer] believe that generally sameness of range is sufficient to exclude the distinctness of two concepts.

This statement is one illustration of the fact that Gödel modified some of his views about classes between the 1940s and the 1970s. On the whole, he seems to have assigned classes a more fundamental position in the Russell paper as compared with his later view that "classes are nothing in themselves." For instance, he seems to have viewed classes and concepts as equally fundamental, when he asserted that, like concepts as properties and relations of things, classes are *real* (*CW*2:128):

8.6.11   Classes may, however, also be conceived as real beings, namely as "pluralities of things" or as structures consisting of a plurality of things existing independently of our definitions and constructions.

Indeed, even in his 1972 formulation (8.5.4 above), Gödel puts special emphasis on the "full concept of class (truth, concept, being, etc.)" and says that the iterative concept of set "may or may not be the full concept of class." In discussions between 1975 and 1976, however, he not only pushed classes to an auxiliary position but obviously implied that the concept of set *cannot* be the full concept of class.

In the context of 8.6.6, Gödel equates classes with "extensional" concepts:

8.6.12   Alternatively, we may deal with "extensional" concepts ("mathematical" concepts) by limiting [them] to concepts such that if A applies to B, then A applies to all concepts with the same "extension" as B.

8.6.13   As usual, classes which are not sets are conveniently referred to as *proper classes*. A natural extension of this terminology is to speak of an *extremely general* concept when its "extension" is not a set (or strictly speaking, it has no extension). Since concepts can sometimes apply to themselves, their extensions (their corresponding classes) can belong to themselves; that is, a class can belong to itself. Frege did not distinguish sets from proper classes, but Cantor did this first.

Even though it is clear that generally the range of a concept need not be a set, it is an open question whether every set is the extension of some concept. Indeed, Gödel conjectures that this is the case. (Compare 8.6.4.)

8.6.14   It is not evident that every set is the extension of some concept. But such a conclusion may be provable once we have a developed theory of concepts and a more complete set theory. While it is an incorrect assumption to take it as a property of the concept of *concept* to say that every concept defines a set, it is not a confusion to say that sets can only be defined by concepts or that set is a certain way of speaking about concept.

For each set a, we may consider a corresponding concept C such that C applies to all and only the objects which belong to a. It might be felt that, in this way, every set is seen to be the extension of some concept. Since, however, sets are extensional, it may not be obvious that there is indeed such a corresponding concept for every set. I do not have a sufficiently clear understanding of the concept of *concept* to give any convincing reason why there may be certain sets for which such representative concepts do not exist. Indeed, I am inclined to assume that they exist for all sets. As far as I can see, such an assumption cannot be refuted and is a reasonable component of the concept of *concept*.

For Gödel, once we recognize the distinction between sets and concepts, the absence and desirability of a satisfactory concept theory, which is not parasitic upon set theory, becomes clear. Even though he is not able to offer more than preliminary suggestions, he considers it an important step to have clarified somewhat the nature of the quest. In the rest of this section I present a group of his disparate observations on this search, as reformulated and edited by me.

8.6.15   For a long time there has been confusion between logic and mathematics. Once we make and use a sharp distinction between sets and concepts, we have made several advances. We have a reasonably convincing foundation for ordinary mathematics according to the iterative concept of set. Going beyond sets becomes an understandable and, in fact, a necessary step for a comprehensive conception of logic. We come back to the program of developing a grand logic, except that we are no longer troubled by the consequences of the confusion between sets and concepts. For example, we are no longer frustrated by wanting to say contra-dictory things about classes, and can now say both that no set can belong to itself and that a concept—and therewith a class—can apply (or belong) to itself.

8.6.16   In this way we acquire not only a fairly rich and understandable set theory but also clearer guidance for our search for axioms that deal with concepts generally. We can examine whether familiar axioms for sets have counterparts for concepts and also investigate whether earlier attempts (e.g., in terms of the lambda-calculus and of stratification, etc.), which deal with sets and concepts indiscriminately, may suggest axioms that are true of concepts generally. Of course, we should also look for new candidates for axioms concerned with con-cepts. At the present stage, the program of finding axioms for concepts seems to be wide open.

The primitive concepts of the theory of concepts are analogous to those of set theory.

8.6.17   A concept is a whole composed of primitive concepts such as negation, conjunction, existence, universality, object, the concept of *concept*, the relation of something falling under some concept (or of some concept applying to some-thing), and so on. (Compare 9.1.26.)

8.6.18   Just as set theory is formulated in the predicate calculus by adding the membership relation, concept theory can similarly be formulated by adding the relation of application: a concept *A* applies to something *B* (which may also be a concept), or *B* participates in the idea [with the Platonic sense] *A*. Logic studies only what a concept applies to. *Application* is the only primitive concept apart from the familiar concepts of predicate logic with which we define other concepts.

If we confine our attention to those objects which are the "pure" sets (mathematical objects) and make the simplifying assumption that every set is the extension of some concept, we may take concepts as the uni-verse of discourse and define sets and the membership relation between them (compare *RG*:310). A more complex and natural formulation would view the universe of discourse as consisting of both concepts and objects, where both concepts and objects consist of both pure ones and empirical ones.

Gödel believes that, however we set up a formal system of concept theory, we already know the primitive concepts and the general principles of forming new concepts by negation, conjunction, existence, and so on. The problem is that we do not know the axioms or the necessary restrictions on applying these correct general principles.

In connection with the determination of axioms of concept theory or the restrictions on the correct principles of forming concepts, Gödel makes several comments on existing ideas. (Compare the Russell paper, CW2:137–138.)

8.6.19   Once we distinguish concepts from sets, the older search for a satisfactory set theory gives way to a similar search for a satisfactory concept theory. For this purpose, however, Quine's idea of stratification [1937] is arbitrary, and Church's idea [1932–1933] about limited ranges of significance is inconsistent in its original formulation. (Compare 8.4.19.)

8.6.20   Even though we do not have a developed theory of concepts, we know enough about concepts to know that we can have also something like a hierarchy of concepts (or also of classes) which resembles the hierarchy of sets and contains it as a segment. But such a hierarchy is derivative from and peripheral to the theory of concepts; it also occupies a quite different position; for example, it cannot satisfy the condition of including the concept of *concept* which applies to itself or the universe of all classes that belong to themselves. To take such a hierarchy as the theory of concepts is an example of trying to eliminate the intensional paradoxes in an arbitrary manner.

8.6.21   A transfinite theory of concepts is an example of trying to eliminate the paradoxes in an arbitrary way: by treating concepts as if they were sets. Consider all concepts whose ranges are included in the universal set V, and merge all concepts having the same range into a class. All these classes make up the power class of V. Repeat the process: in this way the axiom of regularity holds for classes too. But we can obtain no universal concept or class in this manner.

8.6.22   A set having a property is a clearly defined relation between the set and the property. A complete foundation of set theory calls for a study of properties and concepts. And we get more involved in the paradoxes. Compare a footnote in my Cantor paper [CW2:181n. 17, 260n. 118].

8.6.23   When we formulate the paradoxes in terms of concepts clearly defined for everything, we don't see what is wrong. Hence, the concept of clearly defined concept is not a clearly defined concept. A concept, unlike a set, can apply to itself. Certainly the concept of *concept* is a concept. Does the concept of transitive relation apply to itself? [I tried hard to make sense of this question but was not able to come up with a satisfactory interpretation of it.] Concepts are understandable by the mind. Pure concepts are the only kind that we understand without the help of empirical observations.

The obvious obstacle to the quest for concept theory is the intensional paradoxes, of which the most important is that of the concept of not applying to itself. On 18 October 1972 Gödel introduced and explained in detail a simple form of this paradox. He suggested that it would be helpful, for the purpose of developing concept theory, to reflect on it. We may legitimately call it Gödel's paradox, even though he gave it a different name:

8.6.24   There is a simpler version of the familiar paradox of the concept of not applying to itself. It may be called Church's paradox because it is most easily set up in Church's system [1932–1933]. It is particularly striking that this paradox is not well known. It makes clear that the intensional paradoxes have no simple solution. An interesting problem is to find a theory in which the classical paradoxes are not derivable but this one is.

8.6.25   A function is said to be regular if it can be applied to every entity [which may be an object or a function (a concept)]. Consider now the following regular function of two arguments:

(1) $d(F, x) = F(x)$ if F is regular
         $= 0$ otherwise.

[Gödel used a dot between the two arguments, instead of the letter d. I find it clearer to sacrifice the elegance of his notation.]

Introduce now another regular function:

(2) $E(x) = 0$ if $x \neq 0$
         $= 1$ if $x = 0$.

We see immediately:

(3) $E(x) \neq x$.

Let $H(x)$ be $E(d(x, x)]$, which is regular. By (1), we have:

(4) $d(H, x) = H(x) = E(d(x, x))$.

Substituting H for x, we get:

(5) $d(H, H) = E(d(H, H))$, contradicting (3).

This completes the derivation of Church's paradox.

8.6.26   The derivation above has no need even of the propositional calculus. Definition by cases is available in Church's system. It is easy to find functions which are everywhere defined. Unlike the classical paradox, there is no need to assume initially that the crucial concept (or function) of not applying to itself is everywhere defined. The paradox is brief, and brevity makes things more precise. By a slight modification, it can be made into an intuitionistic paradox, using provability.

At this point, I asked Gödel: Is there any paradox that uses nothing else—such as definition by cases—besides provability? He replied that the answer was, he thought, yes. In November of 1975 Gödel, recalling this paradox, added:

8.6.27   It applies also to the concept of all intuitionistic concepts. A. Heyting presupposes the general concept of (intuitionistic) proof in his interpretation of implication: *A* implies *B* if and only if, for every proof of *A*, you can construct a proof of *B*. In contrast, my interpretation uses a narrower concept of proof. (Compare *CW2*:275–276 note h.)

8.7 Principles for the Introduction of Sets

In the 1970s Gödel offered answers—somewhat different ones at different stages—to the question: What are the principles by which we introduce the axioms of set theory? This is different from the related question, What is the precise meaning of the principles, and why do we accept them? He did not say much about the second question, but he seemed to suggest that it should be answered by phenomenological investigations in the manner of Husserl.

In February 1972 Gödel formulated a summary of the five principles actually used for setting up axioms of set theory: (1) intuitive ranges; (2) closure principle; (3) reflection principle; (4) extensionalization; and (5) uniformity. He emphasized that the same axiom can be justified by different principles, which are nonetheless distinct because they are based on different ideas—for example, inaccessible numbers are justified by either (2) or (3).

In May of 1972 he reformulated the five principles, and I quoted them in full in *From Mathematics to Philosophy* (*MP*:189–190). Instead of reproducing these quotations exactly, I combine them here with my notes from less formal discussions.

8.7.1   *Intuitive range.*   For any intuitive ranges of variability—that is, multitudes that can, in some sense, be "overviewed"—there exist sets that represent the ranges. The basic idea of set formation is that of intuitive generation.

8.7.2   *Closure principle.*   If the universe of sets is closed with respect to certain operations, there exists a set that is similarly closed. This implies, for example, the existence of inaccessible cardinals and of inaccessible cardinals equal to their index as inaccessible cardinals. Given any primitive operations of forming sets, [we can] apply them as much as possible and treat the totality as a set. This is how we arrive at the inaccessible and the Mahlo cardinals.

8.7.3   *Reflection principle.*   The universe of all sets is structurally indefinable. One possible way to make this statement precise is the following: The universe of sets cannot be uniquely characterized (i.e., distinguished from all its initial segments) by any internal structural property of the membership relation in it which is expressible in any logic of finite or transfinite type, including infinitary logics of any cardinal number. This principle may be considered a generalization of the closure principle. Further generalizations and refinements are in the making in recent literature. The totality of all sets is, in some sense, indescribable. When you have any structural property that is supposed to apply to all sets, you know you have not got all sets. There must be some sets that contain as members all sets that have that property.

8.7.4 *Extensionalization.* Axioms such as *comprehension* [subset formation] and *replacement* are first formulated in terms of defining properties or relations. They are extensionalized as applying to arbitrary collections or extensional correlations. For example, we get the inaccessible numbers by the closure principle only if we construe the axiom of replacement extensionally. First formulate a principle for definable properties only and then extend it to anything.

8.7.5 *Uniformity of the universe of sets* (analogous to the uniformity of nature). The universe of sets does not change its character substantially as one goes from smaller to larger sets or cardinals; that is, the same or analogous states of affairs reappear again and again (perhaps in more complicated versions). In some cases, it may be difficult to see what the analogous situations or properties are. But in cases of simple and, in some sense, "meaningful" properties it is pretty clear that there is no analogue except the property itself. This principle, for example, makes the existence of strongly compact cardinals very plausible, in view of the fact that there should exist generalizations of Stone's representation theorem for ordinary Boolean algebras to Boolean algebras with infinite sums and products. For axioms of infinity this principle is construed in a broader sense. It may also be called the "principle of proportionality of the universe": analogues of properties of small cardinals by chance lead to large cardinals. For example, measurable cardinals were introduced in this way. People did not expect them to be large.

In the course of stating these principles, Gödel made several incidental observations about them:

8.7.6   These are not mutually exclusive principles. For instance, the Bernays set theory [presumably the system in Bernays 1961] could be founded on the reflection principle or on the combination of extensionalization with the closure principle. The key is similar to the Mahlo principles.

8.7.7   The intended model of set theory includes arbitrarily large cardinals. But in some cases it may happen not to be compatible with the statement that such and such large cardinals exist, because the general concept needed cannot be expressed in the primitive notation of the model.

In the early autumn of 1975, I was revising an earlier draft of my paper on large sets (Wang 1977), in which I considered several forms of the reflection principle quite extensively and in a fairly technical manner. It was natural for me to ask Gödel to comment on the manuscript, and he was quite willing to do so. In the process, he made various observations. Among other things, we discussed the system of Ackermann (1956), which seems to have led Gödel to a drastic reformulation of his five principles for the formation of sets (1972).

Ackermann's system can be viewed as using a language obtained from a language of the Zermelo type by adding a constant V, taken to stand for the universe of all sets. As a result, the universe of discourse contains things other than sets, which are, in familiar terminology, the subclasses of V. The central axiom of the system says that every property expressible in the language without using V determines a member of V (a set), provided it applies only to members of V. (For more details, see Wang 1977:330.)

(A) *Ackermann's axiom.* Let y and z be in V and $F(x, y, z)$ be an open sentence not containing V, such that, for all x, if $F(x, y, z)$, then x is in V. There is then some u in V, such that, for all x, $F(x, y, z)$ if and only if x belongs to u.

In this formulation, y and z are the *parameters*. The main idea is that, if y and z are given sets and all the entities x that satisfy $F(x, y, z)$ are sets, we can collect them into a new set u. In this way, from any given sets y and z, we can find a new set u of all x such that $F(x, y, z)$.

According to Ackermann, (A) is to codify Cantor's 1895 definition of the term *set* (Cantor 1932:282): By a set we shall understand any collection into a whole S of definite, well-distinguished objects (which we will call the *elements* of S) of our intuition or our thought.

Clearly, in order to *collect* certain objects into a whole, the objects have to be *given* first in some sense. A natural interpretation of Cantor's definition is to say that, from among the given sets at each stage, those with a common property can be collected to form a new set. In (A) the objects to be collected are those x which have the property of satisfying $F(x, y, z)$ for given F and given sets y and z, provided only that only sets x can satisfy $F(x, y, z)$. The objects to be collected are in each case determined by suitable y, z, and F.

The requirement that V does not occur in F is needed. Without it, unless we restrict F in some suitable way, we could easily prove that V itself is a set and reach a contradiction: for instance, take "x belongs to V" as $F(x)$: Implicit in the requirement that V does not occur in $F(x, y, z)$ is the principle that V cannot be captured by such expressions. If there were some expression $F(x, y, z)$ not containing V, such that, for certain sets y and z, $F(x, y, z)$ if and only if x belongs to V, then the requirement would be superfluous. Moreover, V would be a set and we arrive quickly at a contradiction.

According to Gödel,

8.7.8 Ackermann's system is based on the idea of the indefinability of V, or the *Absolute*. It is interesting because the system itself is weak in its consequences; but

something weaker may sometimes serve as a better basis for natural strong extensions than a stronger initial system.

Indeed, Gödel tried to find a justification for measurable cardinals by
considering a natural extension of Ackermann's system (see below). At
this stage he seemed to view the unknowability of the universe of all sets
as a reflection principle which unifies all principles by which we set up
axioms of set theory.

8.7.9   All the principles for setting up the axioms of set theory should be reducible to a form of Ackermann's principle: The Absolute is unknowable. The strength
of this principle increases as we get stronger and stronger systems of set theory.
The other principles are only heuristic principles. Hence, the central principle is the
reflection principle, which presumably will be understood better as our experience
increases. Meanwhile, it helps to separate out more specific principles which either
give some additional information or are not yet seen clearly to be derivable from
the reflection principle as we understand it now.

8.7.10   For the present, let us consider the following three principles:

(G1) The principle of intuitive ranges of variability;
(G2) Ackermann's principle, or the reflection principle in a more restricted sense:
V cannot be defined by a *structural* property not containing V—no property
definable from the elements of V can determine V;
(G3) A *structural* property, possibly involving V, which applies only to elements
of V, determines a set; or, a subclass of V thus definable is a set.

As I understand it, Gödel is asserting that the above three principles are
among the special consequences of the general principle of the unknowability of V: as we understand it better, we shall be able to formulate
other and more precise consequences of it. The principle (G1) is the principle we used above to justify the familiar axioms of set theory. It is a consequence of the central principle, because (1) to be able to overview a
multitude is to know it in a strong sense, and (2) a knowable multitude is
a set according to his intended interpretation of the central principle. The
other two principles are also consequences of it, because what is definable
by a structural property is knowable.

The difficult notion is of course that of a *structural* property. Gödel's
association of Ackermann's idea with the inclusive principle suggests that,
for him, the properties in Ackermann's axiom (A) are examples of structural properties. He seems to detect certain distinctive features in the
properties used in (A), apart from the explicit condition that they do not
contain V. He seems to say that any property that shares these features is
a structural property. The problem is to give a moderately precise account
of these features which lends some credibility to the belief that properties
with such features define sets.

Gödel made two observations about (G2):

8.7.11   The positive application of (G2) says that a structural property not containing V must define a set, because the smallest range determined by it cannot go to the end of V. By envisaging a larger universe of entities (say, including also concepts and classes, in addition to sets), we can also have negative applications of (G2): a property or concept not involving V that holds for all sets must have a broader range than V.

8.7.12   (G2) goes beyond (G1) in that what is obtained by (G2) need not be an intuitive range of variability. Disregarding the beginning steps [of forming simple familiar sets], (G2) is the only really evident principle. The building up of the hierarchy of sets depends on this principle: assume you have a clear idea [and have determined thereby a stage or a rank in the hierarchy of sets], you can go on further. Hence, V cannot be defined [or known in such a strong sense]. This is the very idea of the hierarchy. Reflection is a more abstract principle than the principle of intuitive range. To arrive at an intuitive range of variability is only a sufficient condition for finding a set.

On the principle (G3), Gödel made the following comments.

8.7.13   To illustrate the intension of (G3), consider a property $P(V, x)$, which involves V. If, as we believe, V is extremely large, then x must appear in an early segment of V and cannot have any relation to much later segments of V. Hence, within $P(V, x)$, V can be replaced by some set in every context. In short, if P does not involve V, there is no problem; if it does, then closeness to each x helps to eliminate V, provided chaos does not prevail.

8.7.14   There is also a theological approach, according to which V corresponds to the whole physical world, and the closeness aspect to what lies within the monad and in between the monads. According to the principles of rationality, sufficient reason, and preestablished harmony, the property $P(V, x)$ of a monad x is equivalent to some *intrinsic* property of x, in which the world does not occur. In other words, when we move from monads to sets, there is some set y to which x bears intrinsically the same relation as it does to V. Hence, there is a property $Q(x)$, not involving V, which is equivalent to $P(V, x)$. According to medieval ideas, properties containing V or the world would not be in the essence of any set or monad.

8.7.15   In contrast to (G1) and (G2), (G3) is a principle that goes from each to all. Consider a property $P(V, x)$ such that, for each x, if $P(V, x)$, then x is a set and, therefore, belongs to some stage or rank in the hierarchy of sets. By (G3), P then defines a set. But, unlike sets obtained by (G1), the implication (for each x) [of the representability of V by some set in the context of P] does not yield an overview of the range of P, except for the empirical fact that a proof of the implication (for all x) may sometimes yield a survey of the range of the set thus obtained.

Of these observations, 8.7.13 gives the best indication of Gödel's concept of structural properties. As I understand the paragraph, it begins with something like the frame of Ackermann's system and tries to extend the axiom (A) by adding certain expressions that contain V, yet still represent structural properties.

Let $F(x, y, z)$ be an open sentence in the system such that, for given sets y and z, all entities x that satisfy $F(x, y, z)$ are sets. If F does not contain V, it is a structural property. If it contains V, let us rewrite it as $P(V, x)$. The task is to find a notion of structural property for such expressions such that: if $P(V, x)$ is a structural property, then all the sets x that satisfy $P(V, x)$ can be collected together into a new set u.

Gödel seems to say that, for P to satisfy this condition, it is sufficient for the parts of P to be *organically* connected in a suitable sense so that, since x, y, z all are sets and, therefore, small compared with V, only certain initial segments of V are really involved. Consequently, every occurrence of V in P can *potentially* be replaced by some sufficiently large set. This may be seen as another application of the reflection principle: for given x, y, z, if $P(a, x)$ is true when a is V, there is some set v, such that $P(v, x)$ is true. If we extend axiom (A) by requiring that either F does not contain V or it is *organic* in this somewhat vague sense, we get a stronger system because we would expect that in many cases V cannot be *explicitly* replaced by sets in the system.

I am not sure whether this elaboration agrees with Gödel's intention. In any case, there remains, I think, the problem of applying this vague characterization to arrive at precise characterizations of some rich classes of structural properties of the desired kind.

W. C. Powell (in 1972) and W. Reinhardt (in 1974) presented two equivalent formulations of a system in which a lot of measurable cardinals can be proved to exist. As they observed, their systems can each be reformulated by adding a new axiom to Ackermann's system. In particular, the new axiom needed for Reinhardt's system, is his axiom (S3.3) (Reinhardt 1974:15).

On the basis of this technical result, Gödel said, the reformulated system and, with it, the existence of measurable cardinals, can be made plausible on the basis of (G3). Indeed, Gödel formulated the exact wording of this observation and suggested that I include it in my paper:

8.7.16 The combination of (S3.3) with Ackermann's system is the reasonable formulation. The additional axiom (S3.3) says essentially that all subclasses of V obtainable in the system can be defined without reference to V; i.e., V can be eliminated from such definitions. I think that it is this formulation which gives a certain degree of plausibility to this system. Generally I believe that, in the last analysis, every axiom of infinity should be derived from the (extremely plausible) principle that V is indefinable, where definability is to be taken in [a] more and more generalized and idealized sense (Wang 1977:325).

Chapter 9
Gödel's Approach to Philosophy

General philosophy is a conceptual study, for which method is all-important.
Gödel, 23 January 1976

For approaching the central part of philosophy, there is good reason to confine one's attention to reflections on mathematics. Physics is perhaps less well suited for this purpose; Newtonian physics would be better.
Gödel, 24 May 1972

The meaning of the world is the separation of wish and fact.
Gödel, November 1975

For the physical world, the four dimensions are natural. But for the mind, there is no such natural coordinate system; time is the only natural frame of inference.
Gödel, 15 March 1972

During his discussions with me Gödel made many scattered observations on the nature and the method of philosophy. It is not easy to grasp and organize this material so as to give a faithful and coherent exposition of his views; different emphases in different contexts have to be interpreted and reconciled. I find his ultimate ideal in philosophy overly optimistic, and his arguments for his belief in its attainability quite unconvincing. There is a big gap between what he said and an explicit outline of feasible steps that would lead to completion of his seemingly impossible quest. Nonetheless, most of his sayings are, I believe, of interest for their philosophical significance, even to those of us who do not share his rationalistic optimism.

In order to avoid a confusing juxtaposition of Gödel's views and my own, I restrict myself in this chapter to a moderately structured exposition and interpretation of his views—with only occasional interpolated comments. In the Epilogue I compare his conception of philosophy with a few others and propose a loose framework for revealing the complementary character of various serious alternative approaches.

Ultimately, one's *conception* of something consists of all one's beliefs about it, including one's attitude toward it. Effectively communicating someone else's conception of something as complex as philosophy, requires a good deal of selection, interpretation, organization, and articulation. In order to provide an approximation of Gödel's views, I shall try to describe his conceptions of the subject matter and method of philosophy. At bottom, an individual's conception of philosophy is determined by what he or she wants—and believes it possible to obtain—from its pursuit. Hence, both the subject matter and the method are intimately connected to one's aims.

As I understand it, Gödel aimed at a rational and optimistic worldview which puts mind or spirit at the center and, preferably, includes God. Gödel saw metaphysics as the most fundamental part of philosophy; he often identified theology with metaphysics, but sometimes distinguished them, as I prefer to do. The main task of philosophy as he saw it was (1) to determine its primitive concepts, and (2) to *analyze* or *perceive* or *understand* these concepts well enough to discover the principal axioms about them, so as to "do for metaphysics as much as Newton did for physics." On several occasions he said that he had no satisfactory solution even of problem (1). He also said, however, that his own philosophy, in its general structure, is like the monadology of Leibniz.

Gödel's strong interest in objectivism in mathematics, on the one hand, and the superiority of mind over matter, on the other, are closely connected to his main aim in philosophy. The superiority of mind is undoubtedly important for his ontological idealism, which sees mind as prior to matter. A major application of his recommendation to generalize without inhibition is his own generalization from objectivism in mathematics to objectivism in metaphysics. That must be, I think, the reason why he attached so much importance to the philosophy of mathematics for the development of philosophy. Like most philosophers today, however, I am unable to appreciate the plausibility of this extrapolation.

Gödel's enthusiasm for Husserl's method was undoubtedly based to some extent on his wish to believe that this method could enable us to perceive clearly the primitive concepts of metaphysics, and he probably saw his own observations on philosophical method as explicating and complementing Husserl's ideas. Just as Husserl's work is valuable even to those who do not share his aim in philosophy, so too are Gödel's philosophical discussions, though for different reasons.

In his philosophy Gödel tried to combine and go beyond the main contributions by his three heroes: Plato, Leibniz, and Husserl. Leibniz had defined the ideal by giving a preliminary formulation of monadology. Husserl had supplied the method for attaining this ideal. Plato had proposed, in his rudimentary objectivism in mathematics, an approach that could serve as foundation for Husserl's method and, at the same time, make plausible for Gödel the crucial belief that we are indeed capable of perceiving the primitive concepts of metaphysics clearly enough to set up the axioms.

In this first section I outline Gödel's philosophical program and the steps he took to achieve it. In this connection, it is important to remember that Gödel saw the views considered in Chapters 6 to 8 as important parts of his program—even though the significance of this material is, in my opinion, to a considerable extent independent of the program.

Gödel's methodological observations, are discussed in section 9.2; they are related to Husserl's views but contain many distinctive recommendations. In section 9.3 I present some of his general observations on philosophy. His ideal of philosophy as monadology is closely related to his rationalistic optimism and what he took to be "the meaning of the world," a topic I take up in section 9.4.

Both Husserl and Gödel regarded contemporary science as mistaking the part for the whole. They saw this as a consequence of its dogmatic adherence to what Husserl (1954, 1970) called the "natural point of view," which was derived from an unjustified generalization from the spectacular success of the "mathematization of nature." In particular, Gödel points out, this approach does not begin to provide a full treatment of our all-important intuitive concept of time. Gödel emphasizes the great difficulty of the problem of time; nonetheless, he offers some new and stimulating insights on it, in considering the relation between Kant's philosophy and Einstein's physics.—We have here a striking example of his talent for innovation within the broad range of logic as the dialectic of the formal and the intuitive. As he does in his discussion of the interplay between mathematical logic and philosophy, in discussing the problem of time, he restricts the dialectic to that between science and philosophy, which he sees as a special part of logic, broadly understood. I give a brief discussion of this work in section 9.5.

9.1 His Philosophy: Program and Execution

In his manuscript written around 1962 on "the foundations of mathematics in the light of philosophy", which I discussed in section 5.1, Gödel identified philosophies with worldviews and proposed "a general schema of possible philosophical worldviews":

9.1.1 I believe that the most fruitful principle for gaining an overall view of the possible worldviews will be to divide them up according to the degree and the manner of their affinity to, or renunciation of, metaphysics (or religion). In this way we immediately obtain a division into two groups: skepticism, materialism, and positivism stand on one side; spiritualism, idealism, and theology on the other.

Gödel characterized his own philosophy in a general way:

9.1.2   My theory is a monadology with a central monad [namely, God].

9.1.3   My philosophy is rationalistic, idealistic, optimistic, and theological.

9.1.4   As far as the appropriate method of philosophy is concerned, metaphysics, ethics, law, and theology all are different.

According to my interpretation of this last statement, metaphysics is the fundamental part of philosophy; the other three important parts presuppose metaphysics and require more empirical and less certain considerations. Theology or religion in particular, contrary to what the three preceding statements seem to imply, goes beyond metaphysics; one should try to develop first a monadology without a central monad. In any case, I prefer to distinguish metaphysics from theology. I considered Gödel's attempt at theology in Chapter 3. Here I confine my attention to metaphysics in this restricted sense, that is, separate from theology, focusing on Gödel's ideal of a monadology, but, for the present, without the central monad.

At some stage I asked Gödel to give me a systematic exposition of his philosophy, and he replied that he had not developed it far enough to be able to expound it systematically, although he was sufficiently clear about it to apply it in commenting on the philosophical views of others. As I said before, this was undoubtedly why he chose to discuss philosophy by commenting on what I had written—and on the ideas of other relevant philosophers such as Kant, Husserl, and the (logical) positivists.

In November of 1972 Gödel used the occasion of discussing Husserl's "Philosophy as Rigorous Science" (in Lauer 1965) to give what appears to be a summary of the pillars of his own philosophical outlook: that is, (A) to recognize that we have only *probable knowledge*, but to decline skepticism; (B) *monadology*; (C) to appreciate the universality of *observations*; (D) to strive for a sudden *illumination*; and (E) to achieve *explicitness* by applying *the axiomatic method*.

The fundamental ideas seem to be these: By observation we can discover the primitive concepts of metaphysics and the axioms governing these concepts. By the axiomatic method, we can arrive at an exact theory of metaphysics, which for Gödel is best seen as a kind of monadology. In order to pursue this ideal effectively, we must realize that we are capable of only probable knowledge. We should learn to select and concentrate on what is fundamental and essential. Therefore, in order to secure a governing focus to guide our continuous attention, we should strive for a sudden illumination.

Gödel had, on various occasions, made related observations on these five topics, which are reported elsewhere in this book. Moreover, the five pillars are subject to different interpretations, and their implications have to be considered. Nevertheless these five topics can serve as guideposts for organizing and communicating what I take to be Gödel's conception of philosophy, and I reconstruct here the statements he made about them at that time. These statements are exceptional in that, unlike most of his remarks in our discussions, they were presented in a continuous manner on one occasion.

(A) We have only *probable knowledge*, but skepticism is not a tenable position:

9.1.5   There is no absolute knowledge; everything goes only by probability. Husserl aimed at absolute knowledge, but so far this has not been attained. Even if there were absolute knowledge, it could not be transferred to somebody else, orally or through written material. Skepticism is temporary [or provisional].

9.1.6   One conjectures only that there is some probable intuition—and this has to do with being unprejudiced. In the last analysis, every error is due to extraneous factors; reason itself does not commit mistakes.

There are two components in these two observations. One is the theme that we are never infallible, since the empirical component always comes in. The other is the belief that we have ways of correcting our mistakes, as is confirmed by our cumulative experience. (Other ideas related to this point are reported in 9.2.) One general point is that there are degrees of evidence, clarity, and certainty. We have here also a way of dealing with skepticism, because "to acknowledge what is correct in skepticism serves to take the sting out of skeptical objections."

Gödel then considered Husserl's "genuinely scientific ideal" in philosophy and his assertion: "Nor will it ever be realized by a single individual; it would not be science in the modern sense if it could be so realized" (Lauer 1965:15). Gödel said:

9.1.7   The ideal could mean finding the axioms or attaining the whole of knowledge. [He himself was apparently more concerned with the former.] It does not follow from the concept of science that it cannot be realized by a single individual.

(B) *Monadology.* Gödel's own favorite version of the scientific ideal of philosophy is monadology in the sense of Leibniz. In this connection Gödel once used a word that sounded like *bions*. I conjecture that *bion* is formed from *bio-* as *neon* is formed from *neo-* and means something like "elementary life particle." According to Webster's Dictionary, *bion* is the physiological individual, characterized by definiteness and independence of function, in distinction from the morphological individual, or *morphon*.

9.1.8   It is an idea of Leibniz that monads are spiritual in the sense that they have consciousness, experience, and drive on the active side, and contain representations

(*Vorstellungen*) on the passive side. Matter is also composed of such monads. We have the emotional idea that we should avoid inflicting pain on living things, but an electron or a piece of rock also has experiences. We experience drives, pains, and so on ourselves. The task is to discover universal laws of the interactions of monads, including people, electrons, and so forth. For example, attraction and repulsion are the drives of electrons, and they contain representations of other elementary particles.

9.1.9   Monads (bions, etc.) are not another kind of material particle; they are not in fixed parts of space, they are nowhere and, therefore, not material objects. Matter will be spiritualized when the true theory of physics is found. Monads only act *into* space; they are not *in* space. They have an inner life or consciousness; in addition to relations to other particles (clear in Newtonian physics, where we know the relationships between the particles), they also have something inside. In quantum physics the electrons are objectively distributed in space, not at a fixed place at a fixed moment, but at a ring. Hence, it is impossible for electrons to have different inner states, only different distributions.

9.1.10   To be material is to have a spatial position. (The number 2, for example, has no spatial position.) Spatially contiguous objects represent one another. We do not know what the objects are if we know merely that they are in space. We understand space only through the drive of the objects in space; otherwise we have no idea what space is. [But if material objects and space are defined by each other, materialism in this "spatial" sense is untenable.] For this very reason, materialism was given up at the beginning of the century, and "the study of structure" has taken its place. But "the study of structure" is a confession that we don't know what the things are. Real materialism is nonsense.

9.1.11   There is an old idea that description will take on a very concrete form— to make a science out of this. The task is to describe monads on their different levels. Monadology also explains why introspection [self-observation] is so important. What is essential for the understanding of the monads is to observe yourself: This is a monad that is given to you.

I consider Gödel's other observations related to his monadology in 9.4.

(C) *Observation*—especially self-observation—[is] the universal basis.

9.1.12   Everything has to be based on *observation* [watching towards], provided ob- [towards] is understood correctly. Observation includes *Wesenschau* (essential intuition, grasp of essence, categorial intuition, perception of concepts), which is simply left out of what is called *experience* most of the time—in particular, by the empiricists.

This statement is closely related to Gödel's belief in our ability to perceive concepts (discussed in section 7.3) and his objection to the restrictive notions of experience and observation held by the positivists and the empiricists (discussed in section 5.3). His extended observations on self-observation will be consider in the next section.

(D) *Sudden illumination.* On this occasion, Gödel argued that Husserl had attained a sudden illumination some time between 1905 and 1910. Elsewhere he said that he himself had never had such an experience and that philosophy was like religious conversion. In addition, he said:

9.1.13   Schelling explicitly reported an experience of sudden illumination; Descartes began, after his famous dream, to see everything in a different light.

9.1.14   Later, Husserl was more like Plato and Descartes. It is possible to attain a state of mind to see the world differently. One fundamental idea is this: true philosophy is [arrived at by] something like a religious conversion.

9.1.15   Husserl sees many things more clearly in a different light. This is different from doing scientific work; [it involves] a change of personality.

I have at best only a vague guess about what Gödel was suggesting in these observations. Perhaps Husserl was able, after persistent efforts over many years, to understand what is truly fundamental in philosophical investigations, thereby reaching a clearer perspective from which to see things. In any case, I have little to say on this idea of Gödel's. (Compare 5.3.30 to 5.3.33.)

(E) The importance of *explicitness* and the *axiomatic method*:

9.1.16   The significance of mathematical logic for philosophy lies in its power to make thoughts explicit by illustrating and providing a frame for the axiomatic method. Mathematical logic makes explicit the central place of predication in the philosophical foundation of rational thought. [I consider Gödel's related observations in the next section.]

From time to time I expressed skepticism over the realizability of Gödel's project of metaphysics as an exact axiomatic theory and mentioned the familiar objection that such attempts have repeatedly failed in the history of philosophy. On this occasion, Gödel offered the following reply:

9.1.17   One needs some *Arbeitshypothese* or working hypothesis in considering the question whether one should pursue certain metaphysical projects now. My working hypothesis is that the project under consideration has not yet been studied from the right perspective. Specifically, previous attempts have been hampered by one combination or another of three factors: (1) lack of an exact development of science, (2) theological prejudices, and (3) a materialistic bias. The pursuit, unhampered by any one of these three negative factors, hasn't been tried before.

I agree that, by getting rid of the three negative factors, we may hope to do better philosophy. Yet I am not able to see that Gödel's working hypothesis provides us with a sufficient basis for believing that his project is feasible. I do not deny that, by pursuing the project energetically, even though without substantive success, one may arrive at significant new insights. It is, however, unclear to me how far or with what results Gödel himself pursued this project—except that he did say that he had never got what he looked for in philosophy.

Gödel did not think that he himself had come close to attaining the ideal of an axiomatic theory of metaphysics. He said several times that he did not even know what the primitive concepts are. Nonetheless he felt that he had developed his philosophy far enough to apply it in making comments on other views. Moreover, although he discussed extensively various issues which were undoubtedly relevant to his ultimate ideal, he rarely made entirely explicit how the different parts of what he said were related to his overall project.

One general guide is his declaration that his theory is a kind of Leibnizian monadology. Yet he does not discuss the problem of identifying the primitive concepts of metaphysics by reflecting on, say, the monadology already formulated by Leibniz. Nonetheless, in some of the shorthand notes quoted toward the end of section 3.2, he does give what appears to be a tentative list:

9.1.18   The fundamental philosophical concept is *cause*. It involves: will, force, enjoyment, God, time, space. Will and enjoyment: hence life and affirmation and negation. Time and space: being near is equivalent to the possibility of influence.

This list is related to another clue to Gödel's leading idea, the slogan that "the meaning of the world is the separation of wish and fact." He does not explicitly relate this slogan to his project of monadology, but he hints at some link between it and Hegel's system of logic, which he saw as an alternative to monadology. In section 9.4. I consider all these items together—the list in 9.1.18, the slogan, monadology, and Hegel's logic— since I take them to be closely related.

As I said before, Gödel's concern with the superiority of mind over matter is undoubtedly aimed at supporting the fundamental place of mind in monadology. His interest in Platonism has to do with justifying the belief that human beings, as advanced monads, are capable of representing the world more and more clearly.—Yet another problem important for Gödel is the concept of time.

In another direction, Gödel sees his conception of logic as the theory of concepts, including and going beyond mathematics, as cohering with his monadology. He said on one occasion:

9.1.19   Logic deals with more general concepts; monadology, which contains general laws of biology, is more specific.

In the course of a discussion of set theory and concept theory Gödel elaborated on his ontology of the two fundamental categories of being: objects and concepts. Even though he sometimes seems to say that objects consist of physical objects and sets. I now believe that he intends to say, more precisely, that objects consist of monads and sets: that is, (1) monads are objects; (2) sets of objects are objects.

9.1.20   We should *describe* the world by applying these fundamental ideas: the world as consisting of monads, the properties (activities) of the monads, the laws governing them, and the representations (of the world in the monads).

9.1.21   The simplest substances of the world are the monads.

9.1.22   Nature is broader than the physical world, which is inanimate. It also contains animal feelings, as well as human beings and consciousness.

9.1.23   *Being in time* is too special and should not appear so early as in Hegel's scheme, which introduces *becoming* immediately after *being* and *nonbeing*.

Gödel talks about whole and unity, as well as whole and part, in relation to the contrast between concepts and objects and the distinction between primitive and defined concepts:

9.1.24   Whole and part—partly concrete parts and partly abstract parts—are at the bottom of everything. They are most fundamental in our conceptual system. Since there is similarity, there are generalities. Generalities are just a fundamental aspect of the world. It is a fundamental fact of reality that there are two kinds of reality: universals and particulars (or individuals).

9.1.25   Whole and unity; thing or entity or being. Every whole is a unity and every unity that is divisible is a whole. For example, the primitive concepts, the monads, the empty set, and the unit sets are unities but not wholes. Every unity is something and not nothing. Any unity is a thing or an entity or a being. Objects and concepts are unities and beings.

Roughly speaking, concepts and sets are unities which are also wholes; monads are unities but not wholes.—It is better to leave the distinction between unities and wholes in the background.

Gödel does not state explicitly that objects and concepts make up the whole realm of beings, although it is, I believe, convenient—at least in the present context—to assume that they do. His terminology is not always consistent. Once for instance, he proposed a list of "ideal objects" consisting of concepts, values, and sets. He was undoubtedly using the word *objects* in the sense of *beings*. I am inclined to think that he generally construed *values* as special cases of *concepts*. In any case, Gödel did not specify the place of values in his ontological scheme.

9.1.26   *Concepts.*   A concept is a whole—a conceptual whole—composed out of primitive concepts such as negation, existence, conjunction, universality, object, (the concept of) concept, whole, meaning, and so on. We have no clear idea of the totality of all concepts. A concept is a whole in a stronger sense than sets; it is a more organic whole, as a human body is an organic whole of its parts.

Gödel's list of primitive concepts seems to consist only of logical concepts. I do not know whether he regarded the primitive concepts of metaphysics—whatever they are—as primitive in the same sense.

9.1.27 *Objects.* Monads are objects. Sets (of objects) are objects. A set is a unity (or whole) of which the elements are the constituents. Objects are in space or close to space. Sets are the limiting case of spatiotemporal objects and also of wholes. Among objects, there are physical objects and mathematical objects. Pure sets are the sets which do not involve nonset objects—so that the only Urelement in the universe of pure sets is the empty set. Pure sets are the mathematical objects and make up the world of mathematics.

The above formulation is based on Gödel's scattered observations. He read it shortly before 4 January 1976 and commented extensively on my manuscript Q, which included this passage. Although he took it to be faithful to what he had told me, I now believe I oversimplified some of the ambiguities. It seems to me that natural numbers are also mathematical objects and that they are not (reducible to) sets; and I do not think that Gödel wished to deny this. The relation between physical objects and monads is ambiguous. Clearly Gödel takes monads to be objects, even though, as far as I know, he does not mention monads in his published work, but speaks of physical bodies or physical objects. In the above passage, monads and physical objects seem to be identified. As I understand it, physical objects are a special case of monads or are reducible to monads, and so objects consist of monads and mathematical objects. One might even say that physical objects, in Gödel's public philosophy, correspond to monads in his private philosophy.

In other words, objects include monads and natural numbers as well as sets of objects. In any case, Gödel did not state explicitly that these objects—in any of the alternative specifications just suggested—are the only objects. He probably also left open the question of whether pure sets are the only mathematical objects—contrary to what he said on some other occasions.

9.1.28 It is important to have a correct terminology. The essence of a concept is determined by what the concept is composed of, but being a whole is not so determined. A set is a special kind of whole. Sets are unities which are just the multitude; but generally wholes are more than multitudes which are also unities. That is why sets are a limiting case of wholes. A whole must have parts. A monad is a unity but not a whole because it is indivisible: it is only an *uneigentlich* [improper] whole. Primitive concepts, like monads, are unities which are not wholes, because they are not composed of parts.

I do not know what sorts of things the primitive concepts of metaphysics would be for Gödel, nor how he intended to look for them. Occasional hints like the following do not tell us very much.

9.1.29 *Force* should be a primitive term in philosophy.

9.1.30 The fundamental principles are concerned with what the primitive concepts are and also their relationship. The axiomatic method goes step by step. We continue to discover new axioms; the process never finishes. Leibniz used formal analogy: in analogy with the seven stars in the Great Bear constellation, there are seven concepts. One should extend the analogy to cover the fact that by using the telescope we [now] see more stars in the constellation.

9.2 On Methodology: How to Study Philosophy

In different contexts Gödel offered diverse advice on how one is to study philosophy and communicate philosophical thoughts. He emphasized the importance of abstraction and generalization, observation and self-observation, knowing what to disregard, the axiomatic method, appreciating the fundamental place of everyday experience, remembering that we have only probable knowledge and that we cannot explain everything, and so forth. Occasionally he spoke about the necessary qualities and preparations for the pursuit of philosophy. In terms of presentation, he valued brevity and seeing rather than arguing. He applied his methodological ideas to the task of reporting our discussions, notably when he criticized one of my attempts—manuscript Q from December 1975—to report his views on "objectivism of sets and concepts."

I have found it hard to organize these scattered and vaguely related observations on methodology in a perspicuous manner and can only list them arbitrarily under a few general headings.

In connection with the qualities and preparations necessary for the serious pursuit of philosophy, Gödel said:

9.2.1 Philosophers need: (1) good taste in some solid subject; (2) [familiarity with the fundamentals of the philosophical] tradition; (3) general good taste.

9.2.2 My work is the application of a philosophy suggested outside of science and obtained on the occasion of thinking about science.

9.2.3 Everyday knowledge, when analyzed into components, is more relevant [than science] in giving data for philosophy. Science alone won't give philosophy; it is noncommittal regarding what really [is] there. A little bit of science is necessary for philosophy. For instance, Plato stipulates that no one unacquainted with geometry is to enter the academy. To that extent, the requirement is certainly justified.

Since thinking is ultimately an individual activity and its aim is to see things as clearly as one can, it is important to get rid of distractions and to disregard what is not essential. The main thing is to observe what is within yourself:

9.2.4 Philosophical thinking differs from thinking in general. It leaves out attention to objects but directs attention to inner experiences. (It is not so hard if one
also directs attention to objects.) To develop the skill of introspection and correct
thinking [is to learn] in the first place what you have to *disregard*. The ineffectiveness of natural thinking [in the study of philosophy] comes from being over-
whelmed by an infinity of possibilities and facts. In order to go on, you have to
know *what to leave out*; this is the essence of effective thinking.

9.2.5 Every error is caused by emotions and education (implicit and explicit);
intellect by itself (not disturbed by anything outside) could not err.

9.2.6 Don't collect data. If you know everything about yourself, you know
everything. There is no use in burdening yourself with a lot of data. Once you
understand yourself, you understand human nature and then the rest follows. It is
better [in the study of philosophy] to restrict [your view] to the individual than to
look at society initially. Husserl's thoroughly systematic [beginning] is better than
Kant's sloppy architectonic.

Undoubtedly these ideas are related to Husserl's phenomenological
method. But it is hard to know how one is to learn and apply the advice.
It is not even easy to see how Gödel himself applied the advice in his own
work.

E. Hlawka recalls seeing Gödel at work in the department library in the
1930s in Vienna. He was struck by the fact that Gödel customarily spent a
great deal of time on the same page, undoubtedly trying to understand
the material very thoroughly. This suggests a sense of what he meant by
paying attention to self-knowledge or introspection, a sense which is easy
to grasp: select a small amount of important material and try to understand it thoroughly. Similarly, many of us have had the experience of
finding that our most fruitful work is likely to come from reflecting on
what is already in our minds. Moreover, we often realize that extraneous
factors have prejudiced our thinking.

The interplay between our self-knowledge and input from outside us
takes a wide variety of forms. In the process of living, we constantly
respond to what happens to us and in us through certain activities of the
mind which have the effect of modifying consciousness and behavior.
In the process of education, for example, our responses to what we
are taught may include doing problems and taking examinations. How
well we do depends in part on our ability to think with concentration and
persistence.

Gödel's concentration on a brief text involves more thinking about the
same material than can be done by someone who reads the text quickly
and does not return to it. Gödel spent more time in self-observation than
most of us do, looking inward or at the inside. Generally, our thinking
focuses on both inside and outside material, but—at least in philoso-

phy—new insight come principally from looking inward. A crude interpretation of Gödel's advice is to say that the ratio of input to reflection should be small.

Gödel's own manner of thinking and working involved thoroughly digesting and reflecting on the available material—taking advantage of an unusual ability to concentrate and get to the heart of a problem. He located the crucial concepts—such as arithmetical truth, provability, set, ordinal number—and achieved a clear grasp of them. He knew what to disregard, thereby simplifying the data to be examined. And so he proceeded. The rest of us may consciously try to follow this practice, with lesser or greater success, according to our ability, training, and luck. Yet it is hard to see how one can extract a "systematic" method from the relatively successful practice of others or, even, from one's own.

Even though his best-known work is in science or closely related to science, Gödel believed that everyday experience is more important for philosophy than science is:

9.2.7   See 5.3.4.

9.2.8   See 5.3.3.

Gödel considers generalization and idealization to be important components of the study of philosophy and recommends a practice of making uninhibited generalizations, which underlines and follows from his rationalism and optimism.

9.2.9   We can distinguish intuitive generality (and concepts) from blind generality (and concepts). We have also abstract intuition. All blind generality is abstract, but not conversely.

9.2.10   Rationalism is connected with Platonism because it is directed to the conceptual world more than toward the real world. [Compare 9.4.20.]

9.2.11   While we perceive only an infinitely small portion of the world, there is more intentional factual knowledge. In history and psychology, we have [know] only a small part of reality. Even the laws of physics may not be the laws of the whole physical world. There may be another closed system of causal connections in which other laws hold.

9.2.12   Never use terms in a qualified sense unless you specify it [the qualification]; an important example is the term *existence.*

As I reported elsewhere, *existence* in its weakest and broadest sense is for Gödel the clear and correct concept of existence. Statement 9.2.12 concerns not just the communication of thoughts but also the activity of thinking. Gödel is, I believe, recommending that we work with philosophical concepts in their unqualified sense as much as possible.

9.2.13 In philosophy we should have the audacity to generalize things without any inhibitions: [to] go on along the direction on the lower level and generalize in different directions in a uniquely determined manner.

Gödel mentioned as an example his own generalization from our complete success in some parts of mathematics to his rationalistic optimism. It seems to me that his implicit generalization of objectivism in mathematics to objectivism in metaphysics is yet another example. However, as we know, uninhibited extrapolation and use of analogy are notorious for producing incompatible generalizations in situations where our shared beliefs are an insufficient basis for choosing between them.

9.2.14 The essence of mathematics is that it consists of generalizations.

9.2.15 In science we generalize. Mathematics describes possibilities of which only a few have been realized.

9.2.16 We have clear propositions only about a small part of the physical or the mathematical world. Yet we talk about all physical objects and integers. The problem is the same with the concept of all human beings: How can we make general assertions? Only by generalization and idealization.

9.2.17 Generally a better philosophy is more abstract: that is why Kant's is better than Russell's.

Once I asked Gödel about the saying "truth is always concrete." He replied:

9.2.18 This generalization can give no satisfactory explanation of mathematics.

Generalization and abstraction are closely related to idealization, which interacts with our intuition (as illustrated above in section 7.1). Indeed, we arrive at all our primitive concepts by idealization.

9.2.19 What does idealization mean? It is the way you arrive at some concepts with different degrees of abstractness; it is not the cause of the concepts. You reach new primitive concepts by it. All primitive concepts are idealizations.

9.2.20 If one gives up all idealizations, then mathematics, except the part for small numbers, disappears—even mathematics up to ten million. Consequently it is a subjective matter where one wishes to stop. For the purpose of seeing that objectivism is true, it is sufficient to confine one's attention to natural numbers. In principle, we may get these numbers by repetitions of objects.

The oldest and most familiar example of idealization is undoubtedly the use of ideal figures in geometry. Once Gödel cited with approval the following famous statement from Book 6 of *The Republic*:

9.2.21 And do you not know also that although they [the students of geometry, arithmetic, and the kindred sciences] make use of the visible forms and reason about them, they are thinking not of these, but of the ideals they resemble; not of the figures they draw, but of the absolute square and the absolute diameter, and so on?—The forms which they draw or make, and which have shadows and reflections in water of their own, are converted by them into images, but they are really seeking to behold the things themselves, which can only be seen with the eye of the mind.

Other central examples of our idealization include the law of excluded middle, *any* natural number, the real numbers, and the arbitrary sets. Once Gödel gave a brief characterization of what is involved in idealization and provided three examples:

9.2.22   In the description of the way we envisage what could be done we idealize by disregarding the imprecision in what is actual. Kant did this in describing our geometrical intuition. Real numbers are an idealization of the finite sets and sequences. The law of excluded middle is something we imagine in order to increase our capability.

When we idealize, we always generalize our intuition from actual cases to analogous ones. If we find other ways of apprehending the analogous cases, we endow our generalized intuition with additional content and may also be led to modify it to some extent. The following observation by Gödel seems to use this idea to characterize the change in our conception of physical space which resulted from Einstein's theory of relativity:

9.2.23   Physics has eliminated its former dependence on some of the more general intuitions—such as the acceptance on intuitive grounds that space is Euclidean.

At various times, Gödel made a number of scattered observations about intuition:

9.2.24   To apply a position beyond its limit of validity is the most vicious way of discrediting it. This is also true of the emphasis on intuition: appealing to intuition calls for more caution and more experience than the use of proofs—not less. While appeal to intuition continues to be necessary, it is always a step forward when an intuition (or part of it) is replaced and substantiated by proofs which reduce it to less idealized intuitions.

9.2.25   Intuition is not so unreliable. Often a mathematician first has an intuition that a proposition is probably true, and then proves it. If all consequences of a proposition are contrary to intuition, then statistically it becomes very implausible.

9.2.26   The science of intuition is not precise, and people cannot learn it yet. At present, mathematicians are prejudiced against intuition. Set theory is along the line of correct analysis.

9.2.27   The way of how we form mathematical objects from what is given— the question of *constitution*—requires a phenomenological analysis. But the constitution of time and of mathematical objects is difficult. [Compare 9.5.8 below.]

9.2.28 Intuition is different from construction; it is to see at one glance.

9.2.29 The range of intuition is narrower than the plausible but broader than the intuitively evident.

In section 7.1, in discussing Platonism in mathematics, I mentioned Gödel's belief in our fallibility and also in the priority of objectivity. I now list some of his observations on these two topics:

Fallible knowledge. In the first place, like most of us, Gödel believes that we have no absolute knowledge or certainty and that neither a priori knowledge nor intuition is infallible. It is, I believe, desirable to take this recognition of fallibility for granted in interpreting his views. He said, for instance, as I mentioned before, that he was glad to see that Husserl also recognizes the possibility of error.

9.2.30 A priori knowledge is not infallible. In mathematics we are [generally] wrong at the beginning but then we develop [toward what is right].

9.2.31 Even though finitary number theory appears evidently consistent to us, it need not be consistent; it might be that there are only finitely many integers. What is intuitively evident need not be true.

9.2.32 We have no absolute knowledge of anything. To acknowledge what is correct in skepticism serves to take the sting out of skeptical objections. None of us is infallible. Before the paradoxes Dedekind would have said that sets are just as clear as integers.

9.2.33 There is no absolute knowledge; everything goes only by probability.

9.2.34 One conjectures only [that] there is some probable intuition—not exact calculation—to determine the a priori probability; this has something to do with being *unprejudiced.* Probable knowledge defines a certain way of proceeding. In the last analysis, every error is due to extraneous factors: reason itself does not commit mistakes.

9.2.35 We have no absolute knowledge of anything. There are degrees of evidence. The clearness with which we perceive something is overestimated. The simpler things are, the more they are used, the more evident they become. What is evident need not be true. In 10^{10} is already inconsistent, then there is no theoretical science.

At the same time, Gödel has a different notion of absolute knowledge—knowledge that is feasible and applies to central and stable conceptual achievements. He sees this kind of absolute knowledge as the highest ideal of intellectual pursuit. His favorite example is Newtonian physics.

9.2.36 The Newtonian frame is a kind of absolute knowledge. It is a psychological phenomenon. In this sense absolute knowledge is the frame or backbone or axiom system of a good theory. The backbone of physics remains in Newtonism. Experience fills in the gaps after absolute knowledge is obtained. By pure thought, says the Newtonian scheme, we reach the frame. Afterwards one can interpret, for instance, the surface tension of a liquid. Psychology is different from physics; in psychology, you don't know.

9.2.37 The Newtonian scheme was obtained a priori to some extent [compare 9.5.2]. Approximately speaking, Einstein filled some gaps in Newton's scheme and introduced some modifications.—It was a bigger change to go from particles to field theory; a specification of Newton's physics made it into a continuum [physics] just beyond [the theory of] elastic bodies.

Objectivity and objects (priority of objectivity).   According to a widely current policy, it is preferable to put objectivity (the kin of fact, state of affairs, truth, proposition, propositional cognition) before objects; the existence, nature, and knowledge of mathematical objects are considered initially only on the basis of our discussion of mathematical truth and knowledge. This is, I believe, also Gödel's choice, at least in his discussions with me.

By the way, there is a familiar ambiguity in our use of the word *object*. When it means subject matter, all sorts of things—facts in particular— count as objects. The word *object* can also be understood more narrowly; I follow Frege and Gödel in distinguishing *objects* from *concepts*, and so I take it that a more inclusive term—say, *being, entity, thing*— is called for. In contrast with *objects*, Gödel associates *concepts* closely with the objectivity of conceptual relationships.

9.2.38 In connection with our freedom in mathematics, there is something we cannot change: when we define concepts, we cannot assume theorems about them. Also in the physical world, what you define as objects is up to you (e.g., atoms, etc.); but, once [they are] defined, their relations are determined. Only natural concepts exist: they are objective relationships.

9.2.39 Objectivity is a bifurcation of the real, a weaker sense of the real.

I interpret this comment as contrasting objectivity with objects and concepts: objectivity (or objectivism) requires only a bifurcation of propositions into true and false, according to the law of excluded middle— involving a weaker sense of realism than the stronger position which asserts that certain particular objects and concepts are real.

This interpretation seems to be supported by the following more explicit observations:

9.2.40 Out of objectivity we define objects in different ways. Faced with objectivity, how to single out objects is your own child. Is [a] cloud an object? In physics objects are almost uniquely determined by objectivity, if you want to do it in the "natural" way. But not really unique: there may be some different way we don't know [yet] which is more fruitful. It is more probable that natural numbers are uniquely determined by objectivity.

9.2.41   The most natural way of stating objectivism [in mathematics] is the one by Bernays in a recent lecture: The *number* of petals is just as objective as the *color* of a flower.

9.2.42   Confine your attention to objectivity.

9.2.43   There is a large gap between objectivity and objects: given the fact of objectivity, there may be other possibilities of selecting objects which we don't know yet.

As I see it, when we acquire and accumulate beliefs, a crucial and pervasive element that makes knowledge possible is our awareness of and search for "repetitions" that serve to link up certain different beliefs, enabling us to notice that the beliefs are about the *same* thing or to maintain our attention on the *same* thing. This sameness need not focus on something substantial or entirely determinate, but in general requires only some fluid element as a means of tying up certain beliefs more or less in a bundle. As we acquire such bundles of more and clearer beliefs, the objects or entities become more fixed and distinct for us.

9.2.44   Everything is a proposition.

9,2.45   To understand a proposition we must have an intuition of the objects referred to. If we leave out the formulation in words, something general comes in anyhow. We can't separate them completely. Only a picture means nothing; it is always the case that something is true of something.

It seems to me that the "them" in this context could mean "the something general and what it is about" (both of which may be said to be components of the proposition), or "the proposition and its components" or (perhaps, more ambiguously, "the proposition and what it is about"). More significantly, however, Gödel is asserting (if I understand him rightly) that we always see something *general* to be true of something *general*. Hence, the fundamental distinction between the universal and the particular (between concepts and objects) is a distinction within the realm of the *general*.

Statement 9.2.45 was made in the context of contrasting intuition with proof. On this occasion, I mentioned my opinion that, in practice, we do not use the idealized distinction between intuition *de re*—an immediate prehension of some entity—and intuition *de dicto*—an immediate prehension that some relation holds. Gödel agreed. Immediately before statement 9.2.45, he said:

9.2.46   Intuition is not proof; it is the opposite of proof. We do not analyze intuition to see a proof but by intuition we see something without a proof. We only describe in what we see those components which cannot be analyzed any further. We do not distinguish between intuition *de re* and *de dicto*; the one is contained in the other.

9.3. Some General Observations on Philosophy

In December of 1975 I sent to Gödel a manuscript entitled "Quotations from Gödel on Objectivism of Sets and Concepts" (referred to in Chapter 4 as fragment Q), on which he commented extensively. He was critical of this manuscript, but also informative about his views regarding what is important in philosophy and how it should be perceived and presented.

9.3.1   The title should be "Gödel's Framework for Discussing the Fundamental Aspects of Mathematics" or "Sets and Concepts on the Basis of Discussions with Gödel." With your title, you should use only quotations; even the quotations actually used often are incomplete and leave out the contexts. It should be a list of quotations, each of which is to be intelligible and complete by itself. The content is correct but not very interesting. The order could be wrong; indeed, it is chaotic. A clear disposition is missing. It is disorganized and doesn't give the impression of following a line of thought.

9.3.2   It is a mistake to argue rather than report [describe]. This is the same mistake the positivists make: to prove everything from nothing. A large part is not to prove but to call attention to certain immediately given but not provable (primitive) facts. It is futile to try to prove what is given (primitive). There is a clear distinction between just selecting assertions and arranging a list of quotations which point to a line of thought.

9.3.3   One idea is to make a collection of real quotations which are self-contained. On the other hand, if you wish to reproduce the conversations, you should pay attention to three principles: (1) include only certain points; (2) separate out the important and the new; (3) pay attention to connections.

9.3.4   When informal, less disturbing.

9.3.5   It is more appropriate to present my ideas as "remarks" or "discussions with Gödel." The real world may happen to be one way or another.

Gödel recommended self-observation, or introspection, as an important method in philosophy—a notion at the center of Husserl's phenomenology. The perception of concepts, as explained in Chapter 7, is his main example of self-observation, and he spoke about it in commenting on my manuscript Q:

9.3.6   The purpose of philosophy is not to prove everything from nothing but to assume as given what we see as clearly as shapes and colors—which come from sensations but cannot be derived from sensations. The positivists attempt to prove everything from nothing. This is a basic mistake shared by the prejudices of the time, so that even those who reject positivism often slip into this mistake. Philosophy is to call attention to certain immediately given but not provable facts, which are presupposed by the proofs. The more such facts we uncover, the more effective we are. This is just like learning primitive concepts about shapes and colors from sensations. If in philosophy one does not assume what can only be seen (the abstract), then one is reduced to just sensations and to positivism. [Compare the overlapping formulation in 5.4.1.]

This is also why intuition is important, as we see from the following observations:

9.3.7 To explain everything is impossible: not realizing this fact produces inhibition.

9.3.8 To be overcritical and reluctant to use what is given hampers success. To reach the highest degree of clarity and general philosophy, empirical concepts are also important.

Statement, 9.3.7 is reminiscent of Wittgenstein's observation (1953:1): "Explanations come to an end somewhere."

When a concept or a method or a position is either misused or applied beyond its range of validity, it tends to be discredited. It is important to apply the appropriate conception: one that is neither too broad nor too narrow. One's attitude should be critical but not overcritical. Even though these well-worn reminders sound empty in the abstract, they are helpful in practice—especially when current opinion happens to deviate from the golden mean. It is then useful to rethink whether one is applying the right conception.

For example, the positivists, as Gödel and I both believe, have in their philosophy misapplied logic and the axiomatic method, and the concepts of analysis and precision as well. Because of this, I was inclined to question the emphasis on clarity and precision and said so in the draft of *From Mathematics to Philosophy*. Gödel, however, disagreed.

9.3.9 Analysis, clarity and precision all are of great value, especially in philosophy. Just because a misapplied clarity is current or the wrong sort of precision is stressed, that is no reason to give up clarity or precision. Without precision, one cannot do anything in philosophy. Metaphysics uses general ideas: it does not begin with precision, but rather works toward precision afterwards.

In the draft of *MP*, I wrote: "The word 'theory' involves various associations, many of which are likely not to be appropriate to philosophy." Gödel commented:

9.3.10 Philosophy aims at a theory. Phenomenology does not give a theory. In a theory concepts and axioms must be combined, and the concepts must be precise ones.—Genetics is a theory. Freud only gives a sketch of a developing theory; it could be presented better. Marx gives less of a theory.

9.3.11   See 5.3.11.

In section 7.5 I considered Gödel's conception of the axiomatic method. He obviously had a broader conception of the axiomatic method and axiomatic theory than I was used to. For instance, he regarded Newtonian physics as an axiomatic theory—indeed the model for the pursuit of philosophy—but I was under the impression that physicists had little interest in the axiomatic method. So when I wrote, "A sort of minor paradox is the fact that physicists generally show no interest in [formal] axiomatization" (*MP*:18), Gödel said in response:

9.3.12   Max Born, John von Neumann, and Eugene Wigner all do physics with the axiomatic method.

9.3.13   The lack of interest of physicists in the axiomatic method is similar to a pretense: the method is nothing but clear thinking. Newton axiomatized physics and thereby made it into a science.

In the 1970s I was much concerned with the direct social relevance of philosophy. Occasionally Gödel commented on this concern of mine:

9.3.14   Leibniz may have [had] socially relevant philosophical views which he did not publish or [were] destroyed because of the church. Moreover, it would be bad if evil people got to know them and use them only for practical purposes. Evil politicians could use them. The views of Wronski [J. Hoene-Wronski] are obscure.

9.3.15   Practical reason is concerned with propositions about what one *should* do. For example, stealing does not pay. Will is the opposite of reason. This world is just for us to learn: it cannot be changed into paradise. It is not true that only good men are born. It is questionable that it is possible to improve the world.

9.3.16   Learn to act correctly: everybody has shortcomings, believes in something wrong, and lives to carry out his mistakes. To publish true philosophy would be contrary to the world.

Once I suggested to Gödel that philosophy having to do with human relations is more difficult than pure theory, and he replied:

9.3.17   Rules of right behavior are easier to find than the foundations of philosophy.

9.3.18   Strict ethics is what one is looking for. There is a distrust in our capability to arrive at this. Actually it would be easy to get strict ethics—at least no harder than other basic scientific problems. Only the result would be unpleasant, and one does not want to see it and avoids facing it—to some extent even consciously.

In response to my statement that "There is a problem of making a profession into a satisfactory way of life. This problem is specially acute with regard to philosophy" (*MP*:360), Gödel commented:

9.3.19 The question is how to carry on the profession. The intrinsic psychological difficulties in pursuing philosophy today as a profession are unavoidable in the present state of philosophy. On the other hand, many of the sociological factors [which cause this situation] may disappear in another historical period.

9.3.20 Philosophy is more general than science. Already the theory of concepts is more general than mathematics. It is common to concentrate on special sciences. To do philosophy is a special vocation. We do see the truth yet error would reign. The world works by laws; science is an extension of a partial appreciation of this fact.

9.3.21 True philosophy is precise but not specialized. It is not easy to build up the right philosophy. If one concentrates on philosophy from the beginning of one's career, there will be some chance of success, Kant never intended to publish the truth, but just an arbitrary point of view that is consistent. [The] early Middle Ages were a time appropriate for philosophy.

Gödel made some comments on the position of *substantial factualism*, which I proposed in *MP* and which I had renamed at his suggestion. He said he had believed in a similar approach in his younger days. He also suggested an addition to a heading: "Introduction: A Plea for Factualism":

9.3.22 Add after *"factualism"* the specification "as a method in philosophy."

9.3.23 There is no definite knowledge in human affairs. Even science is very heavily prejudiced in one direction. Knowledge in everyday life is also prejudiced. Two methods to transcend such prejudices are: (1) phenomenology; (2) going back to other ages.

9.3.24 Others will call factualism a bias. Historical philosophy is in part true and should be applied to the facts of the sciences. It contains something true and is different from the scientific attitude. Positivists reject traditional philosophy, which is poorly represented by them.

Gödel agreed with me, I think, in believing that factualism, as he understood it, was sufficient to show the inadequacy of the positivistic position. But he wanted more. Over the years, I have thought more about both Gödel's views and my own. In the next chapter I outline what I take to be the agreements and disagreements between us.

Central to Gödel's methodology is the place of the analysis or perception of fundamental concepts; I have reported about this in section 7.3 above, especially in general observations 7.3.20 to 7.3.23.

9.4 The Meaning of the World: Monadology and Rationalistic Optimism

In our discussions in the 1970s Gödel made many fragmentary observations on monadology, Hegel's system of concepts, and the separation of *force* (or wish) and *fact* as the meaning of the world. I now believe that he takes these three lines of thought to be alternative approaches to the same goal. He also relates these ideas to his ontological proof of the existence of God, discussed above in Chapter 3. Moreover, in a discussion with Carnap on 13 November 1940, he recommended that we attempt to set up an exact theory using such concepts as *God, soul,* and *ideas (Ideen)* and spoke of such a theory as meaningful, like theoretical physics (*RG*:217). This sort of thing is, I believe, the kind of metaphysics Gödel has in mind when he says, "Philosophy as an exact theory should do to metaphysics as much as Newton did to physics" (*MP*:85).

The "separation of wish and fact" is an ambiguous phrase. According to one interpretation, it is the recommendation that we keep our wishes separate from our investigation of the facts, not allowing our wishes to distort our vision. The phrase then formulates a familiar warning to guard against our prejudices, and so can be read as a methodological principle. I am, however, concerned here with Gödel's use of this phrase in a special context, a context which suggests that the word *separation* means *discrepancy, gap,* or *distance.* Gödel meant the phrase, I think, to describe the gross phenomenon that, most of the time, we strive to satisfy our wishes because the actual situation does not agree with what we wish for.

In October of 1972 Gödel asserted that one of the functions of philosophy is to guide scientific research and that another is to investigate "the meaning of the world." In November of 1975 he offered the suggestive observation that the meaning of the world is the separation of *force* and *fact.* Wish is, according to Gödel, force as attributed to thinking beings: realizing something. If, as Leibniz and Gödel choose to say, the world consists of *monads* and every monad has wishes (or appetition), we may also say more strikingly:

9.4.1   The meaning of the world is the separation of wish and fact.

I have long pondered over this stimulating aphorism. The word *meaning,* I believe, stands here for "the reason why a thing is what it is." The world develops as the separation of wish and fact and drives the monads to change their states, thereby realizing the world as it is. It seems clear to me that the quest for a systematic explication of aphorism 9.4.1 may be viewed as a succinct characterization of the task of what Gödel takes to be metaphysics, or first philosophy. More specifically, he apparently has in mind the sort of thing exemplified by the Leibnizian monadology. Indeed, he said, in March of 1976, that his own philosophy, or theory, is a monadology with a central monad, namely, God.

Undoubtedly it was for several decades a major wish of Gödel's to develop such a Leibnizian monadology and to demonstrate convincingly that it is a true picture of the world (and is, as Leibniz and Gödel believe, good for mankind). Much had to be done, however, to overcome the wide separation of this "wish" (for a developed monadology) from the "fact" as to what knowledge was then available to Gödel—or, is, indeed available at present to humanity as a whole. It is, as we know, important to know what we know and to avoid wishful presumptions, to separate our wish from the fact as to what we can justifiably claim to know.

In this particular case, most of us today are inclined to think that neither Leibniz nor Gödel has offered convincing reasons to believe that a "monadology"—a Leibnizian picture of the world—can be developed far enough even to be considered plausible. We are inclined to say that their wish for such a philosophy has so colored their judgment in selecting and evaluating evidence that they unjustifiedly see its feasibility as a fact. This seems to be a grand example of the familiar phenomenon of wishful thinking, which results from our natural tendency to permit our wish to prejudice our judgment of (what is or is not) fact.

Gödel says, as I have just mentioned, that his own philosophy agrees in its general outline with the monadology of Leibniz: that his theory is a monadology with a central monad; that his philosophy is rationalistic, idealistic (in the ontological, not the epistemological, sense), theological, and optimistic; and that these characteristics are interlinked. He contrasts his idealistic philosophy with materialism in that it sees mind as real and matter as secondary. His view includes *conceptual realism* as a part, which asserts the absolute and objective existence of concepts, in the Platonic sense. This *realist* doctrine is what is often called objective *idealism*.

According to Gödel:

9.4.2   With regard to the structure of the real world, Leibniz did not go nearly as far as Hegel, but merely gave some "preparatory polemics"; some of the concepts, such as that of possibility, are not clear in the work of Leibniz; Leibniz had in mind a buildup of the world that has to be so determined as to lead to the best possible world; for Leibniz monads do not interact, although C. Wolff and others say that, according to Leibniz, they do.

Let me insert here a brief exposition of what is commonly taken to be the Leibnizian view. According to Leibniz, the actual world consists of an infinite number of individual substances, which he called *monads*, or *units*. These are simple substances; they have no parts, no extension, and no form. The states of a monad are called *perceptions*, and the tendency to go from state to state is called *appetition*. Those monads whose perceptions are relatively distinct and are accompanied by memory are *souls*. Souls that are capable of reason and science, which "raise us to a knowledge of ourselves" are called *spirits* or *minds*. A material object, or a *body*, is a *well-founded phenomenon*, which results from our confused perception of an underlying aggregate of monads. It represents relatively clearly the actual features of that monadic aggregate. One of the monads is the central monad, or *God*. An important feature of the monads is that every monad has an inner life, or consciousness in some form.

What Gödel actually said about the separation of fact and wish is quite brief and cryptic. Much of what I have to say is a conjectural interpretation which results from my fascination with the idea. To me, the following four sentences appear to convey the core of his position:

9.4.3   The meaning of the world is the separation of fact and force. Wish is force as applied to thinking beings, to realize something. A fulfilled wish is a union of wish and fact. The meaning of the whole world is the separation (and the union) of fact and wish.

The following three paragraphs are my interpretation of these sentences:

If we restrict our attention to physical force, the physical world is what it is because at each moment the fact of its state disagrees with the tendency of the force of each of the elementary particles, which produces the next state of the physical world. (If there were no force at all, the world would be dead and there would no longer be any separation of fact and force. Such an unlikely situation could be seen as the limit case, when there would be zero force and zero separation.) Physics may be seen as the study of the laws governing the tendency of the force of each physical particle to overcome the separation of fact (the current state of the world) from its "desired" state. Since the forces continue to interact, the union of a force with fact occurs only when the force of a particle is spent and the particle becomes "contented."

At the same time we tend to think of physical force as "blind" force. Only in the case of wish do we think of an intention (directed to some target) or an ideal. The separation of wish (as a force) from fact is (more or less) the separation of the ideal or the wish from fact. If we compare wish (or force) and fact to appetition and perception in the Leibnizian monadology, it is natural to identify wish with appetition. Perception is then fact as seen by a monad. The replacement of perception by fact yields a common frame of reference for all monads, which is, however, no longer fully within the consciousness of each monad.

I see an affinity of this idea with the view developed by George Herbert Mead in his *Philosophy of the Act* (1938). Mead distinguishes four stages in the *act*: the stage of impulse, the stage of perception, the stage of manipulation, and the stage of consummation. Clearly, impulse and consummation correspond to wish and its fulfillment. Given the separation of wish and fact, one customarily tries to overcome the separation through perception and manipulation.

Gödel makes several other suggestive observations on this point.

9.4.4   Force and fact must occur again and again, repeating a huge number of times.

9.4.5   Force is connected to objects and a concept represents repetition of objects. The general is that which holds the individual objects together. Causation is fundamental; it should also explain the general and the particular.

9.4.6   Multiplicity (or repetition) is mathematics, which does not take primary place in this scheme.

I do not know what Gödel has in mind in making these observations and so can only offer some conjectures. Objects are, in the first place, the monads, whose appetition is force. There are repetitions of all sorts of things, from which concepts arise. Concepts, being general, are what hold things together, in the sense that when the same concept applies to many objects, these objects are connected. Causation is important for attempts to fulfill wishes, since we learn that, in order to bring about B, it is sufficient to get A first. Here we resort to the causal (general) connection that something like (the particular) B succeeds something like (the particular) A. Gödel seems to be saying that, if we leave out all other features in a repetition and consider merely repetition as repetition, we have mathematics. We may also interpret him as saying that, if we consider merely repetitions of successions as successions, then we get mathematics.

He makes the following observations about wishes:

9.4.7   By definition, wish is directed to being something. Love is wish directed to the being of something, and hate is wish directed to the nonbeing of something. These are explicit definitions.

9.4.8   The maximum principle for the fulfilling of wishes guides the building up of the world by requiring that it be the best possible. In particular, [since there are so many unrealized possibilities in this world, it must be a] preparation for another world. Leibniz also gives hints in this direction.

Gödel believes that *force* should be a primitive concept of philosophy. He says that Leibniz puts more emphasis than Hegel does on real definitions so as to get to higher-level concepts from lower-level ones.

Gödel seems to relate the separation of fact and force to the three categories of *being*, *nonbeing*, and *possibility* (instead of Hegel's three initial categories of *being*, *nonbeing*, and *becoming*).

9.4.9   Thesis is always a reinforcement of synthesis, that is, possibility, that is, force; antithesis is an empirical fact. Being in time is too special and should not appear so early as in Hegel. A complete understanding [of the world] should reduce everything to these elements. How you go on may be different from Hegel.

Interpretation.   Being as thesis encounters its antithesis in (empirical) fact. Force brings forth some new possibility (as synthesis), which is reinforced by a new thesis (as being). Somehow force begins as being and turns into possibility after encountering fact. Fact modifies force or wish to get a new force or wish. I am not able to grasp what Gödel has in mind, although it is clear that he wants to put the three categories of being, nonbeing, and possibility (instead of becoming) at the center, as can be seen from the next observation:

9.4.10   Independently of Hegel's (particular choice of) primitive terms, the process is not in time, even less an analogy with history. It is right to begin with being, because we have to have something to talk about. But becoming should not come immediately after being and nonbeing; this is taking time too seriously and taking it as objective. It is very clear that possibility is the synthesis between being and nonbeing. It is an essential and natural definition of possibility to take it as the synthesis of being and nonbeing. Possibility is a "weakened form of being."

Gödel continues with a discussion of time. The relevant point here is that he agrees with Kant in seeing time as subjective. (I further consider the question of time in section 9.5.)

Gödel seems to say that one worthwhile project is to improve on the work of Hegel, which would be a helpful step toward developing the system of concepts. In particular, he states that Karl Ludwig Michelet (1801–1893) provided a better development than Hegel did. In this regard, he mentions Michelet's *Die Entwicklungsgeschichte der neuesten Deutschen Philosophie*, published in 1843 when Michelet was forty-two, as well as *Das System der Philosophie als exacter Wissenschaft* (five volumes, 1876–81).

Gödel believes that there are two philosophies in [Soviet] Russia, one exoteric and one esoteric. The esoteric philosophy, he believes, is a unique system from which all true consequences are derived. He says that Michelet attempts to produce this sort of system with his improved version of Hegel's philosophy.

Gödel offers the following comments on Hegel's logic:

9.4.11   Hegel's logic need not be interpreted as dealing with contradictions. It is simply a systematic way of obtaining new concepts. It deals with being in time. Not Hegel's logic but some parts of it might be related to a proposition (not concept) producing its opposite. For example, if A is defined as in Russell's paradox [namely, A is the set of all sets that do not belong to themselves], "A belongs to A" produces its opposite. In Hegel, a condition produces its opposite condition in history: that is a process in time, and truth depends on time. Hegel's interpretation is like the figures in a puppet show; the second beats the first down. In terms of the unity of opposites and the idea that contradiction gives direction, antinomies receive a different interpretation. The Russell set becomes a limiting case of a succession of belonging-to and not-belonging-to; it is no longer circular.

Gödel is interested in Hegel's system of concepts, but criticizes Hegel on two fundamental points (in contrast to his agreement with Leibniz and Husserl). One point has to do with *meaningful predication* (rendered particularly explicit by mathematical logic but implicitly followed by all clear thinking). The other point seems to be the ideal of seeing primitive concepts clearly and distinctly (such as Husserl's ideal of "intuiting essences"). In both respects, he considers Hegel to be defective.

From time to time Gödel talked informally about monadology, but it was often unclear whether he was expounding his own views or those of Leibniz. It seems desirable to report these observations, even though I do not fully understand them and my reconstruction of the conversations may be far from accurate. I have already given Gödel's concentrated exposition of this topic in 9.1.8 to 9.1.11 above. Isolated observations include the following:

9.4.12 In materialism all elements behave the same. It is mysterious to think of them as spread out and automatically united. For something to be a whole, it has to have an additional object, say, a soul or a mind. "Matter" refers to one way of perceiving things, and elementary particles are a lower form of mind. Mind is separate from matter, it is a separate object. The issue between monadology and materialism depends on which yields a better theory. According to materialism, everything is matter, and particles move in space and exert force in space. Everything has to be governed by material laws. Mental states have to be accounted for by motions and their forms in the brain. For instance, the thought of pleasure has to be a form of the motion of matter.

In this context, Gödel mentions William Harvey and his biological concepts, probably as an influence on the thought of Leibniz. He notes that logic deals with more general concepts and that monadology, which contains general laws of biology, is more specific. He speaks of the limit of science and asks:

9.4.13 Is it possible that all mental activities (infinite, always changing, etc.) be brain activities? There can be a factual answer to this question. Saying no to thinking as a property of a specific nature calls for saying no also to elementary particles. Consciousness is connected with one unity; a machine is composed of parts.

Gödel suggests that:

9.4.14 When an extremely improbable situation arises, we are entitled to draw large conclusions from it. The failure to generalize sufficiently is not confined to philosophy. For example, the calculus of probability is not rightly applied, even in everyday occurrences. It was not a coincidence that Robert Taft and Joseph Stalin died not long after Eisenhower had become president. [To my protest that this seems rather farfetched, Gödel said that] for instance, Eisenhower's policies might have brought distress to Taft and Stalin. There are [laws having to do with] the structure of the world, over and above natural causes. [Gödel made similar observations in his letter of 21 September 1953, which is quoted in section 1.3.]

Gödel posits a direct spiritual field of force in which we live and distinguishes between the explicit factors and a force which is distinct from the sum of the environment. He also speaks of a parapsychological force and of a common force existing for a given time period.

9.4.15 According to a Leibnizian idea, science only "combines" concepts, it does not "analyze" concepts. For example, from this Leibnizian perspective, Einstein's theory of relativity in itself is not an analysis of concepts but it is stimulating for real analysis. It deals with observations and does not penetrate into the last analysis because it presupposes a certain metaphysics, which is distinct from the "true metaphysics" of the Leibnizian science, while real analysis strives to find the correct metaphysics.

Toward the end of section 3.2, I quoted some passages written by Gödel in his "philosophical notebooks" in 1954. The following excerpt is of special relevance to the problem of determining the primitive concepts of metaphysics:

9.4.16 The fundamental philosophical concept is cause. It involves: will, force, enjoyment, God, time, space. The affirmation of being is the cause of the world. Property is the cause of the difference of things. Perhaps the other Kantian categories can be defined in terms of causality. Will and enjoyment lead to life and affirmation and negation. Being near in time and space underlies the possibility of influence.

If we leave out the concept of God, we have to add the concept of being. Will and enjoyment, combined with force, yield the affirmation of being, which is the cause of the world. Properties or concepts cause the difference of things. Clearly there are different ways to try to explicate the pregnant suggestions contained in 9.4.16. Instead of making the futile attempt to interpret them, however, I turn to another outline of his philosophical viewpoint produced by Gödel.

There is among the Gödel papers an undated bundle of loose pages written in the Gabelsberger shorthand, with some words in English mixed in. Cheryl Dawson has recently transcribed these pages, which were probably written around 1960. The first page is headed "Philosophical remarks" and contains a list of categories apparently summarizing what Gödel takes to be the subject matter of philosophy: "reason, cause, substance, *accidens*, necessity (conceptual), value-harmony (positiveness), God (= last principle), cognition, force, volition, time, form, content, matter, life, truth, class (= absolute), concept (general and individual), idea, reality, possibility, irreducible, many and one, essence." I believe the word *class* here means the universal class (of all sets and individuals) and that the identification of this with the absolute harks back to an idea of Cantor's.

On another page, under the rubric "My philosophical viewpoint," Gödel lists fourteen items which appear to be an attempt to outline his fundamental philosophical beliefs:

9.4.17

1. The world is rational.
2. Human reason can, in principle, be developed more highly (through certain techniques).
3. There are systematic methods for the solution of all problems (also art, etc.).
4. There are other worlds and rational beings of a different and higher kind.
5. The world in which we live is not the only one in which we shall live or have lived.
6. There is incomparably more knowable *a priori* than is currently known.
7. The development of human thought since the Renaissance is thoroughly intelligible (*durchaus einsichtige*).
8. Reason in mankind will be developed in every direction.
9. Formal rights comprise a real science.
10. Materialism is false.
11. The higher beings are connected to the others by analogy, not by composition.
12. Concepts have an objective existence.
13. There is a scientific (exact) philosophy and theology, which deals with concepts of the highest abstractness; and this is also most highly fruitful for science.
14. Religions are, for the most part, bad—but religion is not.

These are optimistic beliefs and conjectures. They go far beyond "what is possible *before* all new discoveries and inventions," as Wittgenstein requires of philosophy (1953:126). Unfortunately we know very little of Gödel's reasons for holding them. Undoubtedly the centerpiece is his belief that the world is rational. This key belief is an empirical generalization from his interpretation of human experience, but what is known of his arguments for it is hardly convincing. For instance, in the 1970s, he said to me things like the following:

9.4.18   Rationalism is connected with Platonism because it is directed to the conceptual aspect rather than toward the real [physical] world. One uses inductive evidence. It is surprising that in some parts of mathematics we get complete developments (such as some work by Gauss in number theory). Mathematics has a form of perfection. In mathematics one attains knowledge once for all. We may expect that the conceptual world is perfect and, furthermore, that objective reality is beautiful, good, and perfect.

9.4.19   The world (including the relationships of people) as we know it is very imperfect. But life as we know it may not be the whole span of the individual.

Maybe it will be continued in another world where there is no sickness or death and where all marriages are happy and all work (every career) is enjoyable. There is no evidence against the transmigration of the soul. If there is a soul, it can only unite with a body which fits it, and it can remember its previous life. There are many techniques to train the memory. A very imperfect life of seventy years may be necessary for, and adequately compensated for by, the perfect life afterwards.

As I recall this conversation, I expressed my doubts as Gödel spoke; 9.4.19 is a reconstruction of his answers to my questions about the perfection of the world and about the futility of another life that does not remember the previous one. Gödel smiled as he replied to my questions, obviously aware that his answers were not convincing me.

9.4.20   Our total reality and total existence are beautiful and meaningful—this is also a Leibnizian thought. We should judge reality by the little which we truly know of it. Since that part which conceptually we know fully turns out to be so beautiful, the real world of which we know so little should also be beautiful. Life may be miserable for seventy years and happy for a million years: the short period of misery may even be necessary for the whole.

9.4.21   We have the complete solutions of linear differential equations and second-degree Diophantine equations. We have here something extremely unusual happening to a small sample; in such cases the weight of the sample is far greater than its size. The a priori probability of arriving at such complete solutions is so small that we are entitled to generalize to the large conclusion, that things are made to be completely solved. Hilbert, in his program of finitary consistency proofs of strong systems, generalized in too specialized a fashion.

In the spring of 1972 Gödel formulated a related argument for publication in my *From Mathematics to Philosophy* (*MP*); in it he expressed his agreement with Hilbert in rejecting the proposition that there exist number-theoretical questions undecidable by the human mind (*MP*:324–325).

9.4.22   If it were true it would mean that human reason is utterly irrational [in] asking questions it cannot answer, while asserting emphatically that only reason can answer them. Human reason would then be very imperfect and, in some sense, even inconsistent, in glaring contradiction to the fact that those parts of mathematics which have been systematically and completely developed (such as, e.g., the theory of 1st-and 2nd-degree Diophantine equations, the latter with two unknowns) show an amazing degree of beauty and perfection. In these fields, by entirely unexpected laws and procedures (such as the quadratic law of reciprocity, the Euclidean algorithm, the development into continued fractions, etc.), means are provided not only for solving all relevant problems, but also solving them in a most beautiful and perfectly feasible manner (e.g., due to the existence of simple expressions yielding *all* solutions). These facts seem to justify what may be called "rationalistic optimism."

Gödel's rationalistic optimism is an optimism about the power of human reason. Seven of Gödel's fourteen beliefs may be seen as special cases of this cognitive or epistemic optimism: 2, 3, 6, 7 (a very particular application), 8, 9, and 13. Beliefs 4 and 11 have to do with beings that possess an even higher form of reason. I have discussed in 3.1 some of his reasons for his belief 5, in a life after or a life before, which is based on his belief that the world is rational. Belief 14 suggests the possibility of a *good* religion, perhaps in the sense of one that benefits mankind; his ontological proof is presumably relevant to this belief.

Gödel discussed with me his belief 10—that materialism is false—in the context of physicalism (or psychophysical parallelism) and computabilism (or mechanism), which I discuss above in Chapter 6.

Belief 12—that concepts have an objective existence—is Gödel's well-known Platonism, about which he wrote a great deal over the years; several of the essays focused on this belief have been or will soon be published. In contrast to these articles, his discussions with me suggest a more moderate form of Platonism or objectivism which, in my opinion, is compatible with a wide range of alternative outlooks. Objectivism, which is one of the main topics of this book, is discussed in Chapters 7 and 8.

As I have said before, Gödel favored uninhibited generalization (see 9.2.13). It seems to me that he arrived at most of his fourteen beliefs by applying this principle to certain generally accepted facts of human experience. When these facts are made explicit, however, we do, I believe, see alternative choices. In any case, since I am inclined to adhere closely to what we know, I shall not speculate about those beliefs, given that we have so little knowledge of Gödel's reasons for holding them.

I do not know how these beliefs are interconnected, or how they might convincingly be supported. We may also ask how one who possesses these beliefs would live and behave differently from those who do not have them. In any case, it seems clear to me that we can neither prove nor refute them, although they are certainly of interest in widening the range of possibilities we can envisage.

9.5 Time: As Experienced and as Represented

If we contrast the objective reality of the physical world with the subjective realm of my experience, we see that, even though my mental processes are not spatial, they do take place in time. Since my picture of the objective world is ultimately derived from my experience, time occupies a fundamental place in my life.

We are naturally inclined to think that I should know best whether I have a fever or not, for I know how I feel. In practice, however, we rely with more confidence on what is registered on an instrument that measures my bodily temperature. Similarly, when I wish to know, say, whether I have slept enough, I generally rely more on what the clock says than on my own felling. The thermometer or the clock captures by *objectivation* some aspect of my experience which can be compared across different moments in my life and communicated intersubjectively. On the one hand, objectivation fails, we believe, to capture certain subtle components of my experience; on the other hand, I live my life largely by using the fruits of objectivation—which include conspicuously those derived from science and technology.

Between 1946 and 1950 Gödel wrote several articles on the concept of time from Kant to Einstein. He found certain new solutions for Einstein's gravitational equations and applied them to argue that our intuitive concept of time is, as asserted by Kant, not objective (or objectively representable). (An extended discussion of these articles is contained in Yourgrau 1991.) In addition, Gödel saw Einstein's relativity theory as implying a refutation of "Kant's view concerning the impossibility for theoretical science of stepping outside the limits of our natural conception of the world." I give a detailed exposition of these ideas in "Time in Philosophy and in Physics—from Kant and Einstein to Gödel" (*Synthese*, 102,:215–234, 1995.).

In his discussions with me in the 1970s Gödel made some scattered brief observations on the place of time in our experience as it relates to the pursuit of philosophy. These observations are suggestive, but by no means unambiguous for those, like me, who have only a very partial understanding of many of the subtleties of his thoughts. Before offering my tentative interpretations of them, I present my reconstruction, from rough notes, of his relevant observations:

9.5.1   The four dimensions of space-time are natural for the physical world. But there is no such natural coordinate system for the mind; time is the only natural frame of reference.

9.5.2   The Newtonian scheme was to a considerable extent obtained a priori. Proportionality, space, and time were a priori, while force, which produces acceleration, was empirical. Husserl believed that, by his method, one can get Newton's scheme—or even a better one—even without the scientific knowledge of Newton's time.

9.5.3   What remains in Husserl's approach is the observation of the working of the mind; this is the way to make the concepts of time and so forth, clear—not by studying how they work in science.

9.5.4   We forget how we arrived at the concept of time in our childhood and do not know how we use it. When we try to think about time, our reason is for making certain statements, yet our mind is working and working—on nothing at all. The problem of time is important and difficult. For twenty-five years Husserl worked on just this one problem: the concept of time. [The period from 1893 to 1917 is indicated in volume 10 of *Husserliana*, which is devoted to Husserl's work on internal time-consciousness.] Husserl's work on time has been lost from the manuscripts.

9.5.5   Husserl's unpublished work does not contain more on time than his published work. As we present time to ourselves it simply does not agree with fact. To call time subjective is just a euphemism for this failure. Problems remain. One problem is to describe how we arrive at time.

9.5.6   Another problem is the relation of our concept of time to real time. The real idea behind time is causation; the time structure of the world is just its causal structure. Causation in mathematics, in the sense of, say, a fundamental theorem causing its consequences, is not in time, but we take it as a scheme in time.

9.5.7   In terms of time, there are different moments and different worlds. [One interpretation of this remark is to take it as a reference to the different worlds determined by the spatiotemporal schemes of different observers.]

9.5.8   In sense perception what is originally given is not lost; but in our experience having to do with time and mathematical objects we lose a large part of what is originally given.

9.5.9   Causation is unchanging in time and does not imply change. It is an empirical—but not a priori—fact that causation is always accompanied by change. Change is subjective in the Einstein universe. For Kant, change is the essence of time.

9.5.10   Time is no specific character of being. In relativity theory the temporal relation is like far and near in space. I do not believe in the objectivity of time. The concept of *Now* never occurs in science itself, and science is supposed to be concerned with the objective [all that is objective]. Kant was before Hegel. [I take the last observation to mean that, even though Hegel was later, he regressed from Kant's correct view of time.]

I once asked Gödel to tell me some specific impressive results which had been obtained by using Husserl's phenomenological method, so that I could learn the method by studying such examples. In reply, he mentioned Husserl's work on time, but added that the important part had been lost. Even though Gödel usually praised Husserl's work, he did occasionally express his frustration in studying it. I have a record of what he said on one of these occasions.

9.5.11   I don't like particularly Husserl's way: long and difficult. He tells us no detailed way about how to do it. His work on time has been lost from the manuscripts. [Compare 5.3.20.]

It is clear from the above list that I have not been able to obtain a satisfactory reconstruction of Gödel's pregnant but fragmentary observations on time. Two basic points are, however, clear. (1) Time is subjective, at least when it is understood in the sense of our intuitive concept of it

(9.5.9 and 9.5.10); it is to be clarified by observing the working of the mind (9.5.3). (2) Clarification of the concept of time is fundamental to the study of philosophy, which depends centrally on clarifying how the mind works (9.5.1 and the several references to Husserl's approach); this task is very difficult (9.5.4, 9.5.5, 9.5.9, and 9.5.11).

There are some terminological difficulties in these quotations. Such problems are typically hard to avoid in observations that deal with fundamental issues but are not stated within a comprehensive context. One difficulty is that Gödel calls it a *euphemism* to describe time as subjective (9.5.5). He may be objecting to the idea that, since it is subjective, the concept of time is to be studied in (empirical) psychology, as it is commonly pursued today. The two remaining problems suggested in 9.5.5 and 9.5.6 are indications of his belief that there are specific difficulties to be overcome before we can reach a clear understanding of our concept of time. In other words, he is objecting to those who give up the attempt to clarify our intuitive concept of time, using as an excuse the euphemism that it is subjective. In any case, while acknowledging that we have so far failed to attain a clear understanding of the intuitive concept of time, he believes it is possible—and extremely important for the advance of philosophy—to reach such an understanding.

Indeed, according to Gödel's general philosophical position, objective reality includes both the physical and the conceptual worlds, which we can know better and better. In particular, I think, he believes there is a sharp concept corresponding to our vague intuitive concept of time—but we have not yet found the right perspective for perceiving it clearly. (Compare his discussion of the concept of mechanical procedure in *MP*:84–85.)

In 9.5.6, Gödel contrasts our intuitive concept of time with "real time" and says that the real idea behind time is causation. I take him to be saying that, even though our concept of time is not objective in the sense of being inherent in physical reality, there is an objective relation—that of causation—which lies behind our idea of a real or objective temporal structure of reality and that this relation may, somewhat misleadingly, be called "real time." Under this interpretation of 9.5.6, our natural tendency to think of the physical world as all of spatiotemporal reality is a result of our habit of associating causation with time and change.

Observation 9.5.9 suggests that Gödel wishes to dissociate causation from time and change, which, according to the views discussed in an earlier section, are not objective. When, however, we try to capture the causal structure of the physical world without appealing to the concept of time, we still seem to need something like matter or physical objects to serve as the bearers of causes and effects.

If we begin with one of Gödel's rotating universes (with or without closed time-like lines) as a representation of the causal structure of the whole, completed physical world—that is, as something fixed—we may, theoretically, make do without applying the concept of change and the concept of time linked to it. We would still, however, be thinking in terms of four-dimensional world-points which involve a residue of our intuitive conception of space and time, as embodied in the schemes of Newton and Kant. This situation may be why Gödel continues to speak of "real time" even while asserting that causation is the real idea behind time.

The concept of causation does involve the concept of succession and its iteration, whether or not these are temporal. Gödel's example of causation in mathematics, mentioned in 9.5.6, is probably intended as an illustration of the fact that not all successions occur in time. Once we remove the restriction to the temporal, the order of causal succession need no longer possess all the properties of temporal order as required by our concept of time. Causal succession may be a partial ordering or it may be a relation that is symmetric or circular, so that, within what is ordered by the causal structure, it is possible for A both to precede B and to succeed B in the relation. Clearly, causal dependence in general may involve more complex relations than linearly ordered causal chains. Whether or not effect can precede cause is a controversial issue, which is widely discussed in the literature.

On the whole, Gödel seems to favor the fundamental perspective of seeing objective reality, both the physical and the conceptual, as eternal, timeless, and fixed. At the same time, he believes that it is possible for us, at least partially and step by step, to go beyond every seemingly natural stopping point—such as the Kantian realm of phenomena or appearances—and approach closer to objective reality itself.

On the other hand, our internal consciousness of time is an essential ingredient of our experience, because, as Gödel asserts in 9.5.1, it is the only natural coordinate system for the mind. Gödel's repeated mention of Husserl's lost work on time suggests that he believes that a satisfactory understanding of the working of our time-consciousness would be a decisive advance for philosophy. It would be of interest to ask the related question: What would follow if we had such an understanding?

Gödel's observation 9.5.2 illustrates his belief in the important part which a priori philosophical reflections can play in the study of fundamental science. In particular, even though our intuitive concept of time is not objective, he thinks that by being clear about it and about the other concepts mentioned in 9.5.2, we may be able to arrive at something like Newton's fruitful scheme, or even a better one, on the basis of everyday experience alone.

Chapter 10

Epilogue: Alternative Philosophies as Complementary

Zhi zhi wei zhi zhi, bu zhi wei bu zhi, shi zhi ye. (To know that you know when you do know and know that you do not know when you do not know: that is knowledge.)
Confucius, *Analects*, 2:17

One may now ask: What is to be regarded as the proper characteristic of rationality? It seems that it is to be found in the conceptual element, *which transcends perceiving and (sensual) imagining and which produces a kind of* understanding.
Paul Bernays, 1974

I would like to begin and end with a classification of what philosophy has to attend to. The guiding principle is, I believe, to do justice to what we know, what we believe, and how we feel.
Hao Wang, 1985a

[A philosophical view,] to be acceptable, must accord with our considered convictions, at all levels of generality, on due reflection, or in what I have called elsewhere "reflective equilibrium."
John Rawls, 1993

On the one hand, there is a wide range of philosophical beliefs on which we enjoy agreement—or at least potential agreement, given additional information and reflection. On the other hand, disagreement is prevalent in philosophy, despite its avowed aim to address widely shared concerns and to present views based on widely sharable beliefs. A natural approach to dealing with philosophical disagreement is to break up into parts the process of moving from shared aims and data to the communication of a view, and to search out the sources of disagreement at each stage of this process.

On any given issue we as philosophers aim to say something significant about a shared philosophical concern on the basis of certain sharable—or rational beliefs, derived from what we think we know or are capable of knowing. Initially, we select a shared philosophical concern, come up with a view addressed to it, and then test that view against sharable beliefs. By repeating this process of inventing and testing, we can sometimes obtain and formulate what appears to be a stable and convincing view.

In each case, however, the view may go astray or be unacceptable to others at one or more levels. Those others may not share the chosen concern—finding it of no interest or not seeing it as a philosophical question. Or they may fail to see how the view reached significantly addresses the concern. Or, finally, they may not share some of the beliefs that form the basis of the view.

In order to decompose the disagreement over a given view, we may try to divide the allegedly sharable beliefs into different components, some of which are more solid and more generally shared than others, with one component making explicit the reasons for and against extending the range of application from a more solid component to a less solid one. As a result we will be given a choice at each stage between accepting and rejecting the extension, and the points of disagreement will be localized and brought out in the open. For instance, in Chapter 7 I have tried to decompose the disagreement between Platonism and constructivism in mathematics in this manner. (Compare also Wang 1991:269–273.)

Of course, the whole issue of philosophical disagreement is much more complex than is suggested by my idealized analysis and my specific example of Platonism in mathematics. There are various conceptions of philosophy which differ in appropriate method, subject matter, or central concern, and philosophers differ in their judgments not only over the plausibility of any given philosophical view but also over its significance and relevance to their own central concerns.

Philosophers tend to propose ambitious programs and indulge in uninhibited assimilation and generalization. It is notoriously difficult to agree about the feasibility and fruitfulness of such programs and generalizations. It is equally hard to determine which programs and generalizations are appropriate to present conditions.

Even if we confine our attention to comparatively precise and mature issues with a wealth of sharable relevant beliefs—such as that of Platonism in mathematics—it is hard to agree on whether or why any such issue is important to philosophy. It is difficult to decompose without residue such radical disagreements as that between Gödel and Wittgenstein on Platonism in mathematics. Nonetheless, the significance of their philosophies and the central place of the issue for them both seem to illustrate the appropriateness of my own extended considerations of Platonism in mathematics. Indeed, these considerations are, I believe, an instructive example, not only for the communication of my own approach to philosophy, but also for the current pursuit of philosophy as a whole.

In the first section of this chapter I begin by reviewing my agreements and disagreements with Gödel. Several general observations on philosophical disagreement will be made in the context of trying to determine the appropriate way to benefit from historical philosophy. In specifying the several points on which I disagree with Gödel, I indicate briefly the alternatives I favor.

In section 10.4 I first consider the initial constraints and choices of philosophy by considering its place in our lives. I then try to specify a conception of logic as a kind of metaphilosophy which is to be seen as an adjudicator, a chief tool, and a privileged component of both general philosophy and its distinct parts.

First, however, in order to clarify and support this conception, I discuss in sections 10.2 and 10.3 some of the work of Paul Bernays and John Rawls. I find their views congenial and feel that their outlooks on the study of philosophy are close in spirit to my own perspective.

Unlike Gödel, both Bernays and Rawls adhere closely to what we know. Unlike Wittgenstein, both of them consider certain substantive knowledge relevant to philosophy. Neither of them makes strong categorical statements on the nature of philosophy. Rather, they concentrate on illustrating their conceptions of philosophy by careful work in their chosen areas of research. Occasionally they do make tentative general suggestions on methodology, which I find persuasive and well founded. At the same time, I also find the bold assertions made by Gödel and Wittgenstein on what philosophy should do provocative and stimulating; they challenge me to reflect on the way we choose an approach to philosophy appropriate to what we know.

Bernays has concentrated mainly on the philosophy of mathematics and made major contributions to that field. Unlike Gödel, however, he does not see it as basic to or typical of philosophy. His conception of rationality contrasts the abstract scientific rationality of the concepts of mathematics and physics with the rich rationality of the concepts of life, feelings, and human interaction, including the regulative idea of justice. Specifically, in considering Gödel's sayings, Bernays emphasizes the significance of geometrical concepts and the importance of having a sense of the concept of *concept* different from that which identifies concepts with independent properties and relations.

Rawls is exceptional among contemporary philosophers in having chosen a single topic of research, persisted with it, and developed, with continual refinements, a substantive theory about it. That topic—justice as fairness—is of central importance in political and moral philosophy and has direct relevance to possible improvements in a democratic society. There are, in my opinion, lessons to be learned from his work, even for those who do not specialize in political and moral philosophy. By concentrating on a broadly accessible area of philosophical research, restricted yet rich, Rawls provides us with intimate illustrations of the appropriate way to deal with some of the basic concepts and issues of philosophy and its methodology.

His concepts of *reflective equilibrium* and *overlapping consensus* aptly capture two of the familiar basic tools in methodology. His contrast of *constructivism* with *rational intuitionism* (or moral Platonism) complements the related discussion in mathematics and brings out both the difference and the continuity of different parts of philosophy by using a transparent example. These considerations and the two apt concepts help to clarify the concept of objectivity, which is central to philosophy. Rawls's distinction between political philosophy and comprehensive worldviews teaches us, by example, the value of decomposing disagreements into distinct components, so that, by concentrating on some significant part of the whole, we can replace controversy by specialization, making it possible to study the part without being distracted by conflicts within the rest of the whole. Indeed, once agreement is reached in one part, this agreement usually helps to resolve conflicts in other, related parts as well.

Rawls wrote his first book—*A Theory of Justice* (1971)—in the 1950s and the 1960s, when Anglo-American philosophy was dominated by a special kind of piecemeal linguistic or conceptual analysis. This book, as an example of fruitful substantive philosophy, participated in and strengthened the attempt to go beyond the preoccupation with fragmentary analyses of this type. Moreover, I venture to conjecture that his conscientious efforts to narrow the range of disagreement and to encourage the toleration of reasonable alternative views—explicitly stated and implicitly exemplified by his responses to criticism, especially after 1971—may have encouraged the trend toward replacing debater's criticisms with constructive discussions in philosophy.

10.1 Factualism and Historical Philosophy: Some Choices

As I mentioned before, in discussing my manuscript of *From Mathematics to Philosophy* (*MP*) in 1971, Gödel made several comments on my idea of substantial or structural *factualism*. He saw factualism as a philosophical method and said that in his younger days he had taken something like it to be the right approach to philosophy. He did not deny that the method is of value, but said that it had intrinsic limitations and should be used in conjunction with Husserl's phenomenological method and with lessons from historical philosophy—especially in the pursuit of fundamental philosophy.

In my opinion, the use of lessons from the history of philosophy is an integral part of factualism; but phenomenology is a special type of reductionism, and factualism is an attempt to avoid the pitfalls of all types of reductionism. For Gödel, however, phenomenology is a way to carry out Platonism, which is, he believes, the right view, even though Platonism, too, is in a sense reductive, but acceptable because it is a "reduction" to the universal. It seems to me that Gödel's strong form of Platonism is at the center of the several major points on which I am unable to agree with him. Before considering these points of disagreement, I propose to discuss first the task of using lessons from historical philosophy.

It is likely that Gödel has in mind more decisive and less diffuse uses of these lessons than I do. As the reports in this book make clear, Gödel uses Plato, Leibniz, and Husserl in a positive way, Kant and Hegel in a mixed way, and positivism and Wittgenstein negatively. Since, however, I do not have as strong convictions as he does on most of the fundamental issues in philosophy, my situation is closer to that of a beginner in philosophy who tries to learn from alternative philosophies by checking what they say against what we suppose we know.

Our ideas develop through a complex dialectic of what we learn from the outside versus our own thoughts. In the process, contingent factors interact with our more and more focused and articulate aims, selections, reflections, organizations, and insights. For instance, the interplay of my wishes with my circumstances led me to certain views and to a familiarity with certain parts of human knowledge, including the work of certain philosophers. I found some aspects of these philosophers' work congenial. By reflecting on my agreements and disagreements with them, I have come to understand better my own views, as well as some of the reasons why people disagree in philosophy.

Every philosopher—in the process of developing a philosophy of his or her own—uses in one way or another what other philosophers have said. Some exceptional philosophers, like Nietzsche and, later, Wittgenstein, wish to negate existing trends and make a fresh start. Even they, however, develop their outlooks by reflecting critically on preceding philosophical positions. Most major philosophers, as we know, develop their own views by incorporating and responding to their major predecessors. Gödel, for instance, argued against the positivists and consciously related his own philosophy to the central ideas of Plato, Leibniz, and Husserl.

Plato rejected the views and methods of the sophists and extended the ideas of Socrates. Aristotle, in turn, fully absorbed Plato's teachings and developed an alternative position full of disagreements with his teacher. Kant built his critical philosophy by reflecting on the traditions of rationalism and empiricism. Hegel extended without inhibition the idealistic half of Kant's dualism. Leibniz was outspokenly proud of his own capacity to select and synthesize salient features of alternative views. Characteristically, he said:

10.1.1 I find that most systems are right in a good share of that which they advance, but not so much in what they deny. We must not hastily believe that which the mass of men, or even authorities, advance, but each must demand for himself the proofs of the thesis sustained. Yet long research generally convinces that the old and received opinions are good, provided they be interpreted justly (quoted in Dewey 1888:25–26).

To separate out the part of a system that is right and to interpret familiar opinions justly are ways to learn from historical philosophy. When we are, however, faced with apparently conflicting systems or opinions, we have to find ways to make a large part of them compatible in order to see that each side is right a good deal of the time. Sometimes we are able to detect that two philosophers understand differently the same concepts or words—such as *experience, intuition, concept, theory, fact, observation, the a priori, logic, science, philosophy,* and so forth—and have, therefore, different attitudes toward them.

Wittgenstein and Gödel provide us with a striking example of two philosophers who have different conceptions of and attitudes toward philosophy, its subject matter, method, tasks, and relevant tools. In section 5.5 I report Gödel's comments on Wittgenstein's work and his (Gödel's) position that language is unimportant for the study of philosophy. Elsewhere I have discussed extensively the contrasts between their views (Wang 1987b, 1991, and 1992). Here I confine myself to a brief summary of some of the main points.

Gödel and Wittgenstein agree that everyday thinking is of more fundamental importance for the study of philosophy than science is. They both believe that psychophysical parallelism is a prejudice of the time (see Chapter 6). Both of them believe that science as we know it deals with only a limited aspect of our concerns in philosophy and in life. Wittgenstein expresses this point this way:

10.1.2 Science: enrichment and impoverishment. *One* particular method elbows all the others aside. They all seem paltry by comparison, preliminary stages at best. You must go right down to the original sources so as to see them all side by side, both the neglected and the preferred (1980:60–61).

Husserl and Gödel also aspire to "go right down to the original sources." Indeed, Husserl developed a broad perspective to indicate the one-sidedness of science as we know it in his discussion of the "mathematization of nature" (in Lauer 1965:21–59). The disagreement with Wittgenstein is over the right way to carry out the project of finding and retracing from original sources.

It seems to me that both Gödel and, later, Wittgenstein try to deal with philosophical issues by reducing them to some kind of perceptual immediacy or fundamental intuition—locating this, of course, at different spots.

Gödel endorses the kind of perceptual immediacy (in terms of intentionality and intuition) that is central to Husserl's phenomenology; he puts special emphasis on the feasibility and importance of our power to see universal connections or to have categorical intuition (thus continuing and refining Plato's tradition). Wittgenstein's approach is more novel. It begins and ends with the perceptual immediacy of our intuition of the actual use of words in a given situation. I see this approach as Wittgenstein's way of pursuing the traditional quest for certainty in philosophy.

These different choices of focus are associated with their contrary attitudes toward the abstract and the concrete, the general and the particular, sameness and difference. Gödel puts the abstract and the universal at the center of philosophy and encourages uninhibited generalizations and assimilations. Wittgenstein sees the natural inclination to generalize as the main source of confusion in philosophy.

In an earlier passage I quoted Wittgenstein's declared interest, in contradistinction to Hegel, in showing that apparent sameness conceals real differences. Two of his related observations are:

10.1.3   What Renan calls the *bon sens précoce* of the semitic race is their *unpoetic* mentality, which heads straight for what is concrete. This is characteristic of my philosophy (1980:6).

10.1.4   But assimilating the descriptions of the uses of words in this way cannot make the uses themselves any more like one another. Imagine someone's saying: *All* tools serve to modify something.... Would anything be gained by this assimilation of expressions? (1953:10, 14).

Wittgenstein sees the main force in opposition to his later approach to philosophy in our craving for generality, which is strengthened by the inclination to take science as a model:

10.1.5   This craving for generality is the resultant of a number of tendencies connected with particular philosophical confusions. Our craving for generality has another main source: our preoccupation with the method of science. I mean the method of reducing the explanation of natural phenomena to the smallest possible number of primitive natural laws; and, in mathematics, of unifying the treatment of different topics by using a generalization. Philosophers constantly see the method of science before their eyes, and are irresistibly tempted to ask and answer questions in the way science does. This tendency is the real source of metaphysics, and leads the philosophers into complete darkness (1975:17–18).

That Wittgenstein puts the actual use of language at the center of philosophy is a good illustration of the mentality that "heads straight for what is concrete." Since Gödel believes that we are capable of intuitions of conceptual relations, for him language plays only a minor role. Of course, we are often more sure of concrete details than of general statements about them. At the same time, we are also often more sure of our abstract and universal beliefs—notably our beliefs in mathematics—than of most of our empirical beliefs. It seems to me desirable to take advantage of both kinds of evidence.

In any case, as I have said before (following 5.5.9), the relation of mathematics to language seems to exhibit certain striking peculiarities, which induced Brouwer to speak of "an essentially languageless activity of the mind":

10.1.6   In the edifice of mathematical thought, language plays no other part than that of an efficient, but never infallible or exact, technique for memorizing mathematical constructions, and for suggesting them to others; so that mathematical language by itself can never create new mathematical systems (Brouwer 1975:510).

Brouwer contrasts the effectiveness of communication by means of language in the exclusively intellectual sciences with its ineffectiveness in metaphysics:

10.1.7   Only in those very narrowly delimited domains of the imagination such as the exclusively intellectual sciences—which are completely separated from the world of perception and therefore touch the least upon the essentially human— only there may mutual understanding be sustained for some time and succeed reasonably well.

10.1.8   Language becomes ridiculous when one tries to express subtle nuances of will which are not a living reality to the speakers concerned, when for example so-called philosophers or metaphysicians discuss among themselves morality, God, consciousness, immortality or the free will. These people do not even love each other, let alone share the same movements of the soul (1975:6).

Gödel believes that science—including mathematics—and philosophy can interact fruitfully in several ways. Wittgenstein, by contrast, seems to have devoted a good deal of effort to studying the philosophy of mathematics for the opposite purpose of combatting the bad effects of "the misuse of metaphorical expressions in mathematics" on philosophy (1980:1). He believes that philosophy and mathematics *should* leave each other alone:

10.1.9   Philosophy may in no way interfere with the actual use of language; it can in the end only describe it.... It leaves everything as it is. It also leaves mathematics as it is, and no mathematical discovery can advance it (1953:124).

Given the broad disagreement between the philosophical views of Gödel and Wittgenstein, it is tempting to compare their extended work in the philosophy of mathematics as a way of clarifying that disagreement and, perhaps, deriving some lessons from it. Because they are working here with exactly the same subject matter, one is inclined to believe it possible to arrive at a judgment as to which of them is the more persuasive.

In the case of set theory, I am inclined to think that Wittgenstein fails to do justice to what we know, undoubtedly because he was so strongly convinced that set theory is based on conceptual confusion (compare the last page of his *Philosophical Investigations*) that he did not deem it necessary to study its actual development.

In the case of the theories of natural and real numbers, it is tempting to ask how Wittgenstein would respond to the step-by-step extension through the dialectic of intuition and idealization described in Chapter 7. He did, for instance, uphold the law of excluded middle and, at the same time, a sort of constructivism. The "dialectical" account tries to accommodate both positions.

On several occasions Wittgenstein considered Gödel's theorem, as I have tried to explicate elsewhere (Wang 1991:253−259; Wang 1992:32−40). Here I reproduce only those of his observations on Gödel's work which are easy to understand and accept.

In the early 1930s, according to R. L. Goodstein, Wittgenstein said:

10.1.10   Gödel's result showed that the notion of a finite cardinal could not be expressed in an axiomatic system and that formal number variables must necessarily take values other than natural numbers (Goodstein 1957:551).

10.1.11   Gödel shows us an unclarity in the concept "mathematics," which may be expressed by saying that we took mathematics to be a *system* (1938, quoted in Nedo and Ranchetti 1983:261).

10.1.12   I could say: the Gödelian proof gives us the stimulus to change the perspective from which we see mathematics (1941, quoted in ibid.).

10.1.13   It might justly be asked what importance Gödel's proof has for our work. For a piece of mathematics cannot solve problems of the sort that trouble *us*. The answer is that the *situation*, into which such a proof brings us, is of interest to us. "What are we to say now?" That is our theme (Wittgenstein 1967:388).

It seems to me that, in considering the philosophical views of either Gödel or Wittgenstein, it is necessary to distinguish their general pronouncements on the aims and methods of philosophy from what is revealed through their actual work. In particular, I find a striking divergence between the persuasiveness of Gödel's more or less finished work and what I see as the unreasonableness of his speculations, especially when he simply asserts his philosophical beliefs and recommends the ideal of exact philosophy or the use of Husserl's phenomenological method.

It is, of course, a common experience to find that the methods one has used in doing what one does well are inappropriate to another project, and, accordingly, to see a different method as the best way to approach one's highest ideal. In Gödel's case, however, it is exceptionally difficult to attain a balanced understanding of his philosophy in view of the big gap between his important careful work and his unconvincingly bold speculations. In trying to sort out my agreements and disagreements with him, I find it difficult to reconcile the lessons from his finished work with his recommended method for doing philosophy.

As far as I can determine, even though Gödel may, like many others, have enriched his understanding of the complexity of human experience by studying Husserl's writings, he achieved no significant success by trying to apply Husserl's method. His own spectacular work was obtained otherwise: by applying thoroughly the familiar method of digesting what is known and persisting, from an appropriate reasonable perspective and with exceptional acumen, in the effort to see and select from a wide range of connections. Undoubtedly, careful reflection pointing in the direction of Husserl's method played a part too—but only in combination with thinking based on material other than the act of thinking itself.

Gödel's declared ideal of philosophy as an exact theory aims at doing "for metaphysics as much as Newton did for physics." We can, he believes, by our intuition—using the method of phenomenology—perceive the primitive concepts of metaphysics clearly enough to see the axioms concerning them and, thereby, arrive at a substantive axiomatic system of metaphysics, possibly along the general lines of a monadology. The axioms will be justified because we can see that they are—in the Platonic conceptual world—objectively true; their consequences are true and justified because we can see that they follow from the axioms.

It is unnecessary for me to say that I am unable to see, on the basis of what we know today, how such an ideal is likely to be realized in future. From the perspective of factualism, I believe we know too little to give us any promising guidance in the pursuit of this grand project. At the same time, I recognize that it may be philosophically significant to try to develop a thin—not substantive—monadology, as, say, an extension of an improved version of the system of Wittgenstein's *Tractatus* (compare section 0.2, Introduction).

Quite apart from interpreting and evaluating the feasibility of Gödel's ideal of philosophy as an exact theory, I am not able to subscribe to his idea of the central importance of the method of phenomenology in the study of fundamental philosophy. There are also problems about how to interpret his emphasis on theory, the axiomatic method, and the a priori. In my opinion, these familiar ideas, although useful in a general way, generate confusing controversy when the evaluation of a philosophical position is construed as dependent on a determination of their exact ranges of application.

The distinction between the a priori and the empirical, like that between the innate (or the hereditary) and the acquired, points to something fundamental that is hard to delineate in any unambiguous manner. We would like to distinguish our native mental apparatus for processing information from what comes to us from experience. Yet, more and more components are being added to our receiving apparatus, and, as a result, by the time we are mature enough to try to separate the native from the learned, we are forced to resort to idealization and extrapolation if we are to agree, even, that logic and mathematics belong to the realm of the a priori. Aside from logic and mathematics, disagreement prevails over what is a priori. Undoubtedly, Husserl and Gödel include much more, but I have no clear understanding of their conception of the a priori.

From the perspective of factualism, we are entitled to appeal to concepts and beliefs grounded on our gross experience, or what we take to be general facts, whether or not we choose to consider them a priori. It seems to me that the tradition of seeking to found knowledge on the a priori is motivated by a desire to guard the autonomy of the mind as the universal basis and arbiter of all knowledge. However, the system of universally available and acceptable general concepts and beliefs is, in my opinion, a more accessible and reliable basis for the justification of our beliefs than are those beliefs which fall within the hard-to-determine range of the a priori.

For instance, if we try to develop a philosophical theory, the crucial issue is not whether its principles are a priori but rather whether they are universally acceptable. Even if Gödel's ideal of philosophy as an exact theory were realized, we would be more interested in the acceptability of its axioms than in their apriority. It seems to me, therefore, that we should not confine our attention to looking for a priori results in philosophy. In this connection, I agree with Rawls when, in presenting his substantive theory of justice, he says:

10.1.14   The analysis of moral concepts and the a priori, however, traditionally understood, is too slender a basis. Moral philosophy must be free to use contingent assumptions and general facts as it pleases. There is no other way to give an account of our considered judgments in reflective equilibrium (Rawls 1971:51).

Gödel himself seems to envisage a philosophical theory more along the lines of a physical theory, say, Newton's, than like number theory or set theory. It is not clear that he requires its axioms to be a priori. In any case, the axioms or principles of a theory are usually to be checked by testing those of their consequences which have a fairly direct contact with our intuition.

In philosophy we usually speak of systems rather than theories, and few contemporary philosophies are directly concerned with developing either systems or theories. When the relation between philosophy and theory is explicitly considered, opinions differ. For instance, in contrast to Gödel's statement that philosophy aims at a theory, we have the following statements by Wittgenstein and Rawls:

10.1.15   And we may not advance any kind of theory. There must not be any-thing hypothetical in our considerations. We must do away with all *explanations*, and description alone must take its place (Wittgenstein 1953:109).

10.1.16   I wish to stress that a theory of justice is precisely that, namely, a theory. It is a theory of the moral sentiments (to recall an eighteenth-century title) setting out the principles governing our moral powers, or, more specifically, our sense of justice. There is a definite if limited class of facts against which con-jectured principles can be checked, namely our considered judgments in reflective equilibrium (Rawls 1971:50–51).

When Gödel thinks of a theory, he has in mind an axiomatic theory or system; but his conception of an axiom system is more liberal than the precise concept of a formal system. For instance, concerning Wittgen-stein's statement in 10.1.11 that Gödel shows the unclarity of the concept of mathematics as a system, he would probably say that, although his theorem shows that mathematics is not a *formal* system, mathematics can be captured by an axiom system. He explicitly regards Newton's theory as axiomatic; and he undoubtedly regards a "second-order" system as an axiom system. In reply to a question of mine, he once said that we can add new axioms: in other words, when we have captured the essential axioms, we have an axiomatic theory for the subject, even if we may modify them or add new axioms later. According to his conception of axiomatic theory, he would certainly regard Rawls's theory of justice as such a theory.

I know no precise definition of Gödel's conception of an axiomatic theory or system. His main point in this regard seems to me a recom-mendation that, in studying a branch of philosophy, the crucial step is to find its primitive concepts and the main axioms about them. He declares the phenomenological method to be the central tool for accomplishing this task—but, I think, without any tangible evidence to support that declaration. It seems to me that the ways by which Euclid presented geometry, Newton developed his physical theory, Frege formulated his system of predicate logic, Dedekind found the—now standard "Peano"—axioms for number theory, Cantor arrived at the main axioms of set theory, and Rawls obtained the principles of his theory of justice—all provide us with more instructive and accessible lessons for trying to exe-cute such tasks than do the teachings of phenomenology.

Gödel repeatedly emphasizes the importance of the axiomatic method in the study of philosophy, even saying that it is simply clear thinking. I do not have much information about what he means to include under the axiomatic method. When he talks about metaphysics, he seems to suggest that the main step in applying the method is to use our intuition to find the primitive concepts and their axioms. Still, I am sure he has in mind more flexible applications as well.

Given any set of conceptions, in the sense of concepts with associated beliefs about them, we can try to determine what the reliable basic beliefs about each concept are; whether some of the concepts can be defined in terms of others; and whether some beliefs can be derived from others. Often we find that some concepts can be defined by other concepts, so that we can arrive at a subset of primitive concepts and construe all the beliefs in the set as concerned with them. Those beliefs in the initial set of beliefs which cannot be derived from other beliefs in the set are then taken as the axioms.

In this way, we arrive at one set—or another—of primitive concepts with associated axioms from a given set of conceptions. The axiom system determined by such a set gives order to the original set of concepts and beliefs about them and includes potentially all concepts definable by the primitive concepts and all propositions derivable from the axioms. Once we have an axiom system, we may concentrate our attention on the axioms, to try to determine whether they do indeed agree with our considered judgments and revise them if they do not. Given the revised axioms, their consequences usually have to be changed too, and so we have to check whether the changed consequences agree with our considered judgments according to our intuitive conception of the concepts involved. When this process is repeated, at some stage we may arrive at what Rawls calls *reflective equilibrium* (see section 10.3). In that case, we have an axiom system which provides us with an order of our initial set of intuitive conceptions that is stable with regard to our present beliefs.

In practice, we usually begin with a central intuitive conception of special significance—*point, line, force, existence, number, set, simultaneity, gene, justice,* and so on—and try to find axioms for that conception in various ways. As our knowledge and intuition develop, we may find new axioms or revise old ones. Sometimes we need new information from the outside, such as the experiments and observations of physics and biology.

It seems reasonable to say that looking for and trying to order the connections between concepts and beliefs—on the basis of our intuitive conceptions—are major components of clear thinking and that they can be construed as part of the axiomatic method, in the sense that they are involved in the attempt to arrive at some axiom system for a set of conceptions. But it is not true to say that the axiomatic method is "just clear thinking" in the sense that all clear thinking aims at arriving at some axiom system.

10.2 Some Suggestions by Bernays

Like Gödel, Bernays concentrated largely on mathematical logic and the philosophy of mathematics. But the philosophical views of Bernays are more tentative and open-ended than Gödel's.

It is well known that Gödel and Bernays had a high regard for each other's philosophical views. They corresponded extensively from 1930 on. In Hilbert-Bernays (1939) Bernays gave the first complete proof of Gödel's theorem on the unprovability of the consistency of a formal system within itself. In 1958 Gödel published his *Dialectica* paper to honor Bernays on his seventieth birthday. On several occasions in the 1950s and 1960s he invited Bernays to visit him in Princeton.

In an earlier chapter I quote Gödel's repeated praise of an observation on Platonism in mathematics, which he attributes to Bernays:

10.2.1 There are objective facts of the framework of our intuition which can only be explained by some form of Platonism. For example, as Bernays observes, it is just as much an objective fact that the flower has *five* petals as that its color is *red*.

10.2.2 The most natural way of stating objectivism is the one by Bernays in a recent lecture: the *number* of leaves is just as objective as the *color* of a flower. Not in his paper "On Platonism in Mathematics," which is a misnomer.

A few days later, I asked Gödel for some specific references to his favorite sayings by Bernays. In reply, Gödel said:

10.2.3 I like what Bernays says in a recent paper about inner structure, possible idealized structure, open domain of objectivity, and *sui generis*, different from approximate physics.

Afterwards I located the following:

10.2.4 In the more abstract rationality of natural science we can discern ... the schematic character of all theoretical description. The schemata set up by the theories have their inner structures, which cannot be fully identified with the constitution of physical nature. We have, in fact, between the objects of nature and the schematic representatives, a reciprocity of approximation: the schemata do not fully attain the ample multiplicity of determination of the natural objects; on the other hand, the natural objects do not attain the mathematical perfection and precision of the schemata.

10.2.5 The inner structures of the theoretical schemata have a purely mathematical character; they are idealized structures. And mathematics can be regarded as the science of possible idealized structures. These idealized structures and their interrelations constitute an open domain of objectivity—an objectivity *sui generis*, different from the one we have to deal with in physics as natural science, but indeed, connected with it in the way that by a physical theory some section of physical nature is described as an approximate realization of some mathematical structure (Bernays 1974:603–605).

These observations by Bernays provide a characterization of mathematics as the science of possible idealized structures through its relation to physical theory. The mathematical formulation of physical theories is schematic in that it is more precise than physical nature and leaves out some of the ample specificities of the natural objects. It describes idealized structures. Mathematics can be applied to describe different idealized structures: it studies all possible idealized structures. These possible structures and their interrelation constitute an open domain of *objectivity* which is different from objectivity in the familiar sense of being true of the physical world in every detail.

Gödel's interest in the position expounded by Bernays resulted from his own conviction that it is important to recognize at least the undeniability of some form of Platonism in mathematics; there is room for choice when we come to stronger forms of Platonism in mathematics, but nobody has any good reason to question the parts on which he and Bernays agree.

In December 1975, I sent Bernays a copy of my manuscript Q, which tried to summarize Gödel's Platonism in mathematics. Bernays replied to my request for his comments in a letter dated 23 February 1976, and I sent a copy of it to Gödel in early March. Unfortunately, Gödel never discussed the letter with me, undoubtedly because by that time he had become fully occupied with his health problems and those of his wife.

The Bernays letter summarized some of his own views and raised several questions about Gödel's position as I then presented it:

10.2.6 The questions treated in your text seem to me very delicate. I am of course in favour of objectivism in many respects. You know that I also adopt the distinction of classes and sets and also regard classes as extensions of concepts.

10.2.7 But I doubt if concepts are in the same way objective as mathematical relations. I am inclined to compare the world of mathematical objects and relations with the world of colours and their relations—as also with the world of musical entities and their relations. In all these cases we have an objectivity which is to be distinguished from that one we have in the physical reality. Mathematics, according to this view, is a kind of theoretical phenomenology: the phenomenology of idealized formal structures.

10.2.8 A concept on the other hand is something originally conceived (more or less instinctively) by a mental being which has impressions and sensations, conceived for the purpose of orientation and understanding. Once concepts have been introduced there result of course objective relations between them.

10.2.9 Another point I want to mention is that I think one should not overestimate the philosophical relevance of the possibility of embodying classical mathematics in set theory. It seems to me that for considering the intuitive sources of mathematics we have to keep to the old dualism of arithmetic and geometry. Arithmetical evidence is that one which BROUWER will exclusively admit for mathematics. But this, I think, is an arbitrary and unnecessary restriction.

10.2.10   There is a rich supply of concepts (concerning idealized structures) which is furnished by the geometrical intuition: the concepts of point, curve, surface, connectedness, contact, surrounding, neighbourhood, generally the topological concepts.

10.2.11   It must be admitted that the geometrical concepts are not so fit for discursive use as the arithmetical ones, and therefore an arithmetisation of them is necessary; yet we cannot require a strict arithmetisation but in many cases must content ourselves with a kind of compromise. For such a compromise just the set-theoretic concepts are useful. (It is to be remembered that CANTOR set theory started from the consideration of point sets.)

10.2.12   It seems to me that even the concept of the number series is geometrically motivated. From the strictly arithmetical point of view the progress of numbers is only a *progressus in indefinitum*. It should further be regarded, as I think, that the simplicity and clarity of the concept of subset does not entail an intuitive evidence of the existence of the power set for *any set*. What it entails is only the existence of the *class* of all subsets for any set. The special passing from the set of rational numbers to its power set is motivated for the sake of arithmetizing geometry.

It is clear from this letter that Bernays agrees with Gödel in endorsing some form of objectivism or Platonism in mathematics, to the extent of believing that in mathematics "we have an objectivity which is to be distinguished from that one we have in the physical reality" (10.2.7). The two apparent disagreements are over the objective character of concepts and the importance of geometry "for considering the intuitive sources of mathematics."

In terms of terminology, it is certainly desirable to make some distinction between different uses of the word *concept*. For instance, Gödel drew a distinction between *concepts* and *notions* in his Russell paper:

10.2.13   [On the one hand, one may] understand by a notion a symbol together with a rule for translating sentences containing the symbol into such sentences as do not contain it, so that a separate entity denoted by the symbol appears as a mere fiction. [On the other hand, one may conceive concepts as real entities] as the properties and relations of things existing independently of our definitions and constructions. I shall use the term *concept* in the sequel exclusively in this objective sense (Gödel 1990, hereafter *CW2*:128).

Undoubtedly Bernays had in mind a broader range of concepts than just the *notions* in the special sense specified by Gödel. Quite apart from the difficult issue of common usage, we seem to need a category of concepts or notions which corresponds to what Bernays construes as concepts. Given the fact that I have largely followed Gödel's usage of *concept* in this book, it might be convenient to use the word *notion* for this category in the present context.

It seems to me that Gödel's contrast of concepts with notions in his restricted sense was related to his insistence on restricting the sense of creation to that of making something out of nothing. In both cases, he wanted to limit the range of mental products to what is comparatively poor in content. As a result, a middle range—which plays an important part in everyday experience and philosophical thinking—of creations and of concepts of notions is left out. In my opinion, by paying attention to the category of concepts or notions which Bernays had in mind, we may be able to attain a more accommodating perspective than Gödel's. For instance, if we use Gödel's conception of *concept* (or notion) and of *creativity*, we cannot even express the significant and widely shared belief formulated succinctly by Bernays (1974:604):

10.2.14 [We can] ascribe to rationality a *creativity*: not a creativity of principles, but a creativity of concepts.

It is easy to agree with Bernays that a concept is something originally conceived by a mental being. But Gödel wanted to say that, unless certain concepts are objective, we cannot understand why, for example, we all accept Turing's characterization of the concept of mechanical procedures. At the same time, we can at most infer only that some concepts are objective, not that all concepts are. Gödel seems to suggest that all concepts of philosophical significance are objective. Given, however, our experience from the history of philosophy, that suggestion appears to beg the question.

Specifically, Gödel's central philosophical concern with the feasibility of developing an exact theory for metaphysics seems to depend on his belief that, since we have succeeded pretty well in clarifying the basic concepts of mathematics, we should be able to do the same for metaphysics. It seems to me, however, that, for each concept as originally conceived by a mental being, we can claim it is objective only if it satisfies certain natural requirements: first, it is not a *notion* in Gödel's restricted sense; yet, secondly, our understanding of it is seen to be converging to a unique determination of its content. Indeed, Gödel's examples of our successful perception of concepts, reported above in Chapter 7, do satisfy these two requirements.

The importance of geometrical intuition for the foundations of mathematics is a significant idea which Bernays had already developed in his "On Platonism in Mathematics" (1935). Gödel considered the title a misnomer because the paper was concerned more with clarifying alternative positions than with coming out in favor of Platonism. Indeed, contrary to Gödel's view, Bernays drew from the set-theoretical paradoxes the conclusion: "We must therefore give up absolute Platonism" (in Benacerraf and Putnam 1964:277).

If we begin with our arithmetical intuition of natural numbers, we have only small integers, or at most arbitrary integers. That is why both Kronecker and Brouwer renounce the totality of integers (ibid.:278). The first part of 10.2.12 says that the extension to this totality is geometrically motivated. Like Gödel, Bernays saw this as a jump:

10.2.15   The weakest of the "Platonistic" assumptions introduced by arithmetic is that of the totality of integers (ibid.: 275).

It is, however, when we come to the continuum of the totality of real numbers that Platonistic classical analysis borrows decisively from our geometrical intuition.

10.2.16   The idea of the continuum is a geometrical idea which analysis expresses in terms of arithmetic. [On the intuitionistic conception, the continuum loses its] character of a totality, which undeniably belongs to the geometrical idea of the continuum. And it is this characteristic of the continuum which would resist perfect arithmetization.

10.2.17   These considerations lead us to notice that the duality of arithmetic and geometry is not unrelated to the opposition between intuitionism and Platonism. The concept of number appears in arithmetic. It is of intuitive origin, but then the idea of the totality of numbers is superimposed. On the other hand, in geometry the Platonistic idea of space is primordial (ibid.:283–284).

As Bernays says in 10.2.9, Brouwer arbitrarily and unnecessarily restricted mathematical evidence to the arithmetical. When we try to do justice to geometrical evidence as well, we are led to the power set of integers which "is motivated for the sake of arithmetizing geometry" (10.2.12). Since geometry is not so fit for discursive use and we are not able to attain a strict arithmetization of geometry, we have to resort to a kind of compromise; set theory accomplishes this task quite well (10.2.11).

Bernays did not emphasize the intuitive character of the iterative concept of set, and so we might conclude that we have, in addition to the arithmetical and the geometrical, also a kind of set-theoretical intuition. He did, however, characterize the way we are led naturally to the power set of integers, by using an idealization to satisfy the requirement that classical analysis do justice to our geometrical intuition. Not content with the jump suggested in 10.2.15, Bernays extends Platonism to *sets* of numbers:

10.2.18   It abstracts from the possibility of giving definitions of sets, sequences, and functions [of integers]. These notions are used in a "quasi-combinatorial" sense, by which I mean: in the sense of an analogy of the infinite to the finite (ibid.:275).

Gödel would probably not dispute the claim that geometry is one of the intuitive sources of mathematics. It is likely that, for him, what is essential in geometry for studying the fundamental issues in the philosophy of mathematics is absorbed into set theory. Such a belief would indicate a choice on his part, without having to deny the philosophical relevance of geometry on some level in considering the foundations of mathematics.

In his essay on rationality, Bernays further elaborates the contributions of geometry to rationality. Clearly, the clarification of our conception of rationality is a central concern of philosophy. In this connection I find some of the things Bernays says suggestive and congenial and would like to bring them to wider notice.

To begin his discussion, Bernays gave a sort of definition of rationality:

10.2.19   One may now ask: What is to be regarded as the proper characteristic of rationality? It seems that it is to be found in the *conceptual element*, which transcends perceiving and (sensual) imagining and which produces a kind of *understanding* (Bernays 1974:601).

Bernays distinguishes abstract scientific rationality from rationality in a widened sense, to include also prescientific rationality. Under these two headings he considers a number of major "cases of rationality brought about by the formation of concepts."

Abstract scientific rationality, according to Bernays, includes: (1) a clear understanding of the primitive concepts of predicate logic; (2) the use of abstract concepts in pure arithmetic and algebra; (3) the way we conceive "ideal figures" in geometry; (4) the formation of concepts in theoretical physics; (5) a critical attitude toward the regularities in nature and a positive leading idea—the idea of natural law. Under (3) he mentions a threefold significance of geometrical concepts: (a) experimentally for the physics of space; (b) theoretically for geometry as a domain of pure mathematics; (c) intuitively for a phenomenological theory of intuitive spatial relations (ibid.:602, 605 n. 20).

Comparing Bernays's with Gödel's perspective, we see that the concepts or notions of set theory and concept theory are conspicuously absent in this list. In place of (2) and (3), Gödel concentrates his attention on the concepts of number theory and set theory, assigning to geometry and the abstract concepts of algebra an auxiliary place in his reflections on the foundations of mathematics. As I see it, Gödel need not deny that historically we had developed the concepts of set theory as a way to accommodate a synthesis and an extension of our arithmetical and geometrical intuitions; but the crucial point for him was the belief that we do have intuitions about the concept of set, which is, moreover, more substantive than the abstract concepts of algebra and cleaner than geometrical concepts.

Bernays mentioned four typical examples of prescientific rationality: (1) the fundamental stock of concepts contained in our background knowledge for all empirical investigations of knowledge; (2) the concept of life; (3) concepts for understanding feelings and motives (such as wanting, wishing, love, pride, ambition, jealousy, shame, anger); (4) concepts for describing meaningful intersubjective relations (such as communication, agreement, promise, order, obedience, claim, privilege, duty).

In connection with the concepts of group (4), Bernays made several pregnant observations on the concept of justice, which seem to me to specify a research program of the type pursued extensively and carefully in Rawls's theory of justice as fairness.

10.2.20   Some of these concepts are connected with the *regulative idea of justice*, which is a prominent element of rationality, and which again constitutes a domain of objectivity. An analogy can be made between, on the one hand, the relatedness of a theoretical system of physics to the domain of physical nature that it approximately describes and, on the other, the relatedness of a system of positive law to an intended objectivity of justice to which it approximates in a lower or higher degree (ibid.:604).

It seems likely that Bernays included the concepts of metaphysics under the vague category (1) of "the concepts contained in our background knowledge." Explicitly of the concepts in group (3) but implicitly, I am sure, of all four categories of the concepts of prescientific rationality, Bernays asserts:

10.2.21   By these concepts a distinct kind of understanding is achieved, which in some respects cannot be replaced by any structural explanation, however elaborate it may be (ibid.: 603).

The difficult word *structural* in this context seems to me to be intimately related to Gödel's conception of the axiomatic method and Bernays's own conception of mathematics "as the science of possible idealized structures." If my interpretation of 10.2.21 agrees with Bernays's intention, he implies, contrary to Gödel's belief, that metaphysics cannot be fully treated by the use of the axiomatic method. Most of us, I think, agree that such a conclusion is a reasonable inference from our historical experience.

10.3 Some Lessons from the Work of Rawls

My concern with the work of Rawls is primarily that of an outsider who finds instructive the explicit and implicit methodological ideas it contains. Given this limited concern, I have studied only a small part of his work and, consequently, do not possess anything like a full understanding of his actual methodology. I can only hope that my interpretation of it is of some significance, even if it fails to capture all his intentions.

Of special interest to me are Rawls's ideas on: (1) the concept of objectivity; (2) his conception of reflective equilibrium and due reflection; (3)

the comparison of moral philosophy with the philosophy of mathematics; (4) the relation of moral and political constructivism to rational intuitivism or moral Platonism; and (5) ways to narrow the range of disagreement, in relation to toleration and pluralism.

For more than four decades Rawls has devoted himself to the development of his theory of justice as fairness. He began to collect notes around the fall of 1950. In 1971, after producing a series of articles, he published his *A Theory of Justice*, which aroused a good deal of response. He continued to refine his theory, publishing a number of articles to report on his work in progress. Of these articles, he said in a 1991 interview:

10.3.1   What I am mainly doing in these articles, as I now understand, having written them—you don't always understand what you're doing until after it has happened—is to work out my view so that it is no longer internally inconsistent. To explain: to work out justice as fairness the book uses throughout an idea of a well-ordered society which supposes that everybody in the society accepts the same comprehensive view, as I now say. I came to think that that simply can never be the case in a democratic society, the kind of society the principles of the book itself requires. That's the internal inconsistency. So I had to change the account of the well-ordered society and this led to the idea of overlapping consensus and related ideas. This is really what the later articles are about.

In 1993 Rawls published his *Political Liberalism*, in which he develops these new ideas systematically. According to the 1991 interview, he was working at that time on a related book, tentatively entitled "Justice as Fairness: A Briefer Restatement." Concerning his decision to spend his time—after publishing his original book in 1971—trying to articulate the idea of justice as fairness more convincingly, he says:

10.3.2   I'm not sure that's the best thing to have done, but that's what I have done. I'm a monomaniac really. I'd like to get something right. But in philosophy one can't do that, not with any confidence. Real difficulties always remain (1991:44).

Rarely is a philosopher willing and able to persist so concentratedly and fruitfully on a special topic—even one as rich and important as justice as fairness—which appears to be far removed from what are generally regarded as the central issues of fundamental philosophy. In my opinion, however, Rawls's choice of—and adherence to—this substantive and intimate problem have led to significant illumination of some of the general issues we face in the study of philosophy. The resulting thorough treatment seems to me to provide much food for thought, even for those who have little familiarity with political philosophy. It is an example that stimulates reflection on the ramifications attendant on trying to investigate any philosophical problem seriously.

For example, I find in this work similarities to (and differences from) my own attempt to clarify the objectivity of mathematics, to decompose the disagreement between constructivism and Platonism in mathematics, and to strengthen the relation between mathematical logic and the philosophy of mathematics. It seems to me useful to study both moral philosophy and the philosophy of mathematics with a view to narrowing the range of disagreement within them. Doing so provides us with complementary illustrations of ways of linking persistent philosophical controversies more closely to what we know—in contrast to the usual mutual criticisms limited to a high level of generality.

At one point Rawls distinguished moral philosophy—which considers such problems as the analysis of moral concepts, the existence of objective moral truths, and the nature of persons and personal identity—from moral theory, which is a part of moral philosophy and which is the study of substantive moral conceptions. Rawls questioned the hierarchical conception of methodology—expounded, for example, by Michael Dummett (1973, 1981:666)—which views moral philosophy as secondary to metaphysics and the philosophy of mind, which are, in turn, seen as secondary to epistemology and the theory of meaning. In particular, Rawls urged:

10.3.3 Moral theory is, in important respects, independent from philosophical subjects sometimes regarded as prior to it.... Each part of philosophy should have its own subject matter and problems and yet, at the same time, stand directly or indirectly in relations of mutual dependence with the others. The fault of methodological hierarchies is not unlike the fault of political and social ones: they lead to a distortion of vision with a consequent misdirection of effort (Rawls 1975:21).

10.3.4 Just as the theory of meaning as we now know it depends on the development of logic from, let's say, Frege to Gödel, so the further advance of moral philosophy depends on a deeper understanding of the structure of moral conceptions and of their connections with human sensibility; and in many respects, this inquiry, like the development of logic and the foundations of mathematics, can proceed independently (ibid.:21–22; see also p. 6).

I share Rawls's feeling that the unexamined belief in methodological hierarchies has led to a great deal of misdirection of effort. In 10.3.4 he draws two flexible analogies: (1) the further advance of moral philosophy will depend on the development of moral theory, just as the current theory of meaning has depended on the development of logic; and (2) just as logic and the foundations of mathematics have developed, in many respects, independently, so can moral theory. These analogies, I think, call for some elucidation.

Rawls undoubtedly had in mind his theory of justice as a typical example of moral theory. It seems reasonable to say that his theory is indeed largely independent of alternative comprehensive moral philosophies, especially in light of his continued effort to clarify ideas such as that of overlapping consensus. I do not know whether he would now prefer to change the term *moral theory*, but the intention seems clear to me. One natural question is why Rawls matched moral philosophy with the theory of meaning rather than with the philosophy of mathematics. Another question is whether logic is to be distinguished from the foundations of mathematics—a label that has its familiar ambiguity.

For instance, in 1939 Turing gave a lecture course and Wittgenstein a class at Cambridge—both entitled "The Foundations of Mathematics." Turing's course was on mathematical logic, but Wittgenstein explicitly excluded that topic at the beginning, referring to mathematical logic as "a particular branch of mathematics." In order to borrow a convenient terminology for a distinction I would like to make, I propose to distinguish the *foundations of mathematics* from both *mathematical logic* and the *philosophy of mathematics*.

To begin with, I compare *mathematics* to the realm of our considered judgments on moral matters. In both cases, there is a close contact with our intuitions, which provide us with the data and the tool for our study of moral theory and the foundations of mathematics, as well as of moral philosophy and the philosophy of mathematics. For instance, for Frege, Russell, Hilbert and Gödel, the study of mathematical logic was intimately related to their interest in the philosophy of mathematics. I take this mixed type of work as belonging to the subject of the foundations of mathematics, which I match with moral theory. In this sense, the part in Chapter 7 concerned with the dialectic between intuition and idealization may be said to belong to this middle subject; and it can, in many respects, proceed independently of comprehensive alternative philosophies of mathematics. Indeed, its content seems to me to share with Rawls's theory the desirable characteristic of being close to what belongs to the overlapping consensus.

On a different level, I would hold that, just as the development of logic and the foundations of mathematics from Frege to Gödel played an important part in arriving at the theory of meaning as we now know it, so further development of moral theory (in the sense of Rawls) and of the foundations of mathematics (in my sense) may help us arrive at a more substantive and better structured epistemology.

For the present, it is easier to say something definite about how further advance of moral philosophy and the philosophy of mathematics depend, respectively and perhaps also conjointly, on work on moral theory and the foundations of mathematics. For instance, in both cases the work improves our understanding of the relation between constructivism and Platonism (or rational intuitionism) in mathematics and in moral judgments.

In abstract terms, both moral philosophy and the philosophy of mathematics face two apparently elusive basic questions: (1) In physics we talk

about the physical world, which we believe to be solid and to exist independently; but what are we talking *about* in mathematics or in making
moral judgments? (2) How is it possible to discover what is true about
issues in morality and mathematics, since we seem to appeal—as we do
not in physics—merely to thinking or reasoning about them? In other
words, in both cases we face (1) the ontological question of subject matter
or grounds of truth, and (2) the epistemological problem of justifying our
belief and explaining our agreement (or disagreement) by appealing to the
possibility of some suitable contact between us and the subject matter.

Given these problems, it is easy to see why constructivism is, in a fundamental way, more attractive than Platonism, since we are inclined to
believe that we know what we construct. In contrast, Platonism seems to
have to project from the observed objectivity (in the sense of intersubjective sharability) to an objective reality and then face the problem of
its accessibility to us. However, at least in the case of mathematics, we
have learned through experience that there are many sharable and shared
beliefs which demonstrably go beyond what can possibly be justified on
the basis of constructivism. As a result, we have to choose between
excluding those beliefs and finding some other account of their acceptability. And Platonism is the familiar proposal on the side of toleration.

Initially Rawls seems to suggest that his theory, by constructing the
principles of justice, refutes moral Platonism (1971:39): "A refutation of
intuitionism consists in presenting the sort of constructive criteria that are
said not to exist." Later he distinguishes political constructivism from
moral constructivism, such as Kant's, and emphasizes that a constructivist
political conception is compatible with all reasonable comprehensive
views—including, in particular, moral Platonism or realism or rational
intuitionism.

10.3.5   First, it is crucial for political liberalism that its constructivist conception does not contradict rational intuitionism, since constructivism tries to avoid
opposing any comprehensive doctrine.

10.3.6   The reason such a conception may be the focus of an overlapping consensus of comprehensive doctrines is that it develops the principles of justice from
public and shared ideals of society as a fair system of competition and of citizens
as free and equal by using the principles of their common practical reason (Rawls
1993:90).

Rawls contrasts his political constructivism with both rational intuitionism and Kant's moral constructivism, to indicate that it is compatible
with both views and that it has an account of objectivity which is sufficient for a shared public basis of justification (ibid.:90–116). For my purpose of comparing the relation between constructivism and Platonism in
mathematics with the corresponding relation in morality, I match political

Platonism—which restricts rational intuitionism to the political realm as Rawls contrasts political with moral constructivism—with Platonism in number theory, which restricts Platonism in mathematics to the theory of numbers.

Rawls seems to suggest that, as far as we know, even though political Platonism and political constructivism have different conceptions of objectivity or truth, they lead to the same collection of objective or true considered political judgments, at least with respect to the sense of justice of those reasonable persons who live in a well-ordered democratic society. If something like this is true, constructivism has, as I said before, a clear advantage over Platonism in the applicable universe of discourse.

In contrast, in the realm of number theory, we know that, even though every judgment on the properties and relations of natural numbers that is justifiable (or objective or true) constructively is also objectively true according to Platonism, there are judgments that are true for Platonism but not for constructivism. That is why, in order to narrow the range of disagreement between constructivism and Platonism in number theory, we have to—after agreeing that the judgments which are both Platonically and constructively true have a higher degree of clarity and certainty than those which are only Platonistically true—consider the naturalness and the acceptability of the extensions which lead us from constructive to Platonistic number theory, from the potential to the actual infinite.

Of course, as Rawls emphasizes (1993:118), given the many obstacles in political judgment, even among reasonable persons, we will not reach agreement all the time, or perhaps even much of the time. In this respect, number theory is certainly different: we believe we can reach agreement all the time, at least if we distinguish explicitly between constructively and Platonistically true. This difference suggests to me that reflections on number theory and on political judgments are helpful, in different ways, to our philosophical investigations: the philosophy of number theory serves as a precise, ideal model, and political philosophy as a widely accessible, rich model to illustrate, in a restricted domain, the complexity of philosophy generally.

For example, we may compare Rawls's specification of the essentials of a conception of objectivity (1993:110–116) with Gödel's emphasis on the axiomatic method. In considering mathematical reasoning and judgment, we rarely question their objectivity—at least in the sense of intersubjective agreement. Yet people often question the objectivity of moral and political reasoning and judgment. In this regard, objectivity in philosophy shares more features with the latter than with the former. At the same time, the objectivity of a judgment in mathematics, as in morality, is independent of having a suitable explanation within a causal view of knowledge. In this connection, Rawls says:

10.3.7 Here I should add that I assume that common-sense knowledge (for example, our perceptual judgments), natural science and social theory (as in economics and history), and mathematics are (or can be) objective, perhaps each in their own appropriate way. The problem is to elucidate how they are, and to give a suitably systematic account. Any argument against objectivity of moral and political reasoning that would, by parallel reasoning applied against common sense, or natural science, or mathematics, show them not to be objective, must be incorrect (ibid.:118).

If we compare the conception of objectivity of political constructivism with those of Platonism and constructivism in number theory, we see that the former brings out the full range of the complexity of possible conceptions of objectivity in a more explicit manner. In the case of number theory, we have axiom systems for both classical and constructivist number theory. We are tempted to say that a judgment in number theory is objective or correct if and only if it is provable in the axiom system, and that we can see that the axioms and the rules of inference of the axiom system are indeed objective and correct.

Indeed, we may also be inclined to say that we can see that the principles of Rawls's theory of justice are true, so that a judgment in that theory is objective or correct if and only if it follows from these principles. However, as Rawls indicates, much more is involved in this case than a conception of objectivity based on an idealized interpretation of the axiomatic method. In the first place, we do not arrive at the principles of justice by an analysis or by "intuiting the essence" of the concept of justice. As a matter of fact, we did not arrive at the axioms of number theory in this way either.

It seems to me that generally in every domain, from the concept of natural number to that of justice, each of us begins with certain interrelated firm beliefs which, we assume, are shared by others who are similarly situated in an appropriate way. These beliefs or judgments, which are presumed to be correct or objective, are the initial data from which we try to forge a conception of objectivity for the relevant domain.

In every domain we make considered judgments at all levels of generality. In order to arrive at some sort of systematization of our considered judgments, we reflect at each stage on the relations both between such judgments and between them and our intuition. In this process we continually modify our considered judgments with a view to finding, eventually, a set of considered judgments in reflective equilibrium.

In the case of number theory, we believe we have reached such a state and, moreover, organized the considered judgments in elegant axiom systems—one for the Platonistic view and one for the constructivist view. In the case of the theory of justice, we have not reached such a conclusion. In every case, we develop a conception of objectivity which serves as a framework of and a guide to our quest for a stable system of present and future considered judgments.

As Rawls indicates, all conceptions of objectivity share certain common features. Each proposal specifies a conception of correct judgment, together with its associated public norms, by which we can evaluate the conclusions reached on the basis of evidence and reasoning after discussion and due reflection (ibid.:110, 112, 121). In particular, it implies a criterion for distinguishing the objective from the subjective viewpoint. The ultimate court of appeal is the intuition of every suitably situated person and the belief that agreement can ultimately be reached in a majority of cases for the considered judgments and their systematization, whether we use Platonism (rational intuitionism) or constructivism as the intermediate link (ibid.:112).

Generally, as we know from experience, there are controversies over philosophical and political judgments which our continued efforts have failed to resolve. We feel that two or more incompatible judgments may sometimes be regarded as objective, as far as we can determine. In this sense, *objective* need not always coincide with *true*, since, by definition, incompatible judgments cannot all be true. For this reason, another essential feature of a conception of objectivity is that, as Rawls expresses it,

10.3.8   We should be able to explain the failure of our judgments to converge by such things as the burdens of judgment: the difficulties of surveying and assessing all the evidence, or else the delicate balance of competing reasons on opposite sides of the issue, either of which leads us to expect that reasonable persons may differ. Thus, much important disagreement is consistent with objectivity, as the burdens of judgment allow (ibid.:121; compare 54–58).

Rawls's notion of *reflective equilibrium* aptly captures a fundamental component of methodology which many of us have groped after. He elaborates this notion, and the related notion of *due reflection*, in various contexts, including his two published books and a book manuscript in preparation (see Rawls 1971:48–51, index; 1993: index; and forthcoming: section 10, chap. 1). Even though he confines many of his observations to their application to political judgments related to the concept of justice, it is clear that most are also applicable to judgments involved in many areas of philosophical discussion.

For Rawls, *considered judgments* are those given when conditions are favorable to the exercise of our powers of reason. We view some judgments as *fixed points*, judgments we never expect to withdraw. We would like to make our own judgments both more consistent with one another and more in line with the considered judgments of others, without resorting to coercion. For this purpose, each of us strives for judgments and conceptions in full reflective equilibrium; that is, an equilibrium that is both *wide*—in the sense that it has been reached after careful consideration of alternative views—and *general*—in the sense that the same conception is affirmed in everyone's considered judgments. Thus, full reflective equilibrium can serve as a basis of public justification; which is nonfoundationalist in the following sense: no specific kind of considered judgment, no particular level of generality, is thought to carry the whole weight of public justification.

As I understand these observations, I find them agreeable; indeed, they seem to express my own beliefs better than I can. It is not clear to me, however, that Gödel would also find them congenial. Some of his assertions suggest that for him the weight of justification is primarily or ultimately carried by our perception of the primitive concepts of a domain, with sufficient clarity to determine the correct or true axioms about them—as stable considered judgments which define the range of the conception of objectivity and truth in this domain. Sometimes, however, for example, in his Cantor paper, he also speaks of another criterion for the truth of axioms, namely their fruitfulness (*CW*2:261, 269). It is possible that Gödel's appeal to our intuition to capture the correct axioms, as contrasted with use of reflective equilibrium, is a matter of emphasis for the sake of recommending his belief that we should in the first place concentrate on the fundamental in philosophy.

Since Gödel is in favor of Husserl's methodology, and we have available more extended written considerations of the matter by Husserl, one obvious idea for trying to understand Gödel's view is to study Husserl's work directly.

Dagfinn Follesdal has recently published an essay (1988) in which he analyzes the method of reflective equilibrium and uses quotations from Husserl to show that Husserl accepted this method. We might, therefore, stretch a point to infer that Gödel too can be interpreted as accepting this method. Quite apart from this elusive task of interpretation, I find Follesdal's assimilation of what are commonly regarded as distinct approaches to philosophy somewhat tenuous. My main discomfort is with his characterization and distinction of diverse methodologies. For example, in commenting on "the universally accepted view that Husserl was a foundationalist," he asserts:

10.3.9 There are excuses for this interpretation in Husserl's own writings. Husserl often writes as if he held that we can attain some infallible, absolutely certain insight from which the rest of our knowledge can be built up in a Cartesian fashion.

10.3.10 The way I interpret Husserl, his seemingly foundationalist statements are mere surface appearances. I shall now argue that far from being a foundationalist he is on the contrary a "holist" and has a view on justification very similar to that which has been set forth by Nelson Goodman, John Rawls, and others [e.g., W. V. Quine (1951)], and which I will call the "reflective equilibrium" view (Follesdal 1988:115, 119).

Follesdal seems to identify foundationalism with the very strong view that we can attain certain infallible, absolutely certain insights from which all our knowledge can be built up. In this sense, Gödel was, as he himself emphasized, definitely not a foundationalist. We can also agree that Husserl's mature view was not foundationalist in this sense. Nonetheless, most of us feel that there are major components in Husserl's and Gödel's related approaches to philosophy which are different from those of most philosophers who are *not* foundationalists in this strong sense. In my opinion, this negative characteristic, because it is so inclusive, is not of much help in distinguishing different positions.

According to Follesdal, Husserl, Goodman, Rawls, and Quine are all "holists" who hold the "reflective equilibrium" view. But this grouping seems to me to conceal several crucial differences which are important for one's approach to philosophy. For example, Quine's pragmatic holism is associated with a kind of *gradualism*, which is illustrated by his assertion: "But in point of epistemological footing the physical objects and the gods differ only in degree and not in kind" (Quine 1951, cited in Follesdal 1988:119). In contrast, I prefer to use the term *qualitative factualism* to describe Rawls's approach and my own. In other words, I believe that Rawls agrees with me in recognizing the importance of qualitative differences in the study of philosophy.

Another essential task is to reconcile the view of Rawls with the avowedly a priori approach of Husserl and Gödel. Elsewhere in the present work I have made some tentative observations about the difficult notion of the a priori. In this connection, Follesdal gives an illuminating explication of Husserl's conception:

10.3.11 Also, Husserl characterizes in all his writings phenomenology as a study of the *a priori*. This makes it natural to assimilate him to Kant and Kant's foundationalism. However, Husserl means something different with "*a priori*" than does Kant. For Husserl, the *a priori* is that which we anticipate, that which we expect to find, given the noema we have. Phenomenology studies and attempts to chart these anticipations, but as we know, our anticipations often go wrong, our experiences turn out differently from what we expected, and again and again we have to revise our views and our expectations (Follesdal 1988:115).

I find this explication of the a priori attractive and helpful. It is very likely that Gödel also adopted this conception. Indeed, one might wish to say that this approach to the a priori, with its attempt to chart our anticipations, is a form of foundationalism more reasonable than Follesdal's strong version. However that may be and however we are to apply the a priori element in Husserl's sense, such a view is different—at least in terms of the actual assertions in words—from that of Rawls, who says explicitly: "The analysis of moral concepts and the a priori, however traditionally understood, is too slender a basis" (1971:51). Of course, it is possible that Rawls does not include Husserl's conception of the a priori in this statement.

To understand Husserl's important conception of the a priori, we have to grasp his difficult notion of the *noema*. According to Follesdal, "The noema is a structure. Our consciousness structures what we experience. How it structures it depends on our previous experiences, the whole setting of our present experience and a number of other factors" (Follesdal 1988:109). It seems to me that, in these terms, the thinking process is a succession of thinking acts such that I have a noema at each moment and use its accompanying a priori element in my consciousness to direct myself to obtain additional data from inside and outside my mind so as to arrive at my noema at the next moment. In this process, I go from my noema and my a priori outlook at one moment to those I experience at the next.

In this way it becomes clear that the a priori element is inescapable and plays a central part in all thinking. What distinguishes Husserl's approach from others cannot be just the recognition of this fact. Rather his phenomenology, as the study of the a priori, concentrates on clarifying the general features of this a priori element and charting the fundamental structure of what we anticipate. In contrast, most philosophers, like most people, do not try to study systematically the process of structuring what we experience to arrive at the noema. Rather we make use of the noema and the a priori without attempting to examine systematically what goes on in the bottom region of them. It seems hard to argue that many of us are, unknowingly, using Husserl's method; for he was not himself happy with the way his avowed followers were using what they supposed to be his method.

In my opinion, Rawls's conscientious effort to distinguish his political conception of justice from comprehensive doctrines (1993:13, 175) provides an instructive illustration of how we may be able to carry out the attractive idea of separating and decomposing disagreements so as to reach agreement through an overlapping consensus on some important issues. His discussion on the burden of proof (ibid.:54–62) makes explicit some major reasons why reasonable persons may disagree on certain issues despite their sincere efforts to understand one another. It is, therefore, reasonable to be tolerant in such cases. Moreover, toleration is, for Rawls, a political virtue, and one of the virtues important for political cooperation (ibid.:194,157).

In the pursuit of philosophy, it is generally desirable to have more cooperation and to narrow the range of disagreement. One way to approach this ideal is to try to decompose disagreements, with a view to bringing to light, on the one hand, certain parts which can be seen to suggest promising research problems and, on the other hand, other parts where we can "explain the failure of our judgments to converge by such things as the burdens of judgment." If we can see and communicate convincingly that all or some of the components of an important disagreement are of one or the other of these two types, we shall have narrowed the range of disagreement and increased the feasibility of cooperation. Moreover, with regard to the parts of our disagreements which are seen to be of one of the two types, we have good reason to adopt an attitude of open-mindedness or toleration.

There is, of course, a third type of disagreement, which is typically divisive and which occurs when one or more of the parties misjudge the discrepancy between what they know and what they think they know. In situations where we believe we face a disagreement of this type, Rawls suggests proceeding in the following manner:

10.3.12 Yet disagreement may also arise from a lack of reasonableness, or rationality, or conscientiousness of one or more of the persons involved. But if we say this, we must be careful that the evidence for these failings is not simply the disagreement itself. We must have independent grounds identifiable in the particular circumstances for thinking such causes of disagreement are at work. These grounds must also be in principle recognizable by those who disagree with us (ibid.:121).

10.4 The Place of Philosophy and Some of Its Tasks

A fundamental fact of life is our awareness of gaps between our wishes and their consummation and of conflicts of wishes—both between our own different wishes and with the wishes of others. If all wishes were automatically consummated, there would be no gap between wish and fact, no need to exert ourselves, no conflicts, and no disagreements. If there were no conflicts of wishes, the consummation of any wish would be of positive value.

As it is, we are constantly aware of a gap between a wish and its consummation, which may be easy or hard or impossible to bridge. We have other wishes too, and others have their own wishes. To use our resources and efforts to maximize satisfaction and minimize disappointment, we must select, arrange, and modify our own wishes and even those of others. To do so we need to know the relevant facts about the objective situation, including facts about ourselves and about other people.

Values evolve, through a kind of consensus, as guides for us in our selection and arrangement of our wishes. They are based on our evolving knowledge (or, rather, beliefs) about facts, and they aim to bridge, or at least narrow, the gap between wish and fact. Generally we learn to choose among values in order to simplify the task of finding all the complex facts relevant to the consummation of our various wishes. Occasionally, exceptional people come up with influential value systems which summarize human experience in more or less novel and convincing ways.

Most of the time, most of us are primarily concerned with local problems which arise from the limited contexts of our daily lives, which may include working as a member of some profession. Philosophy is not alone in trying to be coherent and comprehensible (or communicable); what distinguishes it from other pursuits is its ambition to be comprehensive, to look at the most universal in its full richness. Given the ambiguity of this ambition and its formidable range and remoteness from what we really know, it is not surprising that philosophy takes many different shapes; it has been split into many specialized parts and exhibits no clear pattern of accumulation of its fruits.

It is clear that we are all concerned with the interplay of knowledge and action, of wish and fact, and of desire and belief. The gap between wish and consummation produces in us an awareness of the gap between what we know and what we need to guide us to act in such a way that we can consummate our wish. Knowledge is the primary tool to aid us in this pursuit. Freud, for example, speaks of the frequent conflicts between the reality principle and the pleasure principle; we all look for knowledge that would decrease or eliminate such conflicts.

That is why the ideal of philosophy as a guide to action is attractive. Religions and grand doctrines such as Marxism also offer us worldviews that propose to guide our actions by linking them to certain promised future states. We do not know, however, that the promised states will indeed materialize, or what actions are the right ones under many circumstances. Moreover, it is hard to find ways to test objectively whether the beliefs offered to us are plausible or not: we see no way to determine what facts decisively support or disturb the belief that certain humanly possible actions will lead to the desired future states. In Chapter 3 I have discussed some of Gödel's ideas on philosophy as a comprehensive guide to action.

One familiar approach in philosophy is to postpone the task of seeking universal guidance for action—leaving it in the background—and to direct our attention instead to the general concern for attaining a true image of the world in thought. In this task we are immediately faced with the gap between mind and the world, between the inner and the outer.

We cannot help seeing things through our own conceptual or inter-
pretive schemes. It is as though we are always wearing glasses that distort
to some extent what we are seeing. When we think about the relation
between our thoughts and the world, we can think only about *our thoughts*
about the world, about our thoughts, and about their interrelations. For
instance, the distinction between mind and matter is in the first place a
division in experience, in thought. In this sense, whenever we think or
talk about the world, there is an implicit qualification that we refer to the
world *as seen by us*. It is inevitable that we tend to disregard this qualification most of the time.

When we are reminded of it, however, we become aware of a conflict
between two senses of some of the main words or concepts in philosophy—such as *world, truth, knowledge, certainty, object, thought*. We may be
said to have both an ordinary perspective—that drops the qualification—
and an extraordinary one—that attends to it. What underlies this sense of
conflict might be called the *homocentric predicament*, which seems to correspond to what is sometimes spoken of as the *problem of transcendence*. It
is taken seriously in historical philosophy. Kant, for example, answers the
problem by his dualism; Hegel and Husserl strive to bypass it by absorb-
ing realism into their versions of idealism.

This collective theoretical predicament of the species is related to the
egocentric predicament of every person and the *ethnocentric predicament* of
every community or association or society, the consequences of which we
try to overcome in practice by developing ways to communicate with one
another and to reach mutual understanding. Clearly such attempts are important for resolving or reducing disagreements and conflicts between
individuals and between groups.

The homocentric predicament is one indication that, if we are interested
in the whole, the inner and the mind are more accessible to us than the
outer and the world. That is, I believe, the reason why we pay so much
attention to logic and the power of the mind in philosophy, as illustrated
by the extended discussions devoted to these topics in this book. Logic
in the broad sense tries to capture what is universal within the inner, of
which mathematics constitutes an integral part that is conspicuously stable
and powerful. The power of the mind determines the limits of the inner
and the dimensions of the gap between it and the outer. One fruitful, and
less elusive, approach to the delimitation of the power of the mind is to
compare it with the power of bodies and computers.

The gap between a wish and its consummation can be bridged only by
appropriate actions, which require the appropriate application of power or
strength, which, in turn, usually depends on the possession of appropriate
beliefs. We learn from experience that our beliefs often do not agree with
what turns out to be the case. This kind of experience gradually leads us

to the notion of *confirmed belief*, thence to the concept of *knowledge*, which is an idealized limit case of better and better confirmed beliefs. The attempt to study, systematically and globally, the gap between belief and knowledge is, as we know, the central concern of epistemology, or the theory of knowledge, which has become a fundamental part of philosophy from Descartes on.

Philosophy as discourse and conversation uses language and words as its primary, or even exclusive, vehicle in ways which are similar to but also different from those of science, fiction, poetry, and history. The use of words to express and communicate thoughts encounters the problems that arise from the familiar gap between seeing and saying—between what I see and what I say, as well as between what I say and what you see *through* what I say, after hearing or reading it and thinking about it on the basis of the parts relevant to what is in you. Science and literature solve this problem in different ways, with different advantages.

The stage from seeing to saying is part of the move from presentation to representation. The stage from saying by one to seeing by another is part of communication, which produces a presentation in one through a representation by another.

Saying, however, is only one way of communicating. The complex relation between presentation (intention) and representation (expression) leaves room for showing one thing (say the universal or the whole) by saying another (say the particular or a part). Literature, for instance, tries to show the universal by saying the particular; similes and metaphors show one thing by saying something else; action, tone, and gesture can be shown in a drama or film but they can only be said or told in a novel (see Booth 1961: chaps. 1 and 8).

The interest in communication by language shifts our attention to the understanding of what is said as a precondition for determining its truth—from the justification of belief to the clarification of meaning. The subjective and fluid character of the content of seeing stimulates, for the purpose of assuring communication of what is intended, a direct appeal to the connection between words and deeds, to bypass the interference from passing through the mental. The attention to the actual use of words in the work of the later Wittgenstein is an illustration of this tendency.

By being concerned with the whole, philosophy hovers over the limits of thought and language. We represent the world in our thoughts and then represent our thoughts in language. We understand another's thought through what the other person says, with the help of an imperfectly shared correlation between language and reality. It is natural to consider the limits of the power of thought to capture reality, as well as the limits of the power of language to capture thought or reality and to communicate thought between two souls. Indeed, the limits of thought are a central concern of Kant's philosophy, and Wittgenstein often considers, implicitly and explicitly, the limits of language.

Seeing things clearly has value, because, on the whole and in the long run, as we learn from experience, it helps to see things clearly. When a wish is not automatically consummated, we look for possible courses of action that are likely to succeed. For this purpose, it is usually necessary to know certain relevant facts; that is, what is the case. The belief that a course of action is possible and will lead to the desired outcome depends on the belief, based on experience, that certain things are repeated. A crucial part of this belief is the so-called *uniformity of nature:* the same effect follows the same cause.

In other words, we believe not only that there are repetitions, but also that there are *repetitions of succession*. A great deal of our effort in science and everyday life is devoted to the task of learning important and relevant repetitions of succession. At the same time, we are inclined to think that no two concrete things are entirely the same. Indeed, Leibniz has a principle of the *identity of indiscernibles*: "There is no such thing as two individuals indiscernible from each other.... Two drops of water, or milk, viewed with a microscope, will appear distinguishable from each other."

What are repeated are not the individuals, but certain other things, known variously as *properties* (or *attributes*) and *relations, forms, concepts, universals*, and so forth. Our central concern with repetition is the reason why abstraction, idealization, modeling, and so on are so important in life. The "problem of universals" is much discussed in philosophy: whether they exist independently of the individuals, whether they are mental, how they are related to the individuals, and so forth.

Our great interest in the repetitions of succession is probably the fundamental reason why mathematics is so important, for mathematics at its center is concerned with the form of the repetitions of sequences of events, of causal chains, and of chains of means and ends. When we see that a sequence of events leads to a desired outcome, we try to produce a repetition of the first member of the sequence with the expectation that the desired last term of it will also be repeated. In the words of Brouwer,

10.4.1 Proper to man is a faculty which accompanies all his interactions with nature, namely the faculty of taking a *mathematical view* of his life, of observing in the world repetitions of sequences of events, i.e. of causal systems in time. The basic phenomenon therein is the simple intuition of time, in which repetition is possible in the form: "thing in time and again thing," as a consequence of which moments of life break up into sequences of things which differ qualitatively. The sequences thereupon concentrate in the intellect into mathematical sequences, not *sensed* but *observed* (1975:53).

From this perspective, we gain a reliable basis for clarifying the apparent mystery that mathematics, precise and largely autonomous, has turned out to have such wide and rich applications in the study of imprecise empirical phenomena. At the same time, the precision, clarity, and certainty of knowledge in mathematics provide us with a model and an ideal for the pursuit of knowledge. Consequently, reflections on the nature of mathematics are useful in philosophy by supplying us with transparent examples of general issues in the philosophy of knowledge, such as constructivism and realism.

The contrast between the discovery view and the construction view of mathematics may be seen as part of the general issue between realism and antirealism (in particular, positivism). The mathematical world is introduced as an analogue of the physical world. Whether or in what sense the mathematical world exists is a controversial matter. In contrast, few of us doubt that the physical world is real. At the same time, there are also disagreements over the relation between our knowledge of the physical world and what is to be taken as its real situation. For instance, one way of characterizing the famous debate between Einstein and Niels Bohr on the interpretation of quantum mechanics is to say that Einstein is a realist and Bohr is an antirealist.

More generally, the homocentric predicament mentioned above reminds us, not only of the fact that our present knowledge of the world is very incomplete, but also of the possibility that there is a gap between reality as it is and what is knowable by us. We know that there is much we do not know; we do not even know how much of reality we *can* know in principle. Knowledge is part of life and, in the first place, a distillation from our beliefs and attitudes which, together with our desires and feelings, determines what we do under different circumstances. What is known or knowable is more relevant to our conscious efforts in life than what is real but not knowable by us. We would like to believe, but have no conclusive evidence for believing that what is real is always knowable by us.

Kant distinguishes the knowable world of *phenomena* from the largely unknowable world of *noumena* (or *Ding-an-sich*). Buddhism and Taoism, each in its own way, take reality to be something unsayable, something not capturable by language and thought. At the same time, they are much concerned with saying things about the real as it is, with a view to helping us to understand it in order to attain our salvation. Clearly there are alternative ways to construe what is real, and the very attempt to describe reality as it is by propositions imposes a limitation on the extent to which it can be captured.

If we confine our attention to propositional knowledge, the relation between what is real and what is knowable is commonly discussed in terms of the relation between the true and the knowable. In other words, our natural inclination is to adopt what is called the *correspondence theory of truth*: we consider a proposition p true when it corresponds to what is the case, that is, to a fact in the world; this correspondence to a fact is the condition under which p is true. But in order to connect this condition to our knowledge, we also face the related question of the conditions under which we know that p is true.

Given this theory of truth, the (physical or mathematical or whatever) world embodies the real and anchors our concept of truth. Since, however, the real may be, for all we know, less accessible to us than the knowable, we may also choose either to use the concept of the knowable to anchor and define the concept of truth, or to use the former side by side with the latter. For instance, in the case of mathematics, it is common to identify the provable with the knowable. If we were also to identify the true with the provable, there would be no propositions that are true but not provable. Gödel's theorem shows that, for provability within any formal system, there always are such propositions. But we do not know whether there are such propositions for our unrestricted concept of provability. Indeed, both Hilbert and Gödel conjecture that all true mathematical propositions are provable. Since, however, we do not have a good understanding of the unrestricted, or "absolute" concept of provability, we tend to retain truth as a separate concept and use it to measure the power of better articulated, restricted conceptions of provability.

Even though the concepts of real, true, and knowable all are highly abstract and subject to alternative explications, there are certain characterisics of the real and the true which are commonly accepted. Consider the familiar identification of the real with the physical world. We see this world as consisting of physical objects which have certain properties and relations. Given any objects and properties and relations, we believe that either an object has a property or not, but not both, and that either several objects stand in a relation or not, but not both. As a result, when we try to describe the real by means of propositions, we believe that, for every proposition p, either p or its opposite (its negation, its denial), not-p, is true (the principle of excluded middle), but not both (the principle of noncontradiction). We believe that both principles hold for the real, regardless of our capability to know in each case whether p or not-p is in fact true.

If we choose to replace the concept of the real by the concept of the knowable, then it is possible to ask, for each proposed conception of the knowable, whether the two principles (of noncontradiction and of excluded middle) remain true for all propositions. For instance, it may be that the principle of excluded middle remains true for all *simple* (in one sense or another) propositions but not for all *complex* propositions. It may be that, for certain propositions p, neither p nor not-p is knowable; this is Brouwer's position with regard to mathematical propositions. One familiar way of interpreting the "measurement problem" in quantum mechanics is to say that we cannot know both the position and the momentum of a particle at a given instant t. Consequently, if the real is nothing but the knowable, either the position or the momentum may have two different values at t.

A natural choice is to require of our concept of the knowable that, for every proposition p, we are capable of knowing either p or not-p (to be true). If there are things which appear to be propositions but do not satisfy this condition, we may say that they are meaningless propositions or pseudopropositions. For instance, the logical positivists identify the meaningful with the verifiable and the falsifiable and consider metaphysical propositions to be meaningless.

As is well known, it is difficult to design a sufficiently broad and precise notion of verifiability or falsifiability to cover all the intended cases and, at the same time, to retain a distinctive position. For instance, according to Carnap, Einstein once said to him: "If positivism were now liberalized to such an extent, there would be no longer any difference between our [namely, the positivists'] conception and any other philosophical view" (Carnap:963:38). This example illustrates a familiar difficulty with philosophy: views are often so vague that we are not able to see whether or how they are connected with definite and recognizable disagreements.

When such connections are implied or asserted, we have an opportunity both to understand the philosophical views better and to check them, with more confidence, against our own beliefs. For instance, the different views of Einstein and Bohr on the interpretation of quantum mechanics give us a link between specific scientific projects and their different general outlooks. Gödel believes that his discovery view of mathematics played a fundamental part in helping him to accomplish so much in logic. His elaboration of this belief may be studied with a view both to understanding what his relevant discovery view is and to evaluating how much his belief may be seen as evidence for such a discovery view.

We may say that Platonism in mathematics is realism in mathematics. In view of the abstract character of mathematical objects, realism in mathematics is not as widely accepted as physical realism, since few of us would doubt that the physical world is real. However, as physics itself becomes more and more abstract, the fundamental constituents of the physical world, such as the gravitational field and the elementary particles, become more like mathematical objects than familiar physical objects of the type exemplified by tables and chairs. Nonetheless, physics is related to the physical world in a different way than mathematics is. The difference between mathematics and physics is also revealed through the history of the two subjects: development of physical theories consists of refinements and radical changes of view (revolutions) on the same subject matter (namely, space, time, and matter), whereas advances in mathematics have mainly taken the form of expansion of its subject matter.

10.5 Alternative Philosophies and Logic as Metaphilosophy

In his course on the elements of philosophy, C. D. Broad briefly characterized one method of philosophy as "Kant's critical method without the peculiar applications Kant made of it." Wittgenstein commented on this method in his 1931–1932 lectures:

10.5.1   This is the right sort of approach. Hume, Descartes and others had tried to start with one proposition such as "Cogito ergo sum" and work from it to others. Kant disagreed and started with what we know to be so and so, and went on to examine the validity of what we suppose we know (Lee 1980:73–74).

To begin with what we know to be so may be taken as a characterization of factualism. In order to examine the validity of what we suppose we know, we have to locate certain fixed points from which we can approach the task of distinguishing the valid parts of what we suppose we know from the rest. It conforms well with our ordinary conception of logic to say that the fixed points that serve as instruments for examining valid beliefs are what constitute logic. It may, therefore, be asserted that, according to this approach, logic occupies a central place in philosophy. The task is to clarify this conception of logic and consider how it is to be employed in the study of philosophy.

In order to serve their designated purpose, the fixed points themselves have to belong to the valid parts of our beliefs. Factualism solves this problem by identifying them with our considered judgments in reflective equilibrium, on the basis of our present knowledge. The application of logic to philosophy includes both the development of positive philosophical views on the basis of logic and the adjudication of alternative views. For example, to decompose a disagreement is to break it into parts that can then be checked against the fixed points; a philosophical view can be discredited by showing that it fails to do justice to what we know or that it assumes as known things we do not know.

To examine the validity of beliefs is to distinguish between—and develop the appropriate attitude toward—knowledge and ignorance. The task of locating and applying the fixed points is intimately connected with our quest for certainty and clarity, which, as we know from experience, should, ideally, satisfy appropriate requirements that are neither too strong nor too weak.

We constantly face the problem of not possessing the knowledge necessary to realize the purpose at hand. An appeal to unjustified beliefs sometimes does lead to the desired result, but is, as we have learned from experience, likely to fail. The task of separating knowledge from igno-rance, or the known from the unknown, is, in its distinct contexts and forms, clearly a common concern. A related task is to find the appropriate balance of confidence with caution. The "natural attitude" is typically ignorant of our ignorance. To correct this complacency, philosophy tends to demand so much from knowledge that it often denies that we possess knowledge even when we do (to the extent that knowledge is possible at all or is sufficient for the purpose at hand).

Socrates interprets the oracle's answer that "no one is wiser than Socrates," by giving as the reason: "I know that I have no wisdom [knowledge], small or great" (Plato, *Apology*:21). As advice, this story is helpful in that it encourages us to cultivate the philosophical habit of reminding ourselves that we have a natural tendency to adhere to un-examined beliefs. If, however, the implicit recommendation were taken literally, one would be at a loss when actions and decisions depend on a presumption of knowledge. Confucius is more judicious: "To know that you know when you do know and know that you do not know when you do not know—that is knowledge" (*Analects*, 2:17). In my opinion, the attempt to find and communicate this knowledge of our knowledge and ignorance may be seen as a definition of philosophy which agrees quite well with much of the actual history of philosophy.

An appropriate appreciation of the extent and degree of our ignorance offers constraints as well as opportunities. Awareness of ignorance can activate the instinct to overcome it and yield the opportunity to use the open space unoccupied by knowledge for speculations, conjectures, hy-potheses, and solutions of open problems, as well as other interplay of knowledge with ignorance.

We approach the ideal of being both judicious and original with differ-ent mixtures of caution and confidence, in which a major part is played by the felt conclusiveness of our views and their distance from the spirit of the time. Confidence is more or less a free gift to a solid citizen of the community of ideas, which is pervasive in the "village" where he or she works (at least if the village is powerful and confident). At the same time, in philosophy, this gift tends to be accompanied by the danger of paro-chialism, although opinions differ on what is parochial and whether it is a good thing. Each philosopher has an evolving but more or less consistent threshold that separates the thoughts he or she considers meaningful from the others. The assertability, correctness, and significance of these thoughts have much to do with the individual's line between knowledge and ignorance, as well as with the way he or she currently, and inartic-ulately, fits together all parts of the human experience.

In 1929 John Dewey published his Gifford Lectures *The Quest for Cer-tainty: A Study of the Relation of Knowledge and Action*, in which he criticized "philosophy's search for the immutable" and recommended the "naturalization of intelligence." It is obvious that the search in philosophy and science is for objective certainty, not just subjective certainty. The concept of *certainty* (in the objective sense) stands, however, in need of clarification, as we can see by taking into consideration the skeptical position, which denies the possibility of our ever possessing such certainty.

During the last year or two of his life, Wittgenstein studied the concept of certainty; the fruits of this study were afterward published in his *On Certainty* (1969). From the perspective of this study, Dewey's criticism of philosophy's search for the immutable may be seen as saying that it is a quest for a nonexistent kind of certainty. This study may also be seen as a remarkably thorough clarification of what I take to be a missing link between the aim of epistemology and the traditional a priori approach to it.

We see the world through our concepts. Even though we may improve our conceptual scheme, we are bound to it at each stage. This bondage, or relativity, is the source of our feeling that we have no absolute knowledge of anything. But in real life we do not deal with (absolute) certainty in such an ideal sense. That is why we find skepticism idle and, in practice, self-refuting.

The need to clarify the concept of certainty illustrates the close connection between the quest for certainty and the quest for clarity. We think of understanding a proposition as a precondition for knowing it to be true. Clarity is essential to understanding and to knowledge and the theory of knowledge. As Husserl, Wittgenstein, and Gödel all recognize, there are kinds and degrees of certainty and clarity. For instance, mathematical propositions possess a different kind of certainty and clarity from empirical propositions. Calculations with finite numbers have a higher degree of clarity and certainty than propositions involving the infinite. And so on. The relation between propositions and concepts of different kinds and degrees of clarity and certainty is, in my view, a major concern of philosophy.

One heuristic guide to the development of logic as metaphilosophy is the ideal of being able to see alternative philosophies as complementary. The fact that disagreements and conflicting views abound in philosophy is a given. Since the concepts of philosophy are often imprecise and have broad significance, the particularities of each philosopher are hard to exclude. For instance, individual philosophers are affected by and respond differently to the spirit of their times. Conceptions of and attitudes toward religion, art, science and technology, tradition and innovation, feeling and intellect, certainty and clarity, participation and distancing, sameness and difference, the formal and the intuitive, and so on differ from philosopher to philosopher. These conceptions and attitudes all play some part in each person's worldview and general philosophy. Because it is hard to render these factors explicit and articulate, the common desire to have others share our point of view suggests the approach of presenting, at least initially, only the conclusive and definite parts of our thoughts.

In a sense, logic is the instrument for singling out the definite and conclusive parts of our thoughts. And it is tempting to suggest that, within philosophy, such parts all belong to logic. In any case, according to the tradition of including under philosophy only purely a priori concepts and beliefs, one might as well identify philosophy with logic. I am inclined to think of the range of logic as consisting of all those concepts and beliefs which are universally acceptable on the basis of our common general experience—without having to depend on any special contingent experience. But such a conception of the logical is as difficult to render clear and definite as the concept of the a priori. I try, therefore, in the following discussion, to propose a more or less explicit specification of logic in this sense. It will, however, be clear that my tentative suggestions are only first steps toward capturing this vaguely felt natural conception of the logical.

An accessible starting point for me (or anyone) is to begin with the collection of my own considered judgments in reflective equilibrium and try to isolate the logical parts within it. An instructive example is to consider what is involved in trying to use my own convictions to accomplish the significant aim of decomposing philosophical disagreements.

Because each philosophy is such a complex web of belief, it is often difficult for me to attain the ideal of a complete decomposition, even for myself, of disagreements between two philosophers, that is, (a) to isolate those parts of their philosophical views which I can see as true or at least compatible; and (b) to analyze the remaining parts so as to locate their conflicting beliefs in a way that allows me to judge which side is right—because I have boiled them down to beliefs on which I do have considered convictions, pro or con.

Our philosophical beliefs are an integral part of our whole outlook on things, and they depend upon our total experience. They are intricately connected, and they touch the intuitions or considered convictions in reflective equilibrium (on different levels of generality and clarity) of the author and the reader at various (sometimes different) points, positively or negatively. The ideal is for the reader to agree with the author's beliefs at these points of contact and then to extend the agreement to all the other beliefs by way of their connections with these fixed points. On the other hand, if one finds certain points of definite disagreement with the author, one has a base from which to check the other beliefs by examining their connections with these fixed points.

When a philosophy, say Spinoza's *Ethics*, is presented as an axiom system, it is theoretically sufficient to judge the whole by evaluating just the axioms and the rules of inference, since the rest is supposed to follow automatically. In practice, most of us try to understand Spinoza's axioms by finding fixed points among their consequences, even though the axiomatic order makes it somewhat easier to check the interconnections. In any case, it seems clear that the axiomatic method is seldom explicitly used in philosophy.

In philosophy, the fundamental beliefs—as axioms or conclusions—often cannot be expressed both briefly and precisely, and the connections are often not in the form of exact inferences. The dialogue form used by Plato, Leibniz (in his essay on Locke's work), Berkeley, and, later, Wittgenstein (in a disguised form) seeks to spread out both the fixed points of contact with intuition and the formulation of the conclusions. Most philosophers communicate their ideas by using some mixture of deductions, dialogues, and loosely interconnected monologues.

Perennial philosophical controversies usually involve differences for which we are not able to find a sufficient number of stable fixed points to settle. The decomposition of disagreements by fixed points is helpful in such cases, narrowing the range of disagreement and isolating issues on which we have more shared beliefs. In distinguishing political philosophy explicitly from moral philosophy, Rawls seems to be consciously decomposing our major disagreements. When we choose to deal first with a comparatively precise special case of a general problem, we are also instinctively decomposing it. For instance, the large issues of Platonism and mind's superiority over computers are considered in this book mainly through the special case of mathematical thinking.

From a broader perspective, we may also see the development of the sciences such as physics and biology from parts of philosophy as guided by our natural desire to isolate problems we have learned to handle and to make the disciplines that study them as autonomous as possible. Mathematical logic has developed in this way under the decisive influence of the attempts by Frege, Brouwer, and Hilbert to deal in a precise manner with their philosophical concerns over the foundations of mathematics. The attempt at precision is a way to locate and extend the range of shared beliefs and to make that range autonomous.

I can think of several ways of trying to decompose a philosophical disagreement. One guiding principle is to look for situations in which different answers, supposedly to the same question, are in fact directed to different questions. Two philosophers may employ different conceptions or usages of the same crucial concept or word. Different attitudes toward the spirit of the time and toward concepts such as science may lead to different choices of conception and evidence. Another guiding principle is to strive for maximal use of the intuitions derived from what we know. For instance, the belief in classical mathematics may be decomposed into different parts so that one can move from some agreed-upon part, by natural extension, to other parts. Or perhaps one may find that the disputed issue, say political liberalism, actually belongs to the agreed-upon part. Once the disagreement is localized, there remains the task of adjudicating, say, the different conceptions and attitudes, a task in which we expect logic to be useful.

Logic as an activity of thought deals with the interplay, or the dialectic, between belief and action, the known and the unknown, form and content, or the formal and the intuitive. For this purpose, it is useful to select and isolate from what is taken to be known a universal part which may be seen, from a suitably mature perspective, to remain fixed and which can therefore serve as instrument throughout all particular instances of the interplay. It seems natural to view such a universal part as the content of logic.

Even though it seems to me reasonable to accept this vague characterization of logic, it fails, in its application, to determine once and for all the range of logic. There are alternative answers to the question: What is to be required of the concepts and the propositions of this universal part? Different choices can be and have been made with respect to (a) the kind and the degree of their certainty and universality, and (b) the degree of precision and systematic character of their codification. These different choices, which have often been linked to the different conceptions of apriority, necessity, and analyticity, have led to the different conceptions of logic in the history of philosophy.

What is at stake may be construed as a determination of the universal receptive scheme of the human mind, which is to capture the underlying intersection of the diverse schemes actually employed by human beings, which are presumed to be potentially convergent. A convenient starting point is the interactive development of each agent's picture of the world. In his *On Certainty*, Wittgenstein characterizes the origin of this picture thus:

10.5.2 The child learns to believe a host of things. I.e. it learns to act according to these beliefs. Bit by bit there forms a system of what is believed, and in that system some things stand unshakably fast and some are more or less liable to change.... But I did not get my picture of the world by satisfying myself of its correctness. No: it is the inherited background against which I distinguish true and false (1969:144, 94).

As we grow and develop, we do, consciously or unconsciously, try to satisfy ourselves of the correctness of our individual pictures of the world by learning from experience. Indeed, the study of philosophy aims at arriving at a picture of the world that will satisfy us of its correctness. And in this pursuit, logic, with its ideal of capturing the things that stand fast in all reasonable systems of beliefs, occupies a distinguished place as the basis and instrument for organizing our own pictures of the world and adjudicating alternative pictures.

Logic, in this sense, tries to find and apply the sharable fixed points within the range of what we suppose we know. We can begin only with our own fixed points and try to isolate those among them which we believe to be sharable. For example, I have no doubt that mathematics belongs to the sharable part. Once I propose a system of what I take to be the sharable fixed points, others may disagree and wish to add—or subtract from it—certain things. When this process is continued, we may sometimes reach a provisional system in reflective equilibrium for all or most reasonable agents.

Logic in this sense may include certain empirical propositions that are derived from our gross experience and based on what we take to be general facts, even though in some cases we might disagree over which to include or exclude. To this extent the conception of logic suggested here is different from the traditional one, which excludes empirical propositions. Wittgenstein, for instance, asserts:

10.5.3   I want to say: propositions of the form of empirical propositions, and not only propositions of logic, form the foundation of all operating with thoughts (with language) (1969:401).

I am proposing to identify the propositions of logic with those which "form the foundation of all operating with thoughts," rather than beginning with the stipulation that no empirical propositions can belong to logic. In particular, I believe that logic includes mathematics and mathematical logic as we know them, as well as all the propositions intended by Wittgenstein in the above comment.

I am tempted to include within logic certain principles which are not necessarily true come what may, but rather are true come what may within a wide range of allowed-for surprises (see Wang 1985a:57–58) such as: the "principle of necessary reason": there must be special reasons for differences; sameness implies sameness; and the "principle of precarious sufficiency": what survives in nature and in life requires only the satisfaction of certain minimal conditions rather than any abstractly optimal conditions. Clearly, the use of such principles in each instance demands careful consideration of the relevant factors that supply the convincing detailed evidence and arguments.

My main interest here is to consider logic as the instrument for decomposing and resolving philosophical disagreements. Given the conception of logic based on sharable fixed points of different systems of belief, it is possible to introduce also a conception of *local logic*, which embodies the sharable fixed points of the belief systems of the members of a group. For instance, when Rawls conjectures that justice as fairness can gain the support of an overlapping consensus in a familiar type of society, we may view the overlapping consensus as part of the local logic of such a society (Rawls 1993:15).

We consider a belief objective when it is sharable by an appropriate group, or when it is sharable by all human beings, or when it is true in the ideal sense of corresponding to what is the case (in objective reality). On the one hand, we are inclined to think that the subjective component is the ultimate basis of judgment which is directly accessible to each of us. On the other hand, the intersubjective component is, in practice, a less fluid and more reliable guide to the formation of our considered judgments, because of the intimate involvement of thinking with the use of language, which is basically an intersubjective medium. Indeed, the emphasis on what *we* know—rather than what *I* know—implicitly acknowledges the primacy of the intersubjective in trying to determine the content of logic and to decompose philosophical disagreements.

In this sense, when I try to improve my picture of the world by satisfying myself of its correctness or to replace subjective beliefs by objective beliefs, the egocentric predicament is a less troublesome problem than the ethnocentric and homocentric predicaments. Moreover, in the pursuit of truth, much of the time we are striving for objectivity, that is, for beliefs that are expected to enjoy stable universal agreement, potentially if not actually. Indeed, as the work of Rawls illustrates, intersubjective agreement within a suitable group is often of fundamental practical importance.

The slogan about respecting facts is, in practice, a recommendation to respect and fully exploit what we know from our actual cumulative experience. I believe I can single out two guiding principles: that of "limited mergeability" and that of "presumed innocence."—These principles are meant to indicate two general ways in which we can begin to show our respect for facts and move from blind to considered respect. It is probable that there are other principles to which I also appeal but fail to see distinctly enough to formulate.

The first principle is an attempt to get at the asymmetrical relation between having less experience and having more. One famous appeal to this relation is Mill's observation in *Utilitarianism*: "Of two pleasures, if there be one to which all or almost all who have experience of both given a decided preference, irrespective of any feeling of moral obligation to prefer it, that is the more desirable pleasure" (1863, near the beginning of Chapter 2). The difficulties with this principle have been discussed extensively in the literature; it is likely, however, that the comparison of beliefs faces fewer problems than the comparison of pleasures does. I would like to find some suitably qualified analogue with regard to our knowledge and ignorance.

One obstacle to the satisfactory formulation of such a principle is the difficulty of finding a form that would enjoy a reasonable measure of both plausibility and (feasible and broad) applicability. One solution is to provide two alternative forms:

The Principle of Limited Mergeability (PLM).   Of two conflicting beliefs, if there be *one* to which all or almost all who (1) understand or (2) are aware of all the reasons for both of them give a decided preference, irrespective of their other views, *that* is the better justified belief.

Alternatives (1) and (2), both ambiguous, function on different levels. For example, with regard to most of the mathematical propositions believed to be (known to be) true or false, PLM(1) is sufficient to assure us that these beliefs are better justified than their opposites. In order to apply PLM(2), the phrase "all the reasons for" has to be taken with a large grain of salt. If we take constructivism and objectivism as the two conflicting beliefs, we may see Brouwer and Wittgenstein, on the side of the former, together with Bernays and Gödel, on the other side, as among the select few who satisfy (2). If we confine our attention to them or view them as representative of a larger group defined by (2), we have to conclude that a simple application of PLM to the conflict fails to resolve the issue. Indeed, the discussion in Chapter 7 is an attempt to examine more closely "all the reasons for both beliefs," with a view to breaking them up and restructuring them in such a way that PLM(1) and PLM(2) have more room to interact.

There is in PLM(2) an implicit restriction to the views of the experts on a given topic, which is not unreasonable, at least for topics on which one is largely ignorant. Philosophy, however, is more often concerned with topics on which one is not so ignorant, and so dependence on experts is more limited and less direct. For example, we are inclined to think that both Einstein and Niels Bohr knew all the reasons for the two opinions (namely, satisfactory and not so) on quantum theory. As is well known, their preferences were different. If we apply PLM(2) to this case, we will reach the conclusion that "satisfactory" is (at present) the better justified opinion, seeing that "almost all" good theoretical physicists decidedly prefer it—even though less aggressively so in recent years. However, this sort of consensus is of little direct use to philosophy, which, if it is to discuss the issue, is more concerned with the reasons for the two opinions. On the other hand, if what is needed is only the answer to a question, an appeal to the consensus of experts, if there is one, is rational.

The reasons for a belief (such as objectivism) are of different kinds. Roughly speaking, each reason consists of two parts: what is asserted as a fact and what is taken as a consequence of this fact. For example, in

Gödel's two letters to me (in *MP*:8–11), he asserts and convincingly explains that his "objectivistic conception of mathematics ... was fundamental" to all his major work in logic. The content of what he says is a belief which may be evaluated as the report of a fact. It is hard to doubt that in his own case there was indeed such a connection between his objectivistic conception and his results. But what can we infer from such a fact? What is easiest to accept is that, in combination with other circumstances, this conception helped Gödel to obtain important results. This fact, although it certainly lends credence to the conception, does not prove its "truth" (as a necessary condition). Moreover, what is this "conception"?

It seems clear from this example, which may be seen as involving an application of PLM(2), that we are concerned with empirical, probabilistic considerations. Gödel's letters point out to us certain connections we did not see so clearly before, thereby adding to the data in favor of objectivism, on which there is more agreement. Similarly, by pointing out that we are all certain that we accept true beliefs about small numbers and that we all make the "big jump" to the infinite (see section 7.1), we can reduce somewhat the range of apparent disagreement. In each case, alternative choices remain as to what consequences we are willing to assert.

In *Euthyphro*, Socrates asks, "What sort of difference creates enmity and anger?" In reply, he distinguishes different kinds of difference. Differences over a number or magnitudes or about heavy and light do not make us enemies; they are settled by arithmetic or measuring or a weighing machine. Differences that cause anger cannot be thus decided; for "these enmities arise when the matters of difference are the just and the unjust, good and evil, honorable and dishonorable."

The excitement over the issue of Platonism has much to do with the largely implicit association of Platonism with matters of good and evil. That association lends importance to the more restricted issue of Platonism in mathematics, which can also be considered, initially at least, more or less separately from its link to the broader conceptions of Platonism in general. Clearly, the discussion of this issue in the present work aims at sorting out and arranging more easily resolvable differences in order to reduce the range of those which create "enmity and anger." The more definite discussions are, in particular, directed mainly to the easier task of examining Platonism in mathematics. Going beyond this restriction to mathematics seems to call for considerations of a more controversial sort.

As I said before, given the homocentric predicament, there is a sense of certainty according to which we can never attain knowledge that is absolutely certain. If we fail to modulate our inclination toward seeking clear, final solutions, we are naturally led to some form of skepticism. The retrospective task of philosophy to examine the validity of what we suppose we know is largely an internal dialectic within the realm of our beliefs. The principle of presumed innocence is a way to do justice to this fact and, at the same time, guard against the resignation of skepticism.

This principle may be seen as a *method of faith*, in contrast to the famous *method of doubt*. The idea is, of course, a familiar reaction to the repeated failures of the method of doubt. Philosophy is compared to a law court, and "what we suppose we know" is compared to the defendant. The principle says in both cases: one is presumed innocent unless proved guilty. Obviously the method of doubt says that one is presumed guilty unless proved innocent. More explicitly:

Principle of Presumed Innocence (PPI).   What we suppose we know is presumed to be true unless proved otherwise. Instead of "what we suppose we know," we may speak more briefly of "what we believe," which also includes our attribution of different degrees of certainty and centrality to different beliefs. As we know, certainty and centrality often do not go together. Our familiar quest is for what is, to a high degree, both certain and central. But the concept of centrality is ambiguous and relative to the purposes one has in mind. If philosophy is to search for comprehensive perspicuity, to locate what is central to this purpose is itself a problem with alternative solutions. For example, it is hard to deny that everyday beliefs are central in the sense of being fundamental; yet they are notoriously difficult to manage (in the sense of giving them enough structure to see how our other beliefs are "based on" them).

I think of the principle of presumed innocence as an antidote or a corrective measure to what I take to be an excessive concern with local or uniform clarity and certainty. For example, according to this outlook, I need not pay too much attention to skepticism (about the external world, other minds, the past, induction, etc.) or try to eliminate minds, concepts, and so forth.

I do not mean, of course, that we should accept all beliefs on faith, but rather that we should try to reflect on them with as little prejudice as possible and with due respect for such commonly shared beliefs as that killing is wrong, Beethoven's music is beautiful, mathematical beliefs are generally certain, and so on. Just as a law court would—while presuming innocence—try to find all available evidence against the defendant, PPI is not a recommendation to withhold critical scrutiny. Nonetheless, PPI is not neutral; clearly there is a decisive difference between presuming that a given belief is true and presuming that it is false.

I would like to see the discussion of Platonism in mathematics in Chapter 7 as an instructive example of some features of what I envisage as a general approach to philosophy. It illustrates the application of the principles of limited mergeability and presumed innocence to the extent that, on the basis of these two principles, the tentative form of Platonism in mathematics formulated there is the most reasonable position relative to what we know.

It illustrates the desirability of concentrating on a special case—of a large issue such as Platonism—on which we have relatively definite things to say. It recognizes the epistemological priority of our knowledge of objectivity in the sense of intersubjective sharability over our knowledge of truth and objects. By isolating and relating a few domains of different degrees of clarity and certainty, it illustrates the process of enlarging the range of intersubjective sharability through a dialectic of the formal and the intuitive.

In my opinion, an appropriate dialectic between the formal and the intuitive is a characteristic feature of effective thinking. Mathematics and mathematical logic are important in this regard because they provide us with a model and a frame of reference for the interplay between the formal and the intuitive. The idea of logic as metaphilosophy aims at uncovering and also adding other components of the frame of reference we implicitly use.

The *intuitive* is what is obtained by intuition, and intuition is immediate apprehension. Apprehension could be sensation, knowledge, or even mystical rapport. *Immediate* apprehension occurs in the absence of mediation by inference, by justification, by articulation, by method, or by language and thought. The basic ambiguity of the intuitive comes from what was available before the moment of insight. In the rudimentary form, the intuitive is what comes with ease, what is familiar and part of common sense. The range of the intuitive increases as we grow and as we think more and more. The *formal* is the instrument by which we extend the range of the intuitive and the range of personal and public knowledge. Popular exposition aims at making certain formal and technical material intuitive. In learning a subject, we go through the process of transforming the formal into the intuitive. An advanced form of intuition is the end of a process by which one allows facts and ideas to float around until some insight makes sense of them, usually in accordance with a prechosen goal.

When we try to see or perceive or grasp something by thinking, the formal helps us by giving form to different parts of the data, thereby enabling us to have a better command of the material. William James distinguishes knowledge by acquaintance from knowledge about, and Russell similarly distinguishes knowledge by acquaintance from knowledge by description. The former is intuitive; the latter is a mixture of the formal and the intuitive. As we increase the range of the latter, we also increase the range of the former. The former is more intimate and rich in content, but the latter is more objective, public, and communicable.

Forms and concepts are universals, among which words, spoken or written or imagined, are the most regular in the sense that instances of the same word can, in principle at least, be identified without ambiguity. That is why thinking in terms of words often enjoys a greater measure of clarity than thinking in terms of ideas. We may say that in words the formal and the intuitive converge. However, as we know, once we come to the meaning of words, as we must, ambiguity reappears.

The paradigm of the desired convergence of the formal and the intuitive is computation. Computation can, as Hilbert emphasizes, be construed as manipulation of concrete symbols whose shape is immediately clear and recognizable. Concrete intuition (or *Anschauung* in Kant's sense) is sufficient for dealing with such manipulation of symbols. Consequently, computation is a remarkably transparent and univocal region of thinking. In computation we have an attractive focus and basis, which is not only of intrinsic interest but also the gateway that leads us from the concrete to the abstract and from the finite to the infinite. Moreover, the range of computation is potentially so rich that, particularly with the conspicuous prevalence of computers today, it is not surprising that people are debating the challenging question of whether all thinking is nothing but computation.

Computation is also at the center of mathematics. In mathematics, we move from computation to the potential infinite and then to the different stages of the actual infinite, with decreasing transparency, clarity, and certainty. We have by now a good understanding of what is involved in the several steps of expansion. We can see here a substantive and clean example of the operation of the dialectic of the intuitive and the formal, in the form of a dialectic of intuition and idealization—idealization being in this case the road leading to the formal. After we have obtained a good command of computation, which is necessarily finite, we extend the range to the potential infinite by idealization. We then extend our intuition to the potential infinite, and the process of expansion continues.

By reconstituting the broad domain of mathematics through this process of expansion stage by stage, as I have tried to do in Chapter 7, we are able to locate the points at which alternative views on the foundations of mathematics begin to diverge. We then gain a better grasp of what and why alternative choices are made at these points. In this way, the disagreements between conflicting views are decomposed, so that we have a clearer view of what is involved in each case. Moreover, as we familiarize ourselves with our natural tendency to extend further and further what we see, we begin to appreciate the possibility of a reasonable conception of logic which both conforms to one of the traditional intentions and is broad enough to contain mathematics as a proper part.

A further extension of the range of logic is the Frege-Gödel conception of logic as concept theory (discussed in Chapter 8). Because, however, we do not at present have anything like a good understanding even of the backbone of such a concept theory, we cannot yet include it in logic, construed as restricted to the universal part of what we know. At the same time, this attempt to extend logic beyond set theory continues along the direction of limiting logic to what can be precisely systematized. I see this as a somewhat arbitrary requirement. On the other hand, if we restrict logic to what we know and remove the requirement of formal precision, then the extension of logic beyond mathematics and mathematical logic poses the central problem which I have characterized as the quest for logic as metaphilosophy. As I see it, this quest is fulfilled in different ways by Kant's transcendental logic, Hegel's science of logic, Husserl's conception of intentionality, and Wittgenstein's conception of logic in *On Certainty*. While I cannot accept any of these as final, I believe an adequate development of the idea of logic as metaphilosophy, toward which I have offered some suggestions, represents an ideal worth pursuing.

Gödel's confident philosophical views—in particular, his insistence on the objectivity of mathematics—served him in good stead, and benefited mankind, for they provided the groundwork for his spectacular mathematical results. His belief in unlimited generalization, on the other hand, led him in directions where I—and many others—cannot follow him. In contrast, my two methodological principles: the principle of limited mergeability and the principle of presumed innocence, seem to me to provide the basis on which to build a productive philosophical consensus.

References

Ackermann, W. (1956). "Zur Axiomatik der Mengenleher." *Mathematische Annalen* 131:336–345.

Ackermann, W., and Hilbert, D. (1928). *Grundzüge der theoretischen Logik*. Berlin: Springer.

Anderson, C. A. (1990). "Some emendations of Gödel's ontological proof." *Faith and Philosophy* 7:291–303.

Barrett, C. (1967). *Wittgenstein: Lectures and Conversations on Aesthetics, Psychology, and Religious Belief*. Berkeley: University of California Press.

Bernays, P. (1935). "Sur le platonism dans les mathématiques." *L'enseignement mathematique* 34:52–69.

Bernays, P. (1940). Review of Gödel 1939. *Journal of Symbolic Logic* 5:117–118.

Bernays, P. (1959). "Comments on Wittgenstein's *Remarks on the Foundations of Mathematics*." *Ratio* 3:1–22.

Bernays, P. (1961). "Zur Frage der Unendlichkeitsschemata in der axiomatischen Mengenlehre." In Bar-Hillel, Y. (ed.), *Essays on the Foundations of Mathematics*, pp. 1–49.

Bernays, P. (1964). "On platonism in mathematics." Trans. Parsons, C., in Benacerraf, P. and Putnam, H. (eds.), *Philosophy of Mathematics*. Cambridge: Cambridge University Press, pp. 258–271.

Bernays, P. (1974). "Concerning rationality." In Schilpp, P. (ed.), *The Philosophy of Karl Popper*, pp. 579–605.

Bernstein, J. (1991). *Quantum Profiles*. Princeton: Princeton University Press.

Booth, W. (1961). *The Rhetoric of Fiction*. Chicago: University of Chicago Press.

Brower, L. (1975). *Collected Works*, Heyting, A. (ed.). Amsterdam: North-Holland.

Buloff, J., Holyoke, T., and Hahn, H. (1969). *Foundations of Mathematics*. Berlin: Springer.

Cantor, G. (1932). *Gesammelte Abhandlungen mathematischen und philosophischen Inhalts*, Zermelo, E. (ed.). Berlin: Springer.

Carnap, R. (1963). "Intellectual autobiography." In Schilpp, P. (ed.), *Philosophy of Rudolf Carnap*, pp. 1–84.

Cheniss, H. (1962). *The Riddle of the Early Academy*. New York: Russell and Russell.

Cohen, P. (1966). *Set Theory and the Continuum Hypothesis*. New York: Benjamin.

Confucius (1938). *Analects*. London: Allen and Unwin.

Davis, M. (1965). *The Undecidable*. Hewlett: Random Press.

Dawson, J. (1995). "The Nachlass of Kurt Gödel." In Feferman, S., Dawson, J., Kleene, S., Moore, G,. Solovay, R., and van Heijenoort, J. (eds.), *Gödel Collected Works*, vol. 3, pp. 1–6.

Dewey, J. (1888). *Leibniz's New Essays Concerning Human Understanding*. Chicago: Foresman.

Dewey, J. (1929). *The Quest for Certainty*. New York: Balach.

Diamond, C. (1976). *Wittgenstein's Lectures on the Foundations of Mathematics, 1939*. Ithaca: Cornell University Press.

Dummett, M. (1973). *Frege, Philosophy of Language*. London: Duckworth.

Einstein, A. (1949). "Autobiographical notes." In Schilpp, P. (ed.), *Albert Einstein: Philosopher-Scientist*, pp. 1–93.

Einstein, A. (1949). "Reply to criticisms." In Schilpp, P. (ed.), *Albert Einstein: Philosopher-Scientist*, pp. 665–688.

Einstein, A. (1954). *Ideas and Opinions.* New York: Crown.

Elkana, Y., and Holten, G. (1982). *Albert Einstein: Historical and Cultural Aspects.* Princeton: Princeton University Press.

Follesdal, D. (1988). "Husserl on evidence and justification." In Sokolowski, R. (ed.), *Edmund Husserl and the Phenomenological Tradition*, pp. 107–129.

Frank, P. (1947). *Einstein: His Life and Times.* New York: Knopf.

Frege, G. (1884). *Die Grundlagen der Arithmetik.* Breslau: Koebner.

Frege, G. (1950). *The Foundations of Arithmetic.* Trans. Austin, J. Oxford: Blackwell.

Frege, G. (1977). "Der Gedanke." Trans. Geach, P., in Geach, P. (ed.), *Logical Investigations*, pp. 1–30.

Friedman, H. (1971). "Higher set theory and mathematical practise." *Annals of Mathematical Logic* 2:326–357.

Fung, Yu-lan (1948). *A Short History of Chinese Philosophy.* New York: Macmillan.

Gödel, K. (1929). *Über die Vollständigkeit des Logikkalküls.* Dissertation, in Feferman, S., Dawson, J., Kleene, S., Moore, G,. Solovay, R., and van Heijenoort, J. (eds.), *Collected Works*, vol.1: 60–101.

Gödel, K. (1930). "Die Vollstandigkeit der Axiome des logischen Funktionenkalkuls." *Monatshefte für Mathematik und Physic* 37:349–360, in Feferman, S., Dawson, J., Kleene, S., Moore, G,. Solovay, R., and van Heijenoort, J. (eds.), *Collected Works*, vol.1: 102–123.

Gödel, K. (1931). "Über formal unentscheidbare Satze de *Principia mathematica* und verwandter System I." *Monatshefte für Mathematik und Physic* 38:173–198, in Feferman, S., Dawson, J., Kleene, S., Moore, G,. Solovay, R., and van Heijenoort, J. (eds.), *Collected Works*, vol.1: 144–195.

Gödel, K. (1933). "Zur intuitionistischen Arithmetik und Zahlentheorie." In Feferman, S., Dawson, J., Kleene, S., Moore, G,. Solovay, R., and van Heijenoort, J. (eds.), *Collected Works*, vol.1: 286–295.

Gödel, K. (1939). "Constructable sets and the continuum hypothesis." In Feferman, S., Dawson, J., Kleene, S., Moore, G,. Solovay, R., and van Heijenoort, J. (eds.), *Collected Works*, vol.2: 28–32.

Gödel, K. (1944). "Russell's mathematical logic." In Feferman, S., Dawson, J., Kleene, S., Moore, G,. Solovay, R., and van Heijenoort, J. (eds.), *Collected Works*, vol.2: 119–141.

Gödel, K. (1946). "The Princeton lecture." In Feferman, S., Dawson, J., Kleene, S., Moore, G,. Solovay, R., and van Heijenoort, J. (eds.), *Collected Works*, vol.2: 150–153.

Gödel, K. (1947). "What is Cantor's continuum problem? (version 1)." In Feferman, S., Dawson, J., Kleene, S., Moore, G,. Solovay, R., and van Heijenoort, J. (eds.), *Collected Works*, vol.2: 176–187.

Gödel, K. (1949). "A remark about the relationship between relativity theory and idealistic philosophy." In Feferman, S., Dawson, J., Kleene, S., Moore, G,. Solovay, R., and van Heijenoort, J. (eds.), *Collected Works*, vol.2: 202–207.

Gödel, K. (1951). "Some basic theorems on the foundations of mathematics and their philosophical implications." In Feferman, S., Dawson, J., Kleene, S., Moore, G,. Solovay, R., and van Heijenoort, J. (eds.), *Collected Works*, vol.3: 304–323.

Gödel, K. (1953). "Is mathematics the syntax of language?" In Feferman, S., Dawson, J., Kleene, S., Moore, G,. Solovay, R., and van Heijenoort, J. (eds.), *Collected Works*, vol.3: 334–363

Gödel, K. (1958). "On an extension of finitary mathematics which has not yet been used, (version 1)." In Feferman, S., Dawson, J., Kleene, S., Moore, G,. Solovay, R., and van Heijenoort, J. (eds.), *Collected Works*, vol.2: 240–251.

Gödel, K. (1961). "The modern development of the foundations of mathematics in the light of philosophy." In Feferman, S., Dawson, J., Kleene, S., Moore, G,. Solovay, R., and van Heijenoort, J. (eds.), *Collected Works*, vol.3: 374–387.

Gödel, K. (1964). "What is Cantor's continuum problem? (version 2)." *Collected Works*, vol.2: 254–269.

Gödel, K. (1970). "Ontological Proof." In Feferman, S., Dawson, J., Kleene, S., Moore, G,. Solovay, R., and van Heijenoort, J. (eds.), *Collected Works*, vol.3: 403–404, 429–438.

Gödel, K. (1972a). "On an extension of finitary mathematics which has not yet been used, (version 2)." In Feferman, S., Dawson, J., Kleene, S., Moore, G,. Solovay, R., and van Heijenoort, J. (eds.), *Collected Works*, vol.2: 271–280.

Gödel, K. (1972b). "On an extension of finitary mathematics which has not yet been used, (version 3)." In Feferman, S., Dawson, J., Kleene, S., Moore, G,. Solovay, R., and van Heijenoort, J. (eds.), *Collected Works*, vol.2: 305–306.

Gödel, K. (1945–1966). *Letters to mother and brother.*

Gödel, K. (1986). *Collected Works*, vol.1, Feferman, S., Dawson, J., Kleene, S., Moore, G,. and van Heijenoort, J. (eds.). Oxford: Oxford University Press.

Gödel, K. (1990). *Collected Works*, vol.2, Feferman, S., Dawson, J., Kleene, S., Moore, G., Solovay, R., and van Heijenoort, J. (eds.). Oxford: Oxford University Press.

Gödel, K. (1995). *Collected Works*, vol.1, Feferman, S., Dawson, J., Goldfarb, W., Parsons, C,. and Solovay, R. (eds.). Oxford: Oxford University Press.

Gödel, R. (1987). "History of the Gödel family." In Weingarter, P. and Schmetterer, L. (ed.), *Gödel Remembered*. Napoli: Bibliopolis, pp. 13–27.

Hadamard, J. (1945). *The Psychology of Invention in the Mathematical Field*. New York: Dover.

Hallett, M. (1984). *Cantorian Set Theory and the Limitation of Size*. Oxford: Oxford University Press.

Hilbert, D. (1925). "Über das Unendliche." *Mathematische Annalen* 95:161–190.

Hilbert, D. (1967). "On the infinite." In van Heijenoort, J. (ed.), *From Frege to Gödel*. Cambridge: Harvard University Press, pp. 367–392.

Hilbert, D., and Bernays, P. (1939). *Grundlagen der Mathematik*, vol.2. Berlin: Springer.

Hodges, A. (1983). *Alan Turing: The Enigma*. New York: Simon and Schuster.

Hofstadter, D. (1979). *Gödel, Escher, Bach*. New York: Vintage.

Husserl, E. (1910). "Philiosophie als strenge Wissenschaft." *Logos* 1:289–341.

Husserl, E. (1931). *Ideas*. Trans. Boyce Gibson, W. New York: Collier.

Husserl, E. (1960). *Cartesian Meditations*. Trans. Cairns, D. Dordrecht: Kluwer.

Husserl, E. (1964). *The Phenomenology of Internal Time-Consciousness*. Trans. Churhill, J. Bloomington: Indiana University Press.

Husserl, E.(1965). *Phenomenology and the Crisis of Philosophy*. Trans. Lauer, Q. New York: Harper and Row.

Husserl, E. (1969). *Formal and Transcendental Logic*. Trans. Cairns, D. Hague: Martinus Nijhoff.

Husserl, E. (1970a). *The Crisis of European Science and Transcendental Phenomenology*. Trans. Carr, D. Evanston: Northwestern University Press.

Husserl, E. (1970b). *Logical Investigations*, vol.1–2. Trans. Findlay, J. London: Routledge and Kegan Paul.

Jamas, W. (1907). *Pragmatism*. New York: Green.

Jensen, R. (1972). "The fine structure of the constructable hierarchy." *Annals of Mathematical Logic* 4:229–308.

Kant, I. (1933). *Critique of Pure Reason*. Trans. Kemp Smith, N. London: Macmillan.

Kant, I. (1950). *Prolegomena to Any Future Metaphysics*. Trans. Beck, L. Indianapolis: Bobbs-Merrill.

Kreisel, G. (1980). "Kurt Gödel." *Biographical Memoirs of the Royal Society* 26:148–224, corrections in *Biographical Memoirs of the Royal Society* 27:697, and 28:718.

Leibniz, G. (1969). *Philosophical Papers and Letters*. Trans. Loemaker, L. Dordrecht: Reidel.

Leibniz, G. (1981). *New Essays on Human Understanding*. Trans. Remnant, P., and Bennett, J. Cambridge: Cambridge University Press.

Martin, D. (1975). "Borel determinacy." *Annals of Mathematics* 102:263–271.

Mead, H. (1938). *The Philosophy of the Act*. Chicago: University of Chicago Press.

Menger, K. (1994). "Memories of Kurt Gödel." In McGuinness, B. (ed.), *Reminiscences of the Vienna Circle and the Mathematical Colloquium*. Dordrecht: Kluwer.

Michelet, K. (1843). *Die Entwickelungsgschichte der neuesten Deutschen Philosophie*. Berlin: Punker und Humblot.

Michelet, K. (1876–1881). *Das System der Philosophie als exacter Wissenschaft*. Berlin: Nicolaische verlags-buchhandlung.

Mill. J. (1863). *Utiliterianism*. London: Parker, Son, and Bourn.

Miller, G. (1956). "The magic number seven plus minus two: some limits on our capacity for processing information." *Psychological Review* 63:2–5.

Moore, G. (1955). "Wittgenstein's lectures in 1930–33." *Mind* 64:1–27.

Nagel, E., and Newman, R. (1958). *Gödel's Proof*. New York: New York University Press.

Nedo, M., and Ranchetti, M. (1983). *Wittgenstein: Sein Leben in Bildern und Texten*. Frankfurt: Suhrkamp.

Parsons, C. (1983). *Mathematics in Philosophy*. Ithaca: Cornell University Press.

Pasch, M. (1882). *Vorlesungen über neure Geometrie*. Leipzig: Teubner.

Penrose, R. (1990). *The Emperor's New Mind*. Oxford: Oxford University Press.

Perzanowski, J. (1991). "Ontological argument II: Cartesian and Leibnizian." In Smith, B., (ed.), *Handbook of Metaphysics and Ontology*. Munich: Philosophia Verlag, pp. 625–633.

Plato (1993). *Republic*. Trans. Waterfield, R. Oxford: Oxford University Press.

Powell, W. (1972). *Set Theory with Predication*. Dissertation, State University of New York at Buffalo.

Quine, W. (1937). "New foundations for mathematical logic." *American Mathematical Monthly* 44:70–80.

Quine, W. (1951). "Two dogmas of empiricism." *Philosophical Review* 60:20–33.

Ramsey, F. (1931). *Foundations of Mathematics*, Braithwaite, R. (ed.) London: Routledge and Kegan Paul.

Rawls, J. (1951). "Outline of a decision proceedure for ethics." *Philosophical Review* 60:177–197.

Rawls, J. (1971). *A Theory of Justice*. Cambridge: Harvard University Press.

Rawls, J. (1975). "The independence of moral theory." *Proceedings and Addresses of the American Philosophical Association* 48:5–22.

Rawls, J. (1991). "For the record: an interview." *The Harvard Review of Philosophy* 1:38–47.

Rawls, J. (1993). *Political Liberalism*. New York: Columbia University Press.

Reinhardt, W. (1974). "Set existence principles of Shoenfield, Ackermann, and Powell." *Fundamenta Mathematica* 84:12–41.

Rhees, R. (1984). *Recollections of Wittgenstein*. Oxford: Oxford University Press.

Rucker, R. (1984). *Infinity and the Mind*. Toronto: Bantam.

Russell, B. (1919). *Introduction to Mathematical Philosophy*. London: Allen and Unwin.

Russell, B. (1940). *Inquiry into Meaning and Truth*. London: Allen and Unwin.

Schimanovich, W., Buldt, B., Kohler, E., and Weibel, P. (eds.) (1995). *Warrheit und Beweisbarkeit: Leben und Werk Kurt Gödels*.

Skolem, T. (1970). *Selected Logical Works*. Oslo: Universitetsforlaget.

Sobel, J. (1987). "Gödel's ontological proof." In Thomson, J. (ed.), *On Being and Saying*. Cambridge: MIT Press, pp. 241–261.

Spinoza, B. (1941). *Ethics*. Trans. Boyle, A. London: Dent.

Taussky, O. (1987). "Remembrances of Kurt Gödel." In Weingarter, P. and Schmetterer, L. (ed.), *Gödel Remembered*. Napoli: Bibliopolis, pp. 29–48.

Tieszen, R. (1989). *Mathematical Intuition*. Dordrecht: Kluwer.

Toledo, S. (1975). *Tableau Systems*. Springer Lecture Notes in Mathematics, 447.

Ulam, S. (1958). "John von Neumann, 1903–1957." *Bulletin of the American Mathematical Society* 64, no.3, part 2:1–49.

Ulam, S. (1976). *Adventures of a Mathematician*. New York: Scribner.

von Neumann, J. (1961). *Collected Works*. New York: Pergamon.

Waismann, F. (1979). *Wittgenstein and the Vienna Circle*. Oxford: Blackwell.

Wallas, G. (1925). *The Art of Thought*. London: Cape.

Wang, H. (1951a). "Arithmetic models for formal systems." *Methodos* 3:217–232.

Wang, H. (1951b). "Arithmetical translations of axiom systems." *Transactions of the American Mathematical Society* 71:283–293.

Wang, H. (1952). "Truth definitions and consistency proofs." *Transactions of the American Mathematical Society* 73:243–275.

Wang, H. (1954). "The formalisation of mathematics." *Journal of Symbolic Logic* 19:241–266.

Wang, H. (1958). "Eighty years of foundational studies." *Dialectica* 12:466–497.

Wang, H. (1963). *A Survey of Mathematical Logic*. Beijing: Science Press.

Wang, H. (1970). "A survey of Skolem's work in logic." In Skolem, *Selected Logical Works*. Oslo: Universitetsforlaget.

Wang, H. (1974a). *From Mathematics to Philosophy*. New York: Humanities Press.

Wang, H. (1974b). "Concerning the materialistic dialectic." *Philosophy East and West* 24: 303–319.

Wang, H. (1977). "Large sets." *Proceedings of the Fifth International Congress on Logic Methodology, and Philosophy of Science of 1975*, pp. 911–933.

Wang, H. (1978). "Kurt Gödel's intellectual development." *Mathematical Intelligencer* 1:182–184.

Wang, H. (1981a). *Popular Lectures on Mathematical Logic*. New York: Van Nostrand, Reinhold.

Wang, H. (1981b). "Some facts about Kurt Gödel." *Journal of Symbolic Logic* 46:653–659.

Wang, H. (1985). "Two commandments of analytic empiricism." *Journal of Philosophy* 82: 449–462.

Wang, H. (1986a). *Beyond Analytic Philosophy*. Cambridge: MIT Press.

Wang, H. (1987). *Reflections on Kurt Gödel*. Cambridge: MIT Press.

Wang, H. (1986b). "Gödel and Wittgenstein." In Schurz, G., and Weingartner, P. (eds.), *Logic, Philosophy of Science, and Epistemology*. Vienna: Holder-Pichler-Tempsky.

Wang, H. (1991). "To and from philosophy." *Sythese* 88:229–277.

Wang, H. (1992). "Imagined conversations with Gödel and Wittgenstein." *Yearbook 1992 of the Kurt Gödel Society*, pp. 3–47.

Wang, H. (1993). "On physicalism and algorithmism: Can machines think?" *Philosophia Mathematica* 1:97–138.

Wang, H. (1994). "What is logic?" *Monist* 77:261–277.

Wang, H. (1995). "Time in philosophy and physics: From Kant and Einstein to Gödel." *Sythese* 102:215–234.

Webb, J. (1980). *Mechanism, Mentalism, and Metamathematics*. Dordrecht: Reidel.

Weber, M. (1964). *The Religion of China*. Trans. Gerth, H. New York: Free Press.

Williams, R. (1983). *Keywords*. Oxford: Oxford University Press.

Wittgenstein, L. (1953). *Philosophical Investigations*, Anscombe, G. (ed.). New York: Macmillan.

Wittgenstein, L. (1958). *The Blue and Brown Books*. Oxford: Blackwell.

Wittgenstein, L. (1965). "A lecture on ethics." *Philosophical Review* 74:3–11.

Wittgenstein, L. (1967a). *Remarks on the Foundations of Mathematics*, Anscombe, G., von Wright, G., and Rhees, R. (ed.), trans. Anscombe, G. Cambridge: MIT Press.

Wittgenstein, L. (1967b). *Zettel*, Anscombe, G., and von Wright, G. (eds.), trans. Anscombe, G. Oxford: Blackwell.

Wittgenstein, L. (1969). *On Certainty*, Anscombe, G., and von Wright, G. (eds.), trans. Anscombe, G. and Paul, D., Oxford: Blackwell.

Wittgenstein, L. (1974). *Philosophical Grammar*, Rhees, R. (ed.), trans. Kenny, A. Berkeley: University of California Press.

Wittgenstein, L. (1975). *Philosophical Remarks*, Rhees, R., (ed.), trans. Hargreaves, R., and White, R. Oxford: Blackwell.

Wittgenstein, L. (1977). *Remarks on Colour*, Anscombe, G. (ed.), trans. McAlister, L., and Schattle, M. Berkeley: University of California Press.

Wittgenstein, L. (1980). *Culture and Value*, von Wright, G. (ed.) trans. Winch, P. Oxford: Blackwell.

Wittgenstein, L. (1981). *Tractatus Logico-Philosophicus*. Trans. Pears, D., and McGuiness, B. London: Routledge and Kegan Paul.

Woolf, H. (1980). *Some Strangeness in the Proportion*. Reading: Addison-Wesley.

Yourgrau, P. (1989). Review essay of Wang 1987. *Philosophical and Phenomenological Research* 50:391–408.

Yourgrau, P. (1991). *The Disappearence of Time: Kurt Gödel and the Idealistic Tradition in Philosophy*. Cambridge: Cambridge University Press.

Index

Made in the USA
Middletown, DE
31 October 2022